Sonic Strategies

CRITICAL MEXICAN STUDIES

CRITICAL MEXICAN STUDIES
Series editor: *Ignacio M. Sánchez Prado*

Critical Mexican Studies is the first English-language, humanities-based, theoretically focused academic series devoted to the study of Mexico. The series is a space for innovative works in the humanities that focus on theoretical analysis, transdisciplinary interventions, and original conceptual framing.

Other titles in the series:

The Restless Dead: Necrowriting and Disappropriation, by Cristina Rivera Garza

History and Modern Media: A Personal Journey, by John Mraz

Toxic Loves, Impossible Futures: Feminist Living as Resistance, by Irmgard Emmelhainz

Drug Cartels Do Not Exist: Narcotrafficking in US and Mexican Culture, by Oswaldo Zavala

Unlawful Violence: Mexican Law and Cultural Production, by Rebecca Janzen

The Mexican Transpacific: Nikkei Writing, Visual Arts, and Performance, by Ignacio López-Calvo

Monstrous Politics: Geography, Rights, and the Urban Revolution in Mexico City, by Ben Gerlofs

Robo Sacer: Necroliberalism and Cyborg Resistance in Mexican and Chicanx Dystopias by David Dalton

Mexico, Interrupted: Labor, Idleness, and the Economic Imaginary of Independence by Sergio Gutiérrez Negrón

Serial Mexico: Storytelling across Media, from Nationhood to Now by Amy E. Wright

Sonic Strategies

Performing Mexico's War on Drugs, Mourning, and Feminicide

Christina Baker

Vanderbilt University Press
Nashville, Tennessee

Copyright 2024 Vanderbilt University Press
All rights reserved
First printing 2023

Library of Congress Cataloging-in-Publication Data

Names: Baker, Christina, 1985- author.
Title: Sonic strategies : performing Mexico's war on drugs, mourning, and feminicide / Christina Baker.
Description: Nashville, Tennessee : Vanderbilt University Press, [2024] | Series: Critical Mexican studies | Includes bibliographical references and index.
Identifiers: LCCN 2023035276 (print) | LCCN 2023035277 (ebook) | ISBN 9780826505989 (paperback) | ISBN 9780826505996 (hardcover) | ISBN 9780826506009 (epub) | ISBN 9780826506016 (pdf)
Subjects: LCSH: Performance art--Political aspects--Mexico. | Drug control--Mexico. | Sound--Psychological aspects. | Sound in art.
Classification: LCC NX514.A1 B35 2024 (print) | LCC NX514.A1 (ebook) | DDC 700.972--dc23/eng/20230927
LC record available at https://lccn.loc.gov/2023035276
LC ebook record available at https://lccn.loc.gov/2023035277

Contents

Acknowledgments vii

INTRODUCTION   1

1   Sonic Disidentifications and
a *Mexicanidad* for the Twenty-First Century   15

2   Listening to Mexico's War on Drugs:
Necroauralities in Three Movements   59

3   Antigone's Requiem: Sounds against
Death and Disappearance   95

4   Soundtracks of an (After)life:
Radical Geographies of Hope and Survival   137

CONCLUSION   187

Notes 193
Bibliography 243
Index 273

Acknowledgments

Where to start? Writing this acknowledgments section is daunting. I dread making any grave omissions because so many people and organizations have been involved in making this book a reality. Alas, I have to begin somewhere, so I will first thank my partner, Chris, for his eternal patience over the last several years as I sat for hours on end in silence, in front of my computer, often emerging from my office frustrated, confused, and/or hangry. Writing and revising this book during a global pandemic has been a journey, to say the least. I also want to immortalize my writing partner, Scotch, my eighteen-year-old tortoiseshell cat. She may have slept and snored through most of the writing process, but she always remained faithfully by my side.

On a more serious note, I am beyond grateful to Vanderbilt University Press, Ignacio Sánchez Prado, editor of the Critical Mexican Studies series, and Zachary Gresham, acquisitions editor, for taking on this project. What follows would likely have never made it into the world without Ignacio's emphatic belief in junior scholars and wild ideas. Zack is a saint, always willing to calm my anxieties and shepherd me through this process. I also want to recognize members of the Vanderbilt editorial team who have shepherded this book through publication: Joell Smith-Borne and Gianna Mosser. Both of my anonymous readers also deserve commendation for swiftly providing crucial feedback that has made this book stronger.

Now, I will give thanks to a long list of people, institutions, and organizations, beginning with the organizers of the 2019 Hemispheric Institute of Politics and Performance Encuentro held in Mexico City. Due to their expert curation of performances and interventions, I experienced works by Lechedevirgen Trimegisto, Lukas Avendaño, and Violeta Luna. Being able to see and hear these artists' undeniably moving pieces crystalized my vision for this book and the acoustic threads I weave throughout. Moreover, I appreciate that these three artists, who I did not know personally, were willing to communicate with me about this book, sharing insights and emotional stories. During this 2019 trip, I was also able to reconnect with *cabareterxs* whose performances would also become vital to bringing this project to fruition: César Enríquez (La Prietty), Liliana Papalotl (La Mafia Cabaret), Irakere Lima (La Mafia Cabaret and Las Pussy Queers), Larissa Polaco (Las Pussy Queers), and Ana Francis Mor, Cecilia Sotres, Nora Huerta, and Marisol Gasé (Las Reinas Chulas). I express utter admiration and gratitude to each of these figures for sharing their artistic gifts with the world, and for their time, interest, and assistance as I wrote this manuscript. Along this line, I want to thank Hugo Salcedo for his inimitable contributions to contemporary Mexican theater and for the support he has shown me since our first conversation in 2016. I also appreciate the ways Raúl Rodríguez has shared his perspective as a Mexican theater scholar and director. Lastly, I draw attention to Hernán del Riego, David Molina, Edgar Cartas Orozco, and Yurief Nieves, the musicians who kindly took time out of their busy schedules to talk to me about their creative processes. There is also a key artist whose work I could not include in this book but need to acknowledge as an important silent interlocutor: Tito Vasconcelos. Because of Tito's willingness to share his vast knowledge of Mexican cabaret, theater, history, political life, and so much more, I am forever in his debt.

While I did not know it at the time, the 2019 Encuentro would be my last trip to Mexico for nearly three years due to COVID-19. This makes the time I spent discussing the state of contemporary Mexican theater with my dear friends and cheerleaders, Zavel Castro (Aplaudir de Pie founder and *LA crítica de México*) and Pako Reyes (La Mafia Cabaret), even more meaningful. To be honest, Pako has been a lifesaver in so many ways, personally and professionally. In regard to this book, his keen grasp of Mexico's sociopolitical and cultural milieu helped me add layers of nuance to my analysis and his undying support literally ensured the presence of beautiful visual aids (in other words, he helped me secure files and permissions).

Speaking of, I would be remiss not to recognize and emphasize the indispensable role Paola S. Hernández has played in my academic life as my former advisor, career coach, part-time therapist, and number one champion. In fact, with oracle-like precision, she told me I would write this book based on that 2019 trip to Mexico. Sometimes, she knows me better than I know myself. Similarly, without Gastón Alzate and Paola Marín, I could have never navigated the world of *teatro-cabaret*. Not only have they introduced me to artists, but they have also devoted much time and energy to mentoring me since the early stages of my doctoral studies. As key scholars in the field, I cite them regularly in this book, especially Gastón, but I also consider them caring collaborators and friends.

At this point, I want to thank the numerous scholars who have mentored and inspired me over the years (perhaps unbeknownst to them): Gail Bulman, Sarah Misemer, Camilla Stevens, Brenda Werth, Jaqueline Bixler, Josefina Alcázar, Analola Santana, Laura Gutiérrez, Teresa Longo, Silvia Tandeciarz, Jennifer Bickham Mendez, Michael Iyanaga, Adela Amaral, John Lear, Marisela Fleites, Amanda Peterson, Tamara Williams, Emily Hind, Rebecca Janzen, Francesca Dennstedt, Gabriela Pulido Llano, B. Christine Arce, Rafael Figueroa Hernández, Jacqueline Avila, and Alejandro Madrid. I am also deeply appreciative of the people who kept me sane while I wrote this book during a pandemic: Jennifer Baker (sister) and her delightful girls (Kinsley and Addi), Nathan Rabalais and Jorge Terukina (the Giggle Group), Julia Coffin and James Murphy (Best Friends Forever), and my lovely present, past, and future colleagues, Carola Daffner, Shannon Toll, Rachel Wilson-Cotá, Janire Zalbidea, José Manuel Pereiro-Otero, Montserrat Piera, Sabina Madrid-Malloy, Rebecca Barnes, and Erin Riley-López.

Finally, I must acknowledge the institutional arenas that have made this book possible. In chronological order, I thank the College of William & Mary for providing me travel funds as a non-tenure track faculty member. Their support allowed me to see *La Prietty Guoman* performed in and outside of Mexico. Next, I am grateful to have been awarded the Seed Grant while at the University of Dayton. These monies funded my trip to Mexico in 2019, exposing me to many of the works included in this book. Lastly, I express gratitude to Temple University for its generous support in the form of a Summer Research Award. These funds enabled me to complete and submit my manuscript to Zack ahead of schedule. Focusing on events, I want to thank Karina Franco Villaseñor for inviting me to multiple seminars she has organized on sound culture in collaboration with Casa del Lago and Claustro Sor Juana. Additionally, I thank the program selection committees at the Mid-Atlantic Council for Latin American Studies, Latin American Studies Association, and Society of Ethnomusicology for allowing me to present early-stage ideas related to this book.

Introduction

On September 15, 2007, Mexico prepared to celebrate Independence Day marked by military parades, marching bands, concerts, and the presidential "Grito," a galvanizing speech meant to rally the nation. The practice has its origins in Mexico's independence movement, when on September 16, 1810, Father Miguel Hidalgo y Costilla summoned his congregation of poor, rural, and Indigenous followers in the small town of Dolores Hidalgo in Guanajuato, Mexico. There, from the center of the village, he gave an impassioned call to arms, which has since become known as the "Grito de Dolores," or the Cry of Dolores. Remembered more for its emotional delivery than for the actual words spoken, Father Hidalgo's vocalized expression of defiance has become a symbolic act of *mexicanidad* (Mexicanness).[1] To this day, the "Grito" draws massive crowds to central plazas throughout the nation. In Mexico City, onlookers gather in the Zócalo and eagerly wait to see the nation's leader emerge from the National Palace. Towering above the crowds from a balcony, the president addresses the nation while captivated listeners below await their chance to respond, chanting "¡Viva México!" (Long live Mexico!).

Year after year, Mexico City's main plaza fills to the brim with locals, vendors, and tourists from around the world waiting for their chance to experience the "Grito," and 2007 was no different. It was only my third time visiting Mexico City, and I while I was in awe, I could also sense a palpable tension looming in the air. Even though my memory of that September afternoon is fragmented, certain images and sounds have remained with me, guiding me to and through writing this book. The Zócalo was divided in two: one side dedicated in its affirmation of Felipe Calderón's ascent to power, the other adamant that the election had been fraudulent. The latter faction was unwavering in its belief that the "legitimate" president was Andrés Manuel López Obrador, AMLO for short, who would become president in 2018.[2] In addition to waving banners proclaiming AMLO's right to govern the nation, his supporters erected a second stage for musical artists to wage an audible war on those officially chosen to perform at the event. Standing in the middle of the plaza that day, I listened as President Calderón's bands played *rancheras, música norteña,* and *corridos,* among other musical styles deeply aligned with notions of *mexicanidad,* or Mexicanness. Those who supported AMLO, in contrast, had a distinct sound. They played *rock en español,* and the heavy drums and slick guitar licks competed fiercely with the smooth sounds from across the plaza. To my ears, it was cacophony, dissonant chaos. The sonic sparring was unpleasant, but fascinating. It was also an ominous auditory commentary on what was to come and begged those of us in attendance to become engaged auditors. To those of us listening closely, this soundtrack revealed a nation grappling with political outrage and the early stages of Mexico's War on Drugs.

This sonic expression of tension had been building for months, if not years. Upon taking office in 2006, Calderón declared his determination to eradicate violence related to the nation's growing drug trade. Increasing the presence of military forces throughout the country to unprecedented levels, he intended to combat *narco* syndicates and cartel members with overt demonstrations of strength. This approach has resulted in an astounding number of deaths, disappearances, and the displacement of bystanders and everyday citizens.[3] The very tangible stains of death have outlasted Calderón's presidency, as violence continued to rip through the nation under Enrique Peña Nieto (2012–2018), just as it does now under Mexico's current leader, AMLO (2018–2024). Journalists have been targeted for reporting on cartel activity and government abuses; dissident groups, such as the forty-three students of Ayotzinapa, have been forcibly disappeared, never to be seen again; and clandestine mass graves filled with tortured and dismembered cadavers are found all too regularly. To be sure, the government's consistent emphasis on apprehending and dismantling cartels has been a primary factor in the atrocities, but the country is also plagued by political corruption, human trafficking, hate crimes toward LGBTQ+ populations, terrifying levels of feminicide, and neoliberal economic policies that further disenfranchise the poor.[4] Mexico is a wounded country that has waged war not only against drugs, but against itself.[5]

Analyzing various twenty-first-century Mexican theater and performance genres, *Sonic Strategies: Performing Mexico's War on Drugs, Mourning, and Feminicide* contends that artists navigate what survival looks and sounds like following Felipe Calderón's 2006 declaration of war. Since Calderón's pronouncement, Mexico has become a nation where words like "*capo*," "*narcofosa*," and "*cuerno de chivo*" are commonplace vernacular, pointing to the invasive presence of cartels. Mexico is also a country with visual displays of atrocity: lifeless bodies dangle from bridges, mutilated torsos are found strewn on the side of the road, and the news constantly reports on execution-style shootings. After 2006, these linguistic and visual cues characterize daily life. And yet, beyond these signs of a nation suffering from the effects of war, Mexico's sonicscape has also been indelibly marked by massive levels of violence and militarization. The sounds of boots, sirens, shouting, and rampant gunfire typify the War on Drugs, prompting performance artists, ranging from the musicians supporting AMLO in 2007 to La Mafia Cabaret in 2017, to leverage the aural realm to express their dissidence with the nation's state of affairs. Their use of sound recreates, questions, and subverts power structures, shaping the way we, as listeners, understand how the artists themselves experience a nation at war. The performers and practitioners considered in the book use sound to make sense of the violence that surrounds them and to comment on their wounded nation. For example, renowned dramaturge Hugo Salcedo penned *Música de balas* (Music of Bullets) in 2011, and though he leaves many of the sonic decisions up to the directors' discretion, the title of the piece itself captures how he experienced and internalized the sounds of war during Calderón's leadership. Moreover, Violeta Luna, a Mexican performance artist based in San Francisco, makes a consistent and concerted effort to centralize sound in *Réquiem #3: Fosas Cuerpo / Body Graves* (2017). Collaborating with longtime creative partner, musician, and sound designer David R. Molina, her piece deploys sounds to accompany and become an act of mourning for Mexico's innumerable disappeared.

    Engaging conversations from trauma studies, musicology, queer studies, and human geography, *Sonic Strategies* is an interdisciplinary study of sound phenomena that appreciates the sonic reverberations of conflict as a complement to the written text and embodied gesture. As readers will notice, I include music, sound effects, incidental noises, audience participation, onstage voices, and more within the category of sound. This wide definition highlights the diversity of sonic stimuli within theater and performance endeavors as well as their centrality to the overall experience. Even though theater and performance research privileges the visual field and textual production, sound flows through the entirety of a performance by way of stage directions guiding the performance's live soundtrack. It is even fair to state that sound is capable of exceeding anything stage directions could possibly dictate, as there are always unplanned and unscripted interjections produced by artists or audiences that may impact the performance itself. As a whole, then, the aural atmosphere functions to transmit messages, manipulate meaning, make sense of situations, inspire identities, and respond to written, verbally articulated, or visual sites of interpretation. In other words, sound has power.[6] While it is perhaps obvious at this point, it is worth noting that the sonic strategies that I examine throughout this book are as much about the sounds themselves as they are about the choice of musical genre or lyrical composition. Music reveals a deep connection to sociocultural factors, and in this context, the musical and lyrical choices are consciously selected to convey a commentary about living in Mexico after 2006. To this end, *Sonic Strategies* insists that the kinds of sonic stimuli used by artists and performers reveal their personal experiences living in a nation at war and relate how their bodies understand the materiality and affective toll of worsening violence and ongoing corruption. Making sound central to their theater and performance practice, the artists in this book pinpoint the experiences of war from the Global South, refusing a trend to privilege the perspective of English-speaking geographies that situate non-Western beings as dangerous Others. This project proposes that listening to theater and performance showcases what Mexican artists can teach us not just about suffering and surviving, but also about resistance and imagination.

Responding to the necessity to pay attention to the aural realm, *Sonic Strategies* is inspired by Jean-Luc Nancy's philosophical study of sound. In *Listening*, Nancy argues in favor of stretching our ears to absorb the sonic reverberations, pondering, "what secret is yielded—hence also made public—when we listen to a voice, an instrument, or a sound just for itself?"[7] To begin answering this question, it is important to recognize that sound does not represent anything on its own. Instead, it becomes socially significant based on how it is perceived in relation to individual subjectivities and broader social, geographic, and historical contexts. Obviously, then, no sound necessarily evokes the same meaning across cultures, and yet that is not the point. Rather, as Nancy insists time and again, by turning (and tuning) our senses to the sonic realm, we become capable of sensing a subject that resides beyond what we can see, touch, and smell. This quality of constantly shifting meaning depends on one of sound's most intriguing qualities: its plasticity. Sound evades chronological and spatial specificity; via unending arrivals and departures, sound produces a constant continuum of its very existence.[8] Spreading through time and space, sound affects diverse populations who imbue the sonic stimuli with meaning and give its reverberations continued life. That is to say, as aural sensations enter into our bodies, they are transformed into memories that connect emotions, landscapes, and smells with specific sonic triggers. Permeating physical spaces and body cavities, sound upends any notion of fixity or stability, consequently offering continuous opportunities for those of us who listen to analyze, reflect, and reassess.

In many ways, theater and performance share several of the fundamental characteristics of sound I just described. The performative gesture is inherently ephemeral, as are sonic stimuli, but it has the potential to live on in spectators' bodies and memories via what Peggy Phelan has so famously described as "the trace"—that is, the residual elements of the performance that become reactivated in each individual audience member after the event.[9] Like sound, theater and performance pieces can also be enjoyed and evaluated without regard for contextual or biographical information, though considering these details undoubtedly opens new pathways for appreciating and interpreting meaning. In pondering Nancy's key question here, I have adapted it and transformed it into two questions that undergird my analysis: What is gained by actively listening to theater and performance? What is revealed when sound is given intellectual and theoretical treatment equal to that given to visual stimuli? In posing these questions, I am pointing out lacunae within the discipline of theatre and performance studies, as sound often goes undertheorized or ignored entirely. I am also advocating that we, as theater and performance scholars, develop a methodology of listening that pays close attention to dissonance, cacophony, and harmony, among other aural triggers. Similarly, these questions are meant to signal vacancies in sound studies, musicology, and ethnomusicology, as facets of the performance (such as the space, stage design, embodiment, audience proximity), risk being undervalued in comparison to the sonic realm. Above all, *Sonic Strategies* is meant to be read as an invitation to scholars across disciplinary fields to listen to theater and performance as part of their analytical agenda. As I suggest throughout this book, engaging in attuned listening practices produces insights about the lived experience that exist beyond language, embodied gesture, or visual cues.

My interest in Mexico after 2006 is not motivated by a desire to dwell in tragedy, but rather by contemporary Mexican performers who use theater and performance as a mechanism of resistance. In traversing new terrain, literally and metaphorically, the artists considered in this book push boundaries; they challenge "traditional" dramaturgical practices and look beyond the proscenium for staging inspiration. In this sense, *Sonic Strategies* listens to voices that relate daily lived experience rather than to the "official" narratives propagated by government officials. For example, Cecilia Sotres, founding member of the *teatro-cabaret* (cabaret theatre) group Las Reinas Chulas, activist, and scholar, asserts that the absurdity of daily events is beyond logical comprehension, and yet, it provides endless inspiration for theatrical stagings.[10] Many of the artists I consider fervently believe Mexico is a nation continually at war against the *narco* and its own citizens. Reflective of this mentality, members of the theater and performance community routinely describe their performative endeavors using language like "fighting from the trenches" or "taking to the streets in collective struggle." In using these phrases to describe their work, these artists imagine theater and performance as sites capable of creatively fighting back against the violence that plagues the country. Importantly, for the practitioners included in this book, theater and performance offer a mode of expression that does not exist in other mediums.

By turning my attention to sound phenomena in theater and performance, I underscore how sonic vibrations create affective sensations capable of fostering community. Expanding on Jorge Dubatti's *convivio*, the term he coined to describe the shared experience of attending a performance, I posit the aural realm as fundamental to solidifying the act of coming together.[11] By way of conviviality, the ephemeral experience of theater and performance allows audience members to bear witness to creative endeavors, including representations of atrocity, attempts at catharsis, or even radical reimaginings of reality. Foregrounding sonic cues, *Sonic Strategies* contends that audiences also bear auditory witness. In doing so, not only do they perceive the visible materiality of a performance, but they also absorb the invisible resonances that stay with them long after the event has ended. Paying close attention to Mexican theater and performance after 2006, I maintain that sonic stimuli reflect the way practitioners themselves have internalized sounds of violence and fear in everyday life. By integrating them into their works, they share their reality with spectators. These sounds, then, bring into being temporary communities of pain, mutual recognition, and care unique to the realm of theater and performance.

Undeniably, there are numerous ways of conceiving the role of sound in theater and performance. Some that I have come across, and even found compelling, include *escenofonía*, sound universe, musical architecture, and sonic dramaturgy.[12] However, each comes with its own definition, and, I would argue, they cannot be used interchangeably. As a result, my approach reflects the book's title: *Sonic Strategies*. Each of the chapters in this book is a case study on what engaged listening reveals about a nation at war, accentuating different theoretical conversations chosen based on the works themselves. I have allowed each piece to give life to an analytical framework that dialogues not only with the other performance or performances in the chapter but also with the political, social, and cultural realities in contemporary

Mexico. My research tactics pull from scholarship in history, film studies, ethnomusicology, theater, and performance, and I integrate a broad range of secondary sources, such as tweets, Facebook posts, local news publications, press conferences, interviews, blog entries, and government reports. In taking this approach, I rely on academic and nonacademic conversations happening across the border, not just conversations about Mexico from within the United States. By incorporating different voices and disciplinary methodologies, *Sonic Strategies* is a model for what it means to be guided by our sources, to listen to what *they* share with us, not just what *we* want to hear from them.

In researching and writing this book, I have been compelled by ethnomusicologist Samuel Araújo's declaration that the "sounds of violence in the contemporary world are too many and too loud not to be considered carefully" by those of us in humanities-based disciplines.[13] Although my exploration of sonic phenomena is limited to theater and performance in Mexico after 2006, I am indebted to the work of numerous scholars in the fields of ethnomusicology, musicology, and sound studies who examine the relationship between sound and conflict on a global scale.[14] Guided by the premise that "music is a powerful discursive tool," *Sonic Strategies* leans on and into the premise that music, just like other cultural objects, is implicated in power struggles, concepts of otherness, nation building, and exclusionary measures.[15] Most notably, this book has been shaped by the research of Steve Goodman, J. Martin Daughtry, and Suzanne G. Cusik regarding music-turned-torture-tool in the United States' War on Terror. These scholars have informed my thinking about music as part of a "much more expansive field of sonic practices" that can transform acoustic sensations into weaponized modalities.[16] Whether via individual listening devices, such as iPods, or projected over loudspeakers, sonic stimuli impact "the way populations feel—not just their individualized, subjective, personal emotions, but more their collective moods or effects."[17] In other words, music can mobilize populations, and, during times of war, it holds the potential to become mercenary and inflict pain.

While much of this aforementioned research concentrates on the post-9/11 conflict between the United States and Iraq, the examples bear striking resemblance to the way the sounds of Mexico's War on Drugs have indelibly changed the nation's soundscape and the way citizens respond to bellicose action. Throughout my four chapters, I attend to the way Mexico's war has shaped the nation's sonic realm and become a tool used by artists to comment on and reimagine their surroundings. Whether in *Ejercicio de percusión* (Percussion Exercise, 2006) by Enrique Ježik, in which the sounds of an antiriot squad overwhelm onlookers, or *México exhumado* (Mexico Exhumed, 2019) by Lechedevirgen Trimegisto, in which the artist transforms a techno song into a weapon meant to pain and confuse the audience, the sounds of violence permeate physical spaces and assault the body itself.

To reflect on global context of violence, trauma, and war, *Sonic Strategies* contributes to scholarly considerations of what it means to perform and enact the spectacle of war. Carol Martin's detailed consideration of live works and their integration (or manipulation) of diaries, letters, court records, familial photographs, and more has indelibly changed the way the field conceives of "the blurred boundary between the stage and the 'real' world," including the impact of social conflict.[18] Concentrating on global powers involved in the war in Iraq (2003–2011), Lindsey Mantoan's and Jenny Hughes's scholarship claims that "just as the performative and rhetorical dimensions of war can be deployed to manipulate senses . . . so they can be redeployed by engaged scholars, artists, and citizens to generate considered and impassioned resistance to it."[19] Tackling these complicated questions of reenacting and revising atrocities has also shaped much of the recent scholarship in theater and performance studies from Latin America. Blending interdisciplinary theoretical models from human right studies, trauma theory, visual studies, and digital political economy, scholars such as Marcela A. Fuentes, Paola S. Hernández, Sarah Misemer, Brenda Werth, and Cecilia Sosa, among others, showcase the vibrancy, vitality, and variety of theater and performance practices. Notably, the studies produced by these scholars underscore how performative styles including documentary theater, theater of the real, postdramatic productions, street interventions, and hashtag activism offer unique and poignant ways to relate governmental atrocities. These myriad styles also showcase the potential performative efforts have to stimulate commemorative bonds across audiences, time, and space, as well as to effect measurable social change. Importantly, these scholars turn to artists who "do not just examine historical figures with a new lens" but rather "turn to everyday stories . . . that illustrate history's lost, forgotten, or unacknowledged experiences."[20] In doing so, they stress the voices often silenced by official mechanisms and narratives during and following abusive governmental regimes.

Similarly, the examples throughout this book often draw attention to bodies and experiences that challenge official narratives set forth by the Mexican government. For example, AMLO and his representatives continuously attempt to assure the nation that violence against female and female-presenting bodies is not a national crisis. And yet, the statistics present a very different truth. All too often, the eleven women a day murdered are not given names, and for trans women, the situation is even more dire as they are not even considered women by most media outlets, their families, or even investigating officers. As a response to this, *Ni una menos* (Not one Woman Less, 2019) by Las Pussy Queers and *La Prietty Guoman* (The Prietty Woman, 2017) by César Enríquez use music to give the invisibilized and silenced female form new life. Notably, by way of the musical choices, such as a feminist reggaetón song that declares "Ni una menos" or Celia Cruz's rumba version of "I will survive," the artists activate murdered female and feminized bodies from beyond the grave, giving them a chance both to resist their own death and to imagine an alternative world where they do not fear *machista* violence.

Working across disciplinary boundaries to contemplate how Mexican theater and performance efforts interpret atrocity via sonic signifiers, *Sonic Strategies* joins the growing body of work by theater and performance scholars who situate aurality at the center of their investigative practice. Ross Brown, David Roesner, Lynn Kendrick, and George Home-Cook have written critical investigations that work against "the naïve assumption that sound is invisible and intangible," instead situating sound as crucial to our mode of being both in and outside of the performance space.[21] Studying examples ranging from a 2012 London-based performance of *Gatz* (Elevator Repair Service's adaptation of *The Great Gatsby*) to the 1957 BBC production of Samuel Beckett's *All That Fall*, these scholars repeatedly emphasize the "intersensorial process of *dynamic embodied attending*" as an analytical model and imperative for spectators.[22] Yet, this research draws conclusions from performative examples located, most often, within white, Western, and English-speaking geographies. There are, of course, scholars in the field of theater and performance, such as Fred Moten, Alexandra T. Vásquez, and Roshanak Kheshti, among others, whose scholarly praxis notably privileges sound. The work of these scholars also utilizes alternative analytical possibilities to makes room for silenced populations and Otherness within the US and "world music" recording industries.[23] However, much work remains to be done.

By making Mexico my central focus, I am interested in challenging exclusionary geographies and inverting hierarchies of knowledge that generally understand theory as traveling north to south. Instead, *Sonic Strategies* demonstrates what performance and theater studies situated in the Global North can learn by listening closely to the ways Mexican theater and performance practitioners transmit their experiences of living in a nation ravaged by war. For example, the Oaxacan *música fúnebre* (funeral music) compositions that accompany Lukas Avendaño in *Buscando a Bruno* (Searching for Bruno, 2018) are nonverbal symbols of Mexico's dead and disappeared bodies. Moreover, Avendaño, who identifies as *muxe*, embodies an intermediary space within the gender binary. Thus the musical score of the piece, which draws attention to Avendaño's own forcibly disappeared and murdered brother, signifies Mexico's innumerable Antigones who mourn their lost loved ones. Each of the chapters in this book, then, proposes the aural realm as a hermeneutical tool for interpreting individual and collective trauma following the nation's 2006 declaration of war. Thinking about sound in this way emphasizes that it must be understood as an integral part of the contemporary Mexican experience; it underscores the indelible link between sound and the social fabric of the nation.

Just as the perception of war differs from person to person and region to region, no single performance style can represent all individual or collective responses to Mexico's conflict. Leaning into this, *Sonic Strategies* chooses not to fixate on categorizing or reducing pieces to specific genres. When necessary, I note the defining stylistic qualities, such as those used to designate a piece as *teatro-cabaret* or as postdramatic theater, and I also acknowledge the preferred terminology the artists themselves use to discuss their work. My analysis, however, does not hinge on upholding rigid separation of genre; I use sonic cues to emphasize similarities and, by doing so, have included artists who would otherwise not be considered together. This approach is inspired by Josefina Alcázar's declaration that performance (often referred to as *arte acción* in Mexico) is the art of the self, the place where the individual and the collective become entwined.[24] Each of the pieces I have selected for this book do just that; they depart from the personal, centering the body as essential to understanding what it means to live in a nation at war.

Notably absent from this book are the sounds of public protests, such as those in the wake of Ayotzinapa, artistic street interventions like Las Hijas de Violencia's take on street harassment, music productions such as Los Macuano's "Sangre, Bandera, Cruz," and sonorous museum installations like Pedro Reyes' *Disarm* (2013).[25] I have also made the conscious decision to omit theater collective Lagartijas Tiradas al Sol, whose oeuvre is extensively surveyed in Julie Ward's book, *A Shared Truth: The Theater of Lagartijas Tiradas al Sol*. Similarly, I do not include Teatro Línea de Sombra because while the group makes striking auditory decisions, Paola S. Hernández dedicates a chapter to closely detailing several of their pieces in *Staging Lives in Latin American Theater: Bodies, Objects, Archives*. The majority of the artists included here are based out of Mexico City, and many of the pieces were performed there as well. This has as much to do with the fact that the nation's capital is the center of economic, political, and cultural power as it has to do with my own relationships with artists. Traveling to Mexico City since 2007, I am fortunate to have built a network of friends, interlocutors, and acquaintances in a variety of artistic circles. At the same time, the works in this book construct an imagined geography that stretches east from Mexico City to the port of Veracruz and extends north from Mexico City across the US–Mexican border to diaspora sites like San Francisco. Recognizing that many of the performances negotiate the line between life and death, this geopolitical space becomes even vaster. Though I have limited my study to works created and interpreted since 2006, the temporalities invoked on stage offer a much longer view of history. References to Mexico's Golden Age of cinema, from roughly 1930 to 1960, and invocations of Santa Anna's nineteenth-century tyrannical reign not only transport spectators but also expose a nation plagued by repeating wounds and ever-present violent tensions. These performances remind us that the past never stays put but rather makes itself consistently felt in the present.

The book is arranged in four chapters that analyze performances taking place from 2006 to 2019. *Sonic Strategies* begins and ends with chapters centered on *teatro-cabaret*, while the middle includes broad-ranging performative styles. I have chosen to organize the book this way because *teatro-cabaret* nearly always presents its sociopolitical critique immediately to explore the depth of the wound with humor and then concludes with a musical number meant to literally end on a high note. The heaviness of the topics included in these four chapters requires giving my readers, and myself, moments of release from the reality of war—moments of laughter, moments of hope. The analysis presented in each chapter is based on extensive prior fieldwork in Mexico where I attended live performances. For those I could not attend, I have studied recorded material, either provided by the artist or available online. I have also created a personal digital archive of materials that includes video recordings, interviews, unpublished scripts, and critical reviews of the public performances with explicit references to sonic qualities. Each artist included in this book was selected because they created pieces that are individual and collective in nature; they are self-reflexive works, conscious of the greater nation at war. The artists in this book also refuse a singular role in the production itself. There is no cult of the director or emphasis on specific actors in any of the performances. In most cases, the performer wears many hats, including director, costume designer, and playwright. Homing in on aurality, many of the artists in this book either made key decisions about the soundtrack or forged a collaborative, and deeply personal, bond with musicians and sound specialists.

Chapter 1, "Sonic Disidentifications and a *Mexicanidad* for the Twenty-First Century," analyzes how a single *teatro-cabaret* piece, *Nosotras las proles* (We, the Plebs, 2013), by Las Reinas Chulas, imbues quintessential cinema soundtracks from Mexico's Golden Age of cinema (1930–1960) with sociopolitical critiques. I argue that the group showcases how ideal models of citizenry no longer apply to the contemporary nation at war. Additionally, I examine how their rewriting underscores the extent to which "non-normative" beings are especially vulnerable to violence in these times of crisis. I begin with bell hooks's oppositional gaze to dialogue with José Esteban Muñoz's concept of disidentification to claim that, as queer women, the members of Las Reinas Chulas could not accept the heteronormative and patriarchal discourses projected on-screen, discourses that informed definitions of citizenry for much of the twentieth century. By employing what I refer to as sonic disidentifications, the all-female troupe leverages elements of the auditory realm to challenge long-standing discourses that have sought to solidify heteronormativity, masculinity, and white mestizaje as crucial to *mexicanidad*.

"Listening to Mexico's War on Drugs," Chapter 2, interrogates the way military training exercises, ricochet bullets, news reports, and *narcocorridos* resonate throughout city streets daily, creating Mexico's sonicscape of war. I situate J. Martin Daughtry's groundbreaking study, *Listening to War*, in relation to Achille Mbembe's necropolitics to examine the sonic ramifications of the Mexican government's proclamation of war. I draw further inspiration from Ileana Diéguez's work on *necroteatro* (necrotheater) in the Americas to analyze three pieces that forefront the sounds of escalating violence. Applying what I call "necroauralities," the audible contours of brutality that reverberate through the terrain of the body as citizen and performer, I examine Enrique Ježik's *Ejercicio de percusión* (2006) as an auditory signifier of the early stages of Mexico's war; the postdramatic piece *Música de balas* (2012), by renowned dramaturge Hugo Salcedo, as a reference to rampant gunfire; and, finally, *México exhumado* (2019), by performance artist Lechedevirgen Trimegisto, as an aural performance of the wounded body that exists between life and death.

My third chapter, "Antigone's Requiem," studies Lukas Avedaño's performance of mourning for his disappeared brother, *Buscando a Bruno* (2018), and Violeta Luna's *Réquiem #3: Fosas cuerpo / Body Graves* (2017). In considering these pieces together, I showcase the efforts exerted by those who seek to find disappeared family members within a deeply corrupt system and demonstrate the diversity of Mexico's mourning female figures. Departing from feminist philosophical studies on Antigone, like Judith Butler's

Antigone's Claim, I consider how Luna and Avendaño problematize gendered mourning roles, as Luna is not a mother and Avendaño is *muxe* (Zapotec's third gender). Turning to musicological studies of funeral practices, I draw attention to the performed expressions of loss via the nonverbal compositions that create vibrating affective bonds between performer and spectator. In what I call "sounds against death," I maintain that these sonic decisions resist the finality of erasure provoked by forced disappearance and what was very likely a horrific death. The result, I suggest, are pieces that do not give voice to the dead and missing but rather mirror the absence of life. By using haunting aural triggers, they envelop their listeners within the laments of the nation's Antigones.

The final chapter, "Soundtracks of an (After)life," examines music as a creative initiative that breaks the cycle of violence toward female and feminized Mexican bodies. In a country where eleven women are murdered daily, female bodies are treated as disposable commodities. Through the lens of Sayak Valencia's *Gore Capitalism* and Rita Laura Segato's articulations of feminicide as a category of gender-based atrocity, I consider three pieces that expose cruelty against the Mexican female body. As examples of *teatro-cabaret*, *Ni una menos* (2019) by Las Pussy Queers, La Mafia Cabaret's *El Desierto de Las Leonas* (The Desert of the Lionesses, 2017), and *La Prietty Guoman* (2017) by César Enríquez all incorporate music as central to their performative gesture. Inspired by Melissa Wright's work on feminist geographies of resistance, this chapter proposes that musical numbers give the onstage female protagonists agency to perform alternative visions of their fate, to rewrite their tragic endings. In doing so, the characters destabilize chronologies of life and death, simultaneously manifesting radical geographies of hope and survival.

CHAPTER 1

Sonic Disidentifications and a *Mexicanidad* for the Twenty-First Century

I saw Las Reinas Chulas perform live for the first time in the summer of 2013. I was introduced to their work the previous summer when I was in Mexico City searching for inspiration for my research. A dear friend recommended that I check out *teatro-bar* El Vicio in Coyoacán, run and operated by Las Reinas Chulas since 2005. Before they took over the space, it was known as El Hábito, the performance laboratory of Liliana Felipe and Jesusa Rodríguez. Unfortunately, though, during that 2012 trip, I was never able to see one of their shows. Instead, when I returned home, I turned to YouTube, watching nearly every clip of the group I could find. I was fascinated by their performance style; it was broad ranging and multifaceted. There was humor, music, dazzling costuming, and audience participation. Of course, I had seen some *teatro-cabaret* (cabaret theater) performances online, such as older pieces by Astrid Hadad, Tito Vasconcelos, and the inimitable Rodríguez herself, but none were quite like this. In 2013, I returned for the International Cabaret Festival, which, at the time, Las Reinas organized themselves. It was a whirlwind of events that spanned the greater Mexico City area, including outlying neighborhoods like El Faro Oriente and Tlalpán. Shows took place in theatres, community centers, plazas, and even basketball courts behind elementary schools. Little did I know then that *Nosotras las proles* (We, the Plebs, 2013), performed in Coyoacán's public plaza, would become the backbone of my research, and lead me to this book project.[1]

Sitting in the audience that August afternoon, accompanied by a Brazilian friend living in Mexico City, I was amazed by the onstage reenactment of Mexican classic films. Many I recognized immediately, like *Nosotros los pobres* (We the Poor, 1948), but some I had to research afterward. Nonetheless, the whole time I sat there, I was stuck on the title; I did not understand what "las proles" meant, though it seemed to provoke uproarious laughter in the crowd every time the *cabareteras* said it. After the piece ended, my friend explained the term to me. As a presidential candidate in 2011, Enrique Peña Nieto was asked about his favorite books but did not have an answer. Critiqued and made fun of mercilessly by the Mexican public, Peña Nieto's daughter took to Twitter to defend her father: "un saludo a toda la bola de pendejos, que forman parte de la prole y sólo critican a quien envidian!" (hello to the basket of deplorables from the lower class that only critique those they envy).[2] The damage was irreparable, even though Peña Nieto declared that his daughter's response "definitivamente fue un exceso y me disculpo públicamente por ello. Hablé con mis hijos sobre el valor del respeto y la tolerancia, les reiteré que debemos escuchar y no ofender a los demás" (definitively was in excess and I apologize publicly for it. I have spoken with my children about the importance of respect and tolerance, reiterating to them that we should listen to, and not offend, our interlocuters).[3] One thing was clear to the Mexican public: Peña Nieto and his family had clearly defined themselves as part of "the haves" and not the "have nots," the vast majority of the country.

With this context in mind, *Nosotras las proles* is an astute appraisal of a government that disregards its vulnerable in favor of maintaining systematic inequalities rooted in antiquated definitions of the ideal citizen. Weaving together their interpretations of various cinema classics, such as *Nosotros los pobres* (1948), *Ustedes los ricos* (You All, the Rich, 1948), *Angelitos negros* (Black Angels, 1948), *Tizoc* (1957), and *Los tres García* (The Three García, 1947), with references to contemporary and historical events, Las Reinas Chulas subverts present and past master narratives. Bringing archetypes, tropes, and songs from the 1940s into the present, the piece critiques an imaginary of what it means to be Mexican as set forth by audiovisual constructions associated with Mexico's Golden Age of cinema (1930–1960). My analysis follows the structure of the piece itself, first considering *Nosotros los pobres*, followed by *Los tres García*, and finally *Angelitos negros*. While the performance and script include a revised performance of *Tizoc*, I do not analyze this content as it contains no musical numbers. My close listening of the piece is rooted in access to the unpublished script and attendance at a 2013 staging in Coyoacán, Mexico. Notably, the group tackles the melodramatic plot lines devoted to family structures and the musical numbers that sonically reinforce those constructions. In this chapter, I explore the auditory aspect of the performance. This includes, but is not limited to, the choice of songs, lyrical composition (or revision), and sonic elements, such as spoken and singing voices and musical accompaniment. Examined in conjunction, these multiple components point to the way sonic strategies express a relationship to broader sociocultural significance. By employing what I refer to as sonic disidentifications, the all-female troupe leverages the earlier-mentioned elements of the auditory realm as a means of challenging long-standing discourses that have sought to solidify heteronormativity, masculinity, and white mestizaje as crucial to *mexicanidad*. By extension, Las Reinas Chulas also interrogates how these definitions of belonging have established the parameters of those deserving state protections and participation in the nation. The women transmit their critiques in three notable ways: by removing Pedro Infante, and his renowned tenor voice, from his quintessential father-figure roles; by satirizing heteronormative masculinity and homophobic beliefs; and by addressing harmful racial discourses toward Afro-Mexicans.

FROM MELODRAMA TO SONIC DISIDENTIFICATION: REJECTING THE SCREEN STORY AND ITS SCORE

At the heart of *Nosotras las proles*' revision of Mexican cinema classics is a reworking of the films' recognizable melodramatic plot lines and musical numbers that were deployed in order to shape *mexicanidad*. In its very basic sense, the term *melodrama* emerged from the world of theater, meaning a drama accompanied by music.[4] The genre employs music as a separate, subjective element meant to dramatize the narrative. As Thomas Elsaesser argues, this is made possible by the way music punctuates the narrative while also being "both functional (i.e., of structural significance) and thematic (i.e., belonging to the expressive content) because it is used to formulate certain moods."[5] Generally speaking, then, songs are crucial components of melodramatic plots, such as the construction of the family unit. Ana López points out that musical performances in melodramas from this period were "typically invoked as markers of nationality and as sites for national identification," further emphasizing the creation and formulation of the ideal citizen.[6] Expanding on this observation in her groundbreaking work, *Cine-sonidos*, Jacqueline Avila critically engages with sonic structures of Mexican Golden Age cinema, positing that "the continuous reiteration of symbols, myths, memories, and traditions is solidified through specific musical and aural associations."[7] In this sense, music becomes "coterminous" with the screen-story melodrama. That is to say, music became inextricably linked to the films' plots and evolved into aural triggers of *mexicanidad*.[8] In the case of *Nosotras las proles*, I suggest that Las Reinas Chulas homes in on sonic tropes from the 1940s to challenge and dismantle depictions of the heteronormative family unit, phobic masculinity, and the whitened *mestizo* identity that undergird Mexicanness.

The lasting popularity of Golden Age cinema has much to do with its nearly constant accessibility via television programming, video recordings, and streaming services. It is not my intention to offer an in-depth historical study of the relationship between mass consumption and filmic relics of the past. However, according to Néstor García Canclini in *Consumers and Citizens*, this shift was indispensable for the longevity of Golden Age films: "the dissemination of TV channels and video clubs throughout the country, with homogeneous programming designed by monopolies, makes it possible for viewers in large and small cities to have access to almost the same cinematographic repertoire."[9] The seemingly ubiquitous quality of these films and their constant availability for replay has allowed them to inform present generations of what it means to be Mexican, and what it means to be perceived as a "good" family and member of society. Conglomerates like Televisa and TV Azteca (the monopolies to which García Canclini is referring) have further made it possible for the entire country to share a particular vision of the past as well as of the idiosyncrasies that shape the present.

When I asked Ana Francis Mor about the process of recreating *Nosotros los pobres* for *Nosotras las proles*, her response was straightforward and provocative, prompting the questions that have guided this chapter. I want to quote her at length because her words resonate with García Canclini's ideas and point to the continued accessibility and proliferation of the films produced so many decades ago:

> Ese espectáculo, por ejemplo, de *Nosotras las proles*, tiene que ver con una fascinación por ese cine. Lo vimos tantas y tantas veces, todas esas películas las pasaban en un canal de televisión, el canal 4, todos los sábados. Entonces si tu ves que todos los sábados hay una película de esas o dos y entonces, bueno, fue parte de nuestra niñez, nuestra adolescencia durante años así . . . la misma película la viste quince veces y entonces claro la sabemos de memoria y forman parte del pensamiento nacional y de la idiosincrasia nacional.[10]

> *This work, for example, Nosotras las proles, has to do with a fascination for this kind of filmic relic. We have seen these movies so, so many times; they were played every Saturday on channel four. So, you see, for years, watching one or two of these movies every Saturday was part of our childhood, our adolescence . . . You would have seen the same movie fifteen times and, of course, you know it by heart, and it forms part of national thought and national idiosyncrasies.*

Although Mor's words suggest that constant exposure to the films led to them becoming ingrained in national thought and behavior, there are certainly limits to the extent to which viewers bought into these idealized projections of *mexicanidad*.[11] On one hand, as multiple scholars attest, the Mexican melodramas of the 1940s served to "inculcate women and men as 'appropriately' gendered citizens" by projecting a particular image of the heteronormative family unit, masculinity, and a lightened mestizo physique.[12] And yet, there is an argument to be made that the "narrative of post-1940 Mexico," emerging on the heels of a revolution, "fails to accommodate the numerous contradictions and nuances embedded within the daily life of the period."[13] In other words, the state-supported cultural productions that sought to create the images and sounds that characterized Mexican identity were still rife with flaws and could never possibly capture the experience of an entire nation. It is not my intention to enter into a debate about the extent to which Golden Age cinema actually shaped citizenry, but rather I consider the fact that the films did, in no small part, seek to repeatedly project a particular kind of *mexicanidad* that Las Reinas Chulas takes to task in *Nosotras las proles*.

The ways in which Ana Francis, Nora, Cecilia, and Marisol draw attention to and resist fundamental elements of Mexicanness as depicted by Golden Age films echo scholarship that proposes varying degrees of identifying against, rejecting, and opposing the screen-story. Concentrating on the US context and possibilities for black bodies to disrupt white master narratives via cinematic creation, Manthia Diawara and bell hooks offer fruitful sites of departure for my consideration of *Nosotras las proles*. For example, Diawara asserts that when viewers reject the screen-story, they create an intermediary space "where the spectator recuperates his/her identities and interrupts the symbolic system of a master narrative."[14] Similarly, bell hooks proposes the notion of oppositional gazing, an extension of rejecting the screen story, stating that "it is also about transforming the image, creating alternatives, asking ourselves questions" related to the world we live in versus the one we want to manifest into existence.[15] Applying these ideas to the 2013 Coyoacán performance provides an opportunity to understand how Las Reinas Chulas' performance reflects the group's inability to accept master narratives, prompting them to create their own storyline via *teatro-cabaret*.

Importantly, the women's rejection of Golden Age depictions of *mexicanidad* is intimately related to their personal lives. As openly self-identifying lesbian and bisexual women, the members of Las Reinas Chulas could not and cannot see themselves represented within Golden Age characterizations of family and sexuality.[16] The repeated emphasis on heteronormativity, whitened mestizaje, and defined gender roles depicted via plots, characterizations, and musical numbers meant to inspire viewers to replicate and repeat the actions of the past.[17] *Nosotras las proles*, however, is an example of how the cabaret group did not repeat the norms and conventions of the Golden Age, but rather deviated from those expectations. By remaking the melodramatic familial relationships and musical numbers, the piece reorganizes time, and by bringing the past into the present, it unsettles the narratives of the films themselves. Las Reinas Chulas, then, "challeng[es] the singular attributes of the auratic and 'timelessness'" of the original via their dissenting sonic revisions on the 2013 stage.[18] As I argue, the performance transforms the *cabareteras* into "figures for and bearers of new corporeal sensations, including those of a certain counterpoint between now and then."[19]

Las Reinas Chulas' performative reworkings of the melodramatic family plots and their associated recognizable songs are what I call "acts of sonic disidentification." Here, my use of disidentification is a clear reference to the work of José Esteban Muñoz. In his influential text, *Disidentifications: Queers of Color and the Performance of Politics*, he proposes the concept as a means for minority subjects to navigate and negotiate "a phobic majoritarian public sphere that continuously elides or punishes the existence of subjects who do not conform to the phantasm of normative citizenship."[20] He argues that in deploying performance and performative endeavors, artists use popular images to rearticulate meaning in a way that includes previously excluded Others. Muñoz states, "the process of disidentification scrambles and reconstructs the encoded message of a cultural text in a fashion that both exposes the encoded message's universalizing and exclusionary machinations and recircuits its workings to account for, include, and empower minority identities and identification."[21] By scrambling and reconstructing various Golden Age films, *Nosotras las proles* empowers Las Reinas Chulas, as minority figures, to reconfigure exclusionary narratives to be more inclusive of racial, social, and sexual Others. Moreover, the piece's lyrical revisions and sonic reverberations disidentify with the sounds of the past; they become a call to contemplate past and present exclusionary politics deeply embedded in definitions of Mexicanness. As Muñoz would suggest, the sonic element of *Nosotras las proles* gives the social order a "jolt that may reverberate loudly and widely."[22] In this sense, the auditory elements of the performance are a counterpoint to Golden Age soundtracks. They are sonic acts of disidentification that incorporate vulnerable Others previously omitted from definitions of belonging, and, by extension, gain for them the respect and rights they deserve.

TEATRO-CABARET: A BRIEF HISTORY

The theater and performance genre unique to Mexico known as *teatro-cabaret* emerged during the 1980s as a contemporary rendition of early twentieth century *teatro de revista* (revue theater; hereafter *revista*) and *teatro de carpa* (tent theater; hereafter *carpa*) blended with European cabaret styles. *Carpa* and *revista* were known for using comedy, dance numbers, music, stereotypical characters, popular language, and other performance tools organized as individual sketches or connected by an overarching plot. For Armando María y Campos and Socorro Merlín, the Mexican *revista* evolved from Spanish theater styles, such as the opera, *zarzuela*, *sainete*, and "género chico." Brought into the Mexican context after the 1868 Spanish revolution, these models profoundly impacted the sonic qualities and thematic content that evolved into Mexico's own "género chico político," alternatively called *teatro de revista*.[23] According to Merlín, though *revista* and *carpa* are quite similar and share particular elements, including performers, structure, and performance spaces, *carpa*'s concurrent development comes from a different origin: the circus. The first circuses arrived to Mexico in 1790 and "con el circo vienen payasos y toda clase de equilibristas, magos y equitadores, que exaltan la imaginación y el deseo de lanzarse a las pistas de nuestros propios maromeros, graciosos y contorsionistas" (with the circus come clowns and all kinds of tightrope walkers, magicians, and horse riders, all of whom awaken the imagination and desire of Mexico's own acrobats, comedians, and contortionists to get on stage).[24] These body-centric performative repertoires intimately shaped the character types, humor, and emphasis on the body that became characteristic of *carpa* productions. Importantly, both *revista* and *carpa* flourished during the Mexican Revolution, as national upheaval provided the performers and writers with plenty of material. Finding inspiration in revolutionary heroes, battles, and political traitors, *carpa* and *revista* productions laid the foundation for astute political satire that would come to define contemporary *teatro-cabaret*.

The popularity of *carpa* and *revista* traditions can also be attributed to their ability to connect with their audiences by producing relevant and timely content. This is particularly germane because, as Laura Gutiérrez explains, "*revistas* and *carpas* were the first artistic performance format in which popular classes were able to find themselves reflected, a phenomenon that would later be reproduced by the incipient film industry."[25] She goes on to note that part of what made this onstage reflection possible were the representations of Mexican archetypes, and, more specifically, "the emergences of popular types along with a new language that was more popular, urban and 'vulgar.'"[26] Additionally, the structures and low cost of entry facilitated access to content that had otherwise been denied to popular groups, often living on the peripheries of the capital city and without expendable income. Notably, *revistas* often took place in brick-and-mortar structures, meaning that members of the middle class were often in attendance alongside those of lower socio-economic means. In contrast, *carpas* were performed in easily erected and mobile structures like tents or simple wooden canopies known as *jacalones* so that performers could very literally bring cultural productions to the margins of Mexican society.[27] María y Campos and Merlín widely regard the 1920s and 1930s, as the Revolution came to a close and sound cinema became more popular, as the historical moment when *carpa* and *revista* began to disappear from in and around the capital city. Without inspiration for material or audience members, *carpa* and *revista* first became depoliticized and then faded into the background, overshadowed by the silver screen. However, with the appearance of popular stage actors in film, and thus *carpa* and *revista*'s influence over cinematic conventions, these performance styles did not truly disappear. Some genres of Mexico's Golden Age, such as the *comedia ranchera*, borrowed heavily from the musical and narrative structures of the *revista*, fostering a connection between character archetypes, the kinds of songs they performed, and how the music intervened in the overall plot.[28]

Fast forward to the 1980s. *Teatro-cabaret* appeared on Mexico City stages amid a wave of unsettling events, such as the nation's economic collapse in 1982 and the 1985 earthquake that shook the capital city to its core. As a response to this context of crisis and uncertainty, the work of Jesusa Rodríguez, Liliana Felipe, Tito Vasconcelos, and Astrid Hadad represents the artists' anxieties about the kind of art they wanted, and felt they needed, to produce. Officially trained in theater at leading universities, these foundational figures sought new creative means to grapple with the sensation of reality falling apart, very literally, around them. Additionally, identifying against the grain of patriarchal heteronormativity, these figures used *teatro-cabaret* as a powerful mechanism for imagining new definitions of belonging embedded within their revisions of dominant narratives.[29] In using the term *cabaret*, these artists consciously chose to align themselves in relation to models dating back to the eighteenth century. Mexican *cabareterxs* were drawn to the physical space associated with early French cabaret, "where the relationship between performer and spectator is one of both intimacy and hostility."[30] Hadad, Rodríguez, Felipe, and Vasconcelos, and those that followed them, sought to forge bonds between performer and audience by simulating that ambiance of talk, drink, and smoke (when smoking was allowed indoors). Beyond the spatial considerations, the aforementioned performers were inspired by later developments in French cabaret, such as the over-the-top visuals, elaborate costumes, and provocative dance numbers associated with the world-renowned Moulin Rouge. The *cabareterxs* were also captivated by the overtly political commentary in German Kabarett, perceiving parallels with the Mexican context of political abuses. Gastón Alzate proposes that *teatro-cabaret* became, in response to increasing globalization efforts during Miguel de la Madrid's presidency, "una red simbólica contestataria relacionada con una necesidad social frente a mecanismos de marginación" (a rebellious network that responded to social necessity to confront mechanisms of marginalization).[31] In the 1990s, as political corruption became more severe, and the country fell further into economic despair, Rodríguez herself declared, "we're in such a profound crisis, and cabaret always flourishes in crisis—remember the Nazis, how cabaret boomed then? In Mexico, we're in an impossible spectacle, beyond Ibsen or the absurd. We're in a kind of perverse fiction."[32] Even though she made this comment nearly thirty years ago, it resonates with Mexico's current circumstances.

The desire to use *teatro-cabaret* to navigate and interrogate surreal aspects of contemporary Mexican reality continues to inform current practitioners. In her guide to *teatro-cabaret*, Cecilia Sotres, *cabaretera* and foundational member of Las Reinas Chulas, explains that although cabaret encompasses many aesthetics and performative styles, a piece should always have humor and social or political critique.[33] This last point is of particular importance, as Sotres declares that in the Mexico of today, "es claro que vivimos en una época de inestabilidad, de guerra, una guerra velada si lo quieren ver así, pero al fin y al cabo, una guerra. El cotidiano devenir nos obliga a vivir situaciones absurdas que nos sobrepasan, dignas de ser traducidas al lenguaje teatral" (it is clear we live in an epoch of instability, of war, a veiled war, if you want to call it that, but, after all, a war. Daily events force us to live absurd situations that surpass believability, worthy of being translated into theatrical language).[34] In fact, this statement inspired my look to theater as a means of expressing the unfathomable aftermath of Mexico's War on Drugs. Sotres's statement is also perceptible throughout *Nosotras las proles*, which taps into the themes I explore in greater details in later chapters. For example, the onstage characters reference how Mexico's streets became a war zone between the military and *narco* forces, the subject of Chapter 2, and hint at the increasing number of forced disappearances, the topic of Chapter 3. Finally, the performers explicitly comment on the painful and terrifying reality that eleven women are murdered a day in Mexico, the topic of my last chapter.[35] Grappling with these aforementioned grotesque situations and more, Ana Francis, Nora, Cecilia, and Marisol seek refuge in *teatro-cabaret*'s vibrant ability to express dissenting and satirical critiques of the Mexican experience.

LAS REINAS CHULAS AND *NOSOTRAS LAS PROLES*

The four female performers of Las Reinas Chulas are Ana Francis Mor, Cecilia Sotres, Marisol Gasé, and Nora Huerta.[36] As theater performers, the members of Las Reinas Chulas formally studied theater at the National Autonomous University of Mexico (UNAM) under the tutelage of many of the above-mentioned cabaret artists and "cuerpos disidentes" (dissident bodies).[37] In typical *teatro-cabaret* tradition, the women combine awareness of contemporary events, an activist agenda, and artistic practice to critically examine Mexico's current sociopolitical conditions: "para las Reinas Chulas, el cabaret significa fundamentalmente desobediencia civil y resistencia, señalando así la estrecha conexión entre su obra y el activismo social" (for Las Reinas Chulas, cabaret fundamentally signifies civil disobedience and resistance, signaling the intimate connection between their works and social activism).[38] The women are also entrepreneurs; in 2005, they assumed control of El Hábito, once run by Rodríguez and Felipe. Renaming the space El Vicio, Las Reinas Chulas has kept the cabaret tradition alive for the last decade by regularly performing and inviting other local *teatro-cabaret* artists to entertain audiences. Their work also extends beyond the confines of the theatre space and Mexico's national borders. The four women have produced television series, offered workshops on gender inequality and violence in Mexico and Central America, taught classes on how to become a *teatro-cabaret* performer, and founded the annual International Cabaret Festival in Mexico City. To accomplish all of this, the women operate as a civil association. As Teatro Cabaret Reinas Chulas A.C., the members utilize *teatro-cabaret* as "una forma de mirar los problemas sociales desde un enfoque crítico, lúdico y creativo que transgrede y desconstruye la narrativa melodramática ... que a menudo es hegemónica, opresora y patriarcal" (a way of seeing social problems with a critical, ludic, and creative perspective that transgresses and deconstructs a melodramatic narrative ... that is often hegemonic, oppressive, and patriarchal).[39]

These important projects have not gone unnoticed. Las Reinas Chulas has received multiple prestigious grants from the Fondo Nacional para la Cultura y las Artes (FONCA) in categories such as cabaret and career trajectory, and scholarships from the Fondo de Ayudas para las Artes Escénicas Iberoamericanas.[40] In 2014, the legislative assembly of Mexico City awarded the group the medal of honor, which they accepted dressed as celestial beings they interpret in their work (La Virgen Santa Rita, Jesus, Buddha, and Coyolxauhqui). Over the last several years, the group has continued to gain notoriety on the national stage, for example, having been selected to direct the National Theater Company in 2020, an enormous honor and symbolic recognition of *teatro-cabaret*'s cultural value. The COVID-19 pandemic interrupted those plans, however. Long before this, in 2015, Nora Huerta was honored with an Ariel (the equivalent to an Oscar) in the category of stand-out female performance.[41] For years, Cecilia Sotres has offered cabaret training through UNAM and local venues like La Casa del Humor, even pivoting to virtual formats during COVID-19. Beyond *teatro-cabaret*, Ana Francis Mor has directed numerous successful plays such as *La Testosterona* (The Testosterone Woman, 2018) and *Entre Villa y una Mujer Desnuda (Between Villa and a Nude Woman, 2020)*, in addition to writing her first novel, *Lo que soñé mientras dormías* (What I Dreamt while You Slept, 2017), and publishing books on the topic of lesbian love. Upon Andrés Manuel López Obrador's election as president, Marisol Gasé began to emcee public events for the nation's leader and became host of a weekly radio program, *La Hora Nacional*, in 2020. In fact, as of June 2021, both Gasé and Mor were chosen to serve as appointed congresswomen for the Morena party. As evidenced by this partial list of accomplishments, the women of Las Reinas Chulas are making an impact both within and outside the world of *teatro-cabaret*.

The kinds of productions Ana Francis, Cecilia, Marisol, and Nora create do not happen in a vacuum. Part of what inspires their work, and facilitates their success, is their political, cultural, and social postures that operate within and against hegemonic structures. As queer women and feminists, Las Reinas Chulas actively resists heteronormative and patriarchal hierarchies. Moreover, the group's survival as non-normative citizens is appreciated via performance strategies that work "on and against dominant ideology."[42] In attempting to decipher, scramble, and challenge socially pervasive beliefs, such as those promulgated by Golden Age cinema, the group "opt[ed] not to assimilate" to master narratives. In forging relationships with the press and university departments, and by appearing in television and film, the four women have also built a strong presence outside the world of *teatro-cabaret*. This participation in the dominant sector, and their public relationship to the political party currently in power, has raised questions about their ability to be transgressive or dissenting voices.[43] Admittedly, I have noticed a significant depoliticization in their work over the last several years and a reluctance to critique AMLO's presidency, obviously due to their close affiliation with the Morena party and the president himself. And yet, given that I am analyzing a performance from 2013, I do not believe that the current status of Las Reinas Chulas bears significant consequences for my argument or the way I perceive *Nosotras las proles* as an act of disidentification. Rather, I suggest it represents a balancing act as the women navigate being inside and outside of dominant culture.

Performed from 2008 to 2013, the piece combines references to five Golden Age cinema classics: *Los tres García* (1947), *Nosotros los pobres* (1948), *Ustedes los ricos* (1948), *Angelitos negros* (1948), and *Tizoc* (1957). The original title of the piece, *Petróleo en la sangre* (Petroleum in the Blood, 2008), was changed to *Nosotras las proles* in order to engage with a particular 2011 event: the daughter of Enrique Peña Nieto, a presidential candidate later elected to office, called her father's critics "proles," an insult that suggested they were poor and uneducated.[44] The decision to change the name of the piece in response to this comment demonstrates the way *teatro-cabaret* works "se nacen y se modifican según lo que vaya pasando al nivel político" (are born of, and are modified in relation to, what is happening in national politics).[45] Beyond reclaiming the word *prole*, the 2013 updates include references to the following major events: Peña Nieto proposed an "energy reform" that would have privatized part of Mexico's petroleum production; the teacher's union leader, Elba Esther Gordillo, was arrested on fraud charges; PEMEX leader Romero Deschamps was reelected; and teacher strikes took over city centers all over the nation.[46] Hence, *Nosotras las proles* rewrites the aforementioned cinema classics to critique the contemporary "patriarchal" state that, by encouraging neoliberal sociopolitical values, harms, rather than protects, the vast majority of the nation's citizens.

REVISING THE QUINTESSENTIAL MELODRAMATIC FAMILY UNIT AND ITS MUSIC

More than eighty years later, *Nosotros los pobres* (1948) remains one of the most widely viewed films in Mexican history, thanks in large part to being frequently replayed on television.[47] One of the major factors contributing to the film's success was casting acting and singing star Pedro Infante as Pepe "el Toro." In this iconic role, among others, Infante shaped an external (and superficial) representation of *mexicanidad* that generations of Mexican men wanted to achieve. I am talking about his body as spectacle of the mestizo physique. Infante appeared half naked at least once in most of his films, revealing his toned and light-skinned torso. His body came to stand in as the image of beauty and strength. Moreover, as Pepe "el Toro," the actor portrayed a strong patriarchal personality; he was firm, but still sensitive enough to cry at the loss of loved ones. As scholars have repeatedly commented, Infante as Pepe "el Toro" and Blanca Estela as Celia la Chorreada came to embody the virtuous archetypal couple. Their performances in the 1948 classic cemented essential elements of the melodrama genre, such as vertigo-inducing crises and emotional excess juxtaposed by light-hearted songs and jokes.[48] These qualities of the Mexican melodrama, and its representation of the city and its inhabitants, created an idealized vision of what life was like for the urban poor. As the quintessential representation of popular language, urban archetypes, and melodramatic plotlines, the film convinced generations that the way the characters dressed, their social customs, a life without privacy, and the sound of the singsong voice without refined vocabulary represented Mexico.[49] Beyond the screen story, *Nosotros los pobres* demonstrates many elements that Octavio Paz defines as *lo mexicano* in his 1950 *El laberinto de la soledad* (*The Labrynth of Solitude*). For example, the urban poor's resignation to their social status is part of Paz's mythification of *lo mexicano*, a myth that Las Reinas Chulas dismantles as they distance themselves from these oversimplified concepts and state-supported agendas.

Just as Ismael Rodríguez and Pedro de Urdemalas created *Nosotros los pobres* in such a way that the film, its characters, and its melodramatic twists would be sure to garner the public's admiration, Las Reinas Chulas created their own deviant version of the film that disidentifies with major plotlines and crucial sonic triggers. *Nosotras las proles* is an act of "decoding mass, high, or any other cultural field form the perspective of a minority subject who is disempowered in such a representational hierarchy."[50] The 2013 performance begins by projecting the book and neighborhood from the film on a large screen behind the stage, followed by the appearance of the cast. With Ata in his denim overalls, white T-shirt, and cap, Chachita in her modest white dress, la Chorreada in her blue dress and white apron, and Abuela tísica in her wheelchair, covered by her blanket, these onstage costumes visually indicate that *Nosotras las proles* is going to be a remake. The believability of these onstage versions extends to their mannerisms and speech patterns as well; the actors sound and move like their on-screen counterparts.[51] Internalizing qualities of *mexicanidad*, just as Monsiváis, Carlos Bonfil, and many other film scholars propose to be the purpose of Golden Age cinema, Las Reinas Chulas' performative audiovisual decisions

FIGURE 1.1. The cast of *Nosotras las proles* takes the stage looking very much like the original characters from *Nosotros los pobres* (1948). *Nosotras las proles*, 2013. Photo by Daniel Cortés.

reflect the intentionality behind their remake. By deploying similarities to the original, the satirical and politically engaged dialogue is immediately jarring to audience members, and they quickly realize that this is no ordinary different interpretation of the classic film. The act of listening to the piece's overall sonic quality, including musical numbers, lyrical revision, and singing and spoken vocal expression, becomes a point of entry into analyzing the ways in which Las Reinas Chulas disidentify with the original film.

One of the first clues that this is a dissident remake of *Nosotros los pobres* is Pedro Infante's absence from his role as Pepe "el Toro." Only mentioned from within the mimetic space, Las Reinas Chulas does not simply write him out of Golden Age history but make him absent from the stage in order to redefine and reimagine standards of masculine *mexicanidad*. Via female-to-male drag, the troupe still performs masculinity on stage by way of Ata, a character from *Ustedes los ricos*, who, in Pepe's absence, both on screen and on stage, becomes the male figurehead. In this 2013 rendition, Ata is depicted as impotent in his efforts to perform masculine expectations. This "man" stutters, struggles to find the words to express himself, and is definitely not the fearless problem-solver Pepe "el Toro" was.[52] Hence, in place of Pepe's virile body, this powerless Ata communicates Las Reinas Chulas' broader critique of a government that does not take care of its citizens: there is no protective father figure or any other governmental body that ensures basic human rights.

By removing the lead male character, *Nosotras las proles* defiantly rejects the traditional cinematic depictions of the quintessential masculine figure and his family unit. As Monsiváis claims, "en la Época de Oro la industria fílmica potencia y modifica a la Gran Familia Mexicana, y rehace las versiones de la *mexicanidad* al difundir el nacionalismo como *show*, una propuesta aceptada con no demasiadas variantes" (during the Golden Age, the film industry strengthens and modifies the image of the Great Mexican Family, and remakes versions of Mexicanness to disseminate nationalism as a kind of show, an accepted proposal without many variations).[53] Eliminating the father figure from the onstage family and the quintessential image of urban Mexican manliness, Las Reinas Chulas disrupts the tidy package of family values projected on screen and via televised replay, replacing it with a dissident restructuring to show how the expectations of the past no longer meet the needs of contemporary Mexican reality. This decision resists also the master narrative of a benevolent patriarch to instead suggest that the father figure actually functions as an oppressive force, a metaphor for the actions taken by Mexico's powerful political and economic elite.

The production emphasizes this critique through performances of sonic disidentification. Notably, the women of Las Reinas Chulas revise the opening number from *Nosotros los pobres*. In the film, the song "¡Ni hablar mujer!" begins with a promising, joyful tone:

Qué bonito es el reír	How lovely it is to laugh
Qué bonito es el querer	How lovely it is to love
Qué bonito es el vivir	How lovely it is to live
¡Ni hablar mujer!	No way woman!
Qué bonita comezón	What a lovely itch
la que deja el corazón	That the heart creates
Qué bonita sensación	What a lovely sensation
¡Ni hablar mujer![54]	No way woman!

During the musical sequence, many of the neighborhood's figures chime in, sometimes singing verses but most often singing the line "¡Ni hablar mujer!" in unison. Although viewers most certainly enjoy hearing the onscreen drunken female duo, La Guayaba y La Tostada, mumble through a verse, the most important voice is that of the smooth tenor, Pepe "el

Toro." His warm vibrato and clear articulations of happiness welcome listeners into the physical space of the urban barrio. The song unfolds throughout the streets and in Pepe's workshop, transforming it very literally into the soundtrack that accompanies residents and viewers on a journey through the neighborhood. As such, the song forges aurally driven geospatial connections and becomes the sonic anthem of urban life.[55] The vocal performances further posit the neighborhood at the center of romantic love and masculine protection. For example, Infante uses his smooth and seductive voice to deliver lines like "Qué rechula es la mujer / Cuando te quiere de verdad" (How wonderful is the lady / when she loves you really, truly), whereas he reserves his husky, masculine voice to recount "Nací pelado, sí señor / Pero me gusta, qué caray" (I was born poor, yes sir I was / But how I like it, God damnit). Here, Infante's ability to harness sounding firm when singing of masculinity and soft when singing about beauty cements the performance as a blatantly heteronormative love song.

Reflecting Las Reinas Chulas' critique of heteronormative love and patriarchal acts that continue to disenfranchise the poor "ora que ya regresó el PRI" (now that the PRI returned), the group rewrote the song.[56] Without Pepe "el Toro," the protagonist of this version is la Chorreada, supported by Ata and Chachita as her chorus of neighborhood tenants. La Chorreada's female voice dethrones "el tenorio del pueblo" (the village's tenor) from his position of audiovisual significance.[57] Physically and aurally replacing him while singing a tune intimately tied to urban identity and the film itself, this Chorreada gives the original social order a new power structure. Concretely, the centrality of her voice defies the song's very title, "¡Ni hablar mujer!" Using her strong alto range, Ana Francis's vocal production emerges from deep within her body to deliver this updated version. By producing sound from her chest tones, she vocally inhabits a materiality often reserved for men in singing performance.[58] From the beginning of the song, Chorreada's voice enunciates a very different vision of Mexico than the original. The lyrics point precisely to neoliberal practices that wound and further disenfranchise Mexico's urban poor; their words relate a biting satirical commentary on Mexico's state of affairs. Together, the three characters sing:

Chorreada:	Chorreada:
Que bonito es mi país	How lovely is my country
Ora que ya volvió el PRI	Now that the PRI returned
Ya lo vamos a explotar	Now we're going to exploit it

Ata y Chachita:
    Privatizar

Chorreada:
    Aunque nos la dejen ir
    El Progreso viene ya
    Ni lo vamos a sentir

Ata y Chachita:
    Ni a disfrutar

Chorreada:
    Ellos saben negociar
    Algo bueno pasará
    Los tenemos que apoyar

Ata y Chachita:
    Hay que confiar[59]

Ata and Chachita:
    Privatize

Chorreada:
    Even though they let us go
    Progress is soon to come
    We won't even feel it

Ata and Chachita:
    Nor enjoy it.

Chorreada:
    They know how to negotiate
    Something good will come
    We must support them

Ata and Chachita:
    We must believe

Even in these few lines, Las Reinas Chulas' voices satirize what was a commonplace discourse during the 2012 election: that the twenty-first-century PRI was different from its twentieth-century version and ready to enact social change. The references to negotiation, exploitation, and privatization are related to Peña Nieto's 2012 energy reform efforts, which I will discuss in the section about *Los tres García*. Here, I would like to focus on how Las Reinas Chulas reclaims the title of prole to elucidate the harmful impact of "top-down" initiatives. While it bears mentioning that none of Las Reinas Chulas are part of Mexico's lower class, that does not preclude them from critiquing harmful government officials and policies that directly and primarily impact the prole.[60] This solidarity becomes transmitted on stage through the characters' vocal intonation as well as the words they speak. For example, Ata and Chachita's high-pitched voices, in contrast with Chorreada's deep tones, are meant to mimic the sound of the on-screen child actors. These voices also imply a wholesome ignorance with regard to the actual effects of neoliberal political decisions. I want to also suggest that this childlike vocal performance also be heard as Las Reinas Chulas' critical appraisal of the way certain sectors, like those pertaining to the lower class, parroted key phrases used by Mexican politicians to convince voters in the 2012 election. And it worked. The PRI returned to power, though there are, of course, other structural factors that contributed to the party's success. The *cabareteras*' point, however, is that despite repeated experiences of abuse, leaving Mexico's prole with limited access to quality food, education, and respect as a basic human right, the PRI was reelected to power and unsurprisingly, the party had not changed its ways.

Reflecting on Peña Nieto's suggested education reforms, Chachita explains the importance of education:[61]

Ata: ¿Y pa'qué necesitamos educación?

Chachita: Pa' no tener prejuicios, pa'acabar con los méndigos estereotipos que os carcomen la vida. Esta gente nos ve pobres. Pa'que la gente vaya a ver otros shows y no como estos, imagínate que creen que esto es cultura. Está viendo y no ve."[62]

Ata: And what do we need education for?

Chachita: So we suffer from prejudices, to end with pitiful stereotypes that devour us alive. Those people see us as poor. So that the people start to watch other shows, not like this one; just imagine if they think this is culture. They are watching and don't see anything.

Satirizing how Golden Age cinema and melodrama have educated Mexico's public since the 1940s, this onstage Chachita suggests that a different kind of education is needed to break the cycle of prejudices, such as those held by Mexico's First Family and powerful political elite. The 2013 characters also use "el tono de voz canturreado, y el habla carente de refinamiento" (the singsong voice and speech totally devoid of refinement), embedded in popular memory since the 1948 *Nosotros los pobres* classic.[63] This onstage vocal emulation immediately signals socioeconomic separation from the elite as it also showcases the way sonic triggers, such as intonation, have become socially embedded by repetition in national cinema. Employing this particular sonic strategy, the cast of *Nosotras las proles* challenges stigmas associated with poverty and urban life. The onstage Chachita laments, "¿Por qué a los pobres nos toca siempre vivir la tragedia y a estos méndigos (*al público*) no'más reírse?" (Why do we, the poor, always have to live in tragedy, and those (*to the public*) watch us just to laugh?).[64] As if the poor are meant only for entertainment, as would seem to be the case in making box-office hits out of their suffering, this prole directs her question to the audience to provoke an ethical consideration of why the poor continue to be bullied by the rich and powerful.

Using these same singsong voices, often perceived as lacking in refinement, the 2013 characters deliver the devastating news that Pepe "el Toro" will not be the neighborhood savior. The onstage Chorreada says to Chachita, "Pero piensa que ora que regrese el Toro del otro lado, ¿qué cuentas le voy a andar entregando?" (But thinking now that el Toro will return from the other side, what kind of stories are you going to tell him?).⁶⁵ This notion of returning from "the other side" is a play on words: (1) a euphemism for having passed away, and (2) a reference to the vast population of Mexican men that cross the border into the United States searching for work. At the end of the play, these onstage characters reveal that they are working with both meanings. Resonating with the lived experiences of many Mexican families, this diegetic Pepe crossed the border to financially support his family but would not return alive. When the 2013 character La que se levanta tarde (She who gets up late), as she is also called in the film, enters the final scene, she reveals the bad news to Ata: "Son las cenizas de Pepe el Toro, murió electrificado saltando la barda nueva de los gringos, y todo por querer venir a visitar a Celia en su cumpleaños" (These are Pepe el Toro's ashes, he died being electrocuted by the new fence the gringos built. And all because he wanted to come visit Cecilia on her birthday).⁶⁶ The infamously strong Pepe was no match for border politics that utterly disregard the immigrant body, exposing it to intensely painful punishments for crossing over. Although Ata and La que se levanta tarde must figure out how to tell Chachita and Chorreada that Pepe is dead, there is more bad news:

> La que se levanta tarde: Pos así. Y eso no es todo, junto con las cenizas venía una carta donde Pepe el toro confiesa que sí mató a la usuerera, que Chachita es tu hermana y que siempre estuvo enamorado de Jorge Negrete.
>
> Ata: ¿Cómo? ¿Pepe muerto? ¿Chachita mi hermana? ¿El toro puto?⁶⁷
>
> *La que se levanta tarde: Just like that. And that's not all, along with his ashes there was a letter in which Pepe el Toro confesses that he did murder the loan shark, Chachita is your sister, and he was always in love with Jorge Negrete.*
>
> Ata: What? Pepe is dead? Chachita is my sister? El toro is gay?

Throughout this scene, the characters' upbeat intonation and rapid delivery of such tragic news causes a significant dissonance for the audience. In particular, the jarring disconnect between the words and the way they sound becomes an expression of sonic disidentification that highlights the absurdity of the events described on stage as well as the way Golden Age melodramas subjected the on-screen poor to constant trials and tribulations.

In fact, disidentifying with melodramatic conventions, the diegetic death and deathbed confession of the 2013 version of Pepe el Toro destabilizes the bedrock of the traditional Mexican family as per the *Nosotros los pobres* model. This Pepe reimagines the gentile carpenter, wrongly accused of murder, to instead suggest the falsity of the absolute moral integrity classic cinema perpetuated via its screen-story poor. This Pepe also subverts macho heterosexual masculinity, as *Nosotras las proles* rewrites Negrete and Infante as lovers, not enemies, deviating from the path of Golden Age heteronormativity. While the actual death of Pedro Infante shook the nation to its core, it never unsettled his seemingly immortal presence, made possible by his countless cinematic appearances and replay. In fact, his depictions of family and masculinity continued to shape the nation long after his 1957 passing. The diegetic death of this murderous and homosexual version of Pepe, in contrast, immediately and completely dismantles any sense of stability for the onstage characters.

Continuing its performance of overt and over-the-top emotional excess, *Nosotras las proles* emphasizes the failures of the patriarchal state. From center stage, Chorreada emphatically recites the various ways Mexican bodies are excluded and abused. In fact, she doubles over, as if in excruciating pain, while she yells different atrocities that plague Mexico. For example, during this 2013 performance, she screams the words, "Ay, las asesinadas en Juárez, ¡Ay! Sientes que te duele, sientes una punzada en el corazón" (Ouch, the murdered women of Juárez, ouch! You can feel something hurting you, like a knife to the heart). Her high-pitched voice aurally enhances the visual simulation of being stabbed in the torso. Her vocal production also reflects the very real physical and psychic agony caused by the trauma of female citizens being dismembered, stabbed, violated, which I delve into in the final chapter of this book. Chorreada quickly composes herself, however. Bringing her torso back into an erect stance, she calmly and clearly declares in a low-pitched voice: "y nada más dices . . . Resignación." (and like nothing, you say. . . Resignation). This word, *resignación*, becomes her mantra as she continues screaming painful realizations about Mexican reality. After articulating terrifying examples of the state's failures, such as the rising homicide rate or uptick in forced disappearances, she calmly reminds herself: "Resignación." Reaching her breaking point, Chorreada finally declares, "Un día de tantos estar tragando miseria con miseria con tacos de miseria. Un día, eventualmente, que llegue la alegría" (One of these days, after having swallowed so much misery, even tacos filled with misery. One day, eventually, happiness will come). She then bursts into maniacal, guttural laughter, as if on the verge of a mental breakdown. Ata and Chachita run to her, pleading with her not to give up, trying to assure her it does not have to be this way. And yet, Chorreada insists that it does:

Chorreada: No, porque son las reglas del melodrama.

Chachita: ¿Melodrama?

Chorreada: Sí chamaca, que no ves que es el tono del país. Los mexicanos desde siempre vivimos en el melodrama.

Ata: ¡Vóitelas! Pos a lo mejor es momento de cambiar de género.

Chorreada: Que la boca se te haga chicharrón. Ni lo mande Dios. Más vale malo por conocido que bueno . . . ahí nos vicentiamos.[68]

Chorreada: No, because these are the rules of melodrama.

Chachita: Melodrama?

Chorreada: Yes, don't you see, it defines who we are. Us Mexicans have always lived in within the parameters of the melodrama genre.

Ata: Wow! Well, maybe it's time we change that.

Chorreada: Shut your mouth! Better the devil you know than the devil you don't . . . lest we elect another Vicente Fox.

This self-reflexive use of melodramatic excess, including auditory expression, exposes Las Reinas Chulas' astute critique of how the performative conventions of fictional cinematic worlds have become all too real. The way in which the on-screen Chachita, Chorreada, and Ata resign themselves to their situation as poor, marginalized, and exploited bodies is not only a source of the actors' disidentification, but also exposes the ramifications of *resignación*. These onstage counterparts, in contrast, subvert this mentality of acceptance by demonstrating how it is no longer a virtue of *mexicanidad* but a violent and oppressive quality of contemporary Mexican identity. In this sense, Las Reinas Chulas has taken the melodramatic facet of Golden

Age cinema and created a dissenting form, one that exposes the dark and twisted ramifications of passive acquiescence.

At the end of the piece, after interpreting several other classic films, the onstage Ata, Chorreada, Chachita, and La que se levanta tarde circle back to the quintessential neighborhood song, "¡Ni hablar mujer!" Together they sing:

Chorreada:	*Chorreada:*
Que bonito es mi país	*How lovely is my country*
Que bonita es mi ciudad	*How lovely is my city*
Que bonito es trabajar	*How lovely it is to work*
Coro:	*Coro:*
Sin progresar	*Without progress*
Chorreada:	*Chorreada:*
Que bonito Michoacán	*How lovely Michoacán*
Que bonito Yucatán	*How lovely Yucatán*
Que bonito Tultitlán	*How lovely Tultitlán*
Coro:	*Coro:*
Y Coyoacán	*And Coyoacán*
Chorreada:	*Chorreada:*
De estas tragedias hay montón	*Like these tragedies, there's a ton*
Pero hora y media	*But an hour and a half just*
no alcanzó	*isn't enough*
Mira que tal	*But look,*
Si eres uno del millón	*If you're one in a million*
Tu pobreza es bendición	*Your poverty is a blessing*
Coro:	*Coro:*
Ni hablar mujer	*No way woman*
Chorreada:	*Chorreada:*
La democracia es lo mejor	*Democracy is the best*
Si no te importa la nación	*If you aren't worried about the rest*
Porque caray	*Because God damnit*
A la hora de votar	*When voting day comes*
Ni que fueran a contar	*They won't even count*
Coro:	*Coro:*
Ni hablar mujer[69]	*No way woman*

FIGURE 1.2. On stage, Ata and Chachita react to La Chorreada telling them about violence and melodrama. *Nosotras las proles*, Coyoacán, Mexico, 2013. Photo by Christina Baker.

Organizing the piece to open and close with the song, Las Reinas Chulas yet again pays homage to *Nosotros los pobres* while also symbolically calling to a reality characterized by stagnation. Chorreada's strong female vocals not only substitute Infante's vocals, but also repeatedly point out multiple failures in the political system and nation more broadly. Her consciousness-raising words emphasize the state's self-interest but are met with a chorus that responds "Ni hablar mujer," almost as if admonishing her or warning her to keep quiet. Changing the original lyrics once more, instead of praising the qualities of Mexico's poor but morally virtuous citizens, *Nosotras las proles* condemns the nation's repetitive, wounding, and exploitative tendencies.

LOS TRES GARCÍA: FROM MACHO *CHARROS* TO HOMOEROTIC, NEOLIBERAL TRAITORS

Just as the *Nosotras las proles* rewrite of *Nosotros los pobres* examines the abuses of the poor, the 2013 revision of *Los tres García* (1947) exposes how neoliberal decisions have irreversibly impacted Mexico's natural resources and rural communities. The original film, part of the *comedia ranchera* genre, is a story that showcases rural traditions and familial ties. Jesús Amezcua Castillo notes that the three male protagonists represent variants of Mexican masculinity: the womanizing drunk, the self-assured despot, and the shy but proud man.[70] In the film, these cousins compete to please Lupita, the love interest who represented their future family life, and their grandmother, representing loyalty to the family matriarch. Beyond the family unit, "the comedia ranchera synthesized several crucial elements of cultural nationalism."[71] Notably, these cinematic creations solidified "nostalgic visions of Mexican 'traditional' life."[72] As Jacqueline Avila attests, the musical accompaniment, then, reinforced visual signifiers of nationalism and masculinity. A prime example of this is the way "mariachis dressed in full *trajes de charro* (cowboy suits) became one of the genre's musical and visual signifiers" of national belonging and virile manliness during the 1940s.[73] Male actors and singers performing *rancheras* and other originally compositions written primarily from the male point of view completed the construction of the *charro* (cowboy) archetype.[74] In other words, these songs concretized the way cinematic works blended visual imaginaries with aural sensations of gender and citizenry.

Reworking the nostalgic vision of the *comedia ranchera*, its *charro* protagonist, and musical performances of *mexicanidad*, Las Reinas Chulas disidentifies with constructions of acceptable masculinity and breaks down myths of a protectorate state. The group's rendition of the film argues that while external forces, like US-based conglomerates, have pillaged Mexican resources, Mexico's political and socioeconomic elite have also been complicit in selling off national land. Additionally, the women perform using female-to-male drag to parody deeply engrained notions of *charro* masculinity. In his seminal study *Female Masculinity*, Jack Halberstam makes an important distinction between impersonation and drag king efforts, stating, "whereas the male impersonator attempts to produce a plausible performance of maleness as the whole of her act, the drag king performs masculinity (often parodically) and makes the exposure of the theatricality of masculinity into the mainstay of her act."[75] Exposing the theatricality of masculinity through drag is useful for examining visual and auditory cues deployed in this 2013 remake of *Los tres García*. As Ana Francis told me, one of the greater challenges in developing this section of the piece was figuring out "cómo se construye un humor que no sea machista, porque el humor mexicano es muy machista, y hay que empezar con otras líneas de investigación" (how to develop a kind of humor that isn't *machista* because Mexican humor is *machista* and it's important to start from different research avenues).[76] Using drag to re-present Pedro Infante's "breakthrough performance" as Luis Antonio, the renowned tenor, reveals Las Reinas Chulas' intent to unsettle the actor's audiovisual association with heteronormative masculinity.

The *cabareteras* introduce the transition between their rendition of

Nosotros los pobres and *Los tres García* using the centrality of the grandmother figure. Although no costuming or makeup changes occur on stage, the script notes, "La abuela pasa de la paralítica a Sara García" (The grandmother transitions from being paralyzed to Sara García).[77] Because the visual shift from *Nosotros los pobres* to *Los tres García* is imperceptible to audience members, aural cues are vital. The onstage Abuela's first line becomes self-reflexive satire as she says, "¡Ay ya me tienen harta! ¿Por qué no'más hubo una abuela en el cine mexicano? Me traen como su pendeja de una escena a otra" (Uff, I've had enough! What? Why's there only one grandmother in all of Mexican film? You drag me around like an idiot from one scene to the next).[78] The humor in this statement lies in the fact that Sara García, as veteran as she was on screen, was destined to repeat the same role as grandmother for eternity.[79] Following the onstage Abuela's comment, each of the cousins appears on stage, completing the transition to the *comedia ranchera*. Just as the 2013 onstage Abuela is conscious of her role, the way José Luis, Luis Antonio, and Luis Manuel enter reveals a nonlinguistic nod to their satirical and self-aware depictions of their on-screen counterparts. While the image of the *charro* changes over time, "based on specific sociocultural and sociopolitical contexts that allow him to still be recognizable to the popular, urban audience," these 2013 *charros* do not quite fit the 1940s image.[80] The onstage José Luis, Luis Antonio, and Luis Manuel enter the mimetic space with notably unnatural movements; their stances are wide, they take large, heavy steps, and they obviously have padding under their formfitting mariachi jackets and socks in their skin tight pants. With each sock notably larger than the last, these contemporary García "men" make their masculinity abundantly clear. Often posing in profile so the audience can see the size of their "package," they also make a point of adjusting themselves in full-frontal view of the spectators. There is no doubt that these versions of the *charro* cousins critique the "natural" qualities of masculinity, producing overtly theatrical and parodic interpretations.

That these onstage *charros* are aware of their performance of masculinity is further complicated by their reenactment of the fight scene from the end of the original film. In this 2013 version, though, the three cousins are not competing with one another over a love interest.[81] Instead, they attempt to outdo each other in their efforts to sell off the García land and national resources.

Luis Manuel: ¿Vendiste la patente del maguey miserable?

Luis Antonio: Ni digas nada que tu vendiste la patente de la Virgen de Guadalupe a los chinos.

José Luis: Y tú le vendiste los corales de Los Cabos a los koreanos.

Luis Antonio: Y tú vendiste 6 mil kilómetros de litorales junto con la última ballena azul que teníamos a los japoneses.[82]

Luis Manuel: *Did you sell the patent for the miserable maguey?*

Luis Antonio: *Like you have room to talk since you sold the patent for the Virgen of Guadalupe to the Chinese.*

José Luis: *And you sold the coral reefs in Los Cabos to the Koreans.*

Luis Antonio: *And you sold 6,000 kilometers of coastline along with the last blue whale we had to the Japanese.*

Reaching hyperbolic levels, like selling off the last blue whale or destroying Chichén Itzá to invest in a Sheraton hotel, the rivalry between the cousins reflects Las Reinas Chulas' broader critique of the way Mexican politicians have enacted policy at the expense of the nation. More specifically, the *cabareteras* offer a biting critique about how the return of the PRI brought with it a reinvigorated neoliberal agenda. Elizabeth Freeman notes that "the neoliberalist project continues to reconstruct time in these ways as it 'develops' new regions for profit, and additionally depends upon the idea of capital's movement as itself an inexorable progress," one that primarily serves the white, heterosexual, and male constituency.[83] Others, like women, people of color, and queer populations, remain marginalized and bear the brunt of exclusionary politics. In this 2013 rendition, Las Reinas Chulas uses the García family, portrayed as part of a light-skinned wealthy class, to showcase how the nation under the PRI sealed its fate by "buying" into the neoliberal project.

Rather than reaping the benefits of foreign investments and neoliberal modernization efforts, Las Reinas Chulas' version of the Abuela from *Los tres García* points to the more realistic result of loss and exploitation. Directing her fury toward one of her grandsons for having sold the family land, she exclaims: "En veinte años el neoliberalismo ha puesto tantas trampas y hemos ido cayendo en ellas. ¿Y ahora vendes la tierra? ¿Cómo se te ocurre venderla? ¿No tienes escrúpulos! ¿Cuánto dices que te dieron?" (In twenty years, neoliberalism has put up many traps and we have fallen into every last one of them. And now you are selling the land? How dare you? Have you no scruples? How much did you say they paid you?).[84] The following conversation between Abuela and Luis Antonio highlights the failures of neoliberal "development" in the Mexican context:

> Luis Antonio: ¡Juntos los quería agarrar, vendepatrias! De ti Luis Manuel podía esperar que vendieras la tierra donde nacimos pero de ti José Luis ¡nunca me imaginé que vendieras el pozo de agua del pueblo a la Coca Cola, infeliz!

> Abuela: ¡Cálmense, tranquilos todos! Y tu Luis Antonio ni te hagas el bueno, que además de haver vendido el pozo petrolero que teníamos vendiste la patente del maguey a los gringos.[85]

> *Luis Antonio: I want to grab all of you traitors. I am not surprised that you, Luis Miguel, would sell the land we have known since birth, but you, miserable José Luis, I never would have imagined that you would sell the town's water well to Coca Cola!*

> *Abuela: Everyone just calm down! And you, Luis Antonio, don't pretend to be innocent, because in addition to having sold our oil well, you also sold the patent for the maguey to the Gringos.*

As these conversations demonstrate, the 2013 García family is preoccupied with the lost social status caused by decisions to sell Mexico, decisions motivated by the lure of progress and financial gain. Selling water, land, maguey, and petroleum are just some of the ways this revised García family critiques decisions made by Mexico's political elite in the name of "progress" that actually deprive and penalize the majority of the nation.

Just as in the original film, Abuela encourages the three cousins to end their quarrels once and for all. The three men then start to punch, kick, and tackle each other to the ground. When these onstage versions of Luis Manuel, José Luis, and Luis Antonio finish, they stand up, exposing their ripped open shirts and perfectly chiseled padded chests, exploring the queer undertones of the original film as the audience roars with laughter. In *Los tres García*, the three men fight for several minutes, even throwing each other into the fountain. As Abuela shouts at them to "aprender a pelear como hombres" (learn to fight like men), the camera settles on their disheveled hair, wet, tight pants, and bare chests. Having been directed, produced, and filmed by men, this on-screen moment fulfills homoerotic desire wrapped in assurances of macho heterosexual masculinity. As such, the Las Reinas Chulas' over-the-top homoerotic revision exposes the hypocrisy of the master narratives of heteronormativity.

STRIPPING THE *CHARRO*, QUEERING THE *RANCHERA*: A CRITIQUE OF HETERONORMATIVE MASCULINITY

Beyond the visual cues described, the performance includes a musical number that sonically and lyrically disidentifies with the *charro*'s phobic heteronormativity and contemporary neoliberal politics. In itself, *charro* masculinity is intimately related to musical performance; the *charro* sings to "express his innermost sentiments through music, specifically the *canción ranchera*."[86] Scholars such as Alejandro Madrid, Vicente T. Mendoza, and Antonia Garcia-Orozco, among others, have suggested that the *ranchera* genre is the quintessential Mexican music. Broadly speaking, it is also overwhelmingly disapproving of the female timbre and feminine expressions of emotion; the *ranchera* is the music of men. As Madrid and Moore argue, the *ranchera* depicts "paternalistic masculinity such as chivalry, courage, virility, dependability, protection, and domineering control over women" inculcated in popular culture.[87] In *Los tres García*, these ideas are abundantly clear as all three cousins sing *rancheras*, but Luis Antonio's vocals stand out.[88] Pedro Infante, the actor who played the role, was already a singing sensation from radio, known for having a voice that sounded "as though he were singing from the heart, whether he was mourning the passing of a happier past, praising a new love, or declaring that his mother, his nation, or his northern region was the true object of all his affections."[89] This vocal quality, then, only further reinforced Infante's stature as the very embodiment of *mexicanidad*.

In this 2013 stage production, Las Reinas Chulas recreates the scene in which the three cousins serenade their shared love interest with "Cielito lindo." As Avila describes, "the diegetic, foregrounded use of mariachi and small brass bands at the grandmother's house, including a serenade of the traditional 'Cielito lindo,' and the brandish show-off performances of the three cousins at the jaripeo, are all intended to seduce the lovely Lupita."[90] In the original film, this musical performance is critical to establishing the sonic trigger that becomes coterminous with the visual construction of masculinity, heteronormativity, and Mexican identity. With the 2013 version, however, the characters neither attempt to imitate Infante's voice nor perform the iconic song. Instead, this onstage Luis Antonio and his two cousins perform a version of Vicente Fernández's *ranchera* hit, "Para siempre." In the original song, Fernández's deep and seductive vocals croons:

> Olvidemos, el pasado
> Y lo que diga la gente
> La verdad es, que te amo
> Y me amas, Para siempre

> *Let's forget the past*
> *And what the people say*
> *The truth is, that I love you*
> *And you love me, forever*

Olvidemos, el pasado	*Let's forget the past*
Y vivamos, el presente	*And live in the present*
Lo que importa es	*What is important*
Que me amas,	*Is that you love me*
y te amo, para siempre	*And I love you, forever*
Vale mucho, un gran amor	*A great love is worth so much more*
Que en el perdón ha crecido[91]	*Once it has grown from forgiveness*

As evidenced by the lyrics, this would seem to be a love song. While no gender is assigned to the couple, it is a fair assumption that the relationship is between a man and a woman, especially given Fernandez's male voice and the *ranchera*'s proclivity for heteronormative relationships. I want to point out the repeated use of *olvidemos* and *vivamos*, verbal constructions that literally command that the pair forget the past and live in the present. Although the man has made himself part of the romantic unit, his voice and words command the woman to forget something. The references to forgiveness, ignoring rumors, and love would seem to suggest that the man has committed an indiscretion he now expects his companion to overlook. Importantly, the song emphasizes that the woman is expected to overlook mistakes, not that the man is expected to avoid making questionable decisions. Additionally, embedded within Fernández's repeated reminder of their eternal love is the heteropatriarchal control the male figure exerts both within the *ranchera* genre and within broader socio-gendered interactions.

In their 2013 version, Las Reinas Chulas rewrite the original lyrics and give the song a new sound. In doing so, their performance is a double act of sonic disidentification that resists the original performance of "Cielito lindo" as well as the Fernández hit. Mladen Dolar suggests that imitation of another's voice is difficult and often unachievable because "the voice is like a fingerprint."[92] Yet, I propose that the performers substitute Fernández's sound for other reasons. First, the group's goal is not to achieve an exact vocal replica, but a sonic approximation that reinforces the parodic visual construction of the three cousins. Dolar's assertion that the "voice stands at the axis of our social bonds, and that voices are the very texture of the social" is useful here to consider Las Reinas Chulas' performance.[93] The women want to break away from the social bonds and *mexicanidad* represented by the sounds of Infante, *Los tres García*, and Fernández, and as such, use the *ranchera* to point out the homophobia associated with the style and some of its most notorious stars. For example, while Las Reinas Chulas performs their revised version of "Para siempre," the *cabareteras* use visual projection to remind audiences of the 2002 concert in Guadalajara when Vicente Fernández shared an onstage kiss with his son, Alejandro Fernández.[94] At the time, the press immediately seized on the opportunity to emphasize that the kiss was a perfectly normal display of affection between a father and his son and that the two men were not "charros gays."[95] However, Alejandro Fernández has long been rumored to be homosexual or bisexual, rumors he vehemently denies.[96] Over the last few years, as Vicente Fernández's health declined, leading to his death in 2021, his homophobia made international news when he refused to accept a much-needed liver transplant out of fear that the donor was gay.[97] Within this context, the Las Reinas Chulas' rendition disidentifies with what Infante and the 1940s *charros* represent as well as the heteronormative masculinity embodied by contemporary *ranchera* stars, such as the Fernández family.

The 2013 onstage version of "Para siempre" is a stripped-down adaptation meant to emphasize sociopolitical critique and homosexual overtones. Visually, and in a literal sense, the cousins remove the façade of heteronormative masculinity by performing a striptease as they sing. For example, as Luis Antonio belts out the lyrics from center stage, he shows off his exposed padded pectoral muscles. Similarly, behind him, Luis Manuel and José Luis take off their jackets, flexing their foam muscles and shaking their hips. These choreographed movements, considered alongside the vocals and the song's lyrics, become an over-the-top display of masculinity, one that satirizes the macho Mexican as depicted by the *charro* and the *ranchera* genre.

Sonically, the performance is stripped down in the sense that the onstage trio sings live, accompanied only by a single acoustic guitar rather than the guitar, strings, and brass heard in the Fernández original. Therefore, it is easier for the audience to appreciate Luis Antonio's lead vocals and the lyrics that reference the nation's absurd political reality. Much like the rendition of "¡Ni hablar Mujer!," this 2013 musical act collapses individual and collective interests, emphasizing the patriarchal role of the state. Luis Antonio, accompanied by his cousins as backup singers, begins:

Olvidemos el pasado	*Let's forget the past*
Y lo que diga la gente	*And what the people say*
La verdad estoy bien guapo	*The truth is I am very handsome*
Le voy bien al gabinete	*And I'll do well in the cabinet*
Olvidemos el pasado	*Let's forget the past*
Y vivamos el presente	*And live in the present*

Lo que importa es mi bronceado	*What's important is my tan*
Y el peeling de mi frente	*And my facial peel*
Vale más un buen galán	*A good gentleman is worth more*
Pa'secretario de estado[98]	*As the secretary of state*

Throughout this 2013 version, the deep, gravelly tones of Luis Antonio reverberate throughout the performance space. However, I would not consider him, or his cousins, good singers by any stretch of the imagination. That is the point, though. As audience members, we hear their words clearly, slowly, and deliberately. This was a conscious decision that I suggest is part of Las Reinas Chulas' sonic disidentification of the original composition and *charro* identity. In contrast to the way Infante's and Fernández's smooth and romantic sounds make it easy for their Mexican public to passively consume heteronormative masculine messages, the *cabareteras* want their audience to think critically. They want their audience to contemplate plural commands like "let us forget the past and live in the present." Not only do these lyrics and their performance imply forgetting what the morally bankrupt PRI has done to the Mexican public for most of the twentieth century, but they also emphasize the continued presence of an oppressive patriarchal figure.

What makes this performance even more striking is the presence of a biological man and musician on stage. Yurief Nieves, the group's composer and musician, is present throughout the entire performance, playing the guitar and singing back-up vocals. Though the onstage Luis Antonio imitates a male vocal register and timbre, he does not lip-sync or allow Nieves to sing lead. This disidentificatory act challenges the "male only" attitude of the *ranchera* and *charro* world. We hear onstage Luis Antonio's "male" voice loud and clear, though sometimes strained, as if pushed to the limit to stay within a deep alto or tenor range during the song. Because his voice, as well as those of his cousins, belong to biologically female bodies, they provoke disorienting sonic effect. As Muñoz might say, they deliver a jolt to the social order as they underscore incongruities between the performative voice and the artifice and theatricality of *charro* masculinity.

Aside from the scant musical accompaniment, the idea of a stripped-down performance is useful for considering two other elements of the scene: the lyrics themselves and a literal striptease. In this 2013 rendition, Las Reinas Chulas rewrote the lyrics to critique the superficiality of those who hold important political positions, poking fun at the way tan lines and general overall appearance have become indicators of who deserves to hold

FIGURE 1.3. Revised versions of the cousins from the film Los tres García (1947) share center stage. The three "men" show off their notable masculinity with padded muscles. *Nosotras las proles*, Coyoacán, Mexico, 2013. Photo by Christina Baker.

public office. Moreover, their commentaries point to an intellectual stripping down, one that costs citizens proper representation and protections. According to García Canclini, "Latin America's recent history suggests that there are numerous situations in which societies accept the transubstantiation and prefer a political scene in which political heroes resemble those of film and television."[99] Applied to the Mexican context, it is easy to see how the intellectually inadequate, and yet physically attractive, Enrique Peña Nieto (and his soap opera star wife) was elected president. Wishing to see television and movie stars reflected in politics, as the song implies, however, carries the risk of catastrophic political decisions. For example, the 2013 Luis Antonio sings, "Vale más estar mamey / Pa'defender lo privado" (It's more important to be buff / Than to defend private resources), referring to Peña Nieto's plan to privatize Mexico's petroleum production. In this sense, the song critiques the recent efforts of the superficially interested elites to strip the nation of its constitutional rights and resources.

PÍNTAME *ANGELITOS NEGROS*: BLACKFACE THEN AND NOW

In addition to using drag to expose and disidentify with heteronormative gendered constructs, Las Reinas Chulas also addresses the way Golden Age cinema used race to establish a baseline for *mexicanidad* and belonging. In *Angelitos negros* (1948), José Carlos is a gig musician from the working class who rises in social status via marriage. He falls in love with Ana Luisa, a high-society woman, whose light skin hides her racial roots, an African past unbeknownst to her. Throughout the film, she treats dark-skinned bodies with apathy if not cruelty, until she gives birth to a mixed-race child and is forced to reconcile her identity with her racial prejudice. Sergio de la Mora states, "along with *Tizoc*, Infante's only other race melodrama is *Angelitos negros* (Black angels, Joselito Rodríguez, 1948), in which Infante's haughty and racist blonde wife, Ana Luisa is shocked and horrified when she gives birth to a *mulata*, whom she rejects."[100] José Carlos is advised not to tell Ana Luisa about her African roots and decides for quite some time to "shoulder the blame for harboring the black blood that stained their daughter Belén."[101] Following the Golden Age rules of melodrama and excess, however, the family secret is exposed: Ana Luisa's mother is the black housemaid, making her the culprit behind her daughter's dark complexion. After many years, tears, and arguments, the on-screen Ana Luisa eventually accepts her daughter, in spite of her appearance. Joanne Herschfield suggests that this moment of acceptance "exemplifies how film melodrama is able to accommodate cultural uncertainties surrounding issues of race in ways that fit within the limits of proscribed social attitudes and beliefs."[102] Over time, according to the cinematic narrative, the nation would be able to accept its dark-skinned inhabitants, though they would always have the stigma of being racial Others. Yet, for these racial Others to fit within the melodramatic paradigm, and more broadly the social structures of the nation, they should adhere to certain scripts like "victimized servants, innocent children, or resigned friends."[103] Moreover, the characters, like the young Belén, should also demonstrate they are "capable of unquestioning love and friendship for the 'white' characters."[104]

In re-presenting Pedro Infante's performances of *mexicanidad* and masculinity, Las Reinas Chulas exposes how those portrayals are intimately related to whitened depictions of mestizaje. Even in *Angelitos negros*, a film applauded for pushing against the pervasive imagery of light-skinned mestizaje, Pedro Infante is part of a system that reinforces superficial and stereotypical interpretations of nonwhite bodies. Mónica Moreno Figueroa and Emiko Saldívar Tanaka detail how this has much to do with the way "mestizaje's hegemony relied both on its promise of inclusion as well as on the generation and reproduction of racial hierarchies."[105] They add that the state-sanctioned discourses and cultural depictions that posited all of Mexico as "mixed" mestizos has resulted in a deeply entrenched racist normalization precisely because certain races were removed from definitions of *mexicanidad*.[106] As a tangible example, two of the central "black" characters" in *Angelitos negros* are played by "non-black people, literally painted black," including Pedro Infante.[107] Theresa Delgadillo astutely notes that when on-screen José Carlos performs with black musicians, the actor's blackface becomes a "racial masquerade," uncritical minstrelsy that reinforces his character's white privilege.[108] Unlike those who live as Afro-Mexican citizens or black bodies in Mexico, José Carlos is able to move through society performing whichever race is more convenient for personal gain. His onscreen performances, and broader decisions in Mexican Golden Age cinema to use blackface, "abstract the very material nature of blackness" and reduce it to "a performance for the enjoyment of white viewers" with little to no regard for the consequences beyond the screen-story."[109]

The tension between depictions of masculinity and depictions of race in *Angelitos negros* is crucial for my exploration of Las Reinas Chulas' reinterpretation and sonic disidentification in their 2013 performance. By questioning masculinity, itself based on a tacit acceptance of the Mexican male as a whitened mestizo, *Nosotras las proles* interrogates the erasure of black bodies from the nation. In the 1948 film, melodramatic tensions stem from the fact that this family is not an idealized version, but one wrought with contradictory feelings about race and superiority. Just as Las Reinas Chulas absented Pepe "el Toro" from their revision of *Nosotros los pobres*, the group makes absent José Carlos, the father figure who accepted his *mulata* daughter. This decision is not merely an effort to eliminate the father or patriarchal figure, nor does it simply subvert the Golden Age family unit. Rather, the decision exposes the hypocrisy and contrived quality of the on-screen family and paternalism that has informed social bonds since the 1940s. Las Reinas Chulas takes the film and turns it on its head, making the racist mother a prominent figure while removing the supportive masculine presence.

Beyond the erasure of the father figure, the four *cabareteras* situate racial prejudice within a discourse of financial gain, pointing to what scholars like Bobby Vaughn, Herman Bennett, and Theodore Cohen observe as a common connection between race and class privilege. Along with other experts on Afro-Mexicanness, Cohen, Vaughn, and Bennett problematize the pervasiveness of this notion, but Las Reinas Chulas uses the race-class dynamic to emphasize political corruption and the failures of the patriarchal state. For example, the onstage Ana Luisa bears similarities to the screen character, such as her white-passing appearance and outward projection of wealth. But her exaggerated interest in the value of material things stands in stark contrast to the values epitomized by on-screen Pedro Infante/José Carlos. Without his presence, this 2013 Ana Luisa's unrestrained avarice echoes tropes of upper-class interest in economic and political gain. This reorientation of roles, where the benevolent José Carlos is absented, captures how the "idealization of family and of traditional morality" in Golden Age cinema was created to fit the goals of dominant state ideology.[110] By turning away from this framework, the performers expose the nation's deeply rooted systems of inequality and oppression that do unjust harm to vulnerable populations, often those with darker skin.

By way of this 2013 revision of *Angelitos negros*, Las Reinas Chulas attempts to tackle racial exclusion and critique the way racial binaries have been performed and repeated to the point of becoming naturalized constructions. However, it is worth questioning how much the women actually reinforce exclusionary paradigms and further invisibilize Afro-Mexican bodies. Las Reinas Chulas' costuming and makeup decisions—made just two years before the 2015 national census, in which "Afro-Mexican" was to appear as an identity category—are perhaps more problematic than they are critical of Mexico's racial divisions. In what follows, I analyze how the *cabareteras*' sociopolitical rhetoric clashes with their unfortunate decision to use blackface. It is important to recognize that Latin American theater forms have a long history of performing minstrelsy, however my interest in their use of blackface is tied to the original film and its deployment of blackface instead of hiring black actors.[111] On one hand, Laura Gutiérrez explores how Las Reinas Chulas deploys blackness in *Petróleo en la sangre*, later renamed *Nosotras las proles*, and another piece, *El derecho de dudar* (The Right to Doubt, 2006). Gutiérrez suggests that in "recycling black stereotypical iconography from cultural industries," like film, the group generates debate and critical thinking about racial discrimination.[112] Yet, I want to push back against this idea. The women of Las Reinas Chulas are all light-skinned women whose phenotype matches an outward projection of idealized citizenry, providing them with protections and opportunities many darker-skinned Mexicans have never experienced. They have also chosen to use blackface in a series of performances including *Marty, Luty, Kin: I Have a Drink* (2013), a mockery of Martin Luther King's "I Have a Dream" speech, and a collaboration with Regina Orozco called *Está de moda ser negro* (It's Fashionable to be Black, 2009). All these performances took place in a not-so-distant past, between 2006 and 2013, suggesting how "strategic amnesia and disappearance of blackness has permeated Mexican consciousness."[113] Importantly, this strategic forgetting, or ignorance, takes root in Las Reinas Chulas' various productions, highlighting that even the nation's educated progressives are uncritical of how blackface might offend or harm those who experience racism. Possibly more aware of how their racial drag repeats injurious practices now, in 2021, the women no longer seem to perform using blackface. Then again, they posted a video of their blackface *Angelitos negros* sketch on their Facebook page in May 2020 to promote their repertoire.

In the 2013 version of *Angelitos negros*, several members of Las Reinas Chulas use blackface as a double performance of racial drag; the women drag onto their bodies the characters of José Carlos and Belén from the original film who painted themselves in order to perform an exoticized Other. Throughout the film, "blacks are exotic, purely musical and passionate beings from a tropical paradigm," often localized and linked to Cuba.[114] This is exemplified by José Carlos's use of blackface when he performed, accompanied by presumably "authentic" Afro-Mexican and Afro-Cuban musicians and dancers. Reinforced time and again in Golden Age film and other media, this correlation between Afro-diasporic bodies and the Caribbean has made blackness "not something of the here and now" in Mexico.[115] Though José Carlos is absented from their 2013 production, Las Reinas Chulas passes the filmic performative appropriation of race onto the onstage Belén/Negrita. At the beginning of the piece, she wears all white to call attention to her artificially darkened face, hands, legs, and stereotypical afro wig. Later, she seems to take her father's place in a performance of tropicalized Otherness that I analyze further next. In contrast, the remake of Ana Luisa's light-skinned features and blonde hair are made even more noticeable by her black gown, black pumps, and dark fur stole. The power dynamic of victim and victimizer is very literally presented in black and white.

Las Reinas Chulas does not re-present an actual scene from the original *Angelitos negros*, but instead explore the dynamic between Belén and Ana Luisa where the film leaves off. What is abundantly clear from the beginning of the scene is Las Reinas Chulas' critique of melodramatic resolution when Ana Luisa accepts her daughter. The onstage 2013 Ana Luisa/Emilia seeks to replace the honest and hardworking filmic José Carlos with quintessential figures of neoliberal politics, reinforcing the abuses that my previous sections discussed. This reimagined Ana Luisa, referred to in the script as Emilia, the actor's real name, speaks of her desire to be with a powerful Carlos rather than her husband. Her onstage words disidentify with any loyalty she professed in the film to her on-screen husband or family. Instead, in talking to her lover on the phone, she attempts to reassure him that she is not simply interested in him because of his thirty-six mansions. She goes on, "ni tu Ferrari, ni el avión privado de tu hija, no es tu yate, y todas tus pertenencias las que me calientan, eres tú, tus orejitas . . . tu pelona. . . . Grrr. . . . Por cierto, estoy harta de cargar con este marido" (it's not your Ferrari, or your daughter's private plane, or your yacht, or all of your wealth that attract me, it's you . . . your ears . . . your bald head. . . . Grrr. For sure, I am tired to taking care of my husband).[116] The Carlos this onstage Emilia speaks to and of could be one of three powerful and rich options: Carlos Slim, Carlos Salinas de Gortari, or Carlos Romero Deschamps. Throughout the skit, both Slim and Deschamps are mentioned explicitly, but the reference to

FIGURE 1.4. The on-stage Emilia, a modified version of her character in Angelitos negros (1948), yells at her dark-skinned daughter while she cries face-down on the floor. *Nosotras las proles*, 2013. Photo by Daniel Cortés.

baldness rules out the former. While the reference to large ears could easily be a joke about ex-president Salinas's features, the list of properties, riches, and baldness could belong to either him or Deschamps. What is important here is not necessarily identifying which Carlos diegetically impacts the lives of this onstage mother and daughter duo, but rather indicating that all of them represent the socioeconomic inequality and political corruption of contemporary Mexico.

Unlike the racial melodrama that happily resolves itself, the 2013 conversations between Emilia and her daughter, Negrita, call attention to the Afro-Mexicans and other Afro-heritage citizens that are still excluded from the rights and protection they deserve. In many ways, the words they articulate function as a sonic disidentification with the screen story's harmonious resolution. The on-stage Emilia makes comments such as "Ya te dije que no me digas mamacita" (I told you not to call me mamacita) or "Hubiera preferido parir un pollo rostizado que una hija negra como tú." (I would have preferred giving birth to a roasted chicken over a black child like you).[117] In doing so, the character refuses any sense of maternal sensibility that the film suggests she eventually develops. Instead, this 2013 Emilia is frank about her racial prejudice and subsequent rejection of her daughter. Her discourse captures the way blackness and Afro-Mexicanness have been "excised" from the national body "because it has been coded and essentialized as an inferior identity."[118] This is further accentuated by the script itself, which, by referring to Ana Luisa by the actor's real name, Emilia, collapses the space between fictional prejudice and off-screen reality. In contrast, the screen-story Belén is referred to in the script as "Negrita," calling attention to the dehumanizing quality of the insults and the real, lived experience of many dark-skinned bodies in Mexico. As Christine Arce emphasizes, just as in Mexican films where "proper names are displaced and their identities become abstracted into a play of trope" the nameless Negrita in 2013 is yet another cultural nobody.[119] Without a name or body, it becomes easier to inflict violence "on their flesh." [120] This onstage version of Ana Luisa does just that by preying on the young girl's innocence and vulnerability. Telling her daughter, "Porque te odio, odio tu color, tu pelo, tu raza raza de esclavos, deberían seguir encadenados" (Because I hate you, I hate your color, I hate your skin, your race, the race of slaves that should continue to be indentured) even calling her a "cerebrito de chango" (monkey brain).[121] These stomach-churning insults make the racial hierarchy between them excruciatingly clear. By demoralizing her, this Negrita's body is seen as expendable. The following conversation highlights Negrita/Belén's helplessness:

Negrita: Mamita, ¿por qué me quieres vender?

Emilia: Ya te dije que no te voy a vender carboncito, tan sólo es una alianza estratégica, vamos... una reforma, una liberalización, un riesgo compartido, una sociedad de mutua convivencia.

Negrita: Eso me dijiste la vez pasada que me mandaste con el otro señor. Y hasta me dijiste que me ibas a comprar un vestido nuevo, ¿qué pasó, te gastaste el dinero?[122]

Negrita: Mamita, why do you want to sell me?

Emilia: I told you that I am not going to sell you, little dark one, it's just a strategic alliance ... a reform, a liberalization, a shared risk, a society of mutual benefits.

Negrita: That's what you told me the last time you sold me to that other guy. And you even said you would buy me a new dress. What happened, did you spend all that money?

Reworking the melodramatic plot of the original 1948 film, this 2013 version deviates from a tidy happy ending. No, Belén/Negrita's fate as presented onstage is devastatingly heartbreaking and cruel. This mother's sale of and profit from her own daughter's presumably sexual labor dismisses the very real problem of sex trafficking that *La Prietty Guoman* addresses in Chapter 4. This conversation, though brief, showcases the continued legacy of enslaving black bodies, despite Mexico's efforts to erase that colonial past. These painful articulations locate center stage a need to reckon with the way Afro-Mexican bodies "continue only to be buried in the colonial past or to be ahistorically bound" outside of Mexican terrain.[123]

LA NUEVA CANCIÓN AND THE SOUNDS OF RESISTANCE

As a way of bringing some sense of resolution, the onstage Belén/Negrita performs a song that echoes the filmic moment when Nana sings Belén to sleep. Instead of rewriting lyrics, Las Reinas Chulas chose a Latin American protest song about race to further express their sonic disidentification with the original production's depiction of supposed racial harmony. Belén/Negrita is joined by back-up vocalists, and together they sing "Duerme Duerme Negrito," made popular by Mercedes Sosa during the Nueva Canción (New Song) movement of the 1960s and 1970s.[124] Chronologically impossible, this song was not part of the film but mirrors creative decisions made for the cinema classic. Theresa Delgadillo points out that *Angelitos negros* included a song adapted from the 1940s racial protest poem, "Píntame angelitos negros," by Venezuelan Andrés Eloy Blanco, that also inspired the film's title.[125] Performed by Infante/José Carlos, the song "attests to a dialogue about race" within Mexico as well as "conducted through transnational routes of commodity production and exchange."[126]

Las Reinas Chulas similarly perform transnational conversations about race by audibly bringing Argentine Sosa's work to the contemporary Mexican stage. This connection between protest songs and transnational racial considerations is enriched by the fact that, in the film, the black Nana's bedtime song shares similarities with "Duerme Duerme Negrito." In the film, Nana coos, "Belén, Belén, porque tienes tu los ojos así, / despabilao / Belén / Si parece que te han jichao/ ajiguagua / Belén . . . Belén / tu mamai está cansao y se va / si tu no drume Belén" (Belén, Belén, why are your eyes like that / wide awake / Belén / It seems like they got bigger / Belén . . . Belén / Your mother is tired and wants to leave / if you don't sleep, Belén (*Angelitos negros*). The repetition of "drume" in place of "duerme," other hybrid Castilian words, and references to blackness are linguistic means of remembering of an African past. These words also become signifiers of a past "from which this nation (Mexico) on a trajectory of modernity wished to separate."[127] Despite the implicit separation between mestizaje and Afro-diasporic bodies, the *cabareteras* engage in a conversation about race by combining the sentiments behind Nana's bedtime song with Sosa's "Duerme Duerme Negrito." Replacing the screen-story composition with Sosa's protest song, this 2013 act of sonic disidentification comments on continuing racial divisions and prejudices. In Sosa's version, the most well-known, her voice is accompanied only by an acoustic guitar and a drum that Sosa herself plays.[128] Just as Sosa sang, without changing a single lyric or arrangement, the onstage Belén/Negrita and her back-up singers begin:

> Duerme, duerme, negrito
> Que tu mama está en el campo, negrito
> Duerme, duerme, mobila
> Que tu mama está en el campo, mobila
> Te va a traer codornices
> Para ti.
> Te va a traer rica fruta
> Para ti
> Te va a traer carne de cerdo
> Para ti.
> Te va a traer muchas cosas
> Para ti.
> Y si el negro no se duerme
> Viene el diablo blanco
> Y zas le come la patita
> Chacapumba, chacapumba, apumba, chacapumba[129]

> *Sleep, sleep, little black boy*
> *Your mother is in the field, little black boy*
> *Sleep, sleep, Mobila*
> *For your mother is in the field, Mobila*
> *She will bring quails*
> *Just for you*
> *She will bring sweet fruit*
> *Just for you*
> *She will bring pork meat*
> *Just for you*

She will bring many things
Just for you
And if you don't sleep, little black boy
The white devil will come
And zas! He will eat your leg
Chacapumba, chacapumba, apumba, chacapumba

During this first part of the song, the 2013 Belén/Negrita simulates Sosa's deep and emotive quality, a powerful homage to the famed singer. Emulating Sosa also forefronts the lyrical content, easily heard and understood. But as the song progresses, Las Reinas Chulas begin to diverge from Sosa's vocal style. Belén/Negrita and her singers incorporate screen-story Nana's guttural and throaty sound. To some extent, blending the two vocal styles functions to collapse the temporal and regional gaps between the two songs. It emphasizes their united mission to draw attention to the experiences and presence of Afro-Latin American bodies. At the same time, the accentuation of an imagined "African" vocal style becomes a caricature of Nana, falling into the trap of repeating an archetype that involves the "exaggeration of a single quality" intimately linked to "symbolic representation" of Otherness.[130]

By the end of the song, Belén/Negrita and her accompanying vocalists have totally abandoned any semblance of Sosa's style, transforming the song into a tropicalized interpretation via the fast-paced and notably upbeat rhythm. Three back-up singers also follow one another around in a circle, moving their arms from side to side while "playing" güiros and maracas, engaging in a kind of conga line as they sing. Like Belén/Negrita, at this point, the other three Reinas Chulas appear wearing blackface, afro-style wigs, and costumes comprised of form-fitting white pants and white tops with colorful ruffles along the shoulders and down the sleeves. Arguably, their dissidence has been replaced by their own fallible imaginings of the Other as they embody stereotypical *rumba* dancers like those seen in *Angelitos negros* and innumerable other Golden Age films. When Arce contends that Mexican cultural productions dress Mexican blackness "in tropical fanfare" that becomes "woven into the national aural fabric through an acoustics of otherness," she could just as easily have been referring to Las Reinas Chulas' performative decisions.[131]

The group's particular audiovisual decisions invoke the stereotypical cinematic image of dark-skinned *rumbera* dancers and musicians. As Rafael Figueroa Hernández explains, Mexico's geographical proximity to Cuba has facilitated the exchange of people, goods, and cultural practices.[132] Musical forms such as *son*, *danzón*, and *rumba* made their way through the Republic, settling in Mexico City, where they became instrumental in shaping the way bodies and social bonds were conceived. Of specific interest for this discussion is the way Cuban musicians, instruments and musical styles underwent a process of integration in the late nineteenth century, solidified by appearances in Mexican Golden Age cinema. Film was indispensable for the creation of an idealized imaginary of Cuban exoticism filtered through the *rumbera* musical body. Gabriela Pulido Llano notes, "en la temática de las imágenes de 'lo cubano' en México, la rumba se asoció a la imagen del negrito bembón y la mulata que es su adorno" (In Mexico, on the topic of how images created a sense of Cubanness, rumba was always associated with the figure of the black percussionist and the mulata dancer, a kind of adornment).[133] It is important to recognize how this comment reflects the inherent connection between the dancer and musician, and yet the tropical Cuban spectacle was simultaneously divided between "el negrito bembón" and his dancing "mulata." This separation was consistently reproduced and reinforced spatially on stage and in on-screen productions. According to Arce, these repeated depictions via Mexican cinema and popular culture created an "economy of enjoyment that creates excess, pain, and pleasure" rooted in melodrama and its minstrel appropriation of blackness.[134] It's not hard to see that this societal racism and violence continues into the present as evidenced by Las Reinas Chulas' 2013 production.

While reiterating the imagined tropicalization of *cubanidad* from the past, onstage performance does, in some way, make space for possible forms of resistance via their reenvisioned scenarios of protest and sonic disidentification. For example, that the central figure, Belén/Negrita, occupies and sings from center stage, accompanied by her musicians, reflects an effort to resist and reorient the separation of space proliferated by on-screen stories. Through their vocal performance and physical movements, the *cabareteras* juxtapose imagined idealizations of tropical black bodies with lyrics that point to the physical labor and abuse they suffer in the Latin American context. Of course, the representation is disconnected from Mexico's own Afro-diasporic groups and their struggles. As Herman Bennett urges, "our present moment requires us to uncover the Afro-Mexican past in order to arrive at a deeper understanding" of the past and present.[135] Taking this into account, I recognize that this 2013 reworking becomes a means of rejecting and disidentifying with the cinematic rendering of the past. It is an attempt, albeit enormously problematic, at reimagining the screen-story black body as a figure capable of critiquing exclusive racial constructions. However, it is still far from being critical of the way actions such as blackface performative aesthetics and trivialized sonic affiliations continue to exclude Afro-Mexicans.

CONCLUSION

As I have detailed throughout this chapter, *Nosotras las proles* is a rich and complex work that scrambles and rewrites the characters, scenarios, and musical numbers that have come to define *mexicanidad* by way of Mexican Golden Age cinema. As a satirical effort to destabilize the master narratives of Golden Age classics, the piece also reveals how Las Reinas Chulas' inability to accept the screen story's melodramatic plots, characters, and song choices has led them to disidentify with the past. In particular, the performance reflects the troupe's intentional efforts to dismantle notions of heteronormativity, the whitened mestizo physique, and phobic masculinity perpetuated and proliferated by cinematic classics constantly replayed over the last fifty years. By way of their revisions, the cabaret group underscores the wounding tendencies of contemporary neoliberal politics, those that often disproportionately impact already marginalized and vulnerable groups. By focusing on *Nosotros los proles*, *Los tres García*, and *Ángelitos negros*, I have detailed how Ana Francis, Marisol, Nora, and Cecilia's acts of sonic disidentification attempt to offer an alternative to the wounding tendencies of the past and present. Via lyrical revisions, musical accompaniment, and vocal performance, *Nosotras las proles* proposes a more inclusive future vision of *mexicanidad*, one that accepts racial and queer Others.

CHAPTER 2

Listening to Mexico's War on Drugs

Necroauralities in Three Movements

It was a Sunday night, at around 10:30 pm, when I witnessed what I believe to be someone gunned down on a street corner in Mexico City. It was the summer of 2019, and I was in Mexico City finalizing research for this book. On Sundays, Pako Reyes, one of the artists I discuss in Chapter 4, invited me over to watch television, talk about theater, and have dinner with the members of La Mafia Cabaret. He lived right near the Centro Nacional de las Artes (CENART; National Center for the Arts) on Río Churubusco, and I was staying in Roma Norte. On this particular evening, most of the Uber ride was quiet, as it usually was at that time of night. I cannot remember specifics about the date or the street corner. However, I do clearly remember feeling panicked and the fear in my driver's voice as he asked me, "Did you hear that gunshot?" I had. I had also seen what looked to be a group of young men mob a single silhouette right before the bullet rang out. My Uber was just feet away, and I was shaken. While I had certainly read the news over the years describing gun violence and gruesome scenes of terror, I had never heard or seen anything similar. It is entirely possible I still have not. Maybe those boys did not have a gun, but the unsettling metallic sound of that night has stayed with me. These sounds have also stayed with the nation, particularly since the War on Drugs started in 2006.[1]

The rising tension between drug violence and institutionally motivated efforts to eradicate drugs is a source of social conflict. Terms like "militarization," *capos*, "criminal organizations," and "cartels" are part of daily vernacular and bloody scenes of shootouts or mutilated bodies are front-page news. This is a direct result of increased militarization meant to battle drug trafficking. During his presidency, Vicente Fox committed more than 19,000 troops annually, while President Felipe Calderón committed 45,000 troops, a 133 percent increase, and in 2009 alone, "the Army assigned 48,750 men to combating narcotics syndicates."[2] The human toll of Calderón's efforts to dismantle and debilitate drug rings has been estimated at anywhere from 47,000 murdered to 60,000, with figures continuing to rise during Enrique Peña Nieto's reign (the topic of Chapter 3).[3] Yet another study concluded that between 230,000 and 1.6 million people have been displaced by the War on Drugs and homicides have taken the lives of at least 100,000 people, including cartel members, law enforcement personnel, officials, journalists, and innocent civilians.[4] Amaya Ordorika Imaz of La Comisión Mexicana en Defensa y Promoción de los Derechos Humanos (CMDPDH; Mexican Commission for the Defense and Promotion of Human Rights) states that since 2006, more than 150,000 people have been murdered, and since 2011, more than 280,000 have been displaced by violence.[5] Counting the casualties is "a desperate gesture to generate a minimum level of intelligibility"; it does not, and cannot, fully represent the work of violence in daily life.[6] These discrepancies and widely variable figures with regard to Mexico's dead and disappeared illustrate that "although conditions vary from state to state, overall, the presence of military men in top security roles has not diminished the violence afflicting their areas of responsibility."[7]

As a means of rationalizing the decision to mobilize an unprecedented number of troops and the increasing number of Mexican citizens impacted by the War on Drugs, ex-president Calderón deployed skillful linguistic strategies. His rhetorical performances of obfuscation and legitimization consistently reiterated his steadfast dedication to the cause, no matter who it killed. For Mladen Dolar, since the French Revolution, it is the oral performance of political declarations that ushers them into being. By extension, if orality makes law, it can also suspend it: "Life, strength, power, blood, soil—and the voice in continuation of this series, the voice instead of, in place of, the law."[8] This assertion echoes Giorgio Agamben's observation that "it can generally be said that not only language and law but all social institutions have been formed through a process of desemanticization and suspension of concrete praxis in its immediate reference to the real."[9] Hence, by way of oral addresses and media appearances, Calderón repeatedly suspended a sense of reality in favor of an imagined necessity for war, in spite of the costly toll on Mexican citizens. In his first presidential address on December 1, 2006, from Campo Marte, he declared:

> Sé que restablecer la seguridad no será fácil ni rápido, que tomará tiempo, que costará mucho dinero e incluso, por desgracia, vidas humanas. Pero ténganlo

por seguro: ésta es una batalla en la que yo estaré al frente, es una batalla que debemos librar y que unidos los mexicanos vamos a ganar la delincuencia.¹⁰

I know that reestablishing security will not be easy or fast, it will take time, a significant amount of money, and, unfortunately, human lives. However, rest assured that this is a battle which I will be leading, it is a battle that we need to fight, and together, we, Mexicans, will defeat delinquency.

Though brief, this extract showcases how, despite the stark reality that human lives would certainly be lost, Calderón's words emphasize that this would be a battle worth winning, that he too would be on the front line. Over the last several years, his linguistic strategies have been analyzed by numerous researchers, such as Alonso Vázquez Moyers and Germán Espino Sánchez, Melanie del Carmen Salgado López, Rafael Saldívar Arreola, and Ignacio Rodríguez Sánchez, to name a few. Working from Calderón's addresses to the nation and public interviews, these studies track the ways he framed and reframed the continuation of this costly war. Concretely, by establishing a definition of "the narco" for the shared cultural imaginary, Calderón crafted a tangible enemy that invaded national coverage of events.¹¹ Moreover, using collective constructions of "we, the Mexicans," Calderón implored citizens to unite in the fight for what became the good versus the bad, the *narcos* who sought to "secuestrar el futuro de México" (hold the future of Mexico ransom).¹² Crafting speeches in which righteousness outweighed villainy, Calderón consistently positioned himself as a savior of the nation's children, the guardian of the nation's future. In doing so, he elided the realities of the war, and in referring to the loss of life as unfortunate collateral damage, he created the conditions for the state's complicity in eradicating its own citizens.¹³

The surge in violence throughout the nation following Calderón's proclamation of war, lasting into subsequent *sexenios*, prompts a need to briefly consider the limits of political powers to decide who lives and dies. The seemingly constant barrage of violence that exploded in 2006, showcased in the news, on the streets, and across social media, was undoubtedly overwhelming. To think about how this inundation of violent images and acts interrupts daily life, I turn to Slajov Žižek and his categories of subjective and objective violence. He defines subjective violence as "a perturbation of the 'normal,' peaceful state of things"; it disrupts a sense of normalcy and calm.¹⁴ In the case of Mexico, the abrupt militarization and increased level of violence during Calderón's *sexenio* may certainly reflect subjective violence, or at least it may have done so initially. According to Rossana Reguillo, "it is no longer a case of Maria, Pedro, or Juan, but rather of anonymous bodies that are then layered by an ontological dimension . . . converted into units of common sense."[15] Given that the nation has existed in a state of perpetual violence since 2006, I am inclined to suggest the horrific became status quo.[16] Through symbolic acts, like Calderón's language, and systemic structures, such as the government's declaration and support of war, the ensuing scenes of horror are transformed into a new order rooted in "otra gramática corporal, otras mitologías de miedo" (a different embodied grammar, other mythologies of fear).[17] In other words, a *state of exception*. Departing from Foucault's notion of biopower to analyze who holds the power to decide the fate of another, Agamben proclaims, "by means of the state of exception, of a legal civil war that allows for the physical elimination not only of political adversaries but of entire categories of citizens who for some reason cannot be integrated into the political system."[18] This terrifying reality is made possible by the declaration of necessity, and "therefore appears (alongside revolution and the de facto establishment of a constitutional system) as an 'illegal' but perfectly 'juridical and constitutional' measure that is realized in the production of new norms."[19] In the case of Mexico, this necessity came in the form of Calderón's perceived need to combat *narco* violence, and in manifesting Mexico's state of exception, the former president suspended the rule of law, giving total power to a corrupt state and, unwittingly, the *narcos* themselves.

The common result of said states of exception are nations plagued by what Achille Mbembe calls "necropolitics." Referring to colonial systems of oppression and extreme acts of genocide, such as the slave trade, he suggests that "when politics is considered a form of war, the question needs to be asked about the place that is given to life, death, and the human body (in particular when it is wounded or slain)."[20] His observation that within colonial power structures, "the violence of the state of exception is deemed to operate in the service of 'civilization,'" however, could just as easily have been made as a response to Calderón's declaration of war and the mass violence that followed.[21] Mbembe's acute analysis of necropolitics as a "triple loss . . . identical with absolute domination, natal alienation, and social death (expulsion from humanity altogether)" is echoed by innumerable Mexican families who have suffered the death or disappearance of a loved one.[22] For them, because of the War on Drugs, "death remains a spectacle even when the corpse is absent. This takes two forms: absolute or partial erasure. The human condition is absolutely denied as the victim is either dissolved in acid or incinerated."[23] In other words, the state's deployment of necropolitics has transformed the nation into one grappling with what should be unimaginable loss, pain, and fear.

One of the significant ramifications of Felipe Calderón's declaration of war is the way it created a national soundscape deeply tied to the sounds of the military. My use of the term *sonicscape* is indebted to the work of R. Murray Schafer and his aural description of the battleground. Though referring more to early modern settings, Schafer states, "armies decorated for battle presented a visual spectacle, but the battle itself was acoustic. To the actual noise of clashing metal, each army added its battle cries and drumming in an attempt to frighten the enemy. Noise was a deliberate military stratagem."[24] In his groundbreaking study on the sonic contours of war, J. Martin Daughtry analyzes myriad sounds associated with war, ranging from gas generators to sirens to explosions, and the relationship between aurality and listening body.[25] Importantly for my purposes, Daughtry echoes Schafer's observation, but in relation to the US Iraqi War, proclaiming that "to witness war, is in large part, to hear it. And to survive it is, among other things, to have listened to it."[26]

In what follows, I apply sonic considerations of life in "war-torn" Mexico to explore performative gestures. I situate my assessment of the auditory triggers, contours, and geographies of war within the world of theater and performance. Cognizant of the intimate relationship between war, states of exception, and necropolitics, my critical analysis in this chapter is indebted to the work of Ileana Diéguez. Coining the term *necroteatro* her innovative proposition creates an analogous relationship between the performative arts and Mbembe's notion of necropolitics.[27] Diéguez uses this concept to offer precise and impactful analyses of performance trends emerging out of nations impacted by illicit drug trade violence. Taking a hemispheric approach to loss during times of national unrest, including Mexico's War on Drugs, Diéguez posits the purpose of necrotheater as to "poner ante los ojos la evidencia espectacular del sufrimiento, la escena aterradora de un discurso de poder que aniquila el cuerpo humano en vida y *post mortem*" (put before our very eyes the spectacular evidence of suffering, the terrifying scene of how discourses of power annihilate the human body in life and after death).[28] To accompany these ideas, my work thinks about listening to the elements of war that are, in many ways, indelible to the visual component of necropolitics and necrotheater. I propose the term *necroauralities* to contemplate how the audible contours of Mexico's war, state of exception, and necropolitics reverberate through the terrain of the body, as citizen and performer. Concretely, I explore how the sounds deeply connected to wartime practices are refracted through performative practices by putting three pieces into dialogue: *Ejercicio de percusión* (Percussion Exercise, 2006), *Música de balas* (Music of Bullets, 2012), and *México exhumado* (Mexico

Exhumed, 2019). I consider the first piece as an audible performance of the initiation of Mexico's War on Drugs. I listen to the second piece as a reference to necropolitics in its fullest form in the Mexican context, meaning the sounds of rampant gun violence. Finally, I appreciate the final piece as an aural embodiment of the relationship between wounds and deathworlds.

ENRIQUE JEŽIK AND *EJERCICIO DE PERCUSIÓN*

Born in Córdoba, Argentina, Enrique Ježik has been a central figure in the Mexican performance art scene since 1990. After an initial invitation to show his sculpture work in Central Mexico and Oaxaca, the artist decided to permanently relocate to Mexico City. For him, "Mexican chaos is compensated by more freedom. Life in Mexico City brings you to a specific understanding of what is and what is not possible to accomplish."[29] Perhaps the artist exoticizes or romanticizes the metropolitan city, but his description echoes Néstor García Canclini's statement that Mexico City "cannot be encompassed by any description. If we look at it from the inside, from the perspective of local daily practices, we see only fragments, outskirts, locations determined by a myopic perception of the whole."[30] I am interested in the way Ježik uses performance and installation works to enact relational bonds of power and fear. In fact, the titles of his pieces often allude to experiences of violence. His Mexico-based performances, such as *Reforma Agraria* (Agrarian Reform, 2007) in Chiapas, *Seis metros cúbicos de materia orgánica* (Six Cubic Meters of Organic Material, 2009) in Ciudad Juárez, and the series called *Posible Advertencia* (Possible Warning, 2017) in Mexico City, push the boundaries between performance and spectatorship. Outside of Mexico, Ježik has been invited to perform and show his work as an artist in residence in Great Britain (*One and a half miles*, 2004), the Contemporary History Museum in Ljubljana, Slovenia (*Desfile suspendido / Suspended Parade*, 2007), the Eleventh Annual International Festival of Performance in São Paolo (*81 prisões /81 Prisons*, 2015), and the XXII Biannual of Shanghai (*In Hemmed-in Ground*, 2018), just to name a few.

Having lived as a teenager through Argentina's Dirty War (1976–1983), Ježik is no stranger to oppressive regimes or police violence. The artist rarely speaks publicly or through his art about his home country's past, the effect it had on him, or his relationship to current Argentine politics, but the parallels between Argentina and Mexico are palpable. In 2015, Ježik explained the way he broadly conceives of violence, power, and resistance: "La violencia ejercida por el poder abusivo sobre los propios ciudadanos es una preocupación recurrente. Es algo que nos afecta a todos" (Violence exerted over everyday citizens by an abusive power is a constant preoccupation. It is something that affects us all).[31] When he speaks of Mexico, a nation living the aftermath of its War on Drugs, Ježik describes the way that citizens have started to wake up to what was happening around them and have decided not to bury their head in the sand anymore.[32] His performances and art installations also serve as a model of resisting the invisibilizing rhetoric and discursive practices that span Calderón's *sexenio*. In *Valla* (Fence, 2007), the metal grate blockades used against protestors in Oaxaca are reimagined into a map of Oaxaca, transforming the grates into a collective tool for resisting repression, and his installation piece *Práctica* (Practice, 2007) draws attention to twenty life-size silhouettes riddled with bullets, each one a metonym of the lives lost to gun violence.[33] My particular interest is in the piece *Ejercicio de percusión*, in which Ježik fuses intimidation tactics and sounds of battle, mapping them onto the bodies of others via his performative intervention.

The sonic materiality of performance and art installations is a recurring and crucial component of Ježik's repertoire. Starting in the early 2000s, he regularly incorporated bullet holes, the sounds of gunshots, and ricochet noises in his work as a broad critique of gun violence in Mexico.[34] After Calderón's declaration of war, however, Ježik's audiovisual performances found new inspiration. In November 2006, as part of the XII International Festival of Performance, Ježik orchestrated an all-too-real enactment of force.[35] Despite having only been performed once, *Ejercicio de percusión* is one of the artist's most well-known pieces, having much to do with the way he bridges what Diana Taylor calls the "archive" and the "repertoire." Taylor suggests archival memory is comprised of "documents, maps, literary texts, letters, archaeological remains, bones, videos, films, CDs, all those items supposedly resistant to change" while the repertoire "enacts embodied memory: performances, gestures, orality, movement, dance, singing—in short all those acts usually thought of as ephemeral."[36] Starting early in his career, Ježik began documenting and recording as part of performative interventions, creating tangible traces left behind in the wake of a piece's inevitable ephemerality. It is through these traces, the photos and video recordings, that I have come to appreciate *Ejercicio de percusión*.[37] In this chapter's analysis, I explore the way the piece materializes the "unprecedented number of arrests and the magnitude of military deployment" during the first months of Calderón's presidency.[38] In doing so, the brief performance reveals the necroauralities of Mexico's state of exception and the beginning phase of war.

ACOUSTIC TERRITORIES OF INTIMIDATION

Before I delve into details about *Ejercicio de percusión*, I want first to describe where the performance took place: the Ex Teresa Arte Actual (Ex Teresa). Located at 8 Licenciado Verdad, between Moneda and República de Guatemala, the chapel and former convent is around the corner from Mexico City's central plaza. Erected in 1613, the structure was later dedicated to Saint Teresa "la Antigua" by Don Francisco de Aguilar y Seixas on September 11, 1684.[39] Since the nineteenth century, the former convent has undergone a series of changes, such as being used as military quarters, an all-male school, la Universidad de Vasconcelos, and, for a short time, the printing operations of the *Diario Oficial* and the Secretary of Finance's official archive.[40] Since 1989, the space has been used, almost exclusively, for performative and artistic endeavors, gaining both national and international recognition as a site of experimentation and dissidence. Renowned performance artists such as La Pocha Nostra, Xandra Ibarra, Rocío Boliver (La Congelada de Uva), Lorena Wolffer, and Katia Tirado have used the Ex Teresa to create provocative pieces and host workshops. The space is also home to Mexico's most extensive archive regarding national performance artists, especially those who have used the space to present and develop their work.

Aside from its long-standing connection to performance art, the symbolic nature of the building's location as well as its acoustic properties made it an ideal site for Ježik's performance. Since 2006, much of the city center has been constantly patrolled by federal and local police officers. Their presence is a reminder that the nation is at war and serves as a surveillance mechanism deployed against civilians. Just minutes away from the nation's National Palace, built on the ruins of the Aztec capital city, Tenochtitlán, the Ex Teresa is also a reminder of Indigenous conquest and colonialism. Many of the artists who use the space turn to performative means to question both the constant presence of governmental force and neocolonial social practices.[41] Starting with the auditory realm, the bare walls, open floor plan, and high ceilings of the former convent allow for sounds to reverberate, crescendo, and travel through the space. Having myself seen several pieces performed in this location, I can attest that the result is a sonically immersive experience. The aural element often becomes a protagonist, one that assumes a center role but can also be difficult to pin down, isolate, or control. In his consideration of sound in theater, Ross Brown points out that surround sound is seldom integrated into the performance experience, though it has been a staple of cinemas and in-home viewing arenas.[42] As Brown suggests, this is because the sensation of noise enveloping the space and audiences can often be more off-putting than enjoyable in theatre settings. In the case of Ježik's work and the Ex Teresa, this proves to be true; the immersive sounds of militarized activity create an unnerving performance of war.

Though only a mere three minutes and forty-five seconds long, the recorded material of the original performance is an unsettling representation of military stratagem. As I write this in 2021, the images and sounds I detail below could easily refer to Minneapolis or Portland, sites of police terror in the United States. I want to insist, though, that Ježik's piece be understood within the distinct context of Mexico in 2006. Recorded using live feeds from two cameras, the split-pane video offers intimate views of overt force, fear, and confusion. Additionally, the sound is diegetic, meaning it is recorded as the performance progresses rather than added during postproduction editing. In what I will call "feed 1," the camera captures the perspective of the antiriot squad while in what I will call "feed 2," the camera records the unsuspecting participants from within the Ex Teresa. In watching the video, removed from the original moment, feed 1 allows spectators to develop insider knowledge about what is about to happen, knowledge that was not available to those who attended the 2006 performance. Recorded at chest height, similar to the view from a body cam, feed 1 captures an antiriot police squad getting into formation on the streets just outside the former convent. From there, feed 1 records the squad as the officers begin to beat their shields and march toward, and ultimately through, the museum entrance. Feed 2 seems to be mounted on the ceiling, or some comparable elevated location. From this bird's-eye view, feed 2 records the attendees awaiting the next piece. People are standing near an entrance, talking, and the space itself seems to be completely empty. Once the antiriot squad enters, the split-pane view reveals differing approximations of fear. From above, feed 2 offers a holistic view of bodies cowering and being herded into a back corner of the space. Feed 1, on the other hand, documents close-up views of spectators scrambling to move and make sense of the event.

During *Ejercicio de percusión*, the route to, within, and from the Ex Teresa becomes an acoustic territory of war.[43] It is worth noting that both camera feeds are low-resolution and while this may reflect available technology, I would like to suggest that Ježik capitalized on the fact that his performance would take place in the evening to emphasize the aural experience. The dark streets of Mexico's city center and the limited lighting inside the transformed seventeenth-century building made recording a challenge. Yet, the low visibility during that evening's intervention, and in the recording, enhances the bellicose sounds of the antiriot police force. Much like the attendees of the live performance, viewers of the archive footage are also forced to rely on their ear to make sense of what is happening. The quiet street and interior of the museum are abruptly interrupted by the marching boots, batons hitting the plastic shields, and shouted orders. As the sounds of the antiriot squad spread through the street and performance space, they are met with crowd whispers and, later, muffled screams of surprise and terror, demonstrating the way sounds can, and do, become weaponized. This scene, and its auditory elements, echo Bruce Johnson and Martin Cloonan's statement that sound "is part of the larger soundscape, that constitutes our world, and when it inflicts violence, it does not only by virtue of what it means, but what it then is: noise."[44] In *Ejercicio de percusión*, the noises symbolize the intense militarization of the nation resulting from Calderón's proclamation of war. Moreover, the entire event brings to mind Jacques Attali's work on noise, music, and sound politics. He declares, "with noise is born disorder and its opposite: the world."[45] In this case, however, the world and disorder are one and the same; Mexico is a nation in utter disarray. The militarized aurality becomes the perfect "mirror of society" that Attali envisions.[46] Perhaps more accurately, *Ejercicio de percusión* transforms sound into an invisible long arm of the law, used to disorient and terrorize festival participants and unassuming onlookers.

Simulating the way in which Mexican citizens experience the sounds of war, this microcosmic performance highlights the fact that sounds, like bullets themselves, ricochet. On the street, the intensity of the antiriot police squad's aurality is, in some ways, muted. As the sounds bounce between building walls, trailing off down the street, absorbed by bodies and cars, the visual spectacle becomes more menacing than the sonic experience. That is reversed, however, as the squad enters the Ex Teresa. The sounds they make reverberate loudly throughout, increasing in intensity as the squad moves through the space. As Daughtry observes about wartime Iraq, "we can no longer speak of sound as existing phenomenologically at or near the source of vibration. Instead, the event feels like it is taking place *right here*, on the surface of the auditor's skin, or inside the body's cavities."[47] Similarly, the bombastic aurality of *Ejercicio de percusión* becomes delinked from its origin site (the antiriot squad), traveling through space and time to further weaponize the sounds of war. The all-encompassing vibrations create a dizzying sensation for spectators. Reverberating on and through their bodies, they not only see the threat of violence but also feel it coursing through their limbs with no way to protect themselves. Though the forceful presence of the antiriot squad lasts only a mere two minutes, the spectators are not left with feelings of catharsis or relief when the military presence retreats. Rather, they are left without a sense of resolution as their bodies and minds try to process how the sounds of war intruded on their own corporeality.

The performance, much like Calderón's War on Drugs, forces participation on attendees, prompting reactions of fear and confusion. As Agamben notes, for a state of exception to be fully executed, "all social institutions," not only rhetorical strategies and legal jurisdiction, enter into the process of "desemanticization and suspension of concrete praxis in its immediate reference to the real."[48] It is this last observation of the "real" that bears particular importance for *Ejercicio de percusión*. With the antiriot squad simulating an actual training exercise, the performance blurs the lines of performance and reality, much as Calderón's decree blurred the arenas of war and civilian life. As a performance, what Carol Martin would call the "intrusions of the real into the theatrical" are perhaps the most unsettling element for onlookers, festival participants, and video viewers.[49] The entire audiovisual spectacle more than pretends to perform war; it restores embodied memories of antiriot training exercises. Here, Richard Schechner's concept of restored behavior is particularly apt, as it refers to the act of repeating an original behavior that we, as spectators, never see and that can never be completely replicated.[50] The importance of the action is not the original, but instead, how it reveals social bonds.[51] Ježik's performance is a conscious rendition of rehearsing antiriot exercises meant for crowd control and intimidation, and the extent to which *Ejercicio de percusión* may have diverted from "original" training exercises does not matter. What is important is that the piece performs war by way of its restored bellicose behavior. As an enactment of spatial and sonic occupation, the intrusive and immersive aurality of the antiriot squad lays bare the extent to which the War on Drugs became inescapable for so many.

HUGO SALCEDO AND *MÚSICA DE BALAS*

To reflect the continuity of wartime violence, each scene in *Música de balas* begins with a number that refers to Mexican citizens killed because of the War on Drugs. The piece ends as the death toll reaches 30,001, followed by the phrase, "parece no haber fin" (there seems to be no end). Together, the number indicates the massive scale of the nation's trauma while the phrase prophesizes the endless horrors caused by a necropolitical state. Reguillo declares: "we count the dead, but the gesture is useless because we are unable to restore the humanity lost and unable to mend the rupture" created by the state.[52] This seems appropriate for considering the stakes of *Música de balas*, as the numerical figures on the page become enlivened by bodies on the stage. The actors morph into individualized accounts of death that stand in for broader tendencies of terror related to the nation's War on Drugs. The title itself plants the idea that modern-day Mexicans hear gunfire so frequently that it has become a sort of music. Hence, I read and listen to the piece as a continuation of necroauralities, reflective of Calderón's *sexenio* as it intersected with *narco* forces. I apply this analytical model by weaving together analysis of the dramatic text and considerations of three distinct performances: a 2013 staging at the Real Escuela Superior de Arte Dramático in Madrid, directed by Raul Rodríguez; a 2015 performance at the University of Wisconsin–Madison, directed by Paola S. Hernández, where I was also the stage manager; and the 2019 Centro Dramático de Michoacán production, directed by Naoli Eguiarte.[53] I include these sources to showcase not only how Salcedo imbued his dramaturgy with sonic triggers of violence based on his experiences hearing violence, but also to illustrate how directors and performers leveraged their auditory encounters with Mexico's war as part of their artistic practice. My analysis is rooted in engaging listening practices that highlight how Salcedo, the texts' readers, and theater performers across different geographies process the "musiquita de balas" (sweet sound of bullets) that accompanies Mexican citizens "hasta las puertas del infierno" (to the doors of hell).[54] Given the variety of deaths included in the piece, what follows is a close analysis of particular body counts that manifest the threat of gunfire, ex-president Felipe Calderón's dismissive rhetoric, and the *narcocorrido* as a soundtrack to Mexico's War on Drugs.

Originally from Jalisco, Guadalajara, Hugo Salcedo lived on the US–Mexican border for several decades. Before making Tijuana his home, Salcedo studied theater theory at the Universidad Autónoma de Barcelona and received his doctorate in Hispanic literatures from the Universidad Complutense de Madrid. Currently a professor at the Universidad Iberamericana, Salcedo was previously a professor at the Universidad Autónoma de Baja California and was an invited professor at the Université Charles de Gaule Lille III, la Universidad Tecnológica de San Salvador, and his alma mater, la Universidad Complutense. To say his career as a dramaturge has been incredibly prolific is an understatement. Since the mid-1980s, Salcedo has written more than forty pieces, several of which have earned literary prizes at the local, national, and international level. His achievements include the Punto de Partida de la UNAM, Premio Mejor Autor, Premio Nacional de Teatro del INBA, among others. Perhaps his most notable recognition is the prestigious Tirso de Molina prize for *Viaje de los cantores* (The Singers' Journey, 1989), based on an actual case of eighteen undocumented immigrants who suffocated to death in a train car while trying to cross the border. As the first Mexican to earn this award, it was an immense honor for Salcedo, Mexican theater, and the nation.

During his many years residing on the border, Salcedo found inspiration in the way daily experiences of immigration, exploitation, and violence were often met with artistic resistance. Estela Leñero Franco, a theater practitioner and contemporary of Salcedo, praises his critical renderings of Mexican reality. As she explains, his theater incorporates "la frontera, los indocumentados, la cultura popular, y en este caso la violencia y el narcotráfico," (the border, the undocumented, popular culture, and, in this case, violence and drug-trafficking) as themes developed via diverse dramaturgical decisions in his texts and live performances.[55] Appearing in volumes such as *Dramaturgia del Norte* (Dramaturgy from the North), *Teatro de frontera* (Theatre from the Border), and *Teatro del Norte* (Theater from the North), Salcedo is undoubtedly marked by thematic choices as well as his regional placement. His work, though, extends beyond this single designation tied to his geographical location. Jorge Celaya, playwright and editor of *Teatro de frontera*, explains that the kinds of plays that Salcedo writes are ones in which "resultan más importantes los actos, los comportamientos, las relaciones de los actantes ante lo que acontece a su alrededor; más de lo que se dice en el momento" (the actions on stage, the behaviors, and the relationship between the movements are more important than what happens around them; they are more important than what is said in the moment).[56] In this sense, Salcedo's dramaturgical style shares common indicators with postdramatic theater, documentary theater, and theater of cruelty.[57] Scholars have also categorized his work as part of what has recently been designated *novísima dramaturgia* in Mexico. Jaime Chabaud, another contemporary of Salcedo and *novísima* contributor, describes the movement: "en términos generales, la generación reciente se hace menos preguntas categóricas y flexibiliza las reglas. Más bien le valen madre los paradigmas pese a su enorme necesidad de ellos" (in general terms, the most recent generation asks itself fewer questions about categories and, instead, makes the rules flexible. In other words, they do not care about paradigms even though they depend on them).[58] What Chabaud indicates, and Salcedo's work exemplifies, is a tendency to question Mexican reality; it underscores the limits of written and embodied performance to redefine said experiences.

As part of redefining theater and dramaturgy, Salcedo uses sounds as a repeating element in his work. Broadly speaking, Salcedo includes a variety of sonic registers in his pieces, ranging from interrupting noises, like the sound of a train whistle, to musical interludes. According to the playwright, he considers music a "universal language," motivating the way he integrates it into his artistic productions. At the same time, Salcedo confesses that sonic references are not premeditated but rather are unconscious reflections of his own listening practices and understanding of music as a mechanism for creating bonds between people.⁵⁹ One of Salcedo's earliest pieces, *Cumbia* (1987), invokes a widely popular musical style, especially in Northern Mexico and throughout the border area. References to popular music also appear in his other works, for example in his 1997 piece, *Selena, la reina del tex-mex* (Selena, the Queen of Tex-Mex), loosely based on the life of the murdered singer, and in *Música de balas*, which features *narcocorridos*. Considering the ramifications of sounds as backdrops to migratory crossings, *El viaje de los cantores* (The Singers' Journey, 1989) incorporates noises and poetic articulations related to the pain and loss of undocumented bodies.⁶⁰ Continuing the theme of border crossing, *Sinfonía en una botella* (Symphony in a Bottle, 1990), which finds inspiration in the San Ysidro site and Julio Cortázar's short story "Autopista del sur," creates an "efecto irónico del ruido como sinfonía" (an ironic use of sound as a kind of symphony).⁶¹ Time and again, Salcedo's dramaturgy blends the sounds of everyday life with acts of border crossing, prompting readers and spectators to consider unexamined comforts juxtaposed by border dissonance.

Published for circulation in 2012, at the end of Felipe Calderón's presidency, *Música de balas* pushes the boundaries of textual representation and embodied performance of violence. After its initial performance debut in 2011, the piece received the National Prize of Dramaturgy in Mexico.⁶² As scholar Iani del Rosario Moreno notes, "the jury praised the play for its 'innovative dramatic structure, complexity and its link to the reality of contemporary Mexico.'"⁶³ The primary focus of the piece is the rising death toll related to seemingly uncontrollable violence such as police corruption, *narco* territory wars, and feminicides. These staggering numerical figures are used to drive the progression of the play as Salcedo deploys numbers from the nation's death toll, rather than literary titles or words of any kind, to indicate each individual scene in the play. This continues until 30,001, which is the number used to conclude the text and reference the deaths caused by Calderón's sexenio. Given its structure and content, Leñero Franco points out that this play "nos habla sin piedad de las muertes violentas relacionadas con el crimen organizado" (speaks without mercy of the violent deaths caused by organized crime), but does so in a way that also highlights a desperation to find words to describe the horrors. Furthermore, the dramaturgy tests the boundaries of writing conventions by incorporating "letras pequeñas o grandes que invaden toda la página; escribe diálogos o largos monólogos; utiliza los tipos de letra Arial o Courier; incluye fragmentos de corridos o canciones mexicanas; los personajes tienen nombre propio o simplemente son X y Y" (small or large letters that invade the entire page; he writes dialogue or long monologues; he uses Arial or Courier typefaces; he includes fragments of *corridos* or Mexican songs; the characters have names or sometimes are just designated by X or Y).⁶⁴ The words themselves are uncharacteristic of dramatic writing and the visual quality of the text whimpers, declares, screams, and questions the unstable nation. The written version, however, is not the only way in which his play captures these sensations of loss, confusion, and fear. With virtually no production notes included in the text, this openness allows for staging creativity in terms of props, projections, lighting, and costuming. This vagueness also functions to situate the performers' bodies as the central site for communicating the expressive dimensions of gruesome terror. In what follows, my interest is in the acoustic territory of gunfire alluded to and performed.

HEARING CALDERÓN'S WAR AND COLLATERAL DAMAGE

The scene numbered 29,876, referring to that specific death toll figure, recounts listening to Mexico's war rage as its everyday citizens become transformed, unwillingly, into collateral damage as part of militarizing Mexico's streets. In the text, the place, date, and time are undefined; this death could have happened anywhere in Mexico, on any given night of the week. Though there are no stage directions, all three staged performances emphasize the sonic magnitude of the bullets ringing out, juxtaposed by the darkness of night. In Eguiarte's staging, for example, the soundtrack plays a series of loud gunshots, each heard individually, coupled with the high-pitched screams of onlookers. The two onstage performers frenetically run to center stage and throw their bodies flat onto the floor. Barely moving, one friend says to another, "tírate al piso, pérate, no hables, pérate. . . . —un chinguero de balazos. . . ., como noventa o cien, lo menos—que te calles pues, que no te muevas" (get on the floor, wait, don't speak, wait . . . —a ton of gunfire . . . like ninety or a hundred shots, at least—be quiet, don't move).⁶⁵ This act of desperation to find safety is the same across the three performances; despite the characters' best efforts to survey the landscape, the onstage darkness prohibits them from visually understanding their proximity to the origins of the gunshots. The characters are forced to become earwitnesses, intently listening to their surroundings to indicate when they might once again be able to move. Moreover, their inability to pinpoint the source and location from which the bellicose sounds emerge provokes "a degree of unsettledness, anxiety, or insecurity," as the two are immobilized by the sonic threat to their safety.⁶⁶ Nearing the end of the scene, the gunfire wanes in all three performances, and one friend says to the other, "¿Oyes? Ya se acercan las patrullas.

Mejor hay que irnos antes de que lleguen" (Do you hear that? The police are getting close. We should go before they get here).[67] The commentary is an astute observation yet again of the bodily capacity to measure distance by way of invisible sonic waves, as they hear, rather than see, the military or police forces. Like *Ejercicio de percusión*, the acousmatic triggers of militarized troops also reinforce a perceived continued threat to their safety, only now the origin is known: the government. Though just one line, this observation poignantly signals the overt role military figures and state police have in perpetuating violent acts, as well as in provoking terror in Mexico's citizens.

The scene does not end with that imperative to flee the area, but rather in tragedy. The friend who has been nervously talking and trying to make sense of what is happening around them states, "Qué bueno que tardaron en darnos el cambio del billete en el *7-Eleven*, eso fue lo que nos salvó" (Thank goodness they were so slow in giving us our change in the 7-Eleven, that is what saved our lives).[68] Anyone who has tried to make change at a 7-Eleven or OXXO in Mexico knows how frustrating, time consuming, and nonsensical the experience can be. Yet, here, within this context, the observation is a startling commentary about the arbitrary loss of life. At this point, silence consumes the conversation. In Hernández's and Rodríguez's stagings, the body only generates guttural mumbling and gurgling noises. As unpleasant as they are, these sounds become the last audible utterances of life. In all three performances, the scene ends as the friend who had been talking the whole time realizes the other has died from a rogue bullet; they became collateral damage. According to Javier Trevino-Rangel, "in Mexico, euphemisms were used for reframing the status of victims. When referring to them, the Calderón government spoke of 'collateral effects' or 'collateral damage.'"[69] By refusing to name the victims, Calderón's rhetorical strategies easily erased them or rationalized their deaths as part of a greater cause, the ultimate linguistic performance of "an abdication of responsibility."[70] In neither the text nor the onstage representation is the body ever given a name, hobbies, or a physical description. Rather, their artistically rendered anonymity captures the way dead citizens were consciously emptied of value, erased from existence by Calderón's necropolitical state.

In Rodríguez's 2013 performance, Felipe Calderón's rhetorical strategies of obfuscation are presented directly as this scene of collateral damage comes to an end. The stage lighting goes black, and the actors slip out of the space while the audience sees a projection against the back wall. The video montage was created for the performance, juxtaposing fragments of interviews Calderón did during his *sexenio* with clips of mourning resulting from the president's declaration of war. The projection begins with a 2007 clip of Calderón speaking to foreign media.[71] The camera is fixated on Calderón

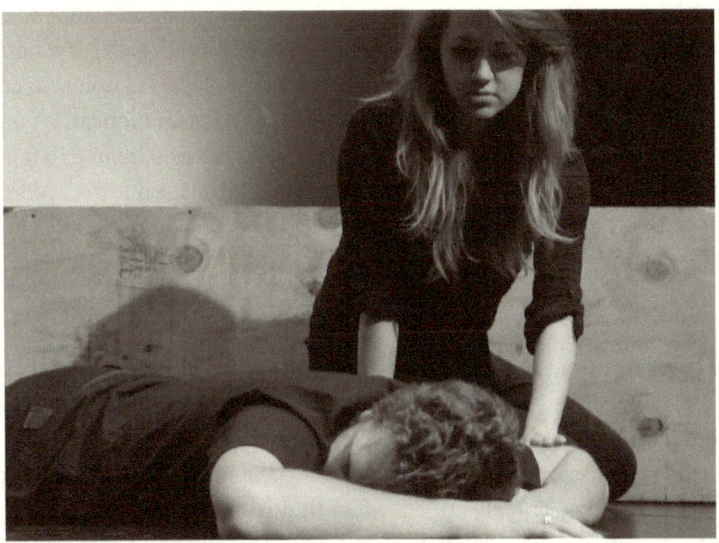

FIGURE 2.1. A pair of friends lie on the ground after hearing gunfire. *Música de balas*, directed by Paola S. Hernández, University of Wisconsin—Madison, Madison, Wisconsin, 2015. Photo by Chris Konieczki.

as his voice calmly states: "We knew, when we started this war, it was going to take time, money, and also cost human lives." As if interrupting the commentary, the video montage then plays a brief interlude of the Mexican national anthem, functioning as a somber soundtrack to the visual depiction of militarized troops and mass mobilization. The video editing strategically brings together Calderón's rhetoric of collateral damage with images of national pride, linking the nationalistic sonic cues with the imperative for war. The montage then cuts back to Calderón in a 2010 interview with the Spanish media program, *Los Desayunos de TVE* (Breakfast with TVE). He fervently explains: "Hay que se equivocadamente dice que la acción del gobierno ha provocado la violencia. No es así, la violencia entre los cárteles es lo que, entre otras cosas, motiva la acción del gobierno" (There are those who erroneously say the government's actions have provoked the violence. That is not the case, the violence between cartels is what, among other things, has motivated the actions of the government).[72] Audibly agitated, Calderón asserts that it would be ridiculous to assume the cartels could, or would, regulate violence among them; "como si fuera arte de magia los criminales se conviertan en santos varones, se les apareciera, como a San Pablo, Jesucristo, y se conviertan en buenos. No va a ser así, hay que enfrentarlos" (as if by some miracle these criminals become saints, having seen the apparitions of Saint Paul, Jesus Christ, and decide to become righteous. It will not be like this, we have to fight them).[73] This declaration, both absurd and firm in its insistence that the government needs to continue supporting the war, is followed by a devastating news segment. The final moments of the montage are from a television program with a banner that reads: "El dolor no cede" (the pain never ends). The visual component showcases mourning family members while the accompanying sounds are of wailing parents and family members who have become, effectively, collateral damage due to Calderón's insistence on militarized action.

OF NECRO AND NARCO AURALITIES

The inner workings of cartel violence, as Calderón notes in the earlier commentary, are also a constant throughout Salcedo's piece. These moments of internal struggle for power and allegiance are depicted in relation to gun violence. The scene corresponding to death toll number 29,880, for example, brings to the stage a reenactment of an interrogation and murder within the *narco* community. One man, Rogelio, is brutally beaten by his interrogator, who accuses him of infiltrating the cartel. As if the infiltration charge is not sufficient to warrant imminent death, Rogelio is also accused of killing "Cerebro de Vidrio," one of the cartel's *capos*. In Eguiarte's and Hernández's productions, the accused is tied to a chair, fully clothed, highlighting his bruised and battered face. In Rodríguez's version, Rogelio is forced to stand blindfolded and bare-chested with his arms raised overhead, tied to a chain. Visually, all three stagings are reminiscent of wartime interrogation and torture tactics, such as those revealed by photos of the Abu Ghraib prison. In both Hernández's and Rodríguez's presentations, the two actors feign the sounds of a beating, flesh on flesh, as the captor pummels the detained with his fist. Eguiarte's presentation, however, takes a different approach, a more symbolic auditory portrayal of violence. The two men are surrounded by supporting cast members who perform a *zapateado*. The acoustic resonances of heels stomping into the floor metonymically become the sounds of slaps, punches, and even gunfire. The dancing is accompanied by a low, pulsing bass, a sonic current that almost mimics the sounds of a racing heartbeat. Together, the crescendo of thumping and metal clashing against the floor create an aural sensation of fear and unrelenting abuse.

Suffering blow after blow, Rogelio finally admits to being a member of the Sinaloan cartel, to being one of those *"shinaloas."* The geographical reference and accent as he pronounces his affiliation clearly situate this experience within the realm of cartel feuds that plague Northern Mexico. Saldívar Arreola and Rodríguez Sánchez note this tendency, stating, "en el imaginario colectivo, incluso se ha vinculado el habla del narco con la variedad

FIGURE 2.2. Rogelio is tied to a chair, brutally beaten, and threatened with a gun. Música de balas, directed by Paola S. Hernández, University of Wisconsin—Madison, Madison, Wisconsin, 2015. Photo by Chris Konieczki.

dialectal del estado de Sinaloa. Hablar como sinaloense se convirtió en emblema y en un elemento identitario de lo narco" (in the collective imaginary, the way the *narco* speaks has been linked to the kind of dialect you hear in the state of Sinaloa. Speaking like you are from Sinaloa has become an emblematic part of the *narco* identity).[74] In this scene, the interrogator reveals that Rogelio did not simply kill "Cerebro de Vidrio," but left him so disfigured that he was unrecognizable. Rogelio left the dead without the commanding presence he was venerated for; "le rompiste todos los faros y la corrocería completa, y lo dejaste allí nada más tirado, con el ojo de payaso bien madreado" (you broke his bones and demolished his entire body, leaving him strewn there, beaten to a pulp).[75] As if using the beating to reinscribe the violence inflicted on Cerebro de Vidrio's body onto Rogelio's, his captor ominously promises the traitor, "y por eso aquí mismito te va a tocar escuchar la musiquita de balas, la que te va a acompañar hasta las puertas del infierno, pinche shinola mal parido" (and for that, right here, right now, it is your turn to hear the sweet sound of bullets, those which will accompany you to the doors of hell, damned Shinola bastard).[76] At this point in Hernández's and Rodríguez's dramatizations, the space goes black, and from within the abyss, the sounds of a final scream and a gunshot ring out. In Eguiarte's presentation, the deceased Rogelio takes center stage and performs a zapateado call-and-response choreography, the culmination of metonymical sounds of gunfire and murder. As his danced rhythms are repeated back to him by a chorus of dancers flanking each side of the stage, Rogelio's singular death becomes sonically linked to greater instances of violence within and beyond the cartel communities.

In addition to the sonic thread (or threat) of gunfire alluded to, or actually heard, the dramatic text includes fragments of *narcocorridos*, a music that reveres violence, masculinity, and *narco* control. Interestingly, aside from a single example, that of the rendition of "500 balazos" by Alacranes Musical, I have yet to encounter trends in *narcocorridos* that literally incorporate the sounds of bullets.[77] Rather, in place of violence transformed into music, *narcocorridos* have been the standard sonic reference point for channeling the ever-growing economic, social, and cultural control *narcos* have over Mexico. Defined as *norteña* musical (or more recently *banda*) accompaniment to lyrical compositions about drug traffickers, *narcocorridos* have become engrained in Mexico's musical culture since the 1970s.[78] This was a pivotal moment for what would become a close relationship between the music industry and the drug trade. The place of this musical genre in Mexican society seems to have reached an all-time high, as hit *narcotelenovelas*—among them *La Reina del Sur* (The Queen of the South, 2011), *El señor de los cielos* (The Master of the Heavens, 2013–), and *Narcos: Mexico* (2018–)—have groups who perform a *narcocorrido* at the beginning of every episode, demonstrating the connections between mass media, drug culture, and the music industry.

Rooted in the *corrido* tradition, the *narcocorrido* genre shares many of its predecessors' sonic and social qualities, although it departs in terms of thematic content. The origins of the *corrido* are difficult to trace, having been linked to both Indigenous and Spanish musical traditions. However, its cultural significance is directly associated to its perception as "la voz del pueblo, del oprimido, del que sufre" (the voice of the people, of the oppressed, of those who suffer).[79] The music became further ingrained in Mexico's musical repertoire from 1910 to 1920, during the nation's revolution. During this period, *corridos* not only vocalized the sentiments of the suffering, but also transmitted information, otherwise inaccessible, to an overwhelmingly illiterate audience.[80] These songs spread information about battles, heroes, landscapes, and other information regarding the state of the nation. Yet, since the 1970s, an updated model that emphasizes archetypes like the valiant, macho drug trafficker, the faithful female companion, and the traitor has replaced the content of the past. A prime example is Los Tigres del Norte's 1973 hit, "Contrabando y traición," which tells of the troubles a drug trafficker and his female companion meet trying to smuggle drugs across the border. Reflecting the song's unprecedented lyrics and popularity, subsequent commercial *narcocorridos* have used this "hit model," emulating what has become known "in popular Mexican imagination as the 'first *narcocorrido*.'"⁸¹ Hermann Herlinghaus explains that part of the success of this genre is the way "these transnational *corridos* draw on a living repertoire of affective dispositions to which they have given a fabulous vitality."⁸² The groundbreaking story line of "Contrabando y traición," giving life to uncharted characterizations in musical form, was crucial in securing the *narcocorrido*'s popularity and consumption along the US–Mexican border and beyond.

Perhaps it is this first-person knowledge and experience that influenced Salcedo's selection process for *Música de balas*. By the time Salcedo published this work, there were many options he could have chosen to include, and yet he only integrated references to, and instructions for, the music of Chalino Sánchez. When I asked Salcedo why he chose this particular artist, he initially said that he doesn't always analyze his motivations and decisions as minutely as scholars do. He then explained that perhaps it was because Sánchez "es un cantante que he escuchado y que además aquí tenemos muchos compañeros que son de Sinaloa . . . y es una música que se escucha en todas partes" (is a singer that I have heard so often, and more than that, here in Tijuana, we have a lot of people from Sinaloa . . . it's a music you hear everywhere).⁸³ Yet, integrating Sánchez's music into the piece creates an opportunity for a more critical exploration of the way the playwright creates a connection to the practices of *narco* culture. Through Sánchez's music, the piece creates an indirect exposure to the violent experiences lived by many outside the bounds of theater. I propose this because after Sánchez was gunned down in 1992 in Culiacán, he was transformed into a kind of patron saint of the *narcocorrido* genre, embodying the sound that many after him would try to emulate.⁸⁴ Not only adored for his raw, unrefined vocal qualities that captured the sound of Sinaloan people, Sánchez was also part of the *narco* lifestyle. César Jesús Burgos Dávila explains, "sus composiciones abordaban una realidad actual. Eran historias de valientes narcotraficantes e inmigrantes" (his songs described reality. They told stories about valiant drug dealers and immigrants).⁸⁵ Hence, the lyrics Sánchez composed recount vivid images of violence, images that have come to represent contemporary Mexican realities during Calderón's War on Drugs.

To accompany death 29,878, a scene in which a mourning *narco* member eulogizes his deceased friend and fellow *narco*, Salcedo includes fragments from two Chalino Sánchez songs in the text. The scene begins with lyrics from "El crimen de Culiacán": "les cantaré este corrido / a dos hombres que mataron / sin tenerles compasión / vilmente los torturaron / y ya muertos con un carro / por encima les pasaron" (I'll sing you all this *corrido* / about two men who were killed / without compassion / viciously tortured / and once dead / were run over by a car).[86] In all three stagings, these lyrics are sung live by the actor. In the case of the Eguiarte's and Hernández's performances, the actor sings along with the actual song, while in Rodríguez's production, the actor sings a cappella, without accompaniment or music. Regardless of the embodied approach, the lyrics are heard clearly throughout the theatre space. The words ring out, understood as a direct reference to violent *narco*-related killings. Furthermore, enunciating the city of Culiacán localizes the events within one of the most dangerous places in all Mexico: Sinaloa. Upon finishing his song, the mourning on-stage *narco* declares, "quien compone para vanagloriar a uno de nosotros, muy probablamente ofenda a otros; y es que con un corrido bien hecho, se exaltan las figuras, las cosas que suceden, los nombres o hasta a cada uno de los miembros que integran una de las familias trabajadoras" (whoever writes songs to glorify one of us probably offends another; but a well-written *corrido*, they can praise important figures, notable events, memorable names, or maybe even members of our working-class families).[87] The mourner is not singing just any *corrido* about landscapes and events, but rather a song deeply tied to gun violence and the drug trade. His friend, "a ese que le apodan El loco," (he who was called "The Crazy One") was killed by *una musiquita de balas*, subsequently putting an end to "sonsonete y todo su conciertito" (his song and concert).[88]

In closing the scene, the eulogizer returns to the music of Chalino Sánchez. To best commemorate his friend, the mourning *narco* promises to sing once more. He declares, "y yo las canto mal, herencia de familia" (I sing poorly, a quality I inherited from my family), though a "good" voice is not necessarily a prerequisite for *narcocorrido* success.[89] He continues, "por aquí les va esta copla, cantada mal, pero eso sí con mucho corazón. Dedicada a la memoria de mi compadre Sebastián Terrazas, que Dios lo tenga en su gloria" (here I am going to sing you this couplet, sun mal, but with a lot of heart. This is dedicated to the memory of my dear friend, Sebastián Terrazas, may God hold him in his glory).[90] At this point, Salcedo integrates lyrics from Sánchez's "Cuerno de chivo," sung by this mourning drug dealer. The song title itself invokes gunfire, as "cuerno de chivo" is slang for an AK-47, now transforming the composition into a promise of future armed combat. The lyrics Salcedo incorporates in the dramatic text further support this idea, asserting that the only certainty in this lifestyle is death, "la suerte cuando se cambia / se convierte en enemigo / un veintidós de noviembre / lo mató un cuerno de chivo / esa cabeza la debe / la gavilla de Chalino" (when luck

FIGURE 2.3. A cartel member cleans his gun while he mourns a friend. *Música de balas*, directed by Paola S. Hernández, University of Wisconsin—Madison, Madison, Wisconsin, 2015. Photo by Chris Konieczki.

changes / it becomes an enemy / one twenty-second of November / he was killed by an AK-47 / that head is due / the vengeance of Chalino).[91] This last part notably relates the desire for revenge, "a continuous motif in contemporary corrido narratives."[92] In enunciating these words, both in the text and on stage, the eulogizer uses Sánchez's lyrics to guarantee future rounds of *música de balas*, a never-ending encore performance of gun violence.

LECHEDEVIRGEN TRIMEGISTO AND *MÉXICO EXHUMADO*

The final piece I consider, *México exhumado*, like *Ejercicio de percusión* and *Música de balas*, enacts symbolic gestures of violence and bullet-ridden bodies. Felipe Osornio, also known by their pseudonym, Lechedevirgen Trimegisto (Lechedevirgen), is a nonbinary performance artist based out of Querétero, Mexico. Incorporating elements of, and references to, postpornography, queer art, dissident sexualities, popular culture, *brujería*, and science, their artist practice is multimodal and multisensorial. Although they are a young performer, born in 1991, Lechedevirgen has collaborated with Lukas Avendaño, whom I discuss in the next chapter, La Pocha Nostra,

Guillermo Gómez Peña, La Fura del Baus, Diana Pornoterrorista, and more. They have performed across Mexico, the Unites States, Canada, France, Italy, Spain, England, Scotland, and myriad digital platforms. Lechedevirgen has also won the prestigious grant for Jóvenes Creadores del Fondo Nacional para la Cultura y las Artes (FONCA) in 2019, and is a faculty member of gender studies at the Universidad Autónoma de Querétaro, where they teach graduate-level courses on performance theory.[93] Their name is inspired by alchemy traditions and the fact that they live with three kidneys, thanks to a transplant that saved their life after ten years of living with kidney failure.[94] This constant sense of their own proximity to death has prompted pieces that explore the ethics of organ harvesting and donation, illness, medical experimentation, and, as in the case of *México exhumado*, rampant violence.

México exhumado was performed during the 2019 Hemispheric Institute of Politics and Performance Encuentro (or Hemi Encuentro) in a blackbox theatre at the Centro Universitario de Teatro (CUT) for an audience of fewer than one hundred.[95] Though the initial reach of the performance may seem limited, its preservation via the Hemispheric Institute's video archive means Lechedevirgen has been able to share the piece across social media platforms, and viewers around the world have been able to partake in the intimate experience of the performance. Using a sketch-based approach, the entirety of *México exhumado* is just under thirty minutes long, organized into four segments linked by the connective thread of perpetual violence in Mexico tied to instances of political corruption and inaction.[96] The opening sequence enacts dark tourism, welcoming foreigners and Mexicans alike to explore the nation's sites of horror. This is followed by a sketch in which a *voice en off* (voiceover) employs a cruel sense of humor to recount some of Mexico's "most unbelievable products," such as a can of fumes with a hint of guayaba, a reference to drug use. The third sketch performs dismemberment and feminicide on the body of an artisanal Indigenous doll, like the kind tourists can purchase at any market. The final segment of the piece collapses individual and collective wounds, showcasing the nation's unhealed traumas across temporal and geographic spaces. *México exhumado*, throughout these four moments, consciously performs in both the visual and auditory realms. With the exception of the opening sequence, during which Lechedevirgen directly speaks to the audience from within the mimetic space, all of the remaining sonic elements are prerecorded. The *voice en off*, noises, and songs accompany and direct the haunting visuals that Lechedevirgen's body creates. While the visual stimuli are a crucial element of the entire performance, my intention is to address the sonic dimensions of the first and final sketches. Concretely, I listen to them as wounding necroauralities; by invoking the fissured, maimed, and marred connective tissues, the acoustic performance blurs the division between life and death.

AURAL TERRITORIES OF FEAR AND HORROR

The piece begins as Lechedevirgen welcomes the public to one of the world's most "surreal" countries. The artist stands center stage, on a slightly elevated black stage, wearing a tightly fitted *charro* suit adorned with streamers under each arm and pointed boots. At first glance, Lechedevirgen conjures the image of *charro* masculinity that, as detailed in my previous chapter, is nearly synonymous with being the "patriarchal protector of women, children, and patria."[97] According to Olga Nájera-Ramírez, the origins of the link between *charros* and masculinity leads back to the late nineteenth century. By the 1930s, the *charro* was depicted time and again on screen by actors like Pedro Infante or Jorge Negrete "not only as a hardworking, noble man of honor, but also as a handsome, romantic singer."[98] Moreover, the link between the *charro*, his costume, and traditions deeply entwined with rural life, family, and Catholicism served to promote "a more conservative view of society."[99] As Jacqueline Avila explains, this view of society was cemented by cinema's repeated projection of a "Mexico removed from its historical or temporal context, tightly bound to tradition and to the social and moral order dictated by religion."[100] The result was a masculinity rooted in overt virility and the tacit acceptance of a heteronormative gender binary as depicted via the *charro* and his polite *china poblana*.[101] Beyond the world of film, Christopher Conway suggests the *charro* is "arguably the most universally recognized emblem of Mexican identity around the world" due to its use in tourism advertisements transmitted globally.[102] It is logical, then, that the reference par excellence for Lechedevirgen's visual construct employs the *charro* as a welcoming figure for an attentive audience.

That the artist dons the *charro* suit is a transgressive act; the nonconforming, nonbinary, and dissident body invigorates the visual with a subversive twist, reinforced by auditory cues. While any color would have worked to create fissures in the heteronormative, patriarchal values associated with the *charro*, Lechedevirgen opted for each piece of clothing to be dyed the emblematic *rosa mexicano*. In contrast to the generally dark hues of the *charro traje*, this abundance of pink, on one hand, can be read as feminizing the *traje*, or imbuing it with queer sensibility. On the other hand, I propose that Lechedevirgen has a more sinister message in mind. In 1951, former president Miguel Alemán proposed a marketing campaign to encourage tourism and enlisted the help of designer, Ramon Valdiosera.[103] Traveling the world with creations lauded as representing Mexico, Valdiosera's pink hues from the cochineal insect were called "rosa mexicano" by the foreign press, and the name stuck.[104] *Rosa mexicano* became yet another government construct, one devised and implemented by men. In similar fashion, in 2012, Mexico City mayor Miguel Ángel Mancera decided to rebrand the capital city as CDMX and painted the town *rosa mexicano*.[105] Lechedevirgen's choice resonates with official efforts and rhetoric rooted in bringing tourism to Mexico, but it is also a performance of resistance: they upend the *charro* and *rosa mexicano* to offer foreigners a glimpse into the nation's dark secrets.[106]

From this central position on stage, with no other décor, props, or projection other than a music stand that holds their document, the artist begins to read aloud a text. Into the microphone, Lechedevirgen's voice is reminiscent of a tour guide persona. On the topic of musical performance, Simon Frith suggests that part of what makes the human voice so compelling to study is that it can occupy four distinct categories: "as *a musical instrument*; as *a body*; as *a person*; and as *a character.*"[107] In this opening sketch, the artist's cheery tone and clear, moderate pace is a conscious manipulation of their bodily materiality into a particular vocal character: the tour guide. This act is solidified and confirmed by the way Lechedevirgen constantly welcomes the audience to Mexico. Echoing many of the comments made by the onstage Chachita in *Nosotras las proles* (We, the plebs, 2013), discussed in the first chapter, this tour guide voice acidly offers up the Mexican landscape. The persona presents Mexico as a series of attractions for those interested in privatized water reserves, expropriated lands, and mass graves, all aspects of contemporary life that make the country one of the "rincones más insólitos del 'tercer mundo'" (most incredible corners of the Third World).[108] Zeroing in on references that call to the nation's necropolitical state, this vocal character directs the listeners: "admire nuestras fosas clandestinas y nuestros socavones de carretera, sea testigo de la más fina brutalidad policiaca y de la corrupción mejor coreografiada" (admire our clandestine mass graves and highway sinkholes, bear witness to some of the finest police brutality and the best choreographed corruption in the world).[109] They continue: "Sorpréndase con la rapidez de nuestros servicios: contamos con *secuestro express* hasta la puerta de su casa, en su plaza favorita o cuándo menos lo espere. Aquí los dedos y las orejas mochadas de sus seres queridos llegan por *Ubereats*" (Surprise yourself with the speed of our services: we have express kidnapping, brought right to your door, your favorite plaza, or even when you least expect it. Here, the severed fingers and ears of your loved ones easily arrive by way of Uber Eats)."⁰ In these observations, the upbeat and friendly intonation exacerbates the nation's wounds: mass graves, filled with bodies perhaps never to be correctly identified, police corruption and abuse, kidnapping on demand, and the dismemberment of victims. The invocation of bearing witness to scenes of public horror exposes the spectacularization of violence so commonplace throughout the country. In this case, however, hearing their description transforms the audience into ear-witnesses of atrocity. This brief journey of dark tourism ends with one final reiteration of welcome. Still dawning that sociable, bubbly vocal character, Lechedevirgen says: "Bienvenidos sean todos Uds. al país donde los food trucks se confunden con las morgues ambulantes, traileres repletes de los cuerpos sin nombre, sin rostro. El país de los desaparecidos y de las asesinadas" (Welcome to a country where food trucks are commonly confused with mobile morgues, semi-trailers filled to the brim with bodies lacking names and faces. This is the country of the disappeared and the assassinated).[111]

The juxtaposition of the voice's welcoming, affable tone and the words they produce creates a jarring sensation for the audience. Considering the depictions of violence enunciated by way of the speaker's warm welcome, their cheery tone generates a startling experience for the listener. As we, the audience, pay attention to the speaker, we hear the obvious sounds of our tour guide's hospitable, instructive tone. However, we also hear descriptions of Mexico's violent realities. The way in which Lechedevirgen conjoins a felicitous voice with terrifying imagery enacts a Brechtian sense of alienation.[112] For Brecht, this means a representation "which allows us to recognize its subject, but at the same time makes it seem unfamiliar."[113] The result of this technique is, ideally, a performance that shakes spectators out of passive consumption and into conscious contemplation. In the case of *México exhumado*, the disjuncture between the upbeat voice and the words it utters accomplishes Brecht's alienation and prompts listeners to consider what is at stake in really listening to what Lechedevirgen has to say about Mexico. Effectively, Lechedevirgen employs this sonic strategy to prompt their audience to contemplate national violences and necropolitical actions.

SONIC WOUNDS AND DEATHWORLDS

This introduction to Mexico's landscapes of horrific violence is reinforced in the final sketch as Lechedevirgen's voice enacts wounds that consume the entirety of their body. During these final minutes of the piece, the artist transforms their body into a geopolitical space reflective of the way violence

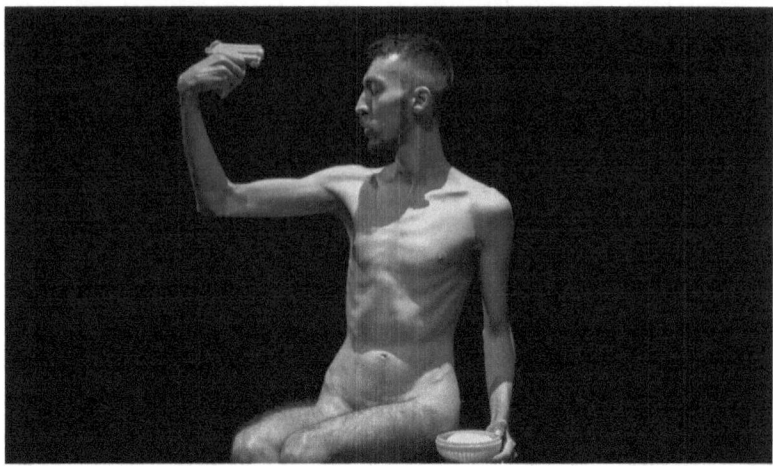

FIGURE 2.4. The artist prepares to shoot themselves in the head with a squirt gun. *México exhumado*, Centro Universitario de Teatro, Black Box Theatre, Mexico City, Mexico, 2019. Photo by Josué Barrera, provided courtesy of INBA/CITRU.

has become normalized throughout Mexico.[114] The examples Lechedevirgen has chosen express the repeated, and seemingly inescapable, necropolitical reality provoked by Mexico's state of exception. As the performer's recorded *voice en off* elaborates a specific act of violence, such as Luis Donaldo Colosio's assassination, on stage, they use a squirt gun filled with red liquid to mark the spot on their body. In this sense, Diéguez's assertion that "*necroteatro* o teatralidades de la muerte son escenificaciones que exponen las muertes violentas como acontecimientos de representación y producción de envíos de un *necropoder*" (necrotheater or theatricalities of death are dramatizations that expose violent deaths as representational events and dispatched productions of necropower) is strikingly apt for this performance.[115] Metonymically, Lechedevirgen's body becomes filled with the deaths that mark the nation's landscapes of past and present terror. At the same time, the performance is not only indelibly linked to bodies murdered and dismembered, but also the wounds that Lechedevirgen carries on and within them as a Mexican citizen living through Mexico's War on Drugs. As R. Guy Emerson notes, inspired by the work of Maurice Merleau-Ponty and the ontology of the flesh, "the wound is violent death rupturing the body to re/inscribe the individual in the death world, and is the unhealable sore that condemns her to an ongoing engagement with death."[116] In the case of this particular performance, Lechedevirgen's body becomes a visual marker, a physical stand-in, for the bodies wounded by immense violence.

Naked, sitting on only a black box in the center of the stage, Lechedevirgen is perfectly still. A voice rings out throughout the silence. The pitch, timbre, and speed of delivery is the same as in previous sketches, but the delivery lacks any emotive triggers. This voice, it seems, is more akin to someone reading off the news of the day as a list of events without differentiation between ghastly happenings and mundane occurrences. According to Dolar, "the voice without side-effects ceases to be a 'normal' voice, it is deprived of the human touch" that separates the human from the machine.[117] In this performance, the disembodied voice seems to lack empathy, suggesting a machine-like production. This aural approach further reinforces the Brechtian alienation of the first scene, once again provoking critical consideration about not just what we hear but how we hear it. For the artist, the flat affect was a deliberate decision, one meant to audibly express the nation's desensitization to, and normalization of, horrific events. I want to suggest another possibility. This voice, deprived of unique qualities and emotion, exists between Dolar's *viva voce* and *mortem voce*; it is a *vulnere voce*, a wounded voice capable of enacting its will to do harm.

The seven wounds that become embodied on stage represent for Lechedevirgen a complete cycle that cuts across temporal moments, geographies, and bodily location.[118] The voice reads the events in the following order:

>24 de marzo 1994, Tijuana Baja California, México
>Luis Donaldo Colosio, candidato a la Presidencia
>Dos disparos, uno en la cabeza.[119]
>
>10 de noviembre 2016, Jalisco, México
>6 personas con manos cortadas.[120]
>
>2 de abril 2006, Guerrero, México
>Decapitación de un policía en Acapulco.[121]
>
>15 de octubre 2012, Sonora, México
>Asesinato de un menor de 16 años en Nogales por disparos de una patrulla fronteriza.[122]
>
>25 de marzo 2018, Ciudad de México, México
>Joven de 21 años con heridas de armas de fuego en el abdomen y pecho.[123]
>
>4 de diciembre 1838, Veracruz, México
>Guerra de los pasteles, Santa Anna amputa la pierna y la entierra.[124]

> 3 de mayo 2019, Ciudad de México, México
> Estudiante del politécnico fue disparada en la pierna saliendo del metro La Raza.[125]
>
> *March 24, 1994, Tijuana, Baja California, Mexico*
> *Luis Donaldo Colosio, presidential candidate*
> *Shot twice, once in the head.*
>
> *November 10, 2016, Jalisco, Mexico*
> *Six people found with their hands severed.*
>
> *Abril 2, 2006, Guerrero, Mexico*
> *A policeman found decapitated in Acapulco.*
>
> *October 15, 2002, Sonora, Mexico*
> *A sixteen-year-old boy was shot and killed by a United States border patrol agent.*
>
> *March 25, 2018, Mexico City, Mexico*
> *A twenty-one-year-old found with chest and abdominal gun-shot wounds.*
>
> *December 4, 1838, Veracruz, Mexico*
> *Pastry War, Santa Anna amputates and buries his leg.*
>
> *May 3, 2019, Mexico City, Mexico*
> *A student at the National Polytechnical Institute was shot in the leg while leaving La Raza subway station.*

While I could elaborate these events as enactments of necropolitics, I want to zero in on the significance of their aurality. In particular, I propose the piece performs sound wounds; as the *voice en off* recounts traumatic memories of the past, it subsequently wounds the body of the present.[126] As the disembodied voice reads the wounds inflicted on past and present bodies, they become inscribed into and onto the flesh of Lechedevirgen. As spectators, we experience the reactivation of these traumas through their visual performance as well as their verbal articulation, so clear and audible. The lack of emotive response from Lechedevirgen's body or the *voice en off* creates an aural objectivity within these sonic memories of trauma and terror. The voice, a disembodied inflictor of pain, comes into contact with

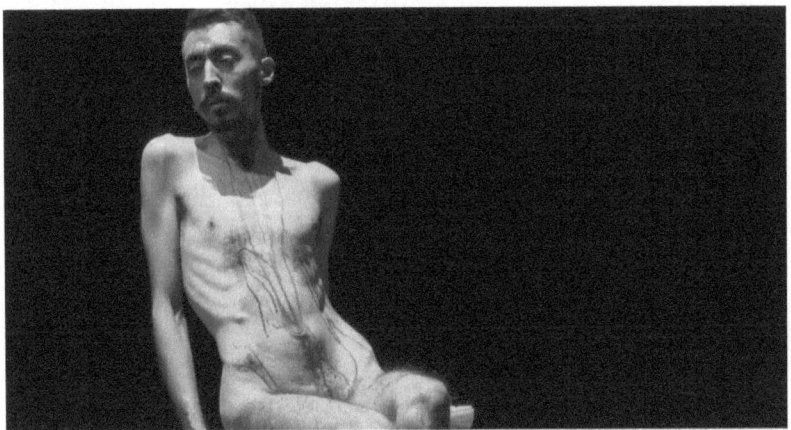

FIGURE 2.5. The artist's body is covered in red spots, representing bullet wounds. *México exhumado*, Centro Universitario de Teatro, Black Box Theatre, Mexico City, Mexico, 2019. Photo by Christina Baker.

the body, transformed into a tangible wound."[127] The invisible soundwaves of pain also travel through the space and bodies of audience members, filling and reverberating through them. While the experience is certainly not the same as marking our own bodies, as Lechedevirgen does, these audible frequencies of past and present violence invade our personal subjectivities. They inscribe within us vibrations of Mexico's long history of public displays of cruelty. These auditory renditions of post-2006 acts of subjective violence become relocated within spectators' bodies as reminders of the nation's state of exception.

As a continuation of the necropolitical performances of *Ejercicio de percusión* and *Música de balas*, Lechedevirgen's (re)enactment of wounds and wounding "does not intend to return the body to wholeness but instead offers an account of the productivity of its opening onto death."[128] That is to say, the artist transforms their body into a vessel that navigates and embodies death in such a way that it evades particular limits of time and space. From the first invocation of the wound, that of Colosio, their 2019 body taps into the wounds of a nation. Although a majority of the wounds are linked to post-2006 acts of atrocity, they enunciate foundational moments of violence to facilitate a sense of continuity across time and space. Conjuring examples from Baja California to Chiapas, Lechedevirgen's body also territorializes terror and abuse that Mexico's powerful political elites cannot, or do not, control. Their body becomes a specter of existence, a liminal signifier of the wound opening itself up to death, a haunting visual cue of the flesh marred and marked by Mexico's War on Drugs.

SHOCK DOCTRINE AND WEAPONIZED SOUND

From this ghastly remnant of a body, Lechedevirgen's wounded body then subjects itself, and the audience, to increasing levels of noise, inflicting a different kind of pain. To further enhance the sense of constant exposure to violence, the remainder of this final sketch weaponizes sound to jar spectators out of any sense of complacency or comfort. The idea of using sound as a kind of "shock doctrine" is not a reference to Naomi Klein, but rather, is precisely how Lechedevirgen describes the motivation behind their audio selection and its deployment.[129] After inflicting the final gunshot, still sitting center-stage, naked, covered in metonymical wounds, the artist then bathes themselves in a blood-like liquid. Their hands run the length of their body, spreading the substance into every nook and crevice until they are covered from head to toe. It is almost as if they are embodying the idea that "death written onto flesh is a different character."[130] For Emerson, "this is the wound, an opening onto death that suggests an impossible co-belonging of body and flesh" meaning that for the *México exhumado*, coexistence ends with the total consumption by death and loss of Lechedevirgen's living body.[131] Moreover, if the performer's body can be read as a geopolitical marker of Mexico's War on Drugs, it then also represents the necropolitical state that consumes the entirety of the nation. So as to emphasize the horrors of war, the artist's sonic intrusion of space ensures that that their public understands; while the audience may turn away or close their eyes to the unsettling sight, they cannot escape the aural barrage.

Rather than cue the sounds of militarized forces or firearms, Lechedevirgen's sonic weapon of choice is a series of jumbled, incomplete news recordings and industrial techno music. As if anticipating Johnson and Cloonan's assertion that "it needs to be emphasized yet again that music is sound, and as such, it is the conflicting decisions as to whether a sound is music or noise and that defines the lines of confrontation along which violence is incipient,"[132] Lechedevirgen consciously deploys music as a signal of violent perturbation. As they begin to paint their body red, the sounds of a radio channel abruptly cut through the sonic calm. Reminiscent of turning the dial on an AM/FM radio, the recorded sounds of static and muffled voices invade the quiet of the black-box theatre. The news clips themselves sound as if they are being transmitted from somewhere remote, and their distance impedes intelligibility. Amid the squeals and white noise, however, voices can be heard describing scenes of exsanguination, goats, and dead bodies. These interjections are from 1990s news broadcasts that provoked widespread panic and conspiracy theories about the famed "chupacabras."[133] These fragments of the past interrupt the present with dissonance and cacophony. Against the backdrop of an ever-increasing sound of metal squeaking, Lechedevirgen uses these jarring media reports as a "fuerza mediática para distraer a la gente" (media force used to distract the people), just as they distracted citizens from the nation's economic collapse under former president Carlos Salinas de Gortari.[134] While spectators stretch their ear to listen to the words, trying to make sense of them through the noise, it is easy to lose track of the other audible sensations, ominously reverberating and occupying the space.

The invisible yet uncomfortable sound waves transform into a sonic mix of guitar reverb, metallic scraping sounds, drumbeats, haunting metal creaks, and more. The visual spectacle of covering the body in red paint, at this point, is far less remarkable than the auditory performance of violence. In his considerations of weaponizing music, Goodman proposes concentrating on "the underlying vibrations, rhythms, and codes that animate this complex and invisible battlefield."[135] Similarly, scholars such as Jonathan Pieslak, J. Martin Daughtry, and Suzanne Cusik have written extensively on the role of music in war zones, used both to "pump up" soldiers heading into battle and as a means of torturing prisoners. As Pieslak explains, perhaps one of the most important contemporary cases of using sound to assail an enemy physically and psychologically was during Operation "Just Cause" in 1989 when US forces blasted heavy metal outside of the embassy in Panama.[136] The goal was to flush out Manuel Noriega. Because he allegedly held great disdain for this musical style, the US Marine Corps filled the sonic space so egregiously he would surrender. Similar techniques were used in Waco, Texas, against the Branch Davidians and have reportedly been used against prisoners in Guantánamo Bay, Afghanistan, and Iraq.[137] In the case of *México exhumado*, I suggest that Lechedevirgen transforms the embodied spectacle of a nation at war with itself into a sonic performance of pain. The distorted and amplified music is deployed as a mechanism for creating fear and used to generate an unsettling ambiance of sounds akin to torture.

The all-out assault on our ears, head, and body lasts less than seven minutes, though it feels like a lifetime. Lechedevirgen and their sound designer, Óscar Betancourt, use and distort the industrial techno music of DJ Black Asteroid. Otherwise known as Bryan Black, the musical powerhouse cut his teeth doing sound design for Prince and has done major remix work for Leonard Cohen and Martin Gore of Depeche Mode.[138] His solo debut album, *Thrust*, "was a statement of artistic intent that went beyond merely the dance floor" by discarding the "endless loops" generally associated with the techno sound and replacing them with a 4/4 structure akin to popular music, but edgy.[139] He did this by turning his ear toward the sounds of "analog, heavy synthesis, and four-to-the-floor kick drums" associated with raw techno.[140] Black Asteroid also integrated melody and vocals into his musical composition. In taking this approach, Black Asteroid highlights the songs' lyrical message while the low number of pre-fabricated layers allows him to achieve an "otherworldly" sound, ominous and tense.[141]

The song "Tangiers," which Lechedevirgen repurposed for *México exhumado*, is a prime example of Black Asteroid's self-described "alien" industrial techno sound. In the original version, French fashion icon and artist Michèle Lamy sings the vocals, switching between English and French.[142] Lamy, who has also performed on a handful of music tracks over the last several years, adds the perfect haunting vocal effect to the song's metallic, rock-driven sounds. I categorize the song on the fringes of rock music following Pieslak's observation that "the use of a distorted guitar timbre and/or power chords is frequently the sole determinant used by scholars to qualify the music as metal, or as exhibiting a metal influence."[143] Much like this description, the song's instrumental composition includes the sounds of reverb, creating a static quality akin to grating metal that distorts the guitar chords set against the backdrop of a thumping 4/4 drum rhythm. This duality, on one hand, envelops listeners in a danceable techno sound while, on the other, unnerving us with uncomfortable noise. Lamy's gravely timbre has a spectral quality that cements Black Asteroid's artistic ambition of "otherworldliness." Slowly enunciating and repeating the phrase "I know now" sounds like a menacing threat, while the remaining lyrics are sung in French and are barely understandable. For Dolar, the singing voice "blurs the word and makes it difficult to understand—in polyphony to the point of incomprehensibility—[and] has served as the basis for a philosophical distrust for this flourishing of the voice at the expense of the text."[144] In the case of Lamy's voice, I propose that the blurring is part of the performance of unintelligibility; the words matter far less than the discomforting sounds they create.

Manipulating the original sonic qualities of "Tangiers," Lechedevirgen achieves an even starker aural performance that becomes weaponized against their audience. The original song, only three minutes and thirty-five seconds, is made to last for about six minutes in *México exhumado*. This edit reveals music's temporal plasticity, its ability to be slowed down and stretched out. Lechedevirgen's reworking also produces an unhurried tempo that magnifies the sensations of reverberation and echo already present in the original recording. The high-pitched sounds of guitar distortion now sound more like a mix of sirens, loudly humming generators, and revved car engines, much like the sounds of war beyond moments of combat, as Daughtry describes

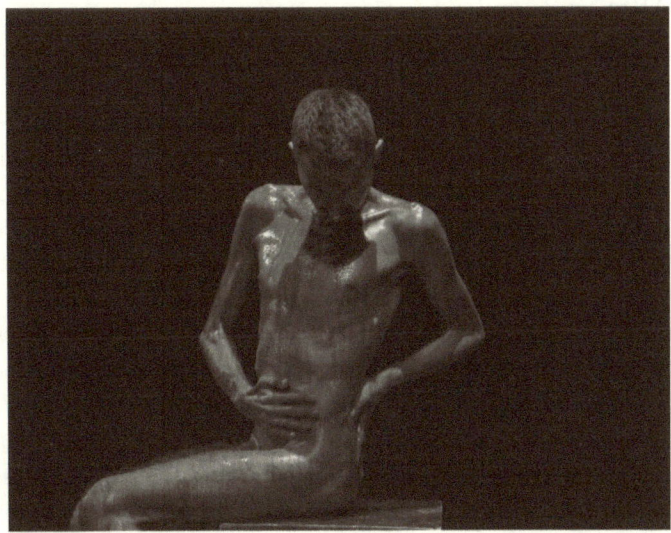

FIGURE 2.6. The artist's body is entirely coated in a red liquid, suggesting violence has consumed them. *México exhumado*, Centro Universitario de Teatro, Black Box Theatre, Mexico City, Mexico, 2019.. Photo by Josué Barrera, provided courtesy of INBA/CITRU.

them.[145] This mix of upsetting noises travels loudly through the space and in our ears. The sustained reverberation, for me, conjures images of frequency waves slicing through the theatre, as if making Elaine Scarry's observations of the torture room come alive. The black box theatre is "literally converted into another weapon, into an agent of pain. All aspects of the basic structure—walls, ceiling, windows, doors—undergo this conversion."[146] During these final minutes of the performance, the sounds bounce off walls, ceilings, chairs, and more, invading the space and the spectators' bodies from all directions. The distorted techno vibrations, accompanied by a strong drumming rhythm, become reminiscent of militarized marching sounds, such as those analyzed in *Ejercicio de percusión*. In addition, having slowed down the original song elongates Lamy's vocals, and the words, "I know now," in their deep, gravelly glory, creep through the theatre. The invisible frequencies of the song now sound even more haunting than previously thought possible. Hence, much like the way sounds are weaponized in wartime scenarios, the performance's noises unsettle any sense of security. The seemingly endless onslaught of vibrations continuously rings out, their constant crescendo provoking sensorial confusion and distortion, perhaps even wounding the audience.

CONCLUSION

In what I have referred to as necroauralities, the three pieces in this chapter sonically chart the initiation, expansion, and effects of Mexico's War on Drugs. From the sounds of increased militarization, as embodied in Ježik's military exercise, to the representation of constant gunfire in *Música de balas*, to the articulations of the wounded body in Lechedevirgen's solo show, these performances are not reparative. They do not seek to heal the bodily and psychic injuries provoked by conflict; they expose them. The artists I analyze in this chapter lay bare through their bodies and sonic reverberations the damaging impact war has had on the nation and their individual subjectivities. Additionally, the broad-ranging historical reference points, exemplified by the occupation of a seventeenth-century convent, the invocation of Santa Anna's nineteenth-century tyranny, and Carlos Salinas de Gortari's vampiric embezzlement in the 1990s, point to a much longer history beyond Calderón's 2006 declaration of war. This long view of history, embedded within performative and sonic discourses of the present, showcase the wounding tendencies that persist from Mexico's past to its present. By offering no sense of healing or catharsis, these performances insist on the ubiquitous nature of violence, one that is likely to accompany the nation into the future.

CHAPTER 3

Antigone's Requiem

Sounds against Death
and Disappearance

Avignon (France), Zurich (Switzerland), The Hague (Netherlands), Guatemala City (Guatemala), and Tabasco (Mexico). These are just some of the cities that have been tagged in photos shared by Lukas Avendaño following his brother's forced disappearance. Traveling around the globe, the performance artist poses with a picture of his brother accompanied by the question, "¿Dónde está Bruno?" (Where is Bruno?). Circulating on social media outlets since 2018, these photos archive his arduous search for justice and are also how I, and many others, have become aware of the artist's horrific loss. Avendaño's posts have also sparked a kind of unofficial international campaign for justice, as countless accomplices have taken a similar photo with Bruno's image asking the same question: Where is he? Taken in airports, in front of governmental and cultural buildings, on busy streets, and in public plazas, these images represent a virtual network of those who support Avendaño in his herculean quest to find his brother. What is striking about these photos, though, is their silence. In contrast to videos shared by news venues or across platforms of Mexican families and friends loudly protesting the missing status of their loved ones, Avendaño's interventions, and those done in solidarity with him, take place in a state of muteness. The broader implication is that the question "Where is Bruno?" has no response. While there is obviously no way to hear what happened before, during, or after the photos, the decision to deny viewers access to sounds that reveal pain and suffering, such as tears, gasps, or even screams, is a conscious one. Avendaño eliminates sonic stimuli associated with the living human voice to underscore the terrible silence that haunts him, a constant reminder of his brother's absence.

In *Why Hasn't Everything Already Disappeared?*, Jean Baudrillard declares, "let us speak, then, of a world from which human beings have disappeared."[1] While he writes of humanity's relationship to technology, I cannot help but think that he writes of twenty-first-century Mexico, or even specifically about Bruno Avendaño's case. Baudrillard's chilling assertion injects itself into my thoughts every time I sit down to write this chapter on Mexico's disappeared and missing persons. Searching for, and pouring over, statistics of the total number of missing and disappeared persons since December 1, 2006, I wonder where so many citizens have gone. Yet, as Rossana Reguillo proclaims, counting the dead, or in this case the missing and disappeared, is a useless gesture "because we are unable to restore the humanity lost and unable to mend the rupture that the machine leaves in its wake."[2] Mexico is filled with ghosts. 95,360 ghosts at the time I write this, of whom 76.48 percent are male, 23.04 percent female, and .48 percent are indeterminate, according to the Comisión Nacional de Búsqueda (CNB; National Search Commission).[3] This number is the most recent figure that represents "official" counts of missing and disappeared citizens since the beginning of Felipe Calderón's War on Drugs. To suggest that this figure is entirely the result of Calderón's presidency would be false. Enrique Peña Nieto inherited a startling number of disappeared and missing persons when he took office in 2012, but the count steadily increased during his presidency.[4] In fact, the exact number of disappeared and missing is unknown, in large part due to faulty reporting practices at local, regional, and national levels. This is compounded by the reality that databases meant to track the information are plagued by inconsistencies. The Registro Nacional de Personas Desaparecidas y No Localizadas (RNPED; National Registry for Disappeared and Missing Persons), created in 2012, was last updated in April 2018, and at that time it reported 37,435 persons.[5] The CNB was created as a result of Mexico's 2018 Ley General en Materia de Desaparición Forzada de Personas, Desaparición Cometida por Particulares y del Sistema Nacional de Búsqueda de Personas (Ley General; General Law on Forced Disappearances of Persons, Disappearances Committed by Individuals, and the National Search Registry). The law was first introduced to Mexico's Congress in 2015, and after years of debate and revision was passed in November 2017 and enacted in January 2018.[6] I want to underscore that the CNB only began offering updated information in the spring of 2021, so for three years Mexico went without publicly available information regarding lost loved ones.

Over the last several years, national and international entities have made numerous inquiries regarding the state of disappeared and missing persons in Mexico. The nation's own Comisión Nacional de los Derechos Humanos (CNDH; National Human Rights Commission) issued a report in 2018 declaring:

> México presenta un grave problema de desaparición de personas a causa, principalmente, de la conjunción de corrupción, impunidad, violencia, inseguridad y colusión de personas servidoras públicas con la delincuencia organizada, que se agudiza con las condiciones de desigualdad y pobreza extrema que impiden el desarrollo social en el país.[7]

> *Mexico presents a grave problem in relation to the disappearance of persons, caused, principally, by the combination of corruption, impunity, violence, insecurity, and collusion of public servants with those involved in organized crime, which exacerbates the conditions of inequality and extreme poverty that impedes social development in the country.*

This same observation was made in various reports published by the Inter-American Commission on Human Rights (IACHR). Their 2015 report, based on a visit in situ in the fall of 2015 found that "more than 98% of crimes committed in Mexico remain in impunity" despite the fact that Mexico has ratified many international human rights treaties.[8] In the 2019 follow-up account, the IACHR repeatedly noted that Mexico had let lapse the timeline for completing many of the original recommendations, particularly the creation of national registries for tracking missing and disappeared persons.[9] Reports issued by the US State Department echo the lack of official infrastructure promised by the Ley General, noting in 2018 that individual states were expected to set up search commissions, but that only seven of thirty-two had done so.[10] By 2019, that number rose to twenty-five of thirty-two, but "the government often merged statistics" on reports of disappeared and missing persons, preventing accurate reports.[11]

In addition to the multitude of official barriers, inefficiencies, and impunity, clandestine mass graves of disappeared bodies also haunt the nation. Mexico's CNB was supposed to also create a national registry of graves, and the 2019 IACHR report claimed "that since 2006, 3,024 clandestine graves have been found, from which 4,974 bodies have been exhumed."[12] The US State Department suggests looking at the state of Veracruz as an indicator of national levels, stating that since 2010, 601 clandestine graves have been discovered "with the remains of 1,178 victims."[13] Even a cursory Google search for mass graves in Mexico yields a terrifying number, both recent and dating back several years. On January 29, 2021, the deputy secretary of human rights, Alejandro Encinas, reported that 559 clandestine mass graves had been found in 2020, unearthing 1,086 bodies.[14] In mentioning these numbers, my goal is to offer a panorama of the loss Mexican citizens have experienced over the last several decades. What should be an unfathomable tragedy continues to plague families across the nation. Without sufficient support from government officials at the federal, state, or local level, family members and nonprofit organizations throughout Mexico have taken it upon themselves to look for their dead.

These startling and constantly growing numbers related to missing and disappeared persons and mass graves are a direct consequence of the purported War on Drugs. Unlike Calderón, whose language I explored in the previous chapter, Peña Nieto's rhetoric referred less often to fighting *narcos* as justification for the war, but he remained steadfast in claiming the necessity of war.[15] Much like Judith Butler contends in *Frames of War*, certain populations became designated as "lose-able," transformed into bodies that could be "forfeited, precisely because they are framed as being already lost or forfeited."[16] Under Peña Nieto, Mexican citizens continued to be framed as collateral damage, already imagined as a needed sacrifice. In doing so, they became "not grievable, since, in the twisted logic that rationalizes their death, the loss of such populations is deemed necessary to protect the lives of the living."[17] In general, linguistic strategies such as these dehumanize living bodies to the point that the state is complicit in preventing families from being able to mourn their loved ones. Though Butler situates her argument within the United States after 9/11 and the War on Terror, her question of what lives count as "mournable" is crucial to the Mexican case.[18] On one hand, Butler argues that all lives are precarious because we are constantly exposing ourselves to risk merely by existing. On the other hand, she defines precarity as the "politically induced condition of maximized precariousness for populations exposed to arbitrary state violence," such as Mexico's War on Drugs.[19] As I detailed in the previous chapter, the transition into a state of necropolitics gave official institutions the right to decide who lives and dies and, by extension, who counts as grievable. Moreover, as the number of mass graves and missing citizens continues to rise, the Mexican state has perpetuated a discourse that does more than merely make them ineligible for mourning; it derealizes them. Melissa Wright contends that authorities make it seem that to be missing—to lack a body—is akin to have never existed at all. And those who have never existed cannot be grieved.[20]

No conversation about Mexico's missing and disappeared persons or about clandestine mass graves would be complete without acknowledging the events of September 26, 2014, in Ayotzinapa, Guerrero. A group of *normalista* students commandeered local buses in anticipation of attending an event in Mexico City, an event to commemorate the massacre of college-aged students on October 2, 1968. However, the students never made it to Mexico City. To this day, only three of the forty-three students have been identified, based on bone fragments, and declared dead. The location and state of their remains continues to be unknown, and the other forty continue to exist in a state of perpetual limbo. Not found, but not present. Yet, due to national and international pressure, the Mexican state has been unable to derealize these students, though it has certainly tried. The horrific scene of that September evening has been replayed in media reports, reenactments trying to make sense of the discrepancies between official reports and the testimonies and recordings from victims. Moreover, the official findings of the Mexican government have been repeatedly challenged by local and international experts. Although former president Peña Nieto, along with many local officials, initially attempted to claim the students had fallen prey to crimes associated with *narco* cartels, eyewitnesses and external investigators have linked the disappearances to federal and state officials, such as the Iguala mayor, José Luis Abarca Velázquez, and his wife, María de los Ángeles Pineda Villa.[21]

The forced disappearance of the *normalista* students is a complex topic, and it is not my intention to delve into more detail. I am compelled to mention the case because it was a turning point for Mexico. The "critical rates of impunity" and "violations of fundamental human rights" irrevocably changed the landscape of protest and human rights advocacy.[22] According to Andreas Schedler, 89.4 percent of people interviewed in 2013 had not taken part in collective protests. However, that changed after Ayotzinapa.[23] Waves of protests across the nation were echoed and supported by individuals and organizations on a global scale. Hashtags such as #Vivosselosllevaronlosqueremos, #Ayotzinapa, #Ayotzinapasomostodos, #nosfaltan generated a massive outpouring of digital support and served to apply pressure to find answers.[24] Importantly, the protests visibly demarcated the labor of mourning; that the forty-three students were all male signals the gendered division of disappearances on a mass scale. The most recent statistics from the CNB reveal that 76 percent of the missing are men and 23 percent are women. In constructing narratives of disappearance, the missing men, including the *normalistas*, have been framed as the nation's lost future.[25] Those who publicly lead the quest for answers in the Ayotzinapa case have also been predominantly men—the students' fathers. These figureheads symbolically stand in as the protectors of the future, a role that Mexico's state has failed to assume. Melissa Wright observes, "the gendered contrast of fathers representing the family and of mothers looking for children reflects the politics of sexual difference within patriarchal organizations of the family."[26] Noticeably, Mexico's innumerable young, missing, disappeared, and murdered women are seldom discussed as embodying the future. In the media and social media discourses, they are framed as "deserving" whatever fate they met because they left the house, went to a party, or wore the "wrong" clothing. These murdered and missing women are demonized, not humanized. Consequently, the female figures who mourn them, those who clamor for justice, do not become rhetorically or symbolically conceived of as protectors, like the Ayotzinapa fathers, but are instead framed as intruders in the public sphere, as bodies that belong in the private space of the home and family. It is as if the lost women and the work their mothers, female friends, and sisters do to return them to the land of the realized is devalued, silenced, invisibilized.

This gendered dimension of mourning and access to public acknowledgment leads me to consider the potency of female and feminine bodies performing acts of mourning in Violeta Luna's *Réquiem #3: Fosas Cuerpo / Body Graves* (2017) and Lukas Avendaño's *Buscando a Bruno* (Searching for Bruno, 2018). The public presence of grieving women is a powerful social, cultural, and historical image that extends far beyond Mexico's borders. The ability to publicly grieve, as Butler observes, "is a political issue of enormous significance . . . since at least the time of Antigone," as her female body defied the king's decree and openly mourned her brother.[27] Over twenty-five hundred years later, Ileana Diéguez contends that Antigone continues to visit us, and throughout Latin America, she is not just a sister but also a mother, daughter, or grandmother.[28] The Greek figure can also be embodied by those who stand in solidarity with the women searching for their missing and disappeared family members. For example, Las Madres de la Plaza de Mayo occupied Antigone's role as they publicly and visibly searched for their disappeared children and loved ones despite official threats and denial. Their brave actions have led to a hemisphere of contemporary Antigones unafraid to bring their grief into the public sphere. By way of their collective search for justice, these women became connected through their profound pain and loss as a *communitas de dolor*, as Diéguez conceives of them.[29] Myriad Latin American Antigones have also taken shape within literary, theater, and performance works such as Griselda Gambaro's *Antígona furiosa* (Furious Antigone, 1986), Luis Rafael Sánchez's *La pasión según*

Antígona Pérez (The Passion According to Antigone Pérez, 1968), *Antígona* (Antigone, 2000) by Yuyachkani, Colombia's *Antígona* (Antigone, 2006) by La Candelaria, and Mexico's recent *Antígona González* (Antigone González, 2012) by Sara Uribe.[30] Undoubtedly, there are numerous other representations not mentioned here, but this list points to the potency of invoking the Greek tragedy to make sense of present political traumas. The continued popularity of Antigone, especially in the twenty-first century, acknowledges how the original "poses questions about kinship and the state" in a way that transcends cultural and historical specificity.[31]

While the word "Antigone" is never used in either piece I consider in this chapter, the symbolic power of a sister seeking to bury her dead brother, despite political ramifications, resonates deeply. Employing Antigone as a conceptual model allows me to explore performances of grief as public, political acts in Lukas Avendaño's *Buscando a Bruno* and Violeta Luna's *Réquiém #3: Fosas Cuerpo / Body Graves*. Each of these pieces enacts modified funeral rituals that serve as reparative acts in the face of terrible loss and pain. In Avendaño's performance, he grieves the loss of his brother Bruno Avendaño, forcibly disappeared May 10, 2018, only to be found in a clandestine grave in November 2020. In Luna's work, she mourns the nation's collective and continual loss of its young. Her piece is an intimate reflection of memories shared, such as those of Araceli Rodríguez Nava, a mother who tirelessly searches for her disappeared son. Considering that these works embody individual and collective loss, yet without actual corpses, I ask myself: What does it mean to perform remains? Whose remains? Who remains?[32]

Despite obvious differences between the performances and the Greek tragedy, the figure of Antigone is a useful mechanism for appreciating the possibilities for performative acts of redress that emerge from a site of liminality. Antigone challenges the state's decree, directly confronting a policy that creates fissures in the political and private realms. In her decision to defy Creon, she enters into a state of exclusion. And yet, in her exclusion, and ultimate death, she fashions what Julia Kristeva refers to as an "imaginary world in which life is possible at the limit."[33] This observation can simultaneously be applied to the world of theater, where the performance space becomes a site of limitless imagination. For instance, Lukas Avendaño and Violeta Luna imagine reparative acts of mourning otherwise not afforded by the state to the families of Mexico's missing and disappeared. From their liminal spaces, *Buscando a Bruno* and *Réquiém #3: Fosas Cuerpo / Body Graves* enact mourning rituals that stand in for formal funerary processions and practices. To consider these performances as rituals is to follow Victor Turner's observation: "I like to think of ritual essentially as *performance, enactment,* not primarily as rules or rubrics. The rules 'frame' the ritual process, but the ritual process transcends its frame."[34] Notably, these works create frames to include those deemed unworthy of recognition by the state. In *How Societies Remember*, Paul Connerton proposes that rituals, such as funeral rites, are meaningful because they have significance for the whole community.[35] Thinking of the performances in this way permits them to "reconfirm social ties and remind the bereaved that they are not alone even though they are in mourning."[36] Luna, Avendaño, and those who participate in the performatically enabled *communitas de dolor* are transformed into bodies "willing and able to face life anew, even if it means, or especially when it means, radically revising and altering the world we share."[37] This collective group of mourners turns to the funeral ritual to imagine an alternative act of redress rather than to continue to appeal to those in power.

The collective nature of Avendaño and Luna's performed funeral rituals act "against death," defying the way death forecloses and annihilates the identity of the deceased. This concept, developed by Tara Bailey and Tony Walter, responds to Douglas Davies's comprehensive study of death rituals.[38] Davies posits "words against death" to describe how language in funeral proceedings allows mourners to resist the definite perception of death and cope with the loss.[39] Antigone's words defying Creon worked against the death of her brother as much as they became "the instrument of political power."[40] Through words and actions, she introduced a new model of the political, "a model based on speech and action rather than tyrannical rule."[41] In the case of Avendaño and Luna, their entry into the political sphere and their attempts to create intelligibility for the disappeared and missing victims are not rooted in speech. On the contrary, their nonverbal acts become instruments of power and mourning, instruments capable of suturing the emotional wounds triggered by the missing corpses.

Réquiem #3: Fosas Cuerpo / Body Graves and *Buscando a Bruno* conjure the spectral body, configuring it through the immateriality of a corpse. It is as if Avendaño and Luna respond directly to Diéguez's question of how to represent the haunting presence of the disappeared. Though Diéguez emphasizes visual aesthetics "fundada[s] en las ausencias y en las siniestras políticas de desapariciones forzadas" (founded in the absences and in the sinister politics behind forced disappearances), Luna and Avendaño's political defiance and laments of loss are channeled through their silences and nonverbal soundtracks.[42] I propose that Luna and Avendaño's sonic decisions mimic the weight of missing bodies themselves. I do not consider the nonverbal choice as reflecting the inability of words to convey pain after atrocity, a kind of unspeakability.[43] Rather, it is a creative choice that purposely reflects the missing's inability to breathe and hence be breathed into words, into a body, and into life.[44] Even without words, Luna and Avendaño, like Antigone, persist in their desire to mourn, in direct defiance of the Mexican state. As contemporary invocations of the Greek figure, Luna and Avendaño's performances enact funeral rites for the disappeared to confront political derealization via what I call "sounds against death." These pieces utilize music, silences, and sounds to forge collectively engaged listening practices that recognize the humanity of the missing and resist their total annihilation caused by death and the state's denial of any existence at all.

VIOLETA LUNA AND *RÉQUIEM #3: FOSAS CUERPO / BODY GRAVES*

Violeta Luna is an internationally recognized performer, known for her politically engaged and deeply moving pieces. Taking a broad view of her work, she explores the relationship between theater, performance art, and community engagement. Over the last several decades, Luna has solidified a style that layers objects, sounds, and images, yielding a performatic architecture where each element of the performance exists autonomously and simultaneously as part of the whole.[45] The artist has also developed a theoretical approach to creation, rooted in works like Rita Laura Segato's *La guerra contra las mujeres* (The War against Women, 2016) and other approaches to human rights abuses. Luna often uses her own body as a territory to interrogate and comment on social and political phenomena, working within what she conceives of as a "multidimensional space that allows for the crossing of aesthetic and conceptual borders."[46] In what she refers to as a cor-po/etics, Luna articulates a tripart consideration of the body, the body as poetic expression, and the body as ethical actor.[47] While she currently lives and works in San Francisco, her pieces are intimately related to her home country of Mexico and the immigrant experience. Paola Marín notes that, "in essence, this artist's work arises from a careful consideration of context, conscientious research, and solidarity across borders with human tragedies that directly appeal to her."[48] Born in Mexico City, Luna earned a degree in acting from the Centro Universitario de Teatro (CUT) at the Universidad Nacional Autónoma de México (UNAM) and has performed and taught workshops throughout Latin America, the United States, Egypt, India, New Zealand, and more. Although Luna primarily works as a solo performer, she is also an associate artist of the performance collectives La Pocha Nostra and Secos & Mojados. She is also a Creative Capital and National Association of Latino Arts and Cultures (NALAC) Fellow, and a member of the Magdalena Project: International Network of Women in Contemporary Theatre. Some of her works include *Body Parted / Cuerpo partido* (2008), *Two Madonnas* (2014), *Vírgenes y diosas / Virgens and Goddesses* (2015), *For Those Women Who Are No Longer Here* (2016), and the *Réquiem / Requiem* series (2011–2017).

Before briefly detailing each piece in the *Réquiem / Requiem* sequence, I want to pause on the series title. As a Latin term used in the mass for the dead, "requiem" translates as "rest." Alexander Stein explains that the music of the commemorative mass "reached a prolonged apogee" from the Renaissance to the present, evolving into "ceremonies performed at rites for the dead."[49] Luna's choice to use "requiem" in the title of her work is a succinct and eloquent indicator of the way these pieces enact efforts to put bodies to rest accompanied by specific sonic cues. With *Réquiem para una tierra Perdida / Requiem for a lost land* (2011), *Réquiem II: Ni una muerta más* (2011), and *Réquiem #3: Fosas Cuerpo / Body Graves* (2017), Luna situates her work within the world of *narco* violence and necropolitics in Mexico following Felipe Calderón's presidency in 2006. Even those unacquainted with Mexico's escalating violent realities can perceive the titles' macabre tone.

To contextualize *Réquiem #3: Fosas Cuerpo / Body Graves*, I offer here an overview of the entire *Réquiem/Requiem* series. The first piece, *Réquiem para una tierra Perdida / Requiem for a lost land* (2011) was performed most notably as part of the Hemi Encuentro held in São Paolo, Brazil, in 2013.[50] Dressed in white, Luna transforms her body into a ghastly image of bloodshed that stands in for Calderón's many casualties of war. The piece culminates in an unforgettable image: Luna's head is overturned, allowing her long, jet-black hair to spread out across the white tile. Placing photographs of Mexico's many dead in her hair, the strands evoke a kind of Medusa. She then douses herself in red paint, transforming into a gory image of a headless body, one commonly seen on Mexico's streets, on television, and in newspapers. A river of metaphorical blood flows over Luna's limbs, cementing a symbolic image of shared pain and gruesome loss. The second work in the series is more aptly considered an intervention that took place in public spaces like San Francisco's streets or Oaxaca City's market. In particular, *Réquiem II: Ni una muerta más* calls attention to feminicide as both a Mexican problem and a global phenomenon. After drawing the outlines of bodies on city sidewalks, Luna's collaborators then embodied the phantoms of female victims by physically occupying the spaces of the departed. Sometimes surrounded by flowers, as if to commemorate them, or even marking themselves with red paint to replicate wounds, the women's aliveness reshaped the scenes of emptiness into tragedy.[51] Finally, *Réquiem #3:*

Fosas Cuerpo / Body Graves was born of Luna's personal experience watching from afar as her country devoured its youth. Watching the news and hearing from friends, family, and acquaintances, she was moved to create this final piece of the trilogy. The totality of her vision came into form after hearing from women searching for their loved ones, "huérfanas de un estado que no protege" (orphans of a state that does not protect).[52] Just as these women seek to repair familial bonds and memory with their searches, Luna's piece invokes their resiliency on stage.

During the Hemi Encuentro in 2019, held in Mexico City, Luna debuted the version of *Réquiem #3: Fosas Cuerpo / Body Graves* that I analyze in this chapter.[53] Development of the piece began in 2016 as she investigated the issue of disappearances in Mexico and documented the formation of community collectives seeking justice. Luna then initiated contact with mothers and activists, speaking on a deeply personal level about their experiences. She was especially moved by Araceli Rodríguez Nava's stories of pain and frustration as she attempts to locate her son, Luis Ángel León Rodríguez, disappeared in November 2009. From these stories, Luna presented an early form of the piece as part of San Francisco's 2017 Fresh Festival. Later that year, she exhibited a more developed version of the piece as part of the Festival of Latin American Contemporary Choreographers (FLAC), also based in San Francisco.[54] It was through these presentations that she settled on embodying the mother who endlessly searches for her missing child. In her creation, it is worth noting that she makes the missing figure a female, to emphasize the gendered element of violence that I consider in Chapter 4. The most recent iteration of *Réquiem #3: Fosas Cuerpo / Body Graves* was performed twice at the 2019 Encuentro in a black box theatre (the same space where Lechedevirgen Trimegisto performed *México exhumado* [Mexico Exhumed, 2019]) for intimate audiences of approximately fifty people each time. Following the Encuentro, Antonio Prieto Stambaugh invited Luna to show the piece for theater arts master's students at La Universidad Veracruzana–Xalapa. Due to COVID-19, Luna has not been able to perform the work since the summer of 2019, as she has chosen not to adapt it for Zoom or other digital platforms. Recordings of both Encuentro performances do exist, archived on the Hemispheric Institute of Politics and Performance website.

Even though I have referred to the *Réquiem* series as pieces or performances, for Luna, the embodied act of commemoration and remembrance is akin to a creating a living altar. Unlike those one might find in a family home or at a gravesite, her altars represent collective brutality rather than individual people. In *Réquiem #3: Fosas Cuerpo / Body Graves*, the visual and spatial elements become an altar rooted in absence, the absence of a body. Even her own appearance invokes invisibility. Dressed from head to toe in black, her figure blends in with the black walls and floor of the theatre space. Though her movements remind us of her body's aliveness, "it must be underscored that the focus of *Requiem* is not the performer's body, but her actions."[55] In effect, Luna's body functions as a vehicle for expressing loss and pain associated with those who are no longer here.

In this void, metaphorical within the theatre space but very real to those with disappeared loved ones, Luna utilizes objects to create polysemic images that symbolize Mexico's generation of lost and disappeared. The work's five chapters recall disappearance, the search for a body, the unearthing of remains, the identification of bones, and memorializing the dead. The first chapter is established by way of an empty chair, placed in the far back left corner of the black box theatre. The search for the body happens center-stage, as Luna unwraps an enormous *bulto*, a blanket resembling the shape of a boulder, sutured together by packing tape. This image is an unsettling reminder of the way Mexico's dismembered, discarded, and disfigured dead are wrapped up, *encobijado*, and tossed away to rot. But what Luna unveils is not a body, but rather the tools used by families to search for their missing and disappeared, such as shovels and metal rods. The third chapter takes place in the back right corner of the stage where Luna pours a mound of dirt onto a table. By the spoonful, the dirt is moved across the stage, sometimes by Luna, sometimes by an audience member, to rest on the seat of the empty chair. The fourth chapter is what Luna calls "the dance of the bones." Luna enacts Quetzalcoatl's descent into Mictlán in order to create the human form from bones guarded by the Indigenous Goddess of the Dead, Mictecacíhuatl, the mother of all beings, dead or alive.[56] Combining the searching Quetzalcoatl with the protective figure of Mictecacíhuatl and Mexico's contemporary mothers, Luna symbolically recovers her dead and adorns her body with their bones. She then dances around each of the objects on stage (the chair, the blanket and tools, the mound of dirt). The piece ends by returning to the empty chair, a symbol of memory, above which now hangs a dirty white dress, a symbol of Mexico's disappeared women and girls. As the garment spins freely in the void, it is accompanied by David Molina's soundtrack and projected poetic texts written by Roberto Varea.

More than a sequence of performatic chapters, the performance fosters a ritual space in which Luna seeks to bridge the distance between performer/audience. During the brief span of twenty-five to thirty minutes, Luna attempts to morph her body and those of her public into one collective being. To accomplish this, Luna assumes the role of the shaman or facilitator, inviting the public to feel included in the action "para ir deluyendo la división entre espacios" (to erase the division between spaces).⁵⁷ This conceptual approach results in the embodiment of Victor Turner's definition of ritual as "a synchronization of many performative genres, and is often ordered by *dramatic* structure."⁵⁸ The piece, organized around the process of moving from loss to commemoration, becomes a ritual of redress, rooted in Luna's belief that ritual practices bring communities together. This echoes Turner's notion of *communitas*, a temporarily formed group "which may be said to exist more in contrast than in active opposition to social structure, as an alternative."⁵⁹ In this case, *Réquiem #3: Fosas Cuerpo / Body Graves* serves to remember those the state has neglected to protect, those the State itself has forcibly disappeared and derealized.⁶⁰ By way of performative gesture, Luna transforms the space and those who occupy it into a temporary *communitas de dolor*, sharing in the act of mourning and pain. In what follows, I explore the way in which Luna's body is a surrogate for contemporary Antigones, but one whose acts of resistance and defiance are expressed via nonverbal sonic acts. In particular, I draw attention to how the piece's music and silences attempt reparative redress through funeral ritual, becoming sounds against death.

ANTIGONE'S CRIES, LUNA'S SILENCE: RITUAL MOURNING

Luna's insistence on a shared moral and performative duty to mourn Mexico's missing and disappeared reflects a deeper understanding and appreciation for ritual as a means of catharsis, or perhaps closure. Without a body, *Réquiem #3: Fosas Cuerpo / Body Graves* relates the immense grief individuals and communities experience in spite of official mechanisms that deny their loss. While Butler explains that "grief attends the life that has already been lived, and presupposes that life as having ended," for Mexico's missing and disappeared, there is no body to assure that a life has ended.⁶¹ And yet, the grief remains very real, especially as the state does not recognize subjects as either alive or dead. In this case, it is not simply that the loss goes unacknowledged by the state, but that families are restricted in their grief, ultimately "denied the power to confer legitimacy on loss."⁶² For Luna, performance pieces become "stubbornly resistant" to the state's efforts of denying life or death.⁶³ The artist's creative endeavors enact memories and experiences that defy the logic of erasure by conferring recognition, and in the case of *Réquiem #3: Fosas Cuerpo / Body Graves*, providing a space of mourning.

Given the work's sense of defiance, the figure of Antigone is an apt means of reading Luna's actions as establishing the legitimacy of loss. For Julia Kristeva, Antigone's actions showcase the extent to which female bodies "have the opportunity and the capacity to generate a new understanding, skill, or even a way of life or survival."[64] Luna, then, becomes one of these many contemporary women whose actions not only create a space of recognition denied by official discourses but also point to the creative potential of performance to redress harm. Her ritual, though brief, breaks a cycle of derealization for her, those who have spoken with her of their traumas, and her audience. Much like Antigone "refuses to let the ruler interfere with private matters such as grief and mourning," Luna too insists on mourning the dead, even if it means doing so without a body or certain confirmation of death.[65]

Although Sophocles' Antigone literally spoke out against injustice, *Réquiem #3: Fosas Cuerpo / Body Graves* is a nonverbal performance similarly "compelled to be courageous . . . moved to fight injustice."[66] Luna was inspired by her own conversations with those who have been directly impacted by disappearance and loss. The experiences that Araceli Rodríguez Nava shared with Luna are of particular importance. Since November 2009, Rodríguez Nava has worked individually and with the collective Movimiento por nuestros desaparecidos en México (Movement for Our Disappeared in Mexico) to find answers about her son's disappearance.[67] Luis Ángel León Rodríguez was a Federal Police officer in Mexico City, sent to Hidalgo, Michoacán, with six other officers and one civilian driver. They never made it to their destination.[68] Not only have the Federal Police insisted that they had no responsibility to protect those officers, the case has been routinely been ignored by the Procuraduría General de la República (PGR; Mexico's Office of the Attorney General), among other federal departments.[69] Despite more recent support for her case from the CNDH, Rodríguez Nava still has no answers about her son's body. Even though Luna is silent, the testimonies of Mexico's many Antigones, like Rodríguez Nava, become metaphorically embodied through the performer and the nonverbal sounds emanating from her body in action. By turning our ear toward the sounds of Luna's body, "aurality offers a way to explore the inherent connection between the corporeal and the conceptual."[70] That is to say, her actions "speak" for the women she carries with her via her body as archive.

Validating the memories of Mexico's Antigones, *Réquiem #3: Fosas Cuerpo / Body Graves* becomes the mechanism through which Luna activates a temporary community of mourners. Throughout the five chapters, Luna is cognizant of her role as "Violeta," the staged incarnation of real-life women.[71] Much like the eulogist in a funeral, the artist becomes a proxy for those whose stories she honors, and she transforms herself and her public into fellow mourners.[72] The result is the ephemeral *communitas de dolor*, solidified by the sounds that Luna's body creates in relation to the space,

FIGURE 3.1. Violeta Luna arranges a variety of tools on a blanket. These tools represent those used in forced disappearances and by families and friends who search for loved ones. *Réquiem #3: Body Graves / Fosas Cuerpo*, Centro Universitario de Teatro, Black Box Theatre, Mexico City, Mexico, 2019. Photo by Christina Baker.

objects, and five distinct chapters. As the sound design falls away at specific, planned moments, the sonic materiality of Luna's body directs and commands our attention. For example, during the second chapter of the piece, "the search," we are directed to the sounds of Luna's bare hands, which work furiously, perhaps much like Antigone's hands hurriedly tried to cover her brother's body with dirt. Luna uses her energy to unwrap the mysterious and bulging *bulto*, or *encobijado*, center stage. The sounds cut through the silent space with a violent force. The jarring noise of plastic adhesive being ripped apart, quickly, furiously, conjures sonic memories of opening presents or packages, though there is no joy in what is revealed. Once the tape has been removed, the blanket falls open to reveal a large black plastic bag, to which I will return later, a pile of metal tools, bundles of rope, and plastic baggies with paper markers. These objects call to mind the tools Mexico's collectives use to recover the remains of loved ones. Painfully, they are also the same tools used to conceal those bodies. The blanket's silence as it falls open is juxtaposed by the sharp pangs of metal pieces hitting one another. Luna proceeds to pick up the pieces, and they collide in her hands and arms. The thud each one makes as she firmly places it back on the blanket is a sonic reminder of the physical weight of the shovel or metal rod. These noises are also a reminder of the emotional and psychic weight of searching for missing bodies.

Following the sounds of searching, Luna's body embarks on a metonymical discovery of a clandestine mass grave. In the moments when the sound design pauses, we hear each of Luna's movements, even those nearly imperceptible. The performer prepares a space to simulate opening the earth or, rather, reopening the wound of unmarked graves. As she wrestles with a blue plastic tarp meant to cover a rectangular table, the unsettling rustling noises echo throughout the space. This brief interlude is followed by Luna spreading a mound of dirt onto the table in relative silence. The gentle hum of earth being poured into a mound on top of the plastic is a notable contrast to the violent sounds that conjure death and decay. Luna then begins to move the dirt, one spoonful at a time, from the table to the vacant chair across the stage. This silent, repetitive act is accompanied only by the sound of careful and quiet footsteps back and forth. The steps evoke, perhaps, the way Antigone herself tread softly in the night as she attempted to reterritorialize her brother within the sovereign realm.[73] In this case, the repetitious steps also become a reminder of the relentless efforts to both find and bury Mexico's missing. These soft steps, back and forth across the theatre, become the sonic act of "confronting *the* death," as Bailey and Walter might suggest, that lies underneath Mexico's soil.[74] But Luna is not alone in her efforts; she invites members of the audience to help her move the dirt. In accepting her invitation, these members enact the ethical dimension she speaks of in her cor-po/etics. The division between performer and audience dissipates, and we all become part of the symbolic deed. Hearing the steps of Luna and audience members reminds us of our corporeality, that our bodies must act for those who cannot.

Symbolically unearthing remains leads to the fourth chapter, which Luna calls "the dance of the bones." As the proxy for innumerable mothers searching for their loved ones, Luna performs travels to Mictlán, the Aztec underworld, to recover the bones and bury them properly. Similar to Antigone, "she is alone in confronting the underground god in order to see—again—if she will survive that solitary ritual."[75] Upon her arrival, Luna finds a large black bag, also visually reminiscent of those used to dispose of dead and dismembered bodies. As she unfolds and pushes away the plastic, the discomforting sound of rustling plastic once again fills the space. From the bag, Luna removes enormous skeletal remains, bound together by an oversized red ribbon. For Luna, the connection to Mictlán is clear, and yet the bones conjure another figure in Mexico's cultural and political imaginary: the skeletons of José Guadalupe Posadas. Following his graphic depictions, "skeletons have been prominent in Mexican popular art as emblems of a playful and resilient 'Mexican spirit' that is the beating heart of the Mexican nation."[76] According to Wright, after Ayotzinapa, Posadas's "resilient" skeletons have been reimagined, used now as "a painful contrast" to convey the current reality of Mexico as "a *dead* skeleton."⁷⁷ Luna secures her dead skeleton to her forehead using the red ribbons, leaving the bones to flow down the sides of her body. As she moves through the space, this time she is accompanied by music, the sounds of pre-Hispanic conches, rocks, and wind instruments to further enhance her depiction of Mictlán. I don't dwell on the sound design here but rather mention these sounds because they are forced into the background by Luna's dance. The bones she carries on and with her collide time and again with the floor. Thud. Thud. Thud. Luna's movements leave no doubt about the solidity of these bones. And yet their sound is absorbed into the floor, swiftly muted. At the same time, the sounds of their materiality are a stark reminder of the way the body to which they once belonged was disappeared and forced into eternal silence.

DAVID MOLINA AND LOOKING WITH THE EAR

Broadly speaking, Violeta Luna considers sound an integral part of establishing a ritual-like atmosphere in her work. In creating *Réquiem #3: Fosas Cuerpo / Body Graves*, Luna turned to her trusted friend and longtime creative partner, David R. Molina, for the piece's soundtrack. Molina is a man of many talents, but he foremost identifies as a composer. From there, he lists multi-instrumentalist, sound artist, music producer, recording engineer, and instrument inventor as some of his many titles. Molina considers what he does music, not sound, because when people hear sound design "they think you're using other people's music and they think you're just editing and doing the technical sound."⁷⁸ In contrast, when Molina collaborates on a piece, he writes the music and also plays all of the instruments. He is adamant about using sounds that originate from instruments and found objects and tries to avoid using synthesizers in his creative process, though he does use software to tweak the recordings.⁷⁹ He has collaborated with Luna for more than fifteen years, working on nearly all of her pieces, and has produced music for an array of performing arts disciplines, films, radio shows, and multimedia installations for over twenty-five years.⁸⁰ Like Luna, Molina's personal connection to social movement work runs deep. Molina's family left El Salvador during its brutal civil war (1979–1992), settling in California. Living in major metropolises like Los Angeles and San Francisco, Molina has been a firsthand witness to socioeconomic disparities running also along lines of race, motivating him to address racial profiling, police brutality, imperialism, and immigrant rights through his work. With such a long career, Molina's collaborations and recognitions are numerous, including, to name just a few of his recent contributions, *King Lear* (2021), included in the St. Louis Shakespeare festival; Migdalia Cruz's translation of *MacBeth* (2021); the two-part series about a Salvadoran immigrant in Los Angeles, *Citizen* (2021); his own 2020 album, *Transient*; Luis Alfaro's *Mojada* (Wetback Medea, 2020); Octavio Solis's *Quixote Nuevo* (New Quixote, 2018); and David Schendel's film *Dead Ink Archives* (2016).

Through his long partnership with Luna, Molina has learned to create and adapt quickly. Sometimes Luna gives him several months to generate the soundtrack for a performance, and at other times only weeks. In the case of *Réquiem #3: Fosas Cuerpo / Body Graves*, Molina had a very short timeline in order to match Luna's production and performance plans. This also meant that he never saw the piece performed in its entirety and, to this day, has not seen it live. Molina wrote, performed, and recorded the entire score based on videos, conversations, and his previous work with Luna.[81] In his poetic homage to sound designers, director Tazewell Thompson writes: "All this created from observation. Imagination. Passion. Sounds that startle. Lull. Soothe. Shock. Jolt. Astonish . . . The sound designer has learned. The art of looking with the ear."[82] Though Thompson does not write specifically of Molina's process, it is a perfect depiction of Molina's creativity and abilities. He produced a profoundly moving score for *Réquiem #3: Fosas Cuerpo / Body Graves* based solely on observation and intuition. By employing what Thompson calls "the art of looking with the ear," Molina translates Luna's visual register and embodied acts into the aural realm.

Analyzing the performance as a requiem for the disappeared means paying close attention to Molina's musical choices. As in the case of theater, coming together to form a temporary community is central to commemorating the dead. Funerals incorporate music as a means of establishing the parameters of the ceremony, reflecting elements of the deceased's personality and becoming a shared soundtrack for mourners.[83] Thinking about *Réquiem #3: Fosas Cuerpo / Body Graves* in this way, Molina's music solidifies the audience's transformation into a *communitas de dolor*. But how does one choose music or sounds for someone whose body is not only missing but disavowed by the state? How does one craft a musical sound that simultaneously represents individuals *and* a collective of missing persons? Molina's soundtrack seeks to engage the audience in a collective act of grieving by way of what he calls "organic sources." For Molina, this means using existing instruments, found objects, and instruments he himself has put together, rather than prefabricated sounds or beats from technological sources.[84] These "organic" sounds emerge from material, tangible sites in opposition to the missing remains of a corpse. The materiality of instruments fills the space in lieu of the missing by way of invisible, yet audibly

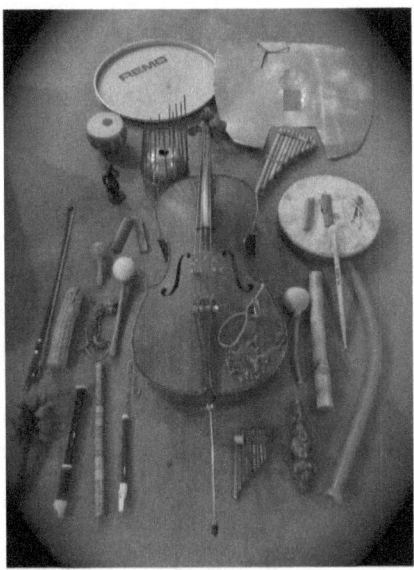

FIGURE 3.2. A selection of instruments used or created by David Molina to create the soundtrack for *Réquiem #3: Body Graves / Fosas Cuerpo* and other pieces by Violeta Luna. Photo by David Molina.

perceptible, presence. Molina's musical score and instrumentation is complex, perhaps the most complex I have ever tasked myself with analyzing, and I will undoubtedly fall short of doing him and his work justice. My intent here is to emphasize the importance of his contribution to the piece's funeral rite and embodiment of Antigone. Paralleling words and funerals against death, Molina's artistic choices function as sounds against death. In what follows, I detail what I consider to be three categories that allow for mourning and redress to occur: the ethereal realm, grounded terrain, and laments.

A VIBRATORIUM OF ETHEREALITY, GROUNDEDNESS, LAMENTS

The aural centrality of Molina's work obliges us spectators to become active listeners. We are tasked with stretching our ears as a means of understanding the gravity and expansiveness of the performance as a whole. Analyzing Molina's musical accompaniment to Luna's onstage actions offers new possibilities for understanding "how meaning is created (and veiled) and how the spectrum of theatrical creation and reception is widened."[85] Specifically, I argue that Molina's sound design transforms Antigone's cries against impunity and loss into a "vibratorium," a term I use based on Nicholas Ridout's observation: "that which brings us together in this momentary communion is that which vibrates, as it were, for ourselves alone, in our bodily reception of the light-sound image."[86] Very literally, Molina's compositions are played at high volume, creating an impressive and invasive tour de force of vibrations. The black box theatre is filled with Molina's reverberating sounds that expand the public's interpretation of the visual elements and connect the audience, forging a temporary community through bodily sensations. The sounds inhabit and travel around us, frequencies bouncing between us, through us. By centering on Molina's musical contribution, the audience becomes "one gigantic communal ear. Their senses shaken. Expanded. Extended. Never the same."[87]

Conjoined in listening practices, we, the audience, that communal ear, acutely perceive that Molina's music does not progress in a linear fashion. At times, the soundtrack seems to follow Luna's logical sequence of five chapters, while at other moments it unfolds at its own pace. Molina's music constantly shifts and moves through both space and time, invoking sensations across the "socially shared experience" of the performance.[88] The soundtrack's vibrations connect us spectators within "affective constellations."[89] That is to say, we become a conglomerate of bodies that transmit energies, affective reactions to the visual and sonic stimuli in *Réquiem #3: Fosas Cuerpo / Body Graves*. Similar to the way objects on stage can become "actants," agents that intervene in "human and non-human worlds," I posit Molina's music as the mechanism through which spectators perceive and experience the affective dimension of Mexico's Antigones and their disappeared.[90]

For nearly thirty minutes, audience members are filled with sometimes-competing sonic registers that express phases of loss and grief. I associate these emotions with what I am calling the sonic ethereal realm. As the piece begins, with the image of the empty chair, Molina used a waterphone to create a constant squeaking noise, one that ripples through the theatre softly and hauntingly.[91] This thin, scraping sound is later accompanied by the sounds of whistles, chimes, and bells. These high-pitched instruments literally ring out, calling to our ears as a whirlwind of chaos that turns the theatre into an echo chamber. Their continuity is disquieting. During the performance's second chapter, the search, these ethereal sounds increase in intensity, as if signaling urgency. Molina juxtaposes these high-pitched sounds with the feathery quality of wind instruments, such as wooden flutes. The result creates further unease. When Luna embarks on her journey to Mictlán, the ethereal becomes otherworldly as Molina integrates conches and rock shakers with the bells, chimes, and wind instruments. These new

FIGURE 3.3. A white dress hangs above an empty metal chair while a pile of bones rests on the floor. *Réquiem #3: Body Graves / Fosas Cuerpo*, Centro Universitario de Teatro, Black Box Theatre, Mexico City, Mexico, 2019. Photo by Julio Pantoja, Hemispheric Institute of Performance and Politics.

sounds do not last long; they fall away, allowing the metallic instruments and flutes to linger in the air. Tia DeNora maintains that the texture and "color" of certain instruments "may connote and perhaps evoke a sense of *what it is like to be* within specific material and corporal aspects of situations and settings."[92] This seems appropriate for considering how Molina returns to the scraping noises near the end of the piece, as Luna places the white dress in its final resting place. The aforementioned instruments, the sounds they create, and the way Molina skillfully combines them cement the ethereal ambience. Molina's composition aurally transmits Luna's visual embodiment of searching for the body that is no longer here but also no longer there, a body between stages of life and death. In this void, the musical selection make tangible the feeling of loss and grief, giving sonic dimension to the missing bodies and efforts for redressive action.

In contrast to the ethereal realm, Molina's composition uses deep, bass-driven music and instrumentation that conjure what I refer to as grounded terrain. I suggest this sonic register is representational of bodies buried beneath the terrain's surface, bodies that are sometimes found but most often lost in the abyss of Mexico's hidden mass graves.[93] To forge this aural connection, Molina turned to a thunder sheet to create roaring thunder-like cracks, a cello for smooth yet deep tones, and metal springs of different sizes to simulate bangs and clashes. This combination of instruments yields tumultuous reverberations. For example, after Luna pours the mound of dirt onto the table, Molina imbues the silent earth with sonic materiality: rolling waves of deep rumbling. Molina's music booms through the theatre, filling it, and the bodies present, with a constant, pulsing rhythm reminiscent of beating hearts. These sounds bring "the minds of mourners to focus on the deceased as an individual human being."[94] The audience in mourning, as a *communitas de dolor*, is provoked to think about the sounds inhabiting their own bodies, those that take the place of bodies denied life and public proclamations of grief. Effectively, or affectively, the soundtrack directs our attention to Mexico's missing. Writing of funeral practices, Janieke Bruin-Mollenhorst states, "the identity of the deceased is no longer constructed by the (deceased) person in his or her sociocultural context but is constructed by the sociocultural context."[95] The nonverbal soundtrack of *Réquiem #3: Fosas Cuerpo / Body Graves*, then, allows for the deceased to be constructed by the sociocultural context of Mexico's impunity, which has permitted missing and disappeared persons to become a constant reality. Performed as an adapted funeral rite, the piece also becomes its own sociocultural context that seeks to recognize the dead, despite their missingness.

The piece's eerie wailing laments provide another aural avenue for mourning. These "mimetic motifs and gestures that call to mind sighs or other vocalizations allied with sadness" give new meaning to the metaphorical act of vocalizing the pain of Mexico's many Antigones, those whom Luna incarnates in her embodied acts.[96] To achieve these haunting "voices," Molina plays what he calls a "whirly tube," an instrument he made himself. It is a large plastic tube that he wears on his head; as it spins, the tube catches the air, resulting in the voice-like noise. The intensity of the "voice" depends on the force and speed at which the instrument rotates around Molina's body.[97] The sound draws my attention to the painful juxtaposition between his living body and those which are not present. There are two notable moments in *Réquiem #3: Fosas Cuerpo / Body Graves* where these sounds of sobs, tears, and wailing punctuate the registers of ethereality and groundedness. The first occurs as Luna, or an audience member, shuffles back and forth through the space, moving the dirt pile one spoonful at a time. The disturbing sound of distant voices breaks the silence within the theatre, prompting unsettled reactions. The vocal productions are not coming from Luna, but our inability as spectators to identify the source is unnerving. Perhaps these voices can be appreciated as those belonging to the dead, but understanding the piece is a ritual of mourning, the voices are more accurately heard as disembodied laments of searching mothers and sisters. This connection becomes clearer at the end of the piece as Luna digs through the remaining mound of dirt. She slowly pulls out a white dress, stained brown by the earth, then carefully hangs it above the empty chair. She proceeds to bury her head in the dirt, frantically covering herself in it, stifling any screams, cutting off her own air supply. As she does this, Molina's composition forefronts the sounds of the whirly tube, furiously wailing and emitting high-pitched squeals. The sounds of heaving sobs, as if from a body unable to fully breathe, move throughout the theatre, through Luna's body, and through the audience. Competing with the ethereal and grounded instrumentation, the emotive cries break through, deeply affecting the spectators, now careful listeners. For this brief period of time, a collective community was engaged in listening to Mexico's grieving Antigones before the laments are silenced to signal the end of the performance.

LUKAS AVENDAÑO AND *BUSCANDO A BRUNO*

Just as Luna's performance enacts stages of grief, loss, and unearthing remains, Lukas Avendaño's *Buscando a Bruno* brings attention to forced disappearances. Born in 1977 in the small town of Santa Teresa, a municipal region located in Tehuantepec, Oaxaca, Avendaño grew up and followed a career trajectory distinct from other practitioners in this book. Avendaño's early life in this firmly Zapotec region of Mexico was marked by a lack of electricity and potable drinking water, experiences of racism because of his indigeneity, and having to make decisions about whether to harvest crops or attend school. Avendaño's family is one of many in the area that have historically earned a modest living by raising a limited number of crops, such as corn, squash, chiles, or bananas.[98] At a young age, Avendaño began working alongside his brothers and father, but always preferred studying. Over the years, as the male members of his family immigrated to the United States, he stayed behind to further his education.[99] He enrolled in a national program run by the Consejo Nacional de Fomento Educativo (CONAFE; National Council on Educational Development) geared toward training teachers to "llevar educación a las zonas marginadas del país" (bring education to the most marginal areas in the country).[100] At fifteen, he was sent to teach in an extremely remote part of southern Oaxaca, reachable only by a twelve-hour walk.[101] Upon completing the program, he pursued a dual degree at the Universidad Veracruzana–Xalapa in anthropology and contemporary dance. Motivated by his desire to convey Indigenous cultural practices through the ephemeral arts, his work is "como un manifiesto, una oda a la diferencia" (as a manifesto, an ode to Otherness).[102]

By the late 2000s, Avendaño's performances had gained national and international recognition. Works such as *Réquiem para un alcaraván* (Requiem for a Stone-Curlew, 2012), about the stages of life and love for *muxe* bodies, and *No soy Hombre, soy Mariposa* (I Am Not a Man, I Am a Butterfly, 2014), a piece that articulates and embraces gender and sexual difference, garnered Avendaño much attention.[103] His most recent work, *Buscando a Bruno* (2018), and subsequent documentary, *Utopía de la mariposa* (The Butterfly's Utopia, 2019), have also made a notable impact in national and international spaces. While he is often referred to as a performance artist, Avendaño prefers to think of his work as "installation for the human body," a notion that reflects his understanding of the body as a site "where meaning and affect are installed."[104] Throughout his career, Avendaño has been invited to perform across Mexico, as well as in Argentina, Colombia, Poland, Canada, Germany, Spain, the United States, and more. Recently, he was included in a Lotería Gucci campaign, and the *New York Times* listed him as one of the most important queer Indigenous artists worldwide.[105] While Avendaño has performed and collaborated with artists such as Guillermo Gómez Peña, La Pocha Nostra, and Lechedevirgen Trimegisto, to name a few, Avendaño often performs alone, presenting introspective pieces about his life and identity.

Buscando a Bruno is one of these solo pieces. The performance is the direct result of the forced disappearance of Avendaño's brother and naval officer, Bruno Alonso Avendaño Martínez. Bruno returned home to Tehuantepec, Oaxaca, on May 4, 2018, for several days of vacation leave, and on the afternoon of May 10, Mother's Day, he was disappeared. Bruno spent that morning helping his mother and was assisting a local contact drive a load of sand out of town that afternoon.[106] At approximately 3 p.m., Bruno got out of the truck at an intersection called "Los Manguitos" and was never seen alive again. It was as if he vanished into thin air.[107] The Avendaño family tried to issue a missing person's report and make a statement that Bruno had been forcibly disappeared, but local authorities refused to file any such claims. Not only that, but the authorities fabricated stories, feigning that Bruno had been seen at a party or that he had even used his cellphone.[108] Yet, because of the family's persistence, the Fiscalía General del Estado de Oaxaca (Oaxaca's District Attorney's Office) eventually opened an investigation.[109] However, by the time Lukas Avendaño was preparing to travel to Barcelona, Spain, in June 2018, there had been no progress, prompting him to make a formal appeal to the Mexican consulate in Barcelona.[110] Finally, in November 2018, the Oaxaca authorities declared themselves unable to pursue the case and transferred it to the Fiscalía General de la República (FGR; Mexico's Office of the Attorney General).[111] Still, despite repeated appeals,

Lukas Avendaño's search for his brother was constantly rebuffed and ignored, and it was not until November 12, 2020, based on an anonymous call, that authorities found Bruno buried in a clandestine grave between the municipalities of Salina Cruz and Tehuantepec.[112] Taking to social media, Lukas Avendaño declared that Bruno was finally home:

> Hoy una vez más podemos decir que nunca nos sentimos solas en estos 927 días de incansable búsqueda por tu regreso Bruno, siempre tuvimos la fortaleza de esta comunidad que aun desde la virtualidad siempre nos ha acompañado.[113]

> *Today, once again, we can say that we have never felt alone during the 927 days that we tirelessly searched for you, Bruno; we always had the strength of our community, which even virtually has accompanied us on our journey.*

It bears pointing out that while Bruno was likely targeted because of his profession and knowledge he possessed about governmental human rights abuses, his disappearance and death as a young Indigenous man is part of a terrifying trend in Oaxaca. Increased violence toward Indigenous populations, especially Zapotec communities, rose to startling levels during the 1990s as groups began to openly oppose neoliberal policies that would irrevocably harm their way of life, such as NAFTA.[114] Grassroots protest movements in Oaxaca came to a head in 2006 when forty thousand teachers protested education reforms and the fraudulent outcome of the presidential election. Lasting over six months, the Popular Assembly of the Peoples of Oaxaca (APPO) occupied public spaces, garnered international attention, and felt the wrath of local and federally sanctioned countermeasures such as using bulldozers, tear gas, and water cannons.[115] Young men, mostly Indigenous, were routinely rounded up, tortured, falsely charged, and imprisoned by agents of the state. Those who survived were released to send a message about the brutality that awaited those who continued to rebel.[116] This crisis eventually waned, notably after APPO spokesmen were promised a meeting with incoming president, Felipe Calderón, only to be tortured and taken to a high security prison, charged with "assault, sedition, and firebombing."[117]

In recent years, Indigenous rights and environmental activists have since become the target of governmental and private security forces, including *narco* cartels. In its 2019 report, the IACHR implored Mexico to "raise awareness of human rights violations against indigenous persons" and the US Department of State Country Report on Human Rights Practices noted that "environmental activists continued to be targets of violence, a majority of them from indigenous communities."[118] As foreign companies have coveted Zapotec community lands for mining and wind energy throughout Oaxaca, dissident voices have been "illegally detained and beaten by police" even being "shot and killed by municipal police" during peaceful protests.[119] Additionally, since Calderón's War on Drugs, at least six cartels have spread into Oaxaca, terrorizing local communities, including the Juchitán, and taking control of natural resources as a further means of monopolizing the local economy.[120] Considered within this particular context, then, Bruno's death is not only part of a larger trend that routinely eliminates Indigenous bodies, but particularly those who represent a threat to corrupt practices.

EL ISTMO DE TEHUANTEPEC AND MUXEIDAD

The work of Lukas Avendaño is in a category of its own. As Antonio Prieto Stambaugh points out, what sets the artist apart from many theater and performance artists in Mexico is the way he interrogates race, class, and gender as intersecting spheres.[121] Moreover, throughout his work, the performances create what Prieto Stambaugh refers to as a queer utopia, one where "political, aesthetic, and sexual dissidence merge, where violence and impunity fail to destroy hope."[122] A central component to Prieto Stambaugh's evaluation, and my own analysis of Avendaño's work, is how the artists defines himself: as *muxe*. Following the artist's own use of pronouns in interviews and public engagements, I refer to Avendaño as him/he throughout my writing, though the performer has often asserted that his gender is what he least thinks about. However, his identity remains a constant site of query for those unfamiliar with *muxe* identity.[123] The list of scholars who have studied this population is short and comprised almost entirely of outsiders, leading to misconceptions and even inaccurate terminology. As a prime example, Heather Vrana details the origin of the Istmo's *muxes* as it is often mythologized:

> Long ago, God sent one of his assistants, Vicente Ferrer, across the Americas with a bag full of queers. Vicente was to scatter the queers across the continent. He began in the South and dropped one in Colombia, then a few in Central America.... When he got to Juchitán, he tripped, his bag tore open, and the remaining queers spilled into Juchitán.[124]

Invoking Saint Vincent Ferrer, this explanation reflects an attempt to make sense of Indigenous gender and sexual practice outside the bounds of Catholicism and Spanish cultural values. What remains unclear is how long *muxes* existed before the arrival of the Spaniards and other colonizing forces. In response to this line of inquiry, Avendaño explains, "all I have are vague intuitions, hypotheses, and speculations; nothing that could be presented as the 'truth.'"[125] Avendaño prefers to respond to the question with his own: Who knows how long? In doing so, his response resists Western anxieties that seek constant categorization and historicization. His response also alludes to an opacity that resides within the *muxe* body and Zapotec community more broadly, an opacity that refuses to be made intelligible by imposed outsider forms of knowledge.

Before I develop notions of *muxe* identity, it is worth mentioning that their perception is indelibly linked to the way Zapotec women have historically been construed. The Istmo de Tehuantepec has long been mythologized as a matriarchy, honored by Zapotec Indigenous familial and social structures.[126] From the early writing of Spanish invaders to colonial travelogues, Tehuana women have been described as nearly mythical creatures: "youthful, slender, elegant, and so handsome that she enslaved the hearts of white men like Cortés's lover long ago."[127] During the first half of the twentieth century, Miguel Covarrubias declared Tehuana women as having a reputation for "beauty and allure," and Sergei Eisenstein described them as ruling "like a queen bee. By some miracle, the matriarchal tribal system has survived for hundreds of years."[128] My aim is not to analyze the rhetoric of these observations, but I note their potency in creating a collective imaginary. This was reinforced visually, as Aída Sierra explains, by Diego Rivera's murals as well as numerous cinematic interventions that depicted the Istmo as a tropical paradise of mythical proportions.[129] More recently, Beverly Newbold Chiñas's *The Isthmus Zapotecs: A Matrifocal Culture of Mexico* (1992), Veronika Bennholdt-Thomsen's *Juchitán, la ciudad de las mujeres* (Juchitán, The City of Women, 1997), and Lynn Stephen's *Zapotec Women: Gender, Class, and Ethnicity in a Globalized Oaxaca* (2005) continue to emphasize the idea of female beauty, power, and exoticism in the region.

This repeated insistence on female Otherness permeates understandings of *muxe* identity. Avendaño accurately points out that those who observe the *muxe* from the outside, and in the singular, tend to draw parallels to a third gender.[130] This not only collapses the cultural complexity and specificity of the *muxe*, but also imposes rigid Western definitions of gender on a non-Western population. For example, in her early studies, Marinella Miano Borruso conflates homosexuality, cross-dressing, and transgenderism with *muxe* identity.[131] These ideas are similarly echoed in much of the scholarship

FIGURE 3.4. Lukas Avendaño, muxe, is bare-chested while wearing a traditional skirt from the Isthmus of Tehuantepec, Oaxaca, Mexico, 2014. Photo by Mario Patiño.

published in the 1990s that continued to define the *muxe* in relation to Western standards of sexuality and gender. Moreover, these anthropological studies emphasize the role of the nongovernmental organization Las Intrépidas, Buscadores de Peligro and their annual gala, known as a *vela*, as indicators of institutionalizing *muxe* presence, though it is more adequately considered tolerance.[132] As Gustavo Subero points out, more recent work, such as Alejandra Islas's documentary *Muxes: Auténticas, intrépidas, buscadores de peligro* (Muxes: Authentic, Daring, Seekers of Danger, 2005) and Nicola Ókin Frioli's photography series *We Are Princesses in a Land of Machos* (2004) reflect more nuanced depictions of *muxe* communities. In these works, *muxes* are conveyed as individuals, with their own ways of referring to themselves, outside the bounds of a "rigid manifestation" of gender.[133]

The fluidity depicted in the aforementioned productions is at the heart of how Avendaño and other *muxes* identify themselves. In the most basic sense, Avendaño defines the *muxe* as a body born according to biological definitions of maleness but does not simulate "being female" as trans-identifying populations may do. Rather, the *muxe* "simply touch[es] up their identity, adding certain signs considered 'non-masculine': painting their nails, wearing thong sandals or 'women's' shoes, curling their eyelashes, using eyeliner, pulling back their hair with clips, and wearing earrings."[134] Amaranta Gómez, fellow *muxe*, community leader, and anthropologist, echoes this definition, adding that "Ser *muxhe* es ser ante todo un ser humano que cuenta con el aval de su sociedad y coexiste con y en ella en un tiempo y espacio específicos" (Being *muxe* means being, above all, a person that counts on the protection of their community and coexists with and among it during a specific time and space).¹³⁵ In referring to the coexistence of *muxes* within a broader social structure, Gómez means the Istmo of Tehuantepec and its Zapotec population. Principally, there is a general sense among *muxe* that the "condición *sine qua non* para definirse muxe' es identificarse como zapoteca, aceptando su herencia y descendencia, incluida la lengua. Es fundamental, entonces tener como primer idioma el zapoteco o ser bilingüe" (the most basic requirement for defining oneself as muxe is to identify as Zapotec, to accept your heritage, including your language. It is fundamental, then, to speak Zapotec as your first language, or at least be bilingual).¹³⁶ The concept that Avendaño uses to describe these considerations is *muxeidad* and insists "that we stop talking about the muxe in the singular or plural and instead talk about *muxeidad* as a 'total social fact.'"¹³⁷ Much like we speak of heterosexuality and homosexuality, Avendaño's *muxeidad* is conceived as a social system that is created and sustained by its context. As such, the way that I approach *muxeidad* attempts to respect how Avendaño envisions himself in relation to this "total social fact."

Avendaño's declaration, "yo no necesito que nadie me legitime" (I do not need anyone to legitimize me), solidifies his *muxe* identity as a challenge to Western binaries of gender and sexuality and communicates a fierce dedication to his right to exist.¹³⁸ In stating he does not need anyone's permission to be who he is, the artist's mantra also embodies, in many ways, the Istmo's place in the collective imaginary as a region of resistance, spanning from pre-Colombian times to the Mexican Revolution.¹³⁹ These notions inform how the *muxe* is understood as a figure of defiance. In the Zapotec community, men are considered the "natural" bastions of authority and power, those who dictate public and political realms. Women, though often seen in public, managing artisan production or maintaining household finances, are still excluded from masculine spheres of control and respect.¹⁴⁰ Avendaño's *muxeidad* within the public eye and in public spaces disrupts, therefore, upends and confronts masculine hegemonic constructs.¹⁴¹ The artist's *muxe* body defies gender, class, and power structures, performing transgressions that refuse to bend to the will of others.¹⁴² In conceiving *muxeidad* in a way that does not foreclose constant reimagining of the self, Avendaño makes one more important declaration: "*Muxeidad* is a frank, open, and deliberate way to question and expose the falsehood of certain patriarchal enunciations as 'standards of truth.'"¹⁴³ In the context of *Buscando a Bruno*, these final reflections resonate deeply with the way Avendaño enacts a ritual of mourning that challenges the state's willful complicity in his brother's disappearance.

EMBODYING ANTIGONE: LUKAS AVENDAÑO'S PUBLIC DECRIES

In many ways, Avendaño's tragic story, subsequent performances, and declarations of mourning are similar to the events that inspired *Réquiem #3: Fosas Cuerpo / Body Graves*. Bruno and Luis Ángel were both federal officers, one on the police force, the other in the navy. They both lost contact with their loved ones at three o'clock in the afternoon and were never heard from again, both seemingly vanished into nothingness. Like Araceli Rodríguez Nava, Avendaño has repeatedly and publicly spoken out against the state's negligence. One major difference between Luna and Avendaño's work is painfully obvious: he is both performer and searching family member. The artist is one of Mexico's Antigones who implores the state to act. The piece was first performed in front of the Mexican consulate in Barcelona, Spain, in June 2018. It has since been performed in Oaxaca City, Oaxaca, in front of the Santo Domingo Cathedral in 2018, in Valladolid, Spain, as part of the 2019 Festival Internacional de Teatro y Artes de Calle, at Mexico City's Museo Universitario el Chopo in February 2019, and finally during the 2019 Hemispheric Institute of Politics and Performance Encuentro. In this chapter, I examine the last two performances in Mexico City to suggest that Avendaño's performance defies the state's attempts to derealize his brother and, through nonverbal cues, enacts funeral rites to honor Bruno.[144] Critically, Avendaño's silence for the duration of the piece draws attention to the soundtrack of Oaxacan funeral music, which I claim serves as sounds against death.

This articulated confrontation between *muxeidad*, and by extension Avendaño's body, and patriarchal enunciations of "truth" leads me back to Antigone. Here, I propose the obvious connection between gender transgression and Antigone, but also draw attention to how patriarchy intersects with power, how Mexican officials manipulate "truth" in relation to missing and disappeared, as in Bruno Avendaño's case. In Sophocles' play, Creon believes "transgression of his orders is possible only by a male and must be interpreted as a political act."[145] Given the act is articulated and enacted by Antigone, a woman, his notion of political actor as male actor is upended. Creon's belief also signals the limits of gendered intelligibility, specifically that women were not intended to inhabit the public—read political—sphere. That was reserved for men. Antigone's body, perceived as female, and her actions, understood as male, create fissures within a binary that predetermines access to political participation. Cecilia Sjöholm's reading of the Greek tragedy maintains that for Antigone, "it is precisely in being problematic and enigmatic that femininity functions as a revelatory power."[146] By articulating her resistance, Antigone breaks the logic and, in doing so, generates new possibilities for gender intelligibility and survival.

Coming back to Avendaño and *muxeidad*, gender fluidity is a transgression that offers possibilities for generating new understandings not only of gender, but also of social justice and human rights.

After forty days without concrete answers regarding his brother's case or whereabouts, Lukas Avendaño entered the Mexican consulate in Barcelona, Spain, prepared to make a formal declaration of negligence. Avendaño demanded that the case be brought to the FGR, which is theoretically equipped with special search commissions to handle cases like his brother's. Avendaño sought to make public the way Oaxaca officials had refused to follow the standards set forth by Mexico's 2018 Ley General.[147] Sjöholm points out that "every law carries in its very edifice the inherent possibility of a transgression, a crime or extreme action that simultaneously violates and affirms its foundation."[148] And yet, that the Mexican state would be the transgressor is a reminder that there is no trusted body to uphold the law. In turn, much like Antigone, Avendaño "attempts to speak in the political sphere in the language of sovereignty that is the instrument of political power."[149]

What is striking about Avendaño's act of defiance and the way he leverages the language of political power is that he does so from the liminal space of gender transgression. Wearing a black Tehuana skirt, large gold earrings, his long hair pulled back, adorned with green ribbons, and wearing a black lace shawl, Avendaño's bare chest disrupts a binary expectation of femininity. This *muxe* body has come to assert its power over silence and its capacity to interrupt the logic of gender, especially as it is performed within this space of government. In stark contrast to the men in dark suits, Avendaño is aware of the symbolic weight of wearing the *tehuana* costume. Specific to the Zapotec women of the Istmo, it visually references racial, civilizational, and regional identity.[150] While the outfit has become a fad in elite Mexican circles and in high-fashion circuits since the early twentieth century, the *tehuana* outfit marks "place and belonging" as much as it functions as "an icon of national identity."[151] Annegret Hesterberg remarks, "clothing may not make the man, but it certainly transmits the image the wearer wishes to project."[152] She goes on to declare that the *tehuana* outfit "is nothing without the woman wearing it."[153] In this case of Avendaño, he consciously chose to present himself as Zapotec and *muxe* during his first performance of *Buscando a Bruno* and all subsequent enactments. He states: "es muy visible y llamativo hacer un acto con tehuanas y el Consulado no me puede decir nada si entro con una de ellas" (it is incredibly visible and powerful to perform using the traditional *tehuana* skirt and the Consulate cannot say anything to me if I enter wearing one).[154] In making this decision, Avendaño links his *muxe* body both to his native Oaxacan terrain and the Mexican consulate in Barcelona. By extension, his aesthetic and physical presence upends the state's desire to create geographies of limitation as his traveling body refuses to remain in a place of silence.

As a living, breathing, contemporary embodiment of Antigone's hybridity, Avendaño's public demands for justice to properly grieve and bury his brother are powerful acts of defiance. They do not stop with his performance in Barcelona but continue through international media coverage, his personal blog, Facebook, and other social media outlets. Via myriad platforms, Lukas Avendaño constantly calls attention to the state's refusal to follow its own laws. As Prieto Stambaugh points out, Avendaño's performances and political articulations are "not mainly concerned within bringing about visibility but rather with the attainment of justice" so that others do not feel the pain he and his family have suffered.[155] The artist's search for his brother's body in the face of rebuttals and ignorance, like the actions of Antigone, are "loud proclamations of grief [that] presuppose a domain of the ungrievable."[156] Butler suggests that the Greek figure's transgressions, both gendered and political, prompt Creon to wonder "who is the man here?"[157] To respond to Creon's question, I ask: Does it matter who the man here is? If the man in Creon's question is meant to be the king and, by extension the Mexican state that does not protect its citizens and violates its own laws, should we not consider alternative structures of gender, power, and leadership? Perhaps we should be compelled to accept Avendaño's *muxeidad* and insistence on juridical procedure as a model of participation and power in Mexico's public sphere.

A VISUAL TABLEAU OF RESISTANCE

Lukas Avendaño's public insistence that local and federal officials were intentionally inactive in Bruno's case sharply differs from his silence while performing *Buscando a Bruno*. For approximately an hour, sometimes more, sometimes less, Avendaño sits in a simple chair with his body facing forward. Seemingly frozen, his feet are planted on the ground as his legs rest slightly open and his torso is completely erect. Despite the seemingly simple positioning of his body, the artist showcases "the art of condensing emotion in expressive gestures, installing silent rage in his body, projecting into the public sphere."[158] The artist's left palm rests facing upward while his right arm firmly cradles a photo of Bruno against his right side. The color photo is approximately the same size of Avendaño's torso, drawing our attention to Bruno, who smiles at the camera and wears a striped blue-and-white polo shirt. Above and below Bruno's body, that of a lively young man, are

FIGURE 3.5. Lukas Avendaño and Ileana Diéguez, author of *Cuerpos sin duelo*, walk down a street following a presentation of *¿Dónde está Bruno?*, Oaxaca City, Oaxaca, Mexico, 2018. Photo by Edith Morales.

words that read: "SEGUIMOS BUSCANDO A BRUNO AVENDAÑO. POR LAS Y LOS DESAPARECIDOS EN MÉXICO" (WE CONTINUE SEARCHING FOR BRUNO AVENDAÑO. FOR ALL THE MEN AND WOMEN DISAPPEARED IN MEXICO). The only part of Avendaño's body that moves during the piece is his neck, allowing his head to slowly rotate from side to side. Next to artist is a single empty chair, a symbolic gesture that underscores Bruno's absence and also functions to invite a series of prearranged, and sometimes improvised, bodies to join Avendaño in still silence.[159] Those who sit with the artist do not fill the void left in the wake of Bruno's disappearance but instead become collaborators in this act of grief and commemoration. Linking hands, and even momentary gazes, these participants become fellow mourners, extensions of the performer's body and pain. Those who participate do so for a series of minutes and then depart, once again leaving the empty seat as a painful reminder of Bruno's absence. There seems to be no set length of time for arrivals or departures, nor a predetermined number of bodies who join Avendaño in his space. The slow pace of each collaborator emphasizes a lack of urgency. These moments of solitude and shared pain are savored, unhurried; they seem to interrupt a logic of linear time, making it feel plastic, drawn out, elongated. This is sustained by the formation of a *communitas de dolor* and the sonic accompaniment that enables the performance of a redressive act.

Before analyzing the sounds of the performance, I want to first acknowledge how the visual elements of the piece contribute to the manipulation of chronologies and geographies. Once in place, the seated bodies in *Buscando a Bruno* become a living tableau that evokes Frida Kahlo's *Las dos Fridas* (*Two Fridas*) and the 1989 rendition of the painting by Las Yeguas del Apocalipsis (Pedro Lemebel and Francisco Casas).[160] The shared performance strategies across the three versions take shape in myriad ways. Kahlo's painting depicts an internal emotional and identitarian struggle: one of her represents her European past, dressed in white, while the other, dressed in colorful *tehuana* clothing, conveys her *mestiza* identity rooted in her mother's Zapotec heritage.[161] A blood-filled vein connects the seated bodies, taking all the blood from the European Frida and giving it to the Tehuana Frida. While the European Frida cuts off the blood supply with a pair of surgical scissors, the Tehuana holds in her palm a small photo of Diego Rivera as a child. The image was revived by Las Yeguas del Apocalipsis during the last years of Augusto Pinochet's dictatorship: the two artists wear light makeup all over their faces, have both painted on Kahlo's iconic unibrow, and style their hair atop their heads just like Kahlo. Both wear *tehuana* skirts, Casas in white and Lemebel in color, but neither wears a top. Their bare chests expose their masculinity, invoking an aesthetic of gender hybridity not present in Kahlo's original painting. These chests also reveal painted-on hearts connected by plastic tubing wrapped around their torsos. The blood-like liquid in the tubing "shared" by these two bodies becomes a very real symbol of both life and death. In the context of Chile, where homosexuals were persecuted, and the 1980s, the height of the global AIDS crisis, Las Yeguas' *Las dos Fridas* is a rebellious act of resistance and survival.

The duality and citationality that Avendaño creates in *Buscando a Bruno* began with a 2017 photo performance called *Lukas y José* (Lukas and José).[162] Incorporating imagery from *Réquiem para un alcaraván*, Avendaño appears as both Lukas and José in the photo, just as Kahlo is doubled in her painting. On the right, José wears a black-and-yellow *tehuana* skirt and colorful ceremonial *itsmeño huipil grande* covering his entire head, chest, and torso, leaving only the face exposed.[163] Lukas, on the left, wears a vibrant pink *tehuana* skirt, no top, and pink ribbon in his hair. As this tableau evolved into the foundation for *Buscando a Bruno*, the artist chose not to wear colorful clothing. Rather, in many renditions, he wears a black *tehuana* skirt and shawl, just as he did on his visit to the Mexican consulate in Barcelona. This look is emblematic of his Indigenous connection to the region and his state of mourning. The one exception to this aesthetic is the June 2019 performance at the MUAC. Avendaño still wears the black skirt, but also dons a white traditional *huipil grande* in which "the wide lace peplum is thrown back over the head, with the rest—collar and sleeves—hanging in the back."[164] He covers his entire body in a cream-colored body suit, erasing

FIGURE 3.6. Lukas Avendaño sits in total stillness and silence, his entire body covered by a white bodysuit, holding hands with a volunteer performer. *Buscando a Bruno*, Museo Universitario de Arte Moderno, Mexico City, Mexico, 2019. Photo by Julio Pantoja, Hemispheric Institute of Performance and Politics.

his identity. At the same time, his body's clothing demarcates a Zapotec origin and, coupled with the black hues, the sentiment of grief. In contrast to Avendaño, his silent accomplices don colorful *tehuana* skirts and vibrant flower crowns in their hair during both 2019 performances. They embody vibrancy, life, futurity. Though there are no painted hearts or veins that connect the bodies, their interconnected hands signal a transfer of energy, compassion, and healing. Informed by his own conception of *muxeidad* and by Lemebel's and Casas's *Las dos Fridas*, Avendaño and his partners appear bare-chested, regardless of gender. In effect, these collaborators join the artist in his transgressive efforts to enact mourning for a body deemed ungrievable by authorities.

EDGAR CARTAS OROZCO

The visual image created by Avendaño, the empty chair, and the accompanying bodies may very well be primordial for the artist, but the soundtrack concretizes *Buscando a Bruno* as a ritual act of mourning. This soundtrack has taken various forms depending on the performance. In Barcelona, the performance occurred in absolute silence, but in Oaxaca City Avendaño's prerecorded voice read personal letters he wrote to Bruno following his disappearance. And in both Mexico City performances, Avendaño is accompanied by the music of a single trumpet played by Edgar Cartas Orozco.

Unfortunately, there is no full recording of the Barcelona intervention or the piece's enactment in Oaxaca City. Thus I focus my attention on the two 2019 Mexico City renditions, as I have been able to watch a video of the full performance at the Museo el Chopo and was present for the intervention at the MUAC.[165] My intention in spotlighting these two performances is to showcase how the trumpet music reverberates through the space, connecting spectators and bystanders and becoming the basis for the piece's soundtrack against death.

Edgar Cartas Orozco was born, grew up, and lives on the outskirts of Tehuantepec, Oaxaca, in the small town of Santa María Mixtequilla. His musical career began at the age of twelve, when he joined the well-known regional Banda Princesa Donahí de Tehuantepec.[166] He performed with the group for eleven years, eventually rising to lead musical arranger and even director.[167] After briefly studying at Oaxaca's Escuela de Bellas Artes and the UNAM in Mexico City, Cartas Orozco settled on a degree in music education at the Universidad Veracruzana–Xalapa. Upon returning to his hometown, he formed and currently directs his own group called Orquesta el Gato Cartas y su combo. Additionally, over the last decades, Cartas Orozco has been passionate about teaching the youth in the Santa María area the value of musical knowledge. He is also passionate about conserving Oaxacan musical traditions that have not necessarily been preserved in formal archives or written scores.[168]

The relationship between Avendaño and Cartas Orozco is professional and deeply personal. The two have worked together for more than twelve years, first collaborating on *Réquiem para un alcaraván* in 2009. Together, they talked through Avendaño's ideas about how to express his *muxe* transformation through visual imagery and dance choreography. From there, Cartas Orozco intuited melodies and compositional structures. For example, at the end of *Réquiem para un alcaraván*, Avendaño's body enters the final stage of life: death. Cartas Orozco chose to accompany this moment with "música sacra del Istmo, música fúnebre, de luto" (sacred music from the Istmo, funeral music, music of mourning). From this final scene, Avendaño created *Buscando a Bruno*, departing from the notion of funeral processions and regional music that conjures mourning.[169] Because the pair have worked closely, Avendaño turned to Cartas Orozco for this commemorative act for Bruno because he does not have to explain himself or what he wants. The two share what Avendaño calls "cultural baggage"; they understand the social function of music, and in this case, funeral music commonly played in the Istmo. Their collaboration has become a natural extension of their shared sociocultural and geographic experiences.[170]

A TRUMPET'S WAILS: AVENDAÑO'S LAMENTS AND RITUAL SOUND

Scholarship on musical practice in Oaxaca is limited, often attending to pre-Colombian findings or state-supported musical groups. In either case, the recurring argument in extant research seems to be that music has historically and consistently played an important role in Oaxacan social life. For example, Sara Barber and Mireya Olvera Sánchez analyze an engraved Yugüe flute found in an ancient burial site in the Río Verde Valley of Oaxaca. In their work, they hypothesize that "music was not simply an aural accompaniment to certain kinds of social action," but an integral part of cultural production."[171] Similarly, Charles Heath surveys the development and social importance of the State Band of Oaxaca through its instrumentation and repertoire. By drawing from European, national, and regional influences, the State Band has created a distinctive Oaxacan sound, recognizable for its brassy, minor-scale tones.[172] While many of the musicians Heath references are men, Xóchitl C. Chávez's research makes a critical intervention into the field, drawing attention to the Indigenous women from Mixe and Zapotec backgrounds that participate in music-making practices. For example, Chávez highlights the all-female wind band, Banda Femenil Regional "Mujeres del Viento Florido" from the Sierra Mixe region and explores musical communities forged as a result of transmigratory routes between this region in Oaxaca and Los Angeles, California.[173] Perhaps most crucial to my considerations in this chapter, however, is Kristin Norget's *Days of Death, Days of Life: Ritual in the Popular Culture of Oaxaca*. Based on years of ethnographic research, Norget's scholarship is the most comprehensive study of funeral practices in the region to date and while music is not her central argument, she recognizes its presence in funerary practice. She observes that "in Oaxaca, biological death is not coincident with the extinction of someone's life as a social actor: the dead continue to exist in the lives of their surviving relatives."[174] Norget goes on, "to give such a voice or presence to the dead is, in a sense, to return them to life ... not as ancestral ghosts or spirits but as persons who linger as present memories," affirming how funeral rites can work "against death."[175] My intention is not to delve into beliefs about the dead but to highlight how the finality of death can be circumvented through social practice by suggesting *Buscando a Bruno*'s sonic acts of memory work against death. By extension, I posit that Cartas Orozco's soundtrack serves to refuse the state's efforts to derealize Bruno Avendaño.

During the performance, Cartas Orozco performs a series of funeral songs often heard at memorials and during Semana Santa (Holy Week); the songs could be characterized as sounding "bleak, somber, desolate, despondent, poignant, sorrowful, melancholic, autumnal, or yearning."[176] As crowds form around the performance to watch the visual spectacle of Avendaño, the chair, and his rotating partners, they are also drawn to the metallic sadness emanating from Cartas Orozco's instrument. He manipulates his sounds, sometimes using a brass mute, walking around the space, or even amplifying the trumpet's sound via a microphone and stereo speaker. Even though the performances at Museo el Chopo and the MUAC were outside, the trumpet's vibrations filled the area, reaching the crowd as well as Avendaño and his partners. The *communitas* formed around this performance of mourning, through their "sight-lines" and "ear-lines," as George Home-Cook would say, are clearly able to identify the source of musical sound.[177] And yet the openness of the MUAC esplanade or front patio at the Museo el Chopo allows people to move freely around the performance, adjusting their viewpoints and their earpoints. These "different positions require different modes of attention," as our ears strain to hear the music or as the music invades our bodily cavities.[178] In relation to *Buscando a Bruno*, all of this depends on where we are in relation to Cartas Orozco and the shared act of listening to his musical choices brings us into relation, turning us into earwitnesses of Bruno's "musical eulogy."[179] Bruin-Mollenhorst describes the way mourners gather at funerals and "set aside their own musical preferences and listen" to the sonic choices meant to represent the deceased.[180] The same occurs during the hour-long commemoration of Bruno Avendaño. Cartas Orozco and Avendaño turned to *música sacra* (sacred music) and *marchas fúnebres* (funeral marches) linked to the Istmo of Tehuantepec, not necessarily as personalized compositions to fit Bruno's life, likes, and dislikes but to represent his origins and last known appearance.

In place of Avendaño's verbal proclamations of defiance and grief, the trumpet emits the artist's unwillingness to accept the state's negligence and ineptitude. The music, emulating a sadness, as if approximating wailing laments, also becomes the sonic embodiment of Avendaño's pain. It is as if Avendaño and Cartas Orozco sonically materialize Rossana Reguillo's assertion that "in the face of these *violencias*, language fails, exhausting itself in its attempt to produce an explanation or a reason."[181] To illustrate this, I home in on two songs in particular: "Luto por derecho" and "Dolor profundo," both by Atilano Morales Jiménez. "Luto por derecho" is considered the masterpiece of Morales Jiménez, a prolific musician and composer originally from San Blas Atempa, not far from Tehuantepec, Oaxaca.[182] The composer wrote the song in 1921 to honor his friend Valeriano López, who was assassinated while serving as municipal president of San Blas.[183] In the song's title, Morales Jiménez declares his just claim to grieve this personal loss, just as Avendaño professes his grief for Bruno. Furthermore, the parallel between the murder of a public figure and Bruno's forced disappearance while serving as a naval officer is clear. The second composition, "Dolor profundo," has become one of the most emblematic funeral songs of the Zapotec region, played while moving the dead to their final resting place.[184] As the title suggests, the composition is meant to audibly translate "the mercurial dimension of emotional experience, the process of feeling."[185] It is meant to translate unutterable pain and sadness of those who mourn. Given that at the time of the Avendaño's 2019 performances, there was still no body to put to rest, Cartas Orozco's musical interpretation transforms "Dolor profundo" into a powerful, symbolic funeral rite. Moreover, including these songs as part of the musical eulogy transforms them into both a reclamation of the state's culpability in Bruno's case and "a device for engaging in emotion work" as we collectively grieve the dead, despite their missing bodies.[186]

Besides these well-known compositions, many of the other pieces Cartas Orozco interprets are numbered minuets and *marchas* also attributed to Morales Jiménez. These songs are commonly heard throughout the region, but many have never been formally written down or archived. This is a music passed down from generation to generation that Cartas Orozco learned and memorized as a young boy.[187] These embodied acts of transfer, as Diana Taylor would call them, depend heavily on the ear as a means of connecting to musical production and commemorative practice. During *Buscando a Bruno*, as a way of honoring this tradition, Cartas Orozco plays entirely from memory and avoids a set list. Rather, he improvises the musical selections to resonate with the energies he perceives from Avendaño and the public. The melancholic and somber energies become affective wavelengths that not only bring the musician into contact with the audience but also integrate all of us in the space into a state of feeling loss. They solidify the funereal ambiance. There are also moments when Cartas Orozco's pace has little to do with Avendaño or the public; it is determined by his own physicality and emotional state.[188] Performing in open-air spaces, with little added amplification, the trumpet's silences remind us of Cartas Orozco's aliveness. As listeners, we become more aware of the musician as he tires and experiences emotional strain, leading him to take breaks. These reminders also highlight the silence of our collective bodies as we remember Bruno's shortened life.

These silences throughout *Buscando a Bruno* create space for nonperformative sounds to permeate the performance, promoting a sonic collision between the ritual and nonritual acts. Although she does not speak of the performance itself, Norget states that Oaxacan death-related rituals "are not ritual arenas carefully cut away from other domains of living."[189] In a similar fashion, *Buscando a Bruno*'s music brings ritual remembrance into the frames of daily life and, by extension, creates "an atmosphere of sacredness even in secular settings."[190] Performed outside and in public spaces, the piece disrupts the quotidian pace of normalcy. It injects a brief interlude of mourning into daily life. I like to think about *Buscando a Bruno* in this way to highlight the symbiotic way ritual time impinges on nonritual spaces and vice versa. The Museo el Chopo's patio is surrounded by two major Mexico City avenues (Insurgentes Norte and Ribera del Cosme), and the MUAC esplanade is part of the UNAM's Centro Cultural Universitario, surrounded by numerous buildings and open to anyone walking by. The way noises, such as honking cars, growling busses, and street vendors become part of the Museo el Chopo performance and the way ambient conversations weave their way into the MUAC rendition add to the sonic complexities of the piece rather than "undo or even shatter sound's organization."[191] The various aural cues, in and beyond the performance, become reminders of the materiality of the living, a painful contrast to Bruno's immateriality. Though Turner claims that the liminality and ephemerality of rituals cause them to "never be much more than a subversive flicker," I maintain that Avendaño's performative intrusion into public space is perhaps enough of a flicker to become a "germ of future social developments, of societal change."[192] The commemorative ritual, musical selection, and temporary *communitas de dolor* refuse to accept a normalized reality of forced disappearances.

CONCLUSION

The ephemeral communities created via Luna's and Avendaño's pieces construct a space that fosters collectively engaged healing practices. Unlike the pieces analyzed in the previous chapter, *Réquiem #3: Fosas Cuerpo / Body Graves* and *Buscando a Bruno* are reparative acts that aim to bring closure to situations of forced disappearance when there is no body to mourn. While Avendaño's work is a personal response to his brother's forced disappearance, Luna's staging relates the experiences of Mexico's collective of mothers, sisters, and loved ones. Both performances embody the nation's Antigones, those who refuse to accept the state's insistence that without a body there is neither proof of life nor death and, hence, no mournable being. Emulating the Greek figure from at least twenty-five hundred years ago, Mexico's Antigones maintain that genealogy of resistance, trespassing into the political sphere, refusing to accept that some lives are destined to become collateral damage so that war can triumph. These bodies impose themselves on the public realm, searching for their loved ones and endlessly clamoring for justice. However, as I have detailed in this chapter, Avendaño's and Luna's artistic interpretations occur in total verbal silence, instead leveraging soundscapes to relate anguish and loss in a way that transcends linguistic capabilities. The sonic accompaniment of trumpets, bells, whistles, thunder sheets, and more fills the performance spaces, becoming a haunting register of what I have called sounds against death, aural efforts to combat the annihilation that comes with death and the state's insane disavowal of ever having existed at all.

CHAPTER 4

Soundtracks of an (After)life

Radical Geographies of Hope and Survival

One.
Two.
Three.
Four.
Five.
Six.
Seven.
Eight.
Nine.
Ten.
Eleven.
. . .

How do I begin a chapter on feminicide and trans feminicide without falling into platitudes and trite refrains? After sitting with this question for months, I still do not have an adequate answer. There are too many names to list, and by the time this is published, some of those will have been forgotten and replaced by even more heinous acts of violence against female and feminized bodies. So, I settled on allowing the eleven women murdered each day to occupy the first page. This is undoubtedly an act that falls short of recognizing the toll of feminicide and trans feminicide on the Mexican female psyche. All the same, my hope is that the numbers give pause, cause discomfort, prompt curiosity, and provoke rage. I suppose I have also taken a cue from the three pieces I consider in this chapter and employ a *teatro-*

cabaret (cabaret theater) methodology. Just like the works I analyze—*Ni una menos* (Not One Woman Less, 2019) by Las Pussy Queers, La Mafia Cabaret's *El Desierto de Las Leonas* (The Desert of the Lionesses, 2017), and *La Prietty Guoman* (The Prietty Woman, 2017) by César Enríquez—I am going to get straight to the point; perhaps the most adequate way to confront the topic of feminicide and trans feminicide is to expose the open, painful wound that motivates artistic defiance.

RESISTING FEMINICIDE: RADICAL GEOGRAPHIES OF HOPE AND SURVIVAL

The three *teatro-cabaret* pieces I consider in this chapter respond to urgent and much needed conversations about violence perpetrated against women. Diana Russell and Jill Radford are two of the earliest scholars to research and document accounts of violence against women, especially violence ending in death, which they referred to as femicide. Russell recounts first hearing the term used in 1974, and she began using it in 1976 when she testified in front of the International Tribunal on Crimes against Women about the misogynist murder of women.[1] Following a similar trajectory, but with a regional focus on the UK, Radford began to integrate the term into her scholarship as well. Together, their edited volume, *Femicide: The Politics of Woman Killing* (1992), has become a key reference for scholars researching gendered violence. The collection of essays established femicide as the appropriate term to signify the killing of women and described its various categories:

> racist femicide (when black women are killed by White men); homophobic femicide, or lesbicide (when lesbians are killed by heterosexual men); marital femicide (when women are killed by their husbands); femicide committed outside the home by a stranger; serial femicide; and mass femicide.[2]

Their work also expands this list to include female deaths resulting from medical procedures, infanticide, and the intentional neglect of women and girls that ends in death. In sum, their work provided the backbone for articulating and describing the innumerable ways female and female-presenting bodies suffer undue harm.

Mexican scholar, activist, and politician Marcela Lagarde y de Los Ríos further expanded the ideas of Radford and Russell when she introduced the concept of femicide into writings in Spanish. As Lagarde y de Los Ríos translated the term, she settled on *feminicidio* rather than *femicidio*. Both terms are used throughout Latin America, sometimes interchangeably, though their meanings are distinct. It is not my intention to delve into why particular countries use *femicidio* over *feminicidio*, but I note that *feminicidio* is commonly used throughout Mexico and, following Lagarde y de Los Ríos's logic, it is the term that I employ throughout this chapter:

> *femicidio* is homologous to homicide and solely means the homicide of women. For this reason, I preferred *feminicidio* in order to differentiate from *femicidio* and to name the ensemble of violations of women's human rights, which contain the crimes against and the disappearances of women. I proposed that all these be considered as "crimes against humanity."³

In flipping the model for the way in which theory and ideas generally flow from North-to-South, *feminicidio* became translated into English as "feminicide." Inspired by Lagarde y de Los Ríos's argument that "*Feminicide* is genocide against women, and it occurs when the historical conditions generate social practices that allow for violent attempts against the integrity, health, liberties, and lives of girls and women," many scholars throughout the English-speaking world have opted for the term.⁴ For example, Rosa-Linda Fregoso and Cynthia Bejarano argue for using feminicide in their edited collection of essays, *Terrorizing Women: Feminicide in the Americas*. In asserting that "low-intensity warfare waged on women's bodies . . . is now routine in many Latin American countries," Fregoso and Bejarano advocate for studying the killing of women as genocide, and hence they give it a proper title that does not diminish its importance.⁵

Framing feminicide as low-grade warfare against both female and female-presenting bodies certainly fits the case of contemporary Mexico. For many, the border town of Ciudad Juárez, Mexico, comes to mind as the epicenter of feminicide, with 1,779 women murdered between 1993 and 2018, and thousands more disappeared during that time.⁶ The countless academic, cinematic, journalistic, musical, and literary productions dedicated to the violence against women has most certainly cemented the city's notoriety. In her research related to the missing and murdered women of Juárez, Julia Monárrez Fragoso declares that a crucial element to these crimes is the way they cement "the relationship of inequality between the sexes: the gender superiority of man over the gender subordination of woman, misogyny, control, and sexism."⁷ In particular, official rhetoric surrounding the female body ingrains a divide between the "good" woman, the one who remains home and fulfills her familial duties, and the "bad" woman, the one who exists within public spaces and, as a result, perhaps provoked her own deadly fate.[8] Not only does this conceptualization around gender become central to the dynamics of violence that assassinate a woman's character and body, but it also reproduces structures of impunity.[9] This is what Rita Laura Segato refers to as the basis for a pedagogy of cruelty: "la repetición de la escena violenta produce un efecto de normalización de un pasaje de crueldad" (the repetition of violent images leads to normalizing acts of cruelty).[10] Women's bodies are converted into landscapes, territories that become the mechanism to express the language of power and violence through mutilation, dismemberment, disappearance, and death (69). For Segato, neither *femicidio* nor *feminicidio* are adequate terms. Instead, she proposes *femigenocidio* to emphasize the intentionality and large-scale collective perpetuation of violence against women as akin to genocide. She states:

> El término *femigenocidio* quedaría reservado para los crímenes que, por su cualidad de sistemáticos e impersonales, tienen por objetivo específico la destrucción de las mujeres (y los hombres feminizados) solamente por ser mujeres sin que haya posibilidad, y, como he señalado, de personalizar o individualizar ni el móvil de la autoría ni la relación entre perpetrador y víctima.[11]

> *The term femigenocidio would be reserved for those crimes which, for their systematic and impersonal quality, have the specific objective of destroying women (and feminine men) solely for being women without the possibility, as I have noted, of personalizing or individualizing either the motive or the relationship between the perpetrator and victim.*

This definition is terrifyingly accurate when looking at Mexico as a whole. Ciudad Juárez is no longer the most dangerous place in Mexico for women. All of Mexico is. Between 1990 and 2016, 46,525 women were reported murdered according to "official" reports; that is one woman every four hours.[12] An independent report prepared by the Instituto Nacional de Mujeres (Inmujeres; National Institute of Women), the Comisión Nacional para Prevenir y Erradicar la Violencia contra las Mujeres (Conavim; National Commision for the Prevention and Erradication of Violence Against Women), and the NGO, Mujeres México, found that between 1990 and 2019, 56,000 women were murdered.[13] In 2022, of the 3,754 women murdered, only 947, or 33.7 percent, were categorized as feminicides.[14] At the time I write this, in 2023, between ten and eleven women are murdered every day in Mexico, and as the statistics make clear, the deaths of female and feminized bodies are rarely considered feminicide and justice is almost never served. Moreover, violence toward women is only exacerbated in situations where the body does not fit a "normalized" vision of the female/male binary. Between 2007 to

2018, 45 feminicides targeting trans women were reported in Veracruz, making it the most dangerous state in the nation to be trans, and, 422 trans feminicides were reported in all of Mexico.[15] Information on trans feminicides is difficult to procure, but the numbers suggest that the violence continues to rise. In 2020, Mexico registered 43 trans feminicides, 55 were recorded in 2021, and 24 were reported in 2022, the year that Mexico City also officially recognized the murder of a trans woman as a trans feminicide for the first time.[16] On a national scale, violence toward trans women is compounded by another layer of brutality: most victims are not even catalogued as female and do not factor into the aforementioned statistics. It is also worth noting that these figures only scratch the surface of the violence female bodies face in Mexico, as they do not account for rapes, beatings, and aggressions, nor do they account for the violence that is never reported.

To consider what is at stake in studying performances that underscore the painful topic of feminicides and trans feminicides, I turn to scholars who analyze systematic and structural efforts that strip bodies of their humanity. Deploying these notions in *Gore Capitalism*, Sayak Valencia outlines the negative and violent impact that neoliberal and capitalist practices have had on Mexico. Detailing how "the many instances of dismembering and disembowelment" are very often connected to "organized crime, gender and the predatory uses of bodies," Valencia offers a gruesome, yet accurate, reflection on the different ways the nation's citizens have suffered due to Calderón's War on Drugs.[17] In the case of female and female-presenting bodies, they are exponentially more vulnerable to becoming a means to express "un tenebroso código de guerra" (a sinister language of war) that operates as an historical and contemporary practice of atrocity toward female subjects.[18] Much like the motivating questions behind my previous chapter on Mexico's disappeared, I feel obliged once again to ask whose lives and deaths matter? Who is worth publicly recognizing and mourning during Mexico's time of bellicose violence? Homing in on gendered violence, Melissa Wright suggests that female bodies in Mexico are especially vulnerable to becoming casualties of war because of official "discursive and material mechanisms for making women and the places and processes associated with them invisible, outside of history and geography, and thereby, unknowable and unthinkable."[19] And yet, the family members of missing and murdered women activate the "political potential of geographical imaginaries" by participating in alternative structures, such as protests, the arts, journalism, and more, to resist the masculine hierarchies of power and, by extension, the cruelty they inflict on female and female-presenting bodies.[20]

Resisting official discursive mechanisms that seek to make missing or dead female citizens unthinkable, *Ni una menos*, *El Desierto de Las Leonas*, and *La Prietty Guoman* are creative initiatives that firmly situate the victims of feminicide and trans feminicide within Mexican history and geography. As pieces that include dark-skinned, trans, lesbian, femme, straight, historical, and ficticious protagonists, they challenge what Wright calls the "myth of the disposable third world woman." In Mexico, this myth generally takes the form of a young woman who "comes to personify the meaning of human disposability: someone who eventually evolves into a living state of worthlessness."[21] These onstage female and trans female characters, however, will not be reduced to the tragic ending that eleven women experience each day. Rather, these protagonists assert their presence and argue that they are, in fact, not disposable citizens. Moreover, representing a spectrum of queer and racialized female bodies, they seek to break the cycle of violence by actively creating "subjectivities that resist feeding into the static loop of white, heterosexual, masculinist formulas."[22] Each of the pieces I consider allow the bodies onstage to become territories that defy acts of violence, transforming into a "terreno-territorio de la propia acción bélica" (territory-terrain of the very same warlike action).[23] That is to say, their female and female-presenting bodies refuse to submit to the cultural passivity and reproduction of cruelty. In doing so, their performances enact feminist solidarity across space and time, forcibly displacing the misogynist control over their ability to exist.

This chapter focuses on the way musical numbers in the aforementioned pieces give the onstage female and trans female protagonists agency to perform alternative visions of violent and untimely deaths. As representational of Mexico's youngest generation of *cabareterxs*, their work establishes new artistic methods and creates pathways of dialogue within *teatro-cabaret*. At the same time, as I discussed in the first chapter in this book, music is an indispensable tool for artists to express dissident discourse.[24] Inspired by Segato's notion of the body as territory and Wright's work on geographies of resistance, I analyze the way *Ni una menos, El Desierto de Las Leonas*, and *La Prietty Guoman* formulate and reconfigure space in the present, past, and imagined futures in order to offer security and safety.[25] The geographies these performances imagine should not have to be "radical," but given the current state of affairs in Mexico, they are. To imagine, communicate, and manifest their respective terrains, the three *teatro-cabaret* acts unsettle the idea that with death comes silence and disappearance by allowing victims of trans/feminicide the ability to communicate from beyond the grave. This approach also echoes how José Esteban Muñoz conceptualizes futurity and utopia in relation to the present. For queer and nonnormative bodies—and, as I suggest, women and trans women in Mexico—"the here and now is a prison house" of violence and humiliation.²⁶ In staging female and trans female (after)lives, these performances "transform contexts and/or situations of vulnerability and/or subalterity into possibilities for action and personal power, thus upending hierarchies of oppression."²⁷ In what follows, I argue that by way of musical selection, the performers and their onstage characters destabilize chronologies of life and death, simultaneously manifesting what I am calling radical geographies of hope and survival.

LAS PUSSY QUEERS AND *NI UNA MENOS*

The burlesque duo known as Las Pussy Queers is comprised of Irakere Lima and Larissa Polaco. Similar to Pussy Riot, the group's name shocks spectators out of complacency; spectators are immediately invited to consider their own internalized heteronormative expectations surrounding burlesque and the female body. While Polaco self-identifies as a queer cisgender woman, incorporating the word "queer" was a conscious decision to conjure a defiant Otherness. At the same time, Lima and Polaco decided to reclaim the word "pussy" as a means of reaffirming strength and pride in their femininity. The two began working together in 2016, blending Lima's theater and cabaret background with Polaco's production expertise.²⁸ They presented their work from 2016 to 2018 at the International Cabaret Festival, held annually in Mexico City. In 2019, they performed as part of the Tiempo de Mujeres festival and were invited to perform as part of the Hemispheric Institute of Politics and Performance Encuentro of 2019 held in Mexico City. The two turned to burlesque as an act of feminist reappropriation of a genre often thought of as purely sexual and heteronormative. According to Las Pussy Queers, burlesque allows them to play with eroticism, "pero al revés, cuando no funciona. Justo esos intentos de ser sensuales, de erotizar y fracasar" (but in reverse, when it does not work. Precisely those moments when sensuality and eroticism fail).²⁹ The drive was born out of Lima's own theater experiences, where women were often asked to undress or appear nude onstage. These requests, made almost entirely by male directors, made her feel as if they dehumanized the female student or actor.³⁰ Departing from this perspective of nudity as an act of invizibilizing women, Lima and Polaco deploy burlesque techniques and choreographies to manipulate expectations related to gender (mis)representation, female sexuality, queerness, and feminicide.

Motivated by their desire to use *teatro-cabaret* to resignify pathways of self-expression, Las Pussy Queers develop choreographies that allow spectators to see themselves reflected onstage. This can mean sensuality or romantic love, but it also means the way the Mexican female body experiences daily threats of gendered violence. Only six minutes long, the cabaret-burlesque piece *Ni una menos* is divided into two segments that reflect escalating violence toward the female body.[31] To express these experiences to their audience, the piece conjoins Maldita Vecindad, Mexican pioneers of *rock en español*, and Chocolate Remix, heralded as "the lesbian reggaeton artist taking on the 'supermachos.'"[32] As the soundtrack plays, the theatre space is completely black. Relying on Maldita Vecindad's "Morenaza," the first half of the piece articulates what Lima and Polanco describe as "el acoso callejero" (street harassment) that plagues women walking down the street, riding the bus, in taxis, and on the metro. During these first several minutes, as the song plays out, the two women onstage embody the uncomfortable sensations we feel when men "nos desnudan con la mirada" (undress us with their eyes), shout, and even try to grab us. The second half of the piece is a sharp departure into the realm of thumping reggaetón bass and the raspy voice of Chocolate Remix's "Ni una menos." As the singer decries "Not one woman less," the performance showcases what happens to the female body once she is derealized, erased, silenced. Effectively, the piece is an audiovisual testament to the terrors of the everyday geographies of Mexico.

REFUSING DEREALIZATION WITH FEMINIST REGGAETÓN: "NI UNA MENOS"

Before the piece begins, an announcement is played over a loudspeaker requesting that everyone put away their cell phones so that the piece can be performed in total darkness. For Las Pussy Queers, "justo estamos enfocando este espectáculo para que la gente lo disfrute a través de los sentidos" (in this piece, we consciously want the audience to enjoy it via their senses).[33] Enveloped in blackness, it is hard to see anything, including your own hands. However, there is no sensation of being alone. The auditory triggers seem to ring out louder throughout the space and in my own ears; every cough, chair dragged across the floor, and sigh heard clearly. Before anything or anyone appears onstage, the first beats of "Morenaza" by Maldita Vecindad play. High-pitched sound of clave sticks beating together mark the beginning of the song. Soon, the booming sounds of the urban city reverberate throughout the theatre. Male voices shouting words like "oralé," "esa," and whistling in the blackness become a disorienting whirlwind. These sounds transport the audience from the Coyoacán theatre to the bustling streets of downtown Mexico City.

As one of the foundational *rock en español* bands, Maldita Vecindad's songs form part of a countercultural musical imaginary geographically tied to Mexico City's urban landscapes. Emerging from the rubble of the 1985 earthquake, Maldita Vecindad became the one of the nation's first household names, and their first album, *Maldita Vecindad y los Hijos del Quinto Patio* (Maldita Vecindad and the Boys from the 5th Ward, 1989) was one of the first CDs that came out in Mexico.[34] From these early days, Aldo Acuña explains that the group's goal was to use music as a vehicle for telling stories about daily life in the capital city.[35] The group never set out to produce songs that could be interpreted as political commentaries, but by exposing the realities of living on the margins of elite society, Maldita Vecindad did just that. Blending samples and various musical styles, Maldita Vecindad's stories are often encased within playful, danceable rhythms, making them easy on the ears. Played over radio waves, on the streets, and at private parties for decades, Maldita Vecindad's songs are a sonically engrained part of the Mexico City experience. Broadly speaking, however, the band stresses the urban male experience. With songs that showcase el Pachuco, los chavos, and even El Santo, their sonicscapes functioned to give agency to and recognize marginalized masculine archetypes.[36] Studying their discography, it is easy to understand Nohemy Solórzano-Thompson declaration that "*la vecindad* of Maldita Vecindad has no space for women."[37] "Morenaza," then, is a prime example of how the group imagines women as objects for the taking. Never giving the female protagonist of the song a face, a name, or even a voice, the song exemplifies how "women are only vehicles that allow male agency to occur."[38] This male agency is a prime example of "acoustic patriarchy," defined by Anthony Rasmussen as "the sonorous enforcement of unequal access to public spaces, one that privileges the free movement of men and restricts women."[39] As in the case of "Morenaza," Maldita Vecindad's musical repertoire reproduces urban power structures, such as the sounds of harassment toward female bodies, reinforcing gendered abuses.

Being that "Morenaza" blatantly fetishizes the female body in public spaces, and having been written with Mexico City in mind, it seems like a perfect choice for Las Pussy Queers. Yet, Lima and Polanco describe the process of choosing a song as difficult and emotionally draining. According to the duo, listening to what seemed like an endless playlist of songs that went from bad to worse, they felt constantly depleted of energy and hope.[40] Finally, though, Lima and Polanco settled on "Morenaza," hoping it would allow spectators to connect with the lyrics in a new way. Betting on the fact that most of the Mexican viewers would know the song, Las Pussy Queers chose it because they were certain it would spark an immediate connection. At the same time, they did not want to simply create a sensation of recognition but instead sought to subvert expectations by highlighting the normalization of harassment as a daily occurrence for the Mexican female body.

In just four minutes, as "Morenaza" plays over loudspeakers, Las Pussy Queers puts on raw display the dehumanizing effect of the male gaze and sexual harassment. The song itself describes the way a man ogles with his eyes, and his words, a random woman on the street. Filling the space of El Vicio, the lyrics, booming male vocals, and upbeat rhythms of the song envelop and invade spectators' bodies. We cannot escape the reverberating sonic scene of street harassment and degradation. On stage, Las Pussy Queers respond to the male *voices en off*, feeling targeted by their words and their imagined gaze. And yet, their bodies do more than just react to the musical composition; they relate the listening strategies and constant calculations that women use when traveling through Mexico City. That is to say, the duo's silent choreography that accompanies "Morenaza" performs the cityscape's transformation into a hellish geography for women, one the male members of Maldita Vecindad sing so cheerily about.

During the song's first minute, as the audience hears clave sticks beating together and mostly inaudible conversation among men, a ghastly figure appears. Wearing an all-white outfit made up of a button-up shirt, skirt, knee-high socks, and gloves, her silhouette disrupts the dark, monochrome space. To ensure the audience understands that the figure is female, she wears a long, wispy pale wig, whose strands cascade down her shirt, and has glow-in-the dark paint on her nose, lips, and eyelashes. The female silhouette rapidly appears and disappears, searing through the vacant stage. From one side to the other, the woman's gestures perform the act of waving down a bus or taxi. Repeating this performance of frustration, the song's chorus begins, and the figure is center stage as she and the audience hear Maldita Vecindad's male vocals warn, "En las calles de la ciudad / Siempre tienes que aguantar / En el barrio o en el camion" (In the city's streets / You have to suck it up / In the 'hood or the bus). The onstage woman starts to feel increasingly more nervous about being alone on the street, constantly being overlooked by public transportation. Responding to her surroundings and the looming masculine *voices en off*, she adjusts her clothing, trying to cover and protect as much of her body as possible. Her efforts are in vain, though. The last line of the chorus ominously advises her, "Siempre tienes que oír la voz, y escucha escucha" (You must always hear the voice, and listen, listen). Then, a black hand emerges, and the woman's body becomes a territory to be dominated. Reaching across her torso to grope her breasts, this hand materializes the way a harasser's audible remarks violently penetrate her personal space. She is no longer in control of her own body but rather has been reduced to an object deemed possessable by an implied male counterpart.

In contrast to this horrific scene, the upbeat rhythm and male singing voice continue:

> Morenaza de mi alma por que tan sola vas
> Con este peloncito te puedes consolar
> Chaparrita preciosa dime qué pensó Dios
> Cuando en vez de naranjas dos melones te dio, te te dio . . .
>
> . . . Como dos gelatinas las meneas al altar
> Como dos cebollitas están para llorar
> No te enojes mi prieta de lo que oyes hablar
> Enojona y coqueta te queremos ahumar aun más[41]
>
> *Brown girl, my dear, why are you alone*
> *You can console yourself with those breasts of yours*
> *Precious short one, what was God thinking*
> *When he gave you melons instead of oranges . . .*
>
> *. . . Like two Jell-O figurines, the way you shake them is divine*
> *Like two onions, they make me cry*
> *Don't get upset about what I'm saying, brown girl*
> *Annoyed and flirty, we want to play with you some more*

While the onstage female figure fears for her safety, the musical accompaniment presents a stark contrast. The words themselves dehumanize the woman, reducing her body to comparisons with fruits and vegetables. As if consuming her, and not just with his eyes, the male vocals suggest the attention is her own fault. After all, as a scrumptious treat, she cannot blame him for wanting to indulge.

As these verses are sung, the ominous black hand becomes two, grabbing the female figure from behind. The hands firmly grip her breasts, hips, legs, and arms. The onstage woman begins to swiftly jog in place, looking from side to side, hoping to find a safe space and respite from the threat of violence. Yet, as the chorus is repeated, it is clear she finds no relief. The line "tienes que aguantar" (you have to suck it up) is repeated, time and again, as the choreography gives it new meaning. Now mimicking a run, the onstage female body relates the fearful, but inescapable, reality that women are forced to deal with in all public spaces. The song's words suggest that women, by inhabiting the public sphere, deserve to be treated as sexual objects and should accept that fate. This belief, entrenched in violence, is made abundantly clear via the performance's visual cues. Just as the male vocals transform the female body into consumable food products, the body is devoured by the darkness, symbolic of the hungry male gaze. Piece by piece, the female figure's clothing is removed, despite her best efforts to resist. Subverting the song's request that she not get upset while men comment on her physical attributes, the female figure is reduced to a mouth that screams out for help. As greedy hands remove her wig, the last remnants of clothing, and even her eyelashes, the grotesque scene ends as her glowing and phantasmagoric mouth opens and closes, seemingly unable to get anyone's attention or help. Mouthing along with the final line of the chorus "siempre tienes que oír la voz, y escucha escucha" (you must always hear the voice, and listen, listen) her pleas are silenced by the overpowering male voice of Maldita Vecindad. The song ends and she disappears entirely. As her clothing disappears piece by piece, so does her humanity. Lost in the dark abyss, her derealized body and humanity resignify "Morenaza" as a sickening *machista* tribute to unwanted advances.

Las Pussy Queers' performance does not stop with the embodied reference to escalating violence toward women. In the final two minutes of the piece, Lima and Polaco utilize burlesque techniques to resist feminicide. The black space of the theatre once again fills with music. The audience hears the grounded, thumping, *boom-ch-boom-chick* sounds of reggaetón, and the steady beat accompanied by a synthesizer echo and the far-off sounds of cheers and chants creates the feeling of being in a dance club. As the overwhelming audio sensations take root in the spectators' bodies, the raspy voice of Chocolate Remix raps, "No hay excusa / para cubrir al que abusa" (There is no excuse / to cover for an abuser). Articulating each syllable clearly, it becomes obvious that what follows is not a typical reggaetón song. No, it is an anthem of female self-preservation and a danceable antithesis to "Morenaza." Hailing from Tucumán, Argentina, Romina Bernardo has taken the music world by storm as her alter-ego, Chocolate Remix. She started producing reggaetón songs in 2013 as a satirical critique of the way the genre "enhances the figure of the man and situates him in a position of constant symbolic authority" all while circumscribing women as objects meant only to fulfill male desire.[42] But with songs like "Ni una menos," Chocolate's music is a blatantly political act of resistance. The title of "Ni una menos" itself is a direct reference to Argentina's *Ni una menos* (NUM;

Not one woman less) movement, which emerged in 2015 in response to the rising number of feminicides.[43] In fact, the artist wrote the song as an homage to Argentina's "feminist warriors" who "took to the streets in October 2016 to protest the country's shocking rate of hate crimes against women."[44]

Concentrating on Argentina and feminist reggaetón may seem like a striking departure from popular reference points, such as Puerto Rico, often understood as the epicenter of the genre, and megastars like Daddy Yankee and Bad Bunny. It would, however, be shortsighted and incorrect to delimit reggaetón to a circum-Caribbean geography and its better known *machista* compositions. The genre itself spans Latin America and US Latinx sites and has even crossed into Spain. The transnational flow is nothing new to the genre, itself a blend of myriad diasporic populations. Wayne Marshall, Raquel Z. Rivera, and Deborah Pacini Hernandez explain that "if anything is certain in the reggaeton narrative, it is that without Jamaican dancehall reggae there would be no reggaeton."[45] The editors of *Reggaeton* are keen to elaborate those early forms of reggaetón, like *reggae en español*, which "more often describes Panamanian recordings from the 1980s and early 1990s" and reflects Jamaican immigrant flows to Panama and New York.[46] From these early roots and cartographies of artistic exchange, reggaetón if often seen as coming out of Puerto Rico, mixing together the local style *underground* with *reggae en español* and US hip-hop.[47] Ultimately, the genre itself reflects a history and aesthetics that "do not abide by nation" but rather follow language as an organizing principle.[48]

With these global flows in mind, it is important to note that Chocolate Remix's work is groundbreaking because it forefronts a woman's vocals. Female voices have long been situated in reggaetón as objects of "male-directed and male-created" fantasies.[49] Perhaps Glory's orgasmic groans and famous line, "dame más gasoline" (give me more gasoline), from Daddy Yankee's 2004 hit "Gasolina," are most emblematic of this "male-bound synecdoche."[50] Until the last few years, the artist who was most successful in rejecting this aural role was Ivy Queen, la Diva, la Caballota, la Potra. She has "troubled many of the questionable aspects of race, gender, and sexuality" in reggaetón, such as in her 2003 "Yo quiero bailar."[51] Remixed again in 2019 with an all-female production team, the song defends women's "freedom on the dance floor" and women's right to say no to any man.[52] Ivy Queen is often credited by younger reggaetón artists like Becky G (United States), Natti Natasha (Dominican Republic), and Karol G (Colombia) for inspiring them. While these commercially successful women perform bold songs about their sexual pleasure, reggaetón artists like Chocolate Remix (Argentina), Tomasa la Real (Chile), and Ms. Nina (Spain) demonstrate a growing global feminist trend.[53]

Chocolate Remix's voice is not the only reason her music breaks boundaries and challenges reggaetón's male dominance. As she states bluntly, "ya es un hecho político que una mujer lesbiana cante" (it is already a political act that a lesbian sing).[54] By having a nonheteronormative body, she and her content subvert and upend the so-called hit model of the genre. While Chocolate Remix has certainly been criticized for using the same obscene, sexual language as famous male reggaetón stars, she refutes claims that she reproduces tropes and violence against women. The singer explains: "me pareció un acierto total poder hablar del sexo desde otro lugar" (it seemed to me to be a wise choice to tackle sexuality through a completely different lens), one that is both female and queer.[55] Though it seems obvious to point out, it is impossible to draw an equivalency between Chocolate Remix and most of her male reggaetón counterparts because she will never possess the same privileges and power as heterosexual men. Moreover, as a woman in Latin America, Chocolate Remix is constantly reminded of the war being waged against female bodies.

Representative of reggaetón's transnational and global cultural exchanges as well as the war on women's bodies, Chocolate Remix's "Ni una menos" sounds out a call to create hemispheric female solidarity. Her words, "Aquí llegó pa' molestarte esta intrusa / Todas las que mataste, hoy son mi musa" (I came here today to bother and disrupt you / All of those women you killed, today are my muse), showcase the extent to which she retools the musical genre in order to reflect a feminist agenda, one that knows no borders. As if manifesting Segato's declaration to imagine female and female-presenting bodies as new territories that demand protection, Chocolate Remix's song is a rallying cry for women across the Americas. More important than the quality of her voice or the musical accompaniment are the lyrics themselves. Her words are a means of resisting the hell of the here and now female bodies experience; they refuse the harassment, fear, violence, dismemberment, and abandonment women experience throughout Latin America. Translated into choreographed movements by Las Pussy Queers, "Ni una menos" does more than resonate through the space, it becomes heard and seen as a battle cry for justice from Argentina to the stages of Mexico City.

Enveloped in the stark blackness of the space, the audience's ears make sense of the new sounds, just as they did when "Morenaza" began to play. Just as Chocolate Remix's voice enunciates the lyrics quoted above, slivers of green and blue lines cut into the dark stage. The tempo speeds up, and the song begins to sound more like a dance tune. And yet, Chocolate Remix's strong, deep voice declares: "¡Culpable, es todo aquel que no acusa! / Complicidad, se llama este juego / Ya dejemos de hacernos los ciegos" (Guilty, all those who stay silent! / Complicity is their game / Let's stop pretending to be blind). At this point, the audience becomes fully aware that the abused woman from "Morenaza" has multiplied to reflect Mexican national statistics more accurately. Before their eyes stand not just one naked and brutalized female body, but three.

These female figures slowly begin to reappear, seemingly activated by Chocolate Remix's voice and lyrics that condemn violence against women. Still rapping in her gravelly tone, she declares:

> Vamos, cabrón, que yo no valgo tu ego
> Vamos, que aquí nos están prendiendo fuego
> Si se fue de casa, ¡ni una menos!
> Si se puso minifalda, ¡ni una menos!
> Si se pintó los labios, ¡ni una menos!
> ¡Ni una menos!, ¡ni una menos!, ¡ni una menos!
> Si baila reggaetón, ¡ni una menos![56]

> *Look, asshole, I don't care about your ego*
> *Look, don't you see they're setting us ablaze*
> *If she left home, not one woman less!*
> *If she put on a miniskirt, not one woman less!*
> *If she put on lipstick, not one woman less!*
> *Not one less! Not one woman less!*
> *If she dances reggaetón, not one woman less!*

During this part of the song, the singer's voice articulates her point with increasing urgency, eventually shouting the words "¡ni una menos!" Chocolate Remix's voice is filled with rage as she repeats the emblematic refrain "Not one woman less!" As a response to the singer's emotion-filled cries, the onstage bodies reappear. One glowing handprint at a time, the audience witnesses the reconstruction of spectral skeletons representing bodies that once were, bodies marked by horrific acts of violence. Together, we bear witness to the realization of legs, torsos, arms, and faces.

Having painted what they could on their own bodies, the three women band together, embracing one another. The three are covered in red, blue, and green glow-in-the-dark paint, signifying the way their stories are intermingled. They symbolically bind themselves to the horrific trend that kills eleven women a day in Mexico. Linking hands as Chocolate Remix's voice rapidly repeats "ni una menos" over and over and over again, the piece ends, and the lights come on. The audience sees the three women in their entirety. This vulnerable "desnudo franco" (frank undressing), as Lima calls it, lasts a mere three to five seconds, but feels like an eternity to the performers onstage. However, they felt ending the piece in this way was necessary; it was their silent "grito de basta" (scream to say "Enough!"). After each performance, Las Pussy Queers always hopes the audience leaves understanding that they did not merely watch an interesting choreography set to popular music, but that they bore witness, visibly and audibly, to the toll feminicide takes on the Mexican female psyche. Standing together, their paint-covered bodies communicate the imperative: "vamos juntas y enfrentamos juntas nuestra realidad" (Together we go and together we confront our reality).[57] Together, their bodies declare there will be not one woman less.

LA MAFIA CABARET AND *EL DESIERTO DE LAS LEONAS*

That acts of solidarity can combat the erasure of murdered women is the central argument of *El Desierto de Las Leonas* by La Mafia Cabaret. The group is comprised of three members: Pako Reyes, Liliana Papalotl, and Irakere Lima. They met during a workshop on *teatro-cabaret* methodologies led by Cecilia Sotres and Paola Izquierdo. Papalotl, from Mexico City, and Lima, from Tlaxcala, studied theater in leading university programs at the UNAM. Like cabaret practitioners before them, they could not reconcile performing pieces far removed from everyday life with their interest in using theater to make political interventions. Reyes, with previous studies in journalism, moved to Mexico City from Veracruz with the intention of studying theater, but once he stumbled across the work of Las Reinas Chulas, was immediately drawn to *teatro-cabaret*. Collaborating in a workshop, the three learned how to transform their sociopolitical commentaries into scripts and studied the intricacies of staging a piece to fit the content. Since 2012, La Mafia Cabaret has written and performed a series of *teatro-cabaret* pieces, most notably *La casa de los celos (o quien la tiene más grande)* (The House of Jealousy [Or, Who Has the Biggest Member], 2016), *Sueño de una noche medieval* (Dreaming of a Medieval Night, 2014), and *El Desierto de Las Leonas* (2017). With performances at the XLIV Festival Internacional Cervantino, Mexico's premier theatre festival, the Festival Internacional de Cabaret in Mexico City, the Festival Internacional de Cabaret in Morelos, and independent presentations in Hermosillo, Tlaxcala, Puebla, and more, La Mafia Cabaret is active in the development and proliferation of cabaret throughout the nation.

El Desierto de Las Leonas tells the story of three female protagonists,

Martiniana/Martín (Lima), Cacahuata (Reyes), and Juana Gallo (Papalotl), brought together under circumstances of violence, silence, and near erasure. Cacahuata and Juana are held captive in a convent as punishment for their crimes against the patriarchy, but a fire erupts, threatening to burn them alive. However, without a moment to spare, they are saved by Martiniana/Martín, a mysterious figure who turns out to be Cacahuata's estranged daughter dressed as a man. Having emerged from the tutelage of Las Reinas Chulas, the three members of La Mafia Cabaret generally ascribe to the basic quality that defines *teatro-cabaret*: a piece should have social or political critique and humor. Although *El Desierto de Las Leonas* follows this premise, there are many moments that do not provoke laughter but rather prompt quiet reflection. This was a deliberate choice the group made. The topic of feminicide is a serious social affliction that puts the lives of women very literally on the line every single day. As a collective, they did not feel moved to laugh at this point of great pain, and this decision is notably reflected in the piece's overall structure and musical selection.[58] Since the piece's debut in 2017, La Mafia Cabaret has performed it in various theatre and cabaret spaces throughout Mexico City such as El Vicio and Foro A Poco No. The group was also commissioned to bring the piece to Hermosillo, Sonora, as part of a feminist festival and spent a month performing for various audiences in the state of Puebla. Prior to the start of the COVID-19 pandemic, the group was completing an application for funding that would enable them to perform in high schools around the state of Morelos.[59]

The musical compositions are crucial to how the three characters stage acts of defiance and rebellion. Of the five musical numbers, three are heavily influenced by Hernán Del Riego's creative ingenuity. Del Riego has performed, directed, sung, composed, and produced over ninety theater pieces throughout Mexico, and has been recognized for his work, honored as "best actor," for "best original music," and "best bi-nacional production," to name a few his many accolades.[60] Additionally, his love of music has led him to direct some of the nation's leading orchestras and operas. Born from a belief that "una canción es mucho más que sus palabras y sonidos. Como la patria no es solo el pedazo de tierra que habitamos" (a song is much more than its words and sounds. Similarly, the country is not simply a piece of land we inhabit), Del Riego uses musical performance to resignify the sounds of a nation wounded by enormous amounts of violence and instability.[61] Del Riego also understands and appreciates the importance of music in the world of *teatro-cabaret*. Over the years, he has collaborated with some of *teatro-cabaret*'s biggest names like Tito Vasconcelos and Nora Huerta (Las Reinas Chulas). Given his performative talents and understanding of the genre,

La Mafia Cabaret instinctively knew they needed to work with him for their piece. Del Riego worked with the group and musician Sabrina Maytorena, modifying the complexity of his original compositions to match the limited instrumentation, space, and musical training of La Mafia Cabaret. At the same time, his adaptations for *El Desierto de Las Leonas* maintains the songs' original tone, rhythm, and message. As Papalotl, Lima, and Reyes sing live, Maytorena accompanies them with just her electronic keyboard, providing the actors with instrumentation and occasionally interjected sound effects.

REVOLUTIONARY UTOPIA: VISUAL CUES AND CHRONOLOGICAL SLIPPAGES

Before analyzing the soundtrack, I want to briefly examine the visual elements of *El Desierto de Las Leonas*.[62] The plain backdrop is manipulated by lighting to indicate movement through time and space, and the only notable prop is a large, dark brown chest, filled with women's stories, that the three characters take turns moving around throughout the piece. The costumes are juxtaposed with the sparse stage decor; all of their outfits conjure images of the early twentieth century, specifically the era of the Mexican Revolution (1910–1920). Juana Gallo, who appears first, wears an adapted nun's outfit. Her habit, comprised of a white tunic and black apron, is secured to her person by way of bandoliers, conjuring the *soldadera*, and her coif is more reminiscent of an oversized hat worn by many of the female heroes and notable male figures like Emiliano Zapata. Covered head to toe in dirt, soil, and ash, the character is of indiscernible age, a conscious decision that adds to the sense of temporal fluidity that I will discuss shortly. Juana Gallo's nod to the Revolution is visually solidified by the remaining characters. Cacahuata is a sight for sore eyes, entering the stage in pastel pink. Wearing a skintight corset, complete with nipple tassels, a long pink skirt, and petticoat for added volume, her arms are adorned with ruffle fabric, her neck encircled by pearl and gold necklaces, and her ringlet curls gently covered by a matching pink bonnet. She truly is the image of the erotic "fallen woman" associated with saloons and cantinas. Lastly, Martiniana, also known as Martín, appears. Her/his visual representation is the most masculine presenting of the three characters, wearing leather chaps, gun holsters on each hip, a handkerchief around the neck, boots, and a series of belts with oversized buckles clothing. Cementing the image of masculinity, Martiniana/Martín wears a hat like the one Pancho Villa was often photographed in, and her/his face is covered by a large mustache. Emphasizing further this visual sense of manliness, Maytorena, always present on the side of the stage, is dressed the same way as Martiniana/Martín, with a hat, leather pants, and boots. As a result, these outward images channel revolutionary war heroes and their associations with masculine energy.

From this description of the plot, character names, and visual triggers, *El Desierto de Las Leonas* would seem to be a piece set in the period of the Mexican Revolution. All the character names were inspired by Revolutionary figures: Juana Gallo has a *corrido* named in her honor; Cacahuata is also the title of a *corrido*; and Martiniana/Martín's name is doubly significant. First, Martiniana evokes the *son* Oaxaqueño made famous in the early twentieth century while Martín Corona references the fictional character played by Pedro Infante in *Ahí viene Martín Corona* (Here Comes Martin Corona, 1952).[63] Considering the ramifications of interpreting one of Pedro Infante's roles via drag aesthetics would be an interesting endeavor that echoes Chapter 1, but that is not my intention here. Rather, I want to emphasize the fact that despite these cues, the group never actually articulates a specific date. According to Papalotl, "si hubiéramos querido que fuera 1914 lo hubiéramos dicho" (if we had wanted it to happen in 1914, we would have said so). By not specifying a time period, the group leverages *teatro-cabaret*'s flexibility to insert contemporary references to Netflix and pop singers.[64] Moreover, the way the characters speak about Revolution goes beyond explicitly discussing the national struggle, at times pointing to the sexual revolution of the 1970s or even the need for a twenty-first-century feminist revolution. As Reyes explained, in turning to the overarching theme of the revolution, "la idea central de estas tres personajas era que hacían una revolución, pues la idea detonadora era a qué te recuerda la revolución porque alguna forma te plantea un espacio, justo un universo imaginario" (the central idea is that these three characters were what propelled a revolution, the detonating idea was that the piece makes you think of the Revolution because, one way or another, the space invokes the idea, but as a kind of imaginary universe).[65] Expanding on Reyes's observation, Papalotl declares, "igual es una utopía la Revolución mexicana, como la rusa, ¿no? O sea, es una utopía y nunca ocurrió en realidad, pero sí simbólicamente es importante para los mexicanos" (In any case, the Mexican Revolution, just like the Russian Revolution, is a utopia, is it not? I mean, it is because the utopia never really arrived, but for us Mexicans, it is a symbolically important aspect of the historical event).[66]

In this imagined universe, the slippages, or perhaps more adeptly considered disruptions of linear time and physical space allow these female characters to create a radical geography of hope and survival in times of crisis. As if echoing Wright's myth of the disposable woman, the testimonies of Cacahuata, Juana, Martiniana/Martín, and those archived in the chest become a chorus of fear, abandonment, and abuse that spans centuries. The spatial and temporal uncertainty become a nod to the reality that violence could happen anywhere, at any time. For Papalotl, women throughout history have always been subjected to misogynist cruelty. Now, the point is to change that by way of feminist revolutionary tactics. For this very reason, the protagonists escape from the convent in Salispuedes, an undefined and oppressive geographical space in Mexico. They leave in search of "La Haya," another geographically undefined space that challenges existing masculine hierarchies of power. Though Cacahuata jokes about finding "la haiga," La Haya represents a future for the three women and for those whose stories they carry with them. On the one hand, a literal translation of La Haya is The Hague, a city deeply connected to questions of human rights through the work of the United Nations, and Cacahuata's "haiga" could be understood as a humorous mispronunciation. Instead, though, I want to offer a different reading of how La Mafia Cabaret conceives of this a radical terrain of hope. In opposition to *hoyos* (holes), turned into *fosa* (mass graves) where bodies are dumped to disintegrate and never be found, La Haya "es el lugar al que vas cuando en tu pueblo es más peligroso exigir justicia que asesinar a una mujer. . . . La Haya, Cacahuata, es un lugar hermoso con jardines colgantes y fuentes de todos los colores, ahí todas las mujeres son libres, tienen derechos y las respetan" (the place you go when, in your city, it is too dangerous to seek justice for a murdered woman. . . . La Haya, Cacahuata, is a beautiful place, with floating, colorful gardens and flowing springs, there the women are free, have rights, and are respected).[67]

If the description of La Haya reads like a utopia, that is the idea. Representing a hopeful future on the horizon, the piece ends with our protagonists in the middle of the desert. While they don't know exactly what to do, they do know they are not going to give up until they reach La Haya. In the same way that Muñoz proposes futurity as always on the horizon, the promised land lies just outside of reach for our three protagonists. Their performance reflects the constant tension between the concrete pressures of the here and the potentiality of a better alternative. That is to say, *El Desierto de Las Leonas* occurs within the inferno of the present while also approximating a safety assured by a future unknown. These three characters inhabit a continuum of frustration and pain that fuels their consistent efforts to make revolution in spite of challenges and setbacks.

JUANA GALLO AND GLORIA TREVI: THE VOICES OF FEMINIST REBELLION

The characters' feminist resilience and rebellious spirit is apparent from the performance's opening lines. For example, Martiniana/Martín and

Cacahuata debate whether Juana Gallo, revolutionary heroine, ever existed. By way of cultural representations, such as María Félix's interpretation of her in the 1961 film *Juana Gallo* and her namesake *corrido*, she is a mythical figure of the popular imaginary who represents female courage and bravery. Trying to convince Cacahuata to flee the convent engulfed in flames, Martiniana/Martín declares: "No Cacahuata, ya estás bien intoxicada por los humos del incendio, Juana Gallo nunca ha existido es sólo una leyenda" (No Cacahuata, you must be high from all the flames, Juana Gallo never existed, she is only a legend).[68] Insisting that Juana not only exists but is also her friend and fellow feminist, La Cacahuata retorts, "yo me acuerdo clarito como platicábamos, me contó todas las historias de la revolución y de cómo la traicionaron, ¡Juana! Juana la de las mil batallas, pues no hasta un corrido le hicieron" (I very clearly remember how we used to talk, she told me all about the Revolution and how they betrayed her. Juana! Juana, she of a thousand battles, so brave that they even wrote a *corrido* about her).[69] Emerging valiantly from the wings, Juana introduces herself by belting out the *corrido* that tells her story:

Entre ruidos de cañones y metrallas	Between the rumbling of cannons and Gunfire
De una joven que apodaban Juana Gallo	A young girl they called Juana Gallo
Por ser valiente a no dudar	For her unwavering bravery
Siempre al frente de las tropas se encontraba	Always leading the troops She was found
Pelando como cualquier Juan	Fighting like any other John
En campaña ni un pelón se le escapaba[70]	In battle, not a single man Escaped her

In this verse, Juana describes her bravery, strength, and fearlessness in battle. Importantly, the lyrical references to military troops, cannons, and campaigns also make clear the song's tie to war and, in particular, to the Mexican Revolution.

The musical style known as the *corrido* is intimately connected to the Mexican Revolution. Its origins can be traced to the nineteenth century; as Alejandro Madrid explains, the *corrido* singers were considered "storytellers" whose songs were used to disseminate news "from town to town and informing people of events."[71] The style rose to popularity during the Revolutionary years, as *corridos* were used in place of printed sources to transmit

FIGURE 4.1. Juana Gallo stands tall, wearing a bandolier bullet belt, holding a cigar. *El Desierto de Las Leonas*, 2018. Photo by Juan Boites

information to the masses, as events transpired quickly in a context of instability and with high rates of illiteracy, which limited the effectiveness of newspapers. According to Helena Simonett, most compositions follow a particular structure: they have an opening statement of time and place; a reference to the song as a *corrido*; a nod to either the singer, audience, or the song itself; a description of a journey or particular event; and the use of dramatic speech.[72] Because of this narrative style, lyrical composition has always been more important than musical melodies or vocal competence.[73] Over the last centuries, some well-known *corridos* have been archived, "handed down on leaflets," while others remain in the oral imaginary, passed down through performative repertoire. In either case, these songs serve to relate national events, political heroes and villains, natural disasters, family feuds, romantic adventures, and more, ultimately constructing and performing social imaginaries.[74]

Although the majority of *corridos* are centered around masculine figures, historical and fictionalized, there are several that recognize the importance of women. Anna Fernández Poncela points out, "predominan las soldaderas—las juanas, adelitas o galletas, como popularmente eran conocidas" (the female soldiers are most common—the Juanas, Adelitas o Galletas, as they were popularly known), as well as the figure of the *coronela*, the female leader who breaks boundaries.[75] María Herrera-Sobek notes that while many *corrido* scholars such as Merle E. Simmons, Vincent T. Mendoza, and Américo Paredes have studied the genre as a social and historical phenomenon, she applies a feminist reading to the female figures. Placing them into three major categories, Herrera-Sobek outlines women as following a "true historical dimension," being depicted as a "love object," or being recounted as "mythical archetypal figure."[76] Given that Juana Gallo does not represent a verifiable person or a specific event, her namesake *corrido* falls into the last of the three categories. By all accounts, the song, composed by Ernesto Juárez Frías, was first performed in 1958 and was made into a film soon after. As a late addition to the *corrido* genre, the song bends some of the generally accepted norms detailed above. "Juana Gallo" is an example of a *corrido* that mythologizes an archetype outside of specific geographic or temporal markers. In general, the *corrido* tells the story of a woman who strikes fear into the hearts of generals and suffers the grave consequences of frail masculinity, even betrayed by her own husband, as the lyrics detail: "El marido le había puesto un cuatro / que la había traicionado, / la llevaron a prisión, / por envidia le había entregado" (Her own husband had put a mark on her back / he had betrayed her, / they took her to prison, / out of envy he turned her in).[77] Even so, she does not give up, screaming "pinche traidor" (damn traitor) as she is carried away. By integrating this song into *El Desierto de Las Leonas*, the *corrido* comes to emphasize the promise of a radical feminist utopia. The lyrical ambiguity regarding the when and where allow her to be reimagined for the twenty-first century, and her notorious skills in battle and fearless attitude make her the perfect candidate for resisting the effects of Mexico's War on Drugs and the nation's all-out assault on female bodies.

The onstage Juana Gallo, as indicated in the script, sings the *corrido* in the style of Lucha Moreno, a contemporary heiress of the *voz bravía* (untamed voice) tradition. Inspired by Lucha Reyes, this vocal technique emphasizes and relies on the singer's body. This approach emerged not from *corrido* performance, but from Reyes' performances of the *ranchera* genre. Singing acoustically, she used her voice, and the materiality of her body, to be heard over live musicians. Yolanda Moreno Rivas explains, this style "fue el resultado de una conjunción de elementos. La nueva forma de ejecución daba una nueva impostación a la voz" (was the result of a variety of elements. This new delivery style gave a new form of projecting the voice).[78] Speaking specifically about Reyes, the sound came "directamente la garganta, aunque esto significara en ocasiones una enunciación rasposa y poco musical (por lo tanto más bravía)" (directly from the throat, even though this meant, at times, a raspy enunciation that was not very musical [and for that, more untamed]).[79] The primary objective became pushing the body to its limits rather than expressing the highest quality singing voice. It is also important to note that this public display of a female body dominating male musicians as well as expressing emotions reserved for men is equally important in the development of *la voz bravía*.[80] According to Olga Nájera-Ramírez, "whereas men who sang softly or tenderly in their performances were read as 'romantic' rather than feminine, 'masculine' qualities were regarded as vulgar and therefore not appropriate for a lady" until Lucha Reyes' defiance broke down barriers for later female singers like Lucha Moreno.[81]

Accompanied by a single keyboard, the onstage Juana Gallo's voice rings loud and clear. Papalotl sings "Juana Gallo" in a low vocal register, occupying the spaces of the body generally related to masculine vocal projection such as the throat and chest.[82] While she lacks the vocal training and prowess of the trailblazing women who came before her (such as Las Luchas), the onstage Juana Gallo's intention is not necessarily to achieve a sound associated with refined singing but rather to use her voice to tell a story of radical feminist resistance. Her body represents Segato's call for female bodies to become territories unto themselves that make public demands for protection and respect.[83] The strength and low timbre of her voice also reinforce a model of strength and resiliency generally not associated with female bodies nor common across many *corridos* that concentrate on female figures. Lyrics like "Sin piedad se los tronaba con / su enorme pistolón" (Without mercy she took her shot / with her enormous pistol), conjure an image of ferocity as well as phallic endowment.[84] At the same time, she is a wife, suggesting adherence to some social scripts assigned to women, like the presumption of heteronormativity. And even though her husband betrays her, the song closes with the following refrain:

> Ábranla que hay viene Juana Gallo
> Va gritando en su caballo
> Viva la revolución
> Para los que son calumniadores
> Para todos los traidores
> Trae bien puesto el corazón[85]

> *Make way, for here comes Juana Gallo*
> *She comes screaming from atop her horse*
> *Long live the Revolution*
> *Beware those who slander*
> *Beware those who betray*
> *For she has the heart of a lion*

As the onstage Juana's voice transitions from singing voice to speaking voice, the implication is clear. She has not given up despite her circumstances. Though in the mimetic space of the performance she faces being burned alive while imprisoned, she still has the heart of a lion. She will shout her values and resistance, in this case against men who abuse the female body. In this geographically and temporally ambiguous setting of Salsipuedes, the lyrics ring out: "Viva la revolución" (Long live the Revolution). Effectively, this Juana Gallo reaffirms that "la revolución será feminista o no será" (the revolution will be feminist, or it will not be at all).[86]

The word "revolución" is also used to connect the three protagonists to myriad movements, past, present, and future, that refuse to normalize violence against women. During her younger years, Cacahuata enchanted men night after night with her music and dance routines while working in a saloon called "La Valentina." After meeting Porfidio Malrostro, the most enigmatic man she'd ever encountered, she fell head over heels in love and became pregnant. Upon hearing the news, he "se desinfló, como nuestro amor, o sea . . . salió corriendo y no lo volví a ver jamás" (he went flat, just like our love . . . I mean, he ran out on me and I never saw him again).[87] Raising her child alone, Cacahuata became her town's feminist love advice expert. As women came to her house looking for support, Martiniana/Martín heard it all. She listened to her mother tell María Madgdalena to leave her controlling husband and heard her talk with María Resignación about how she works from morning to night on household chores while neither her husband nor her two sons help. She even heard her mother assure Teresa Rubí that her husband "se merecía que le reventaras el hico de un chingadazo" (deserves a good beating) for cheating on her.[88] In less than a month, all three of these women were found dead: "María Magdalena muerta en una zanja, a María Resignación en bolsas de plástico y Teresa Rubi en un tambo con cemento" (María Magdalena dead in a trench, María Resignación in plastic bags, and Teresa Rubi in a barrel of cement).[89] Contemplating stories of abuse and feminicide, Martiniana/Martín asked her mother, "¿Ese es el futuro que me espera?" (Is this the future that awaits me?), to which Cacahuata had no words.[90] After that, Martiniana/Martín watched her mother organize self-defense workshops and other trainings so that collectively they could change their fates.

Inspired by her mother's work, Martiniana/Martín internalized feminist rhetoric and practices. In studying performative strategies in the wake of Southern-cone dictatorships, Diana Taylor suggests the notion of DNA of performance: "just as the generations share genetic materials, which these

FIGURE 4.2. Cacahuata and Martiniana/Martín link arms center stage. *El Desierto de Las Leonas*, Teatro Bar El Vicio, Coyoacán, Mexico, 2018. Photo by Daniel Cortés.

groups have actively traced through DNA testing, there are performance strategies (DNA of performance) that link their forms of activism."[91] In the case of *El Desierto de Las Leonas*, discourses and actions of feminist resistance are passed down from mother to daughter, as well as between generations of strong women—from Juana Gallo to Cacahuata to Martiniana/Martín—regardless of shared genetics. Beyond the mimetic space of the stage, reflective of the slippages in chronological time, Martiniana/Martín's musical selection binds her to a more contemporary figure of female ferocity: Gloria Trevi, who is known for her dramatic onstage antics and offstage story that is stranger than fiction. Fabio Correa aptly asks, "¿Constituye Gloria Trevi un mito feminista, en el cual se desmitifica a la mujer mexicana?; ¿Encarna Gloria Trevi un acto socialmente simbólico de representación del inconsciente político de la sociedad Mexicana a través de un discurso antagónico?" (Does Gloria Trevi constitute a feminist myth in which she demystifies the Mexican woman?; Does Gloria Trevi embody a socially symbolic representation of the political unconscious of Mexican society by way of her antagonistic discourse?)[92] It is not my intention to enter into debates about Trevi's role as a political or feminist figure; rather, I accentuate here her rebellious qualities. Described by Olivia Cosentino as appearing with "untamed hair, racy, self-made outfits and scandalizing dance moves," La Trevi quickly became known as La Atrevida (The Daring One).[93] The daring one had no qualms representing herself as an antithesis to contemporary television stars like Lucerito and feminine icons like the Virgin of Guadalupe.[94] Her performative emphasis on dominating men, exposing her sexuality, and generally refusing to be submissive resonate with the onstage Martinana/Martín, Cachuata, and Juana Gallo.

As a teenager, Martiniana/Martín had a close group of female friends who called themselves "Las Leonas." They chose this nickname because "ya estábamos hasta la coronilla de no poder salir, de no sentirnos libres" (we had had enough of not being able to move freely, of feeling restrained). At this point in the performance, Martiniana/Martín turns to Trevi's "Todos me miran" to express herself. The original lyrics are as follows:

Y me solté el cabello	And I let my hair down
y me vestí de reina	And dressed like a queen
Me puse tacones	I put on my heels
me pinté y era bella	I got made up and I was gorgeous
Y caminé hacia la puerta	And I walked toward the door
te escuché gritarme	Where I heard you call out
Pero tus cadenas	But your chains
ya no pueden pararme	No longer bind me
Y miré la noche	And I looked to the night
y ya no era oscura	And it was no longer dark
era de lentejuelas[95]	It was filled with sequins

Trevi's raspy voice has invited many women to acknowledge and explore their inner angst over the years. Additionally, the lyrics "y me solté el cabello / me vestí de reina" (I let my hair down / and dressed like a queen) have become an unofficial anthem for rebellious women, drag queens, and gender-bending performers throughout Mexico. The unrestrained hair and empowered dress described in the lyrics echo Cosentino's observation about the artist's own appearance. With newfound confidence, the singer declares her independence, and as a "reflejo de la postura contemporánea antimachista de las mexicanas (reflection of the contemporary antimachista posture of Mexican women), she leaves behind a man who sought to control and restrict her.[96] As he screams after her, she only looks forward, toward the bright future that awaits. In Martiniana/Martín's revised version, she sings:

y me amarré el cabello,	*And I tied back my hair*
me vestí de lencha,	*And dressed like a lesbian*
me puse espolones	*I put on my spurs*
y unas carrilleras.	*And my ammunition belts*
caminé como fiera	*I was ferocious*
fui a enfrentarles	*I went to confront them*
porque mis temores	*Because my fears*
ya no pueden atarme,	*Could no longer bind me*
y miré la noche	*And I looked at the night*
y ya no era oscura,	*And it was no longer dark*
era de las leonas.[97]	*It was for the brave*

Martiniana/Martín's voice is not nearly as intrepid as Trevi's, but her lyrical revision describes an image in opposition to the free-flowing hair and glamor the pop singer paints with her lyrics. On one hand, she is playing with tropes—that lesbians are masculine types who wear combat boots. On the other hand, she stays true to the overarching theme of revolution in the elastic temporal moment of the early twentieth century. Rather than leaving behind a specific man, her declaration of independence is one that sets her free from fear; she becomes unburdened by the fear of violence that faces many women. Like Trevi, the future that awaits her is not dark but full of promise. Her futurity reiterates her utopic sense of strength and fierceness.

Once she finishes her brief interlude, Martinana/Martín turns to the audience and tells them, "Ahí se me ocurrió hacerme llamar Martín Corona y armar la revolución sin que nadie me anduviera chingando" (And just like that it occurred to me to call myself Martín Corona and start a revolution without anyone getting in my way).[98] At one point in the performance, Juana Gallo even comments, "Se decía que un joven de nombre Martín Corona era el líder de la nueva revolución, se rumoró que se había enfrentado al gobierno, exigiendo tierra y libertad . . . y equidad de género" (It is said that a young man named Martín Corona was the leader of a new revolution, it is rumored that he confronted the government, demanding liberty and land . . . and gender equality).[99] Martiniana/Martín's fame for fomenting a revolution rooted in protections against gendered violence is an example of what arriving at utopia would look and sound like. At the same time, the reality that Martiniana had to dress like a man in order to accomplish her goals and merely survive reminds us that she lives in the hell house that is the "here and now" even if that "here and now" is a fluid construct of time and space. As a woman, Martiniana knew she couldn't survive the violence and abuse that awaited her, but through the disguise of Martín, she would be able to enact change and be reunited with her mother, Cacahuata.

IN SOLIDARITY WE GO: "SOMOS MÁS"

As a final effort to find a way out of systemic violence against women, the onstage protagonists haul a *baúl* (chest) alongside them as they search for La Haya. This plain brown chest does not inspire much visually, and yet, it prompts continuous panic as Juana and Cacahuata refuse to leave the burning convent without it. Facing an unthinkably painful death, these women insist on carrying this enormously heavy, large, and awkward piece with them. Even Martiniana/Martín does not immediately seem to grasp why. Juana and Cacahuata reveal at the very end that this *baúl*, one of one hundred, is a kind of memory storage space.[100] Inside, it houses and protects the stories and voices of women murdered, beaten, and otherwise forgotten. Juana Gallo somberly explains, "empezamos a juntar las historias de las mujeres y guardarlas en el baúl de Juana, un día el baúl ya no fue suficiente, así llenamos otro y luego otro, y así, un día tuvimos cien baúles repletos de historias de mujeres" (We began collecting and storing the stories of women in Juana's chest and one day, one chest was no longer enough, so we began to fill another, and another, and like that, one day, we had a hundred chests overflowing with women's stories).[101] This singular structure, capturing only a fraction of the oral histories destined to never make it into the archives of official history, represents the ninety-nine others burned. This *baúl*, then, metonymically keeps those stories alive. Disheartened, Cacahuata asks, "¿esto es todo lo que lograste rescatar?" (Is this all you were able to save?). Juana Gallo confirms the unfortunate truth, but not deterred, Cacahuata declares: "No importa, si es necesario volveremos a empezar" (It does not matter, if we must, we will start collecting stories all over again).[102]

Dragging this *baúl* through a seemingly endless desert, the women are exhausted and ready to give up. Cacahuata pleads to take a break, to give her aching knees a rest after having already walked for forty days and forty nights. She also reveals that they are out of water, which Juana Gallo is quick to point out is Cachuata's own fault: "te lo acabasete igualito que te acabaste los cuatro kilos de Jameson, los diecisiete tamales de chiltepín, las cuatro bolas de quesillo" (you finished it just as you finished the four kilos of Jameson, the seventeen chiltepín tamales, the four bags of quesillo), and much more.[103] As Juana Gallo and Cacahuata continue to bicker, Martiniana/Martín interrupts them with the piece's final monologue. Speaking slowly and deliberately, she asserts:

> Yo también tengo sed, sed de dignidad, tengo la boca adolorida de tanto exigir y gritar, ya no estoy dispuesta a seguir caminando por la calle con miedo, siempre alerta y con miedo de ser la siguiente, ser una de las siete que matan a diario en este lugar, de desaparecer y que mi madre no tenga ni donde llorarte, de dejar de ser Martiniana y convertirme en un número en una estadística, las lágrimas no me alcanzan, el miedo me paraliza y sin embargo, voy a seguir caminando, tenemos que seguir caminando.[104]
>
> *I too am thirsty, thirsty for dignity. My mouth is dried out from all my screaming, and I am no longer willing to walk down the streets in fear, always on guard, and scared to be the next woman murdered, to be one of the seven killed each day in this place, to disappear and leave my mother to have no idea where to find me or mourn my body, to no longer be Martiniana y become just another statistic. I have no more tears to cry, and fear paralyzes me, but I am going to keep going, we have to keep going.*

Although the words convey a strong message of no longer tolerating the fear of living as a woman, characterized by violence and discrimination, the sound of her voice is not filled with anger. Instead, as she declares her desire not to end up as one more dead, to not become just another number, her voice is shaky, as if on the edge of tears. The rebellious tone she invokes through Trevi's lyrics gives way to a frank vulnerability and raw display of emotion. However, she ends her statement recuperating an unwavering tone, firmly avowing to continue searching for La Haya, no matter what.

The three women have no idea how they are going to reach La Haya, or if they ever will, but one thing is abundantly clear: they will not give up. Closing the piece, Cacahuata, Juana Gallo, and Martiniana/Martín occupy center stage and sing "Somos más," an original composition by Hernán Del Riego. For Del Riego, music is used "para inventar el país que queremos y no encontramos" (to invent the country we want but that does not exist).[105] Thinking about the piece's search for a radical geography of hope, La Haya, Del Riego's musical philosophy and composition come to life in "Somos más."[106] The song itself is only two minutes and thirty seconds long, and the only instrumentation is provided by an electronic keyboard played by Maytorena. Yet, despite its brevity, the three protagonists express a range of emotions. Repeating the first verse twice, the three proclaim:

> No nos vamos a callar
> No nos vamos a esconder

No nos vamos a morir aún más.
No se trata de voltear para no ver
No se trata de callar para vivir.[107]

We will not be quiet
We will not hide
We will not die anymore
It is not about turning a blind eye
It is not about being silent to survive.

These first lines, sung in unison and in a minor tone, create a powerful, albeit haunting sensation. The delivery of the song is reminiscent of a lullaby or something you might sing to soothe fears. The steady, hypnotizing rhythm of the protagonists' voices is further enhanced by the piano, whose notes are calm and consistent. Singing the lines as they push the *baúl* around the stage, Juana Gallo, Cacahuata, and Martiniana/Martín's collective activism reverberates by way of their soft voices that defy erasure.

When the trio reaches the chorus, the tone and rhythm become notably different. The keyboard produces the sounds of a drumbeat, creating a sensation similar to R. Murray Schafer's battle soundscape. Reproducing new sound through their bodies, the onstage protagonists begin to march. As if the song were a call to battle, the women get in formation like a military troop. Moving steadily across the stage, the protagonists sing in unison and in harmony. With a stronger vocal projection, they declare:

Los vamos a enfrentar diciendo más
Los vamos a enfrentar saliendo
Los vamos a enfrentar levantando la voz
Para vivir, para vivir.
Los vamos a enfrentar alegres
Los vamos a gritando
Los vamos a de frente valientes
Porque somos más, porque somos más.[108]

We are going to confront them speaking up
We are going to confront them in public
We are going to confront them raising our voices
In order to live, to live
We are going to confront them with joy
We are going to scream

We are going to be brave
Because we are more, we are more.

Following the piano's lead as Maytorena plays an upbeat tempo, the onstage characters begin to approach their audience. Face to face with the spectators, the three very literally embody the words that ring out throughout the stage: "los vamos a enfrentar" (we are going to confront them). Repeating the chorus once more to drive home the message, the three protagonists perform the song as a chant. With a deeper chest-tone range and vocals that are almost spoken rather than sung, the final repetition of the verse and chorus is less musical and more of a declaration of presence. These onstage characters and the stories of the women protected by the *baúl* will not be silenced. One way or another, the women will make it to La Haya, that radical geography of hope and survival. At this point, the performance ends and the actors' voices echo throughout the mimetic desert, resounding in the physical space of the theatre, and hopefully reverberating beyond the performance itself. As the house lights come on, audiences are left to consider the importance of resisting gendered violence, as well as being able to literally hear female voices and preserve their stories. Ending the piece on this somber note, La Mafia Cabaret sends a strong message: despite moments of reprieve and relief, violence toward women and trans women is no laughing matter. And much like Las Pussy Queers' *Ni una menos*, the closing refrain emphasizes a sense of solidarity and collective action.

CÉSAR ENRÍQUEZ AND *LA PRIETTY GUOMAN*

Echoing the strategies of the artists described earlier, César Enríquez blends his personal experiences as a dissident citizen with formal studies to produce complex *teatro-cabaret* pieces and protagonists.[109] Having studied Brechtian technique and commedia dell'arte, among other theater traditions, for five years with Ludwik Margules at El Foro Teatro Contemporáneo, Enríquez has an intense routine for developing the personality and physicality of his characters. And as a dark-skinned, self-identifying gay man, many of Enríquez's artistic decisions express elements of his autobiography as a form of resistance. Moreover, just as many *cabareterxs* are recognized for being avid researchers and political commentators in the public sphere, Enríquez leverages his university studies in political science to craft characters who push the boundaries of what informed citizenry looks and sounds like.[110] Enríquez's earlier works, such as *Disertaciones de la chingada* (Dissertations of the Screwed, 2012) and *Petunia sola en Sanborts* (Petunia,

FIGURE 4.3. The three women, Juana Gallo, Cacahuata, and Martiniana/Martín face the spectator, and in solidarity, they refuse to be victims of gender violence. *El Desierto de Las Leonas*, 2018. Photo by Juan Boites.

Alone in Sanborls, 2014), incorporate male-to-female drag aesthetics to critique monolithic stereotypes of Mexican identity. In *Por jodidos y hocicones mataron a los actores* (For Being Messed Up and Loudmouths, They Killed the Actors, 2018), Enríquez reelaborates popular aesthetics of Mexican *teatro de carpa* to shine light on the nation's forced disappearances.[111] Beyond the world of *teatro-cabaret*, he has also directed theater pieces such as *Amor en la Obrera* (Love in the Obrera, 2018), a commentary on queer love in one of Mexico City's working-class neighborhoods, and was a cast member in the Mexican version of Julie Taymor's stage adaptation of *The Lion King* (2015), performing as Banzi and Scar.

Crafting a protagonist who retools perceived weaknesses, such as being dark-skinned, trans, dyslexic, and a prostitute, *La Prietty Guoman* is a prime example of bringing marginalized communities to center stage. Since its debut in August 2016 as part of the Annual International Cabaret Festival held in Mexico City, the piece has been offered runs in well-known spaces throughout the nation's capital, including El Vicio, La Capilla, Teatro NH, and the Centro Cultural Helénico. At the national level, Enríquez and his protagonist were invited to close the Thirty-Eighth Muestra Nacional de Teatro (2017) in Guanajuato, and have traveled to Tijuana, Tlaxcala, and Oaxaca to present at other events. Enríquez has also performed this piece for international audiences in Cádiz, Spain, for International Women's Day, and in Chicago for the Annual Chicago Latino Theatre Alliance. In 2019, the piece was programmed as part of the Hemispheric Institute of Politics and Performance Encuentro in Mexico.[112] Enríquez was also awarded the prestigious Lark Fellowship, which allowed him to work with performers in New York City to translate the piece with the goal of producing a version based in the United States.

By way of mesmerizing visual aesthetics and sonic triggers, César Enríquez's brand of dissident comedy makes a pointed sociopolitical critique about discrimination and violence in contemporary Mexico. Moreover, through the myriad identities embodied in one figure, La Prietty makes the impossible seem possible. To arrive at these stages of im/possibilities, Enríquez pushed his protagonist to the limits in order to include "a todas las minorías, minorías entrecomillada, a todos los grupos vulnerables" (all the minorities, "minorities," and vulnerable groups).[113] Yet, following a basic tenet of *teatro-cabaret* humor, he is keenly aware of the need to develop jokes and satirical commentaries that avoid further victimizing the subject.[114] One of the many ways La Prietty showcases the struggles of intersectional and marginalized identities without further abusing them is precisely by way of lyrical revisions and drag re-presentations that aim to incorporate the protagonist into definitions of belonging and to impress upon the audience her humanity and mournability as a dark-skinned trans woman. By way of audiovisual transformations, La Prietty's performances of an (after)life stage hope and survival for myriad marginalized Others and resist the erasure of trans women murdered in contemporary Mexico.

When Enríquez first imagined the piece, the protagonist was not trans, but rather a female prostitute who loved to sing. The character was inspired by the real-life story of a sex trafficking victim in Lydia Cacho's *Esclavas del poder* (*Slavery Inc: The Untold Story of International Sex Trafficking*, 2010), a journalistic study of female sex slavery around the globe.[115] In her chapter on Mexico, Cacho reveals the deeply troubling sex-trafficking industry in Mexico through the heart-wrenching story of Arely, a nineteen-year-old Venezuelan girl trafficked to Monterrey, Mexico, under the premise of a modeling career.[116] Forced to work as a prostitute, she found refuge in a young man who brought her jewelry and stuffed animals and gave her his favorite film, *Pretty Woman*. Out of the blue, Arely and a group of girls were told: "Ya son muy professionals y esto se pone aburrido, así que les tenemenos una sorpresa. Se van a Cancún, allí trabajarán en un lugar muy bonito frente al mar" (You all are ready and must be bored here, so we have a surprise for you. You are going to Cancún where you will work in a lovely place on the shore).[117] In a sickening twist of fate, her knight in shining armor actually worked for the club bosses. Upon hearing the news, he simply told her he would come visit her; a vacation on the beach sounded nice.

In the summer of 2016, the Pulse massacre of forty-nine people in Orlando, Florida, garnered international attention and a Facebook filter while the assassination of four trans women in Veracruz the week before barely made any headlines.[118] That juxtaposition led Enríquez to redefine his protagonist as trans and relocate her to Veracruz.[119] Arguably the disparities between coverage of the Orlando and Veracruz tragedies could be related to the number of victims, yet Enríquez felt a division within the queer community between the First World and Third World. As if following Sayak Valencia's imperative that "First World discourse should pay attention to what Third World discourses have to say about the evolution of the world of capital and of the world more generally," Enríquez then made drastic changes to the piece.[120] He renamed his protagonist and connected her narrative to gendered trans violence in Veracruz. In order to ensure his piece was humorous, in the style of *teatro-cabaret*, but avoided becoming a caricature of trans communities, he worked with several trans activists and trans sex workers to ensure trans women could see themselves reflected in La Prietty.[121] He translated this ethnographic work into the language she uses in her jokes and articulations of self, and incorporates it into a visual aesthetic that pays tribute and calls attention to the trans experience. Though the plot still limits the trans woman of color to sex work, humiliation, and abuse, this imagined life performs many of the strategies of recognizing the humanity of an Other.[122] That is to say, in giving La Prietty a name, a face, and a body, and by recognizing her hobbies, likes, dislikes, and slogans by which she lives, Enríquez ensures that the fictional protagonist is not an abstract notion of a trans woman, but rather stands in for the many trans bodies beyond the performance space.

CARTOGRAPHIES OF CRUELTY AND IMAGINATION: THE ORIGINS OF A DIVA

For many people, Roy Orbison's catchy pop tune, "Oh, Pretty Woman," conjures memories of the cinema classic, *Pretty Woman* (1990). The film is often considered a romantic comedy, even though the entire plot revolves around the fact that Julia Roberts's character is a sex worker on the streets of Los

Angeles, hired by a wealthy businessman (played by Richard Gere) to accompany him to events. César Enríquez's *teatro-cabaret* piece, *La Prietty Guoman*, was inspired by the romantic side of the film as well as the gritty realities of prostitution. However, the protagonist, La Prietty, differs from Roberts's character in two notable ways: she is a dark-skinned trans woman and tells her story from beyond the grave. The piece's focus on transfemicide, racial marginalization, and sexual labor would seem to make it difficult to sit through. However, as an example par excellence of *teatro-cabaret*, La Prietty deploys costume changes, quick wit, impeccable comedic timing, and stunning punch lines to keep the audience engaged. Here, I underscore how *La Prietty Guoman* filters sociopolitically driven humor through audiovisual revisions of US pop songs and divas from the 1990s. For example, embedded within her fierce aesthetic and revised lyrical performances of "Pretty Woman," "Vogue," "I Have Nothing," and more, La Prietty recounts the horrific violence and tragedies she experienced.

In bringing La Prietty to life, a car is a pivotal reference point for our protagonist's journey, just as in the original film. The first scene begins: "(En el escenario se enciende la luz, se ve la parte trasera de un coche. Ella está sentada en la cajuela. El coche saca humo como si estuviera andando. Se forma una nube blanca, que nos asemeja la luz de una estrella internacional)" (The lights come on, and in the back, the audience sees a car trunk. Prietty is sitting on the trunk while the car blows smoke from the exhaust like it's running. The smoke forms a white cloud, similar to soft lighting for an international movie star).[123] The audience is constantly reminded of the car, which is constructed of plywood and painted white, by its centrality on stage. In the original film, cars very literally become the means by which Julia Roberts is transported to a new life, one where she gains riches and respect. For La Prietty, this onstage car also holds the key to her destiny. Not only does it house her costumes and extra wigs and become a canvas for projecting images, but it also metonymically transports the protagonist to different stages in her life. The car becomes a mechanism for imagining her ultimate arrival at a radical geography that secures hope and survival. As she recounts, when she was thirteen, she told her father that she was a woman: "¡Que quede claro! Yo nunca me travestí" (Let me be clear! I never dressed in drag!), but her parents forced her to present as male.[124] In response to her desire to look like a woman, her father retorted, "en mi pueblo a las mujeres se les venden. ¿Eso quieres?" (In my town, women are sold. Is that what you want?). Deploying a discourse "that refuse[s] to appeal to victimization and the nullification" of her subjectivity, La Prietty does not dwell on the possibility of being sold.[125] Rather, she pokes fun at her horrific situation, confessing, "y ahí supe que yo era una mujer de la 'High'. Me vendió a un gringo por unos tenis Nike, y a los trece me llevaron en un coche a Veracruz a trabajar" (And in that moment, I knew I was destined to be part of the upper class. My father sold me to some gringo for a pair of Nike shoes, and at thirteen, I was taken away in a car to work in Veracruz).[126]

Although the protagonist imagined she would be going on a journey to find her romantic ending, just like the Hollywood film, this white onstage car metaphorically and metonymically takes her to a gruesome end. As a story told from beyond the grave, giving life to a body deemed unmournable, La Prietty showcases the perspective of the spectral as she tells her spectators about the song that gave and ended her life, "Oh, Pretty Woman." She details:

> A los 13 años fui vendida, me subí a ese coche con felicidad en el rostro imaginándome una vida así, llena de vestidos hermosos mientras mi canción preferida La Pretty Woman sonaba en la radio relatando mi camino hacia la muerte. Terminé con los brazos anudados a mis tobillos, quemada por las colillas del cigarro apagadas en mi piel, violada y torturada satisfaciendo los deseos reprimidos de unos cuantos y así después de escuchar un 'Por puto' es que en la oscuridad de una cajuela viajé para siempre.[127]

> *At thirteen, I was sold, and I got into the car with a smile across my face, imagining a glamorous life, one filled with beautiful dresses while my favorite song, "Oh, Pretty Woman," played on the radio, not knowing it foretold my death. I ended up with my arms tied to my ankles, burned by cigarette butts put out in my skin, raped, and tortured until I had satisfied the repressed desires of a handful of men, and then, after hearing a "This is what you get for being a faggot," the lights went out and I would spend eternity in that trunk.*

As if taking cues from José Esteban Muñoz's *Cruising Utopia*, the queer utopia La Prietty imagines for herself exists as a hopeful revision of the violence and discrimination she and other queer bodies and nonnormative bodies face in the "prison house" of the present.[128] It makes sense, then, that the imagined (after)life of La Prietty still limits the trans woman of color to sex work, humiliation, and abuse, and takes her through cartographies of pain. But by retooling those experiences, they become sources of inspiration for her empowerment, resistance, and continued search for a place where she would be safe and accepted. The images and meanings Muñoz associates with cruising are especially apt for considering La Prietty's movement through time and space. On one hand, cruising refers colloquially to picking up lovers and prostitutes for lax affairs, while on the other, it invokes a sense of traveling through life with ease, like driving down the highway in a convertible with the wind in your hair. In cruising from Tlaxcala to Veracruz, La Prietty creates a new world from beyond the grave, one that unsettles heteronormative chronologies and geographies, circumventing the vacancy created by way of her horrific murder. Rather than dwell on that painful truth, this imagined (after)life affords the protagonist the freedom of self-expression and the opportunity to experience desire on her own terms. Specifically, she aligns her image with the divas who inspire her, and through staging their images, her body becomes an empowered site of pleasure and pride, something unattainable in her material realm.

The audiovisual aesthetic that defines La Prietty is not a frivolous choice; it is an act of queer resistance. The piece's lyrical revisions and performances offer hope and survival amid spaces associated with terrible atrocity. Enríquez's decisions surrounding the protagonists' visual construction were inspired by a night in a Mexico City queer bar several years ago; he still laughs at the memory of how different a particular drag performer looked from the artist she was actively trying to mimic.[129] As La Prietty lyrically and sonically interprets the work of famous female singers, she employs a style of drag commonly referred to in Mexico as *personificaciones*, meaning imitation. At the same time, her costuming choices consciously poke fun at what can be a startling disconnect between a drag artist's visual image and the singer they seek to recreate. Though speaking firmly of the United States, Esther Newton's claim that "as female impersonators see it, 'beauty' is the closest approximation, in form and movement, to the mass media images of glamorous women" is useful in considering La Prietty's look.[130] In turning to pop culture divas, her (after)life is imagined in relation to glamor, success, and fame. At the same time, these recreations, sometimes laughably bad, are arguably "merely 'citational,' and can only thereby consolidate the authority of a fantasized original."[131] In thinking about *La Prietty Guoman*, I suggest that Enríquez's citationality of the pop divas, however, does not simply consolidate an authorized vision of stardom or heteronormativity. Rather, the performances allow him to "interrogate the ideals of the past."[132] By this, I suggest that in turning to divas, Enríquez and La Prietty use drag to imagine trans beauty and belonging—and also simply to live.

The divas that Enríquez chose are intimately related to *La Prietty Guoman*'s soundtrack, which includes musical interpretations spanning from the late 1970s through the mid-1990s, with heavy reliance on US dance hits. Rewriting lyrics to fit her particular circumstances, La Prietty allows herself an escape mechanism from the reality of a gruesome end. At the same time,

FIGURE 4.4. La Prietty stands in front of a white car, showing off her outfit and spectacular body. *La Prietty Guoman*, Teatro NH, Mexico City, Mexico, 2018. Photo by Christina Baker.

the protagonist's (after)life performances are "an insistence on potentiality or concrete possibility for another world," one where she becomes, very literally, a mouthpiece for renouncing gendered violence.[133] Representing a collective through her monologue, La Prietty, stands in and for a utopic vision of future possibility.[134] One way she does is this is by singing live, accompanied only by a single piano played by La Muda. Simon Frith suggests that "the voice, in short, may or may not be a key to someone's identity, but it is certainly a key to the ways in which we change identities, pretend to be something we're not."[135] In this sense, Enríquez's singing voice is one of the crucial ways he brings the protagonist to life and transforms into La Prietty. Throughout the piece, her vocals fill the theatre space, adeptly shifting between deep tenor ranges and alto-soprano notes, showcasing the spectrum of gendered associations she experiences in trying to make her inner identity match her outward appearance. Singing live becomes a performance of La Prietty's self, of what it means to be a trans woman without surgery or hormone replacement therapy.

Starting with Julia Roberts, her first muse, La Prietty takes shape. From the beginning of the piece, the protagonist appears dressed like Roberts's on-screen counterpart, wearing a red curly-haired wig, a crop top, a blue miniskirt, and thigh-high black patent leather boots. La Prietty jokes that she and Roberts's character are basically the same: "Es que somos igualitas, no más yo autóctona pero la nariz idéntica, bueno la mía expansiva. Altura 1.75 con tacón, igualitas" (I mean, we are basically twins, only that I am Indigenous, but we have the same nose. Well, mine is wider. Height, 1.75 meters in heels, identical).¹³⁶ She goes on, "Les digo igualitas no más ella puta en Hollywood y yo acá en Catemaco, ¿Cuál es la diferencia?" (Like I said, twins, only she's a whore in Hollywood and I'm one here in Catemaco. What's the difference?).¹³⁷ Through the humorous discourse and appearance, Enríquez parodies the film. However, he remains dressed as the sex-work version of Roberts's character for the entire hour and a half long show because he felt that he needed to perform the piece in heels to accurately reflect the lives of female sex workers on the street.¹³⁸ In the beginning, La Prietty tells the audience that she tries imitating Roberts, posing on the street, generally looking fabulous as she cruised for her wealthy businessman "en los coches, en los camiones, en el bici taxi . . . En la lancha, la banana, la acuamoto, el parachute pos a lo mejor ahí venía volando" (in cars, in buses, in bicycle taxis . . . In boats, canoes, water boats, and even parachutes, in case he was flying around up there in the sky).¹³⁹ Sadly, she has no luck. Provoking laughter, her comments are an astute critique of the way prostitution is glamorized in popular culture, but in her lived reality, searching for profitable clientele was both exhausting and rarely successful.

What makes this comparison even more humorous is that fact that La Prietty is aware that she looks nothing like the Hollywood star. By way of her rendition of "Pretty Woman," she makes that abundantly clear. She declares, "¡Esto es el soundtrack de mi vida!", and begins to sing her rendition:

> Prietty Guoman,
> Con el sol crecí
> Prietty Guoman
> y más me oscurecí
> Prietty Guoman
> Soy mexicana igual que tú pero parezco de Perú
>
> Prietty Guoman
> Los cocos sé partir
> Prietty Guoman
> Y mojarras freír
> Prietty Guoman
> Rostro rupestre con gracia mil, soy totonaca del Tajín.¹⁴⁰

Prietty Woman
Grew up under the sun
Prietty Woman
Now I'm the darker one
Prietty Woman
I'm Mexican just like you but I look like I'm from Peru

Prietty Woman
I know how to break coconuts
Prietty Woman
And fry up a nice tilapia
Prietty Woman
With strong features and a lustrous sheen, I'm Totonaca from Tajin.[141]

In this lyrical selection, the references to Peru and Tajín, sites linked to Indigenous histories, signal La Prietty's melanin-rich skin, as well as her intention to express belonging in a society that values light-skinned bodies. La Prietty engages master narratives such as those in the Mexican context, as in many sites throughout Latin America, where imagined racial construction has been essential to defining belonging and social recognition. From José Vasconcelos's seminal work, *La raza cósmica* (The Cosmic Race, 1925), to Mexico's Golden Age of cinema (1930–1960), official discourses of the twentieth century sought to blend Mexico's ethnic variability into an almost mythical Mexican mestizo, a light-skinned body that venerated an Indigenous past as long as it was delinked from Mexico's dark(er) skinned ancestors.[141] By way of lyrically integrating herself into the nation and appearing as a dark-skinned woman, La Prietty embodies "historically situated struggles" of a collectively marginalized group, even in her imagined utopic space.[142]

This is not the only time that La Prietty references her skin tone or pokes fun at Mexico's racist social stratification. Instead of claiming her indigeneity when she meets her captors in Veracruz, La Prietty tells them she was from a Caribbean island, letting them surmise she means Cuba. She openly admits to the audience that she has never been and has, on more than one occasion, had to improvise knowledge of her "homeland":

¿A poco sí eres cubana? ¿De qué parte de Cuba eres? . . . —De la playa—le dije. Porque hay que ser chava lista. Que me vuelve a preguntar ¿Quién gobierna Cuba me dice? —El pueblo—le dije—porque el pueblo manda—¡Yo totalmente anti-Trump! ¡Y porque no nada más hay que ser lista también hay que ser culta!¹⁴³

Are you really Cuban? What part of Cuba are you from? . . . —The beach—I said. It's important to be quick on your feet. And then he asks me another question: Who governs Cuba? —The people—I said, because the people rule—I am totally anti-Trump! And of course, more than witty, it's important to be intelligent!

La Prietty's humorous decision to construct herself as an historically exoticized dark Cuban body was strategic. Anita González explains that, the way *mexicanidad* has been imagined and repeated "obscures the presence of African, Asian, and other populations that have contributed to the growth of the nation."[144] By not including these dark-skinned bodies in the conceptualization of the new mestizo, the nation racially distanced itself from nations with larger African populations, such as Cuba; continuously and consistently, blackness has been displaced onto the Caribbean.[145] This state-sanctioned practice turned modern-day refrain effectively delinks blackness "from the modern imagination of *mexicanidad*," localizing it outside the bounds of the mestizo nation.[146] Mexico's geographical proximity to the island has facilitated the exchange of people, goods, and cultural practices. These tangible and embodied practices first entered through the most geographically accessible locations, like Yucatán and Veracruz, and later throughout the rest of the country, ultimately facilitating a fictionalized understanding of blackness and Afro-cultural transmission throughout the nation. At the same time, it begs pointing out, as Ben Vinson III and Herman Bennett have on numerous occasions, that during the colonial period, there were moments when free and enslaved black bodies outnumbered Spanish settlers, particularly in the metropolitan Mexico City.[147] Additionally, the archeological sites throughout Veracruz reconstruct Maroon survival tactics after Yanga's slave revolt, pointing to Mexico's Afro-diasporic populations beyond the Costa Chica regions of Oaxaca and Guerrero.[148] The repeated postcolonial construct of black Otherness has played out on the national stage, such as by way of Mexico's Golden Age of cinema. Cementing representations of *cubanidad* has become one of few ways for dark-skinned Others to exist, to be made intelligible, within the cultural imaginary of the nation.[149] In inventing a Cuban past, La Prietty attempts to localize herself within a narrative that may accept her as an exoticized sexual commodity rather than subject her to painful discrimination, as in the case of Indigenous citizens.

FROM MADONNA TO CELIA: A SOUNDTRACK OF SURVIVAL AND SOLIDARITY

After these elaborations of (racial) difference, La Prietty confesses one more thing that sets her apart from Roberts's character: talent. She states, "esa no canta, ni actúa, ni hace nada ... No más es bonita" (she doesn't sing, she doesn't act, she doesn't do anything ... She's just pretty).[150] Our protagonist reveals that to earn a living, she began impersonating others, who according to her had more talent and whom she resembles. She lists the following divas: Whitney Houston, Celia Cruz, Mariah Carey, and Madonna. This selection of icons speaks to La Prietty's connection to women of color, with the exception of Madonna, who arguably is the most crucial of all the divas for La Prietty's journey.

The protagonist channels the master chameleon herself, performing selections from "La Isla Bonita," "Like a Virgin," and "Vogue," each one mapping her body's trafficked movement and abuse. On the day she was driven to Veracruz to work in a brothel, she was inspired by the lyrics of "La Isla Bonita." Still dressed like Roberts's character, La Prietty does not yet visually interpret the US pop singer, but to make her performative intentions clear, she tries very hard to dance a box step with exaggerated gestures while repeating the one line she knows: "La isla Bonita ... La Isla Bonita ... La Isla Bonita ...."[151] She admits to the audience, "No hablo muy bien inglés pero sé claramente que esta canción habla de La isla bonita: Me imagino que habla de los arrecifes, de las cascadas, de los aborígenes; también es poeta la Madonna como yo" (I don't speak English very well, but I know this song speaks of a beautiful island. I imagine it describes coral reefs, waterfalls, aborigines; Madonna is a poet, just like me).[152] Just as Muñoz suggests, in this new stage of her life, La Prietty turns to hope in what could very easily be a time of despair. Rather than stress her horrible situation, she imagines herself surrounded by a tropical paradise. By way of her imagination, La Prietty manifests a radical place that provides hope and possibility for safe existence.

In addition to dealing with her captors' cruelty, La Prietty was constantly harassed and abused by other young, kidnapped women because of her trans identity and dark skin. That is, until she won them over with an assist from Madonna. In preparation for being trafficked abroad from Veracruz, which is an accessible port city, the protagonist taught them a choreography she made, set to "Like a Virgin." The irony is not lost on the audience members, who often burst into laughter at this revelation. Singing a few bars of the easily recognized tune, La Prietty reveals: "Nos la aprendimos en inglés y en español porque a todas nos habían dicho que nos iban a llevar pa los United" (We learned it in Spanish and English because they told us we were being sent to the United States).[153] In this brief assertion, the protagonist makes a searing commentary about how female bodies in Mexico "are conceived of as products of exchange," shipped across borders as dehumanized remnants of citizenry.[154] La Prietty's revelation is also reminder to spectators that underneath her optimistic tone lies horrific truths. Her voice shifts, now flat and serious as she states: "Porque no sólo en Tlaxcala se venden a las mujeres, en el mundo las mujeres somos de exportación" (because it's not just in Tlaxcala that women are sold, but all over the world women are seen as exportable goods).[155] Then, quickly dancing across the stage, as if performing a *jarabe tapatío*, La Prietty sings a list of more than thirty Mexican cities and states where women are kidnapped and sold into the sex trade. In this hard transition between seriousness and playfulness, the protagonist highlights cartographies of sexual labor, cruelty, and impunity in which many Mexican women are forced to participate.

Turning back to her own story, La Prietty recounts that after memorizing the lyrics and her dance routine, she is prepared to be sent abroad. This time, a boat rather than a car was to bring her to the next stage of her journey. Out in the open sea, she details how her male captor realizes she is trans after sexually assaulting her. Potential death by drowning or shark attack seemed preferable to what would happen if she stayed aboard. Remembering that all of this action occurs in La Prietty's afterlife, the fear and violence she experiences in her own imagination are a terrible reminder of the way trans women are murdered "a veces más de dos veces en una misma vida" (sometimes twice in the same lifetime).[156] In 2014, Mexico City passed a law that recognizes a person's identity may not match the gender they were assigned at birth, though the frequent disparity between the law and its enforcement further dehumanizes the trans body.[157] On a national scale, the murders of trans women are compounded by another layer of brutality: most are not even catalogued as feminicide. La Prietty explains:

> Se nos mata de distintas maneras y a veces más de dos veces en una misma vida. Se nos mata poniéndonos el nombre masculino que nunca quisimos llevar, se nos mata después de muertas llevándonos al féretro con la ropa del sexo que nunca quisimos portar, se nos mata saliendo en la portada del periódico cuando se burla de nosotras diciendo ¡Joticidio! Siendo esto un feminicidio.[158]

> *They kill us so in so many ways, and sometimes even twice in the same lifetime. They kill us by using the masculine name that we never wanted to use, they kill us after death dressing us up like men for our funeral, using the clothes we never wanted to wear, they kill us again in the newspapers when they make fun of us, calling us victims of "Faggicide" even though it was it was feminicide.*

As if these bodies cannot rest in peace, La Prietty's efforts to emphasize hope

FIGURE 4.5. La Prietty, transformed into her version of Madonna, prepares to sing her rendition of "Vogue." *La Prietty Guoman*, Teatro de la Ciudad Esperanza Iris, Mexico City, Mexico, 2018. Photo by Secretaría de Cultura CDMX.

and resist erasure are always marred by the fact that the "here and now" is often an awful experience for Othered bodies who do not fit "white, heterosexual, masculinist formulas" of power.[159]

Our protagonist, however, is a symbol of survival. When she washes up on shore and sees the sun, she assumes she made it to Miami. Basking in the light of her imagined future with Gloria Estefan, she echoes Muñoz's utopic queerness as the "warm illumination of a horizon imbued with potentiality."[160] La Prietty very quickly realizes, however, she only made it to Tabasco when she is greeted by the woman who would change her life. La Muda would become her new best friend, musician, and entrepreneur. Gesturing with sign language and writing on small sheets of paper, La Muda invites her to become a performer in her nightclub, but as an artist, not a prostitute or sex slave. In this new place, La Prietty is afforded an opportunity to start anew, again, crafting new stages and spaces of hope.

At La Dorothy, a comfortable place for all kinds of people, no matter how they identify, La Prietty seems to have found a tangible, radical place that shields her from violence. Here, she starts a new life filled with characters that accept her for who she really is. This club, "su lugar jotero y especial" (your queer and very special place), is a sanctuary for LGBTQ+ people like her and embodies the very literal stages that Muñoz imagines filled with utopic potential.[161] Just as Muñoz analyzes the stages of Los Angeles, filled with amateur aesthetics, drag queens, and a sense of belonging, La Dorothy offers La Prietty a space not just to imagine inclusivity, but to live it.[162] Approaching the white car onstage, the protagonist opens the trunk and pulls out a curly blond wig and a gold corset with pointy brassiere. Transformed into Madonna in front of the spectators' eyes, she gives her first show, "Vogue," at La Dorothy.

Pointing out her beauty, nerve, and talent, La Prietty declares the club a place of queer culture and appreciation. Just as Madonna raps in her version of "Vogue," the protagonist does so as well, but La Prietty creates her own version of the lyrics:

> Anda ven sal ya del closet Ponte orgullo y los tacones
> Sor Juana y Sara García las tortillas aplaudían
> Pedro Infante y Frida Kahlo le daban a los dos bandos
> La Chavela y Monsiváis reinas de la Marcha Gay
> Bienvenido gay, lesbiana si es obvia mejor mana. Bisexual, intersexual judío y musulmán.
> Negras, blancas, pelirroja, las albinas, tu pecosa;
> gorda, flaca, musculosa, qué importa somos personas.[163]

> *Come on, come out of the closet, get proud and put on your heels*
> *The lesbians Sor Juana and Sara García applaud you*
> *Pedro Infante and Frida Kahlo played on both teams*
> *Chavela and Monsiváis were queens of the Gay Parade*
> *Welcome gays, lesbians (yes, it is that obvious), bisexuals, intersexuals, Jews, and Muslims.*
> *Blacks, whites, redheads too, albinos, and you with freckles*
> *Fat, skinny, muscular or not, what does it matter, we're all people here.*

Enunciating the list of diverse public figures, with varying sexual orientations, physical attributes, and more, La Prietty emphasizes a discourse of belonging, one that resists silence and erasure from the public eye. In doing so, the protagonist signals how some of the nation's cultural treasures are part of a queer community. Just as Madonna invites listeners to let their bodies "move to the music," La Prietty makes it clear that any, and every, body is welcome to groove with her at La Dorothy. In doing so, La Prietty transforms the imagined space of La Dorothy and the actual theatre stage into imagined queer utopias.

Despite professional success at the bar and her friendship with La Muda, La Prietty's goal throughout the various stages, and spaces, was to find her Richard Gere. Even the audience becomes invested in her search for a wealthy gentleman to love and rescue her from the horrors of sex work. After much praying and asking around in La Dorothy and on the streets, the protagonist finally finds her leading man. Driving a 2013 Volkswagen Jetta, La Prietty's Richard, the owner of an avocado stand, brings her flowers, writes her poetry, and says he loves her.[164] Not quite the limousine or profession she imagined from the film, but she is thrilled. When he pulls up to the club, she faces a bittersweet end to her partnership with La Muda, but a promising new chapter for her future. She is ready to embark on a journey once again across new lands in an effort to secure hope.

As a farewell gesture, La Prietty transforms before our eyes, putting on a tight, floor-length red dress, covered in sparkles from head to toe, and a black-haired wig. She then dedicates Whitney Houston's "I Have Nothing," from the 1992 *Bodyguard* soundtrack, to La Muda. Accompanied on piano, La Prietty performs, word for word, Houston's hit. There is no double entendre, there are no mispronounced English words, and La Prietty pauses at all the right moments. Belting out, "Don't make me close one more door / I don't want to hurt anymore / Stay in my arms if you dare / or must I imagine you there," the audience gets goosebumps. She even attempts Houston's iconic vocal arpeggio runs at the end, transforming the words, "Don't you dare walk away from me / I have nothing, nothing, nothing / If I don't have you, you / If I don't have you, oh, oh," into expressions of raw emotion.[165] Seamlessly maneuvering between deeper chest tones and soprano notes, La Prietty gives the performance of a lifetime to her enraptured audience and La Muda.

In looking to pop culture divas, La Prietty's staged (after)life is imagined in relation to glamor, success, and fame. Yet, Enríquez's overall creative vision is always conscious that this storyline never existed because, well, La Prietty never existed. Seated in front of the audience, she asks them if they have liked her story, one in which after much struggle and violence, she does find love. Unfailingly, the audience responds with resounding cheers, to which she responds that she too would have like to have lived that life, but never had the chance. Much like Valencia's assertion that "contemporary history is no longer based on the experiences of survivors, but rather on the vast numbers of the dead," she then becomes a voice for all the trans women murdered.¹⁶⁶ She proclaims:

> ¡Por Paola, por Viviana, por Alessa, por Agnes, por Tavita! Por la Julia por Alaska que la coronaron hace poco como reina de belleza y después le pusieron un alambre de púas como collar. Por cada mujer asesinada, por todas las que se les oculta, por todas las que se les embolsa, por las miles más que no somos ni si quiera una estadística ante una sociedad feminicide.¹⁶⁷

> *For Paola, Viviana, Alessa, Agnes, and Tavita! For Julia and Alaska, who just after being named a beauty queen was killed and crowned with barbed wire tied around her neck. For every woman murdered, for each one of them who is forgotten, for all of those put in plastic bags, and for the thousands more who are not even a statistic in this feminicide-ridden country.*

Relating the contemporary statistics and names of trans women killed in Mexico, her voice breaks, and she begins to cry. But she is not alone. Gasps of horror and held back sobs can be heard throughout the theatre, whether in Mexico City, Chicago, or Cádiz. In these profoundly moving silences, her spectral existence becomes indelibly linked to Mexico's veiled war and violent acts that excluded her from protections afforded to gender- and sexuality-normative beings. Moreover, these silences represent, time and again, the audience's recognition not just of La Prietty's humanity and mournability, but of the humanity and mournability of the litany of murdered trans women.

But rather than end on that note, La Prietty wipes her tears and performs one last song, "I Will Survive" a la Celia Cruz. Transforming before her audience's eyes, she removes from the car trunk a bright yellow dress with arm ruffles, reminiscent of the *rumberas* from Mexico's Golden Age of cinema. Channeling Justin Torres's proclamation after the Orlando shooting, "the only imperative is to be transformed, transfigured in the disco light. To lighten, loosen, see yourself reflected in the beauty of others. You didn't come here to be a martyr, you came to live, papi. To live, mamacita. To live, hijos," La Prietty gives life.¹⁶⁸ With a salsa beat, our protagonist proclaims: "Yo viviré, ahí estaré / Hoy armemos la comparsa yo está rumba cantaré" (I will survive, I will be there / Tonight, let's have a party and I'll provide the beat).¹⁶⁹ Standing among the audience members, La Prietty instructs spectators to shout the word "fuera" as she lists a litany of discriminatory practices ranging from derogatory language to political corruption. The audience then joins her in condemning these practices. Then, in a final gesture, La Prietty invites everyone to sing along with her. In this symbolic move, La

FIGURE 4.6. La Prietty prepares to sing "I Have Nothing" by Whitney Houston. La Mudita helps the protagonist zip up her red dress. *La Prietty Guoman*, Teatro NH, Mexico City, Mexico, 2018. Photo by Christina Baker.

Prietty's strained voice becomes intertwined with the voices of those in the audience. This chorus of voices, ringing out firmly, commanding the space, and demanding change, is a powerful sensation. The unified proclamations of acceptance and resilience are loud and proud. In this moment, La Prietty and her audience seem capable of "trac[ing] out paths of defiance that allow them to live in struggle through effective, micropolitical resistance."[170] Via this collective clamor, the audience joins La Prietty and La Muda in their efforts to solidify their radical geography of hope and survival. The reverberating message, that of recognizing the protagonist's humanity, extends to the collective struggles of trans women and minorities. La Prietty dominates the stage as she sings:

>Para ti mi gente siempre aquí estaré
>Yo te doy mi azúcar caramba y sobreviviré
>(Rompiendo barreras, voy sobreviviendo
>cruzando fronteras, voy sobreviviendo)
>Yo viviré, yo viviré, yo viviré y sobreviviré[171]

>*For you, my people, I will always be here*
>*I'll give you my sugar and I will survive,*
>*(Breaking boundaries, I am surviving*
>*Crossing borders, I am surviving)*
>*I will survive, I will survive, I will survive*

CONCLUSION

"I will always be here, I will survive." These final lines reverberate throughout the three performances I have analyzed in this chapter. Though arguably *Ni una menos* and *El Desierto de Las Leonas* end on a more somber note than *La Prietty Guoman*, all three conclude with the insistence on continued existence. Even in the face of death, these mimetic figures refuse to accept the finality of their situation. They refuse to accept their violent and tragic feminicide and trans feminicide. Instead, the onstage figures engage musical practice to reimagine a life unrestrained by death, constant threats of *machista* violence, and daily harassment. Musical numbers like La Prietty's "I Will Survive" capture the way each of the works in this chapter envisions what I have referred to as radical geographies of hope and survival. The resurrection of female bodies to the sounds of "Ni una menos," the determined search for the utopic La Haya while singing "Somos más," and the club space of La Dorothy where La Prietty becomes Whitney and Madonna underscore the power of music to transport us from a desperate situation to a hopeful alternative. Maneuvering beyond time, space, and even linguistic barriers, music allows these onstage women and trans women to evade what is most certainly a heinous end. Their soundtracks of an (after)life become the escape mechanism where they can imagine an alternative, one in which they are not only safe from harm, but also find solidarity in the arms of other women and trans women.

Conclusion

At approximately 5 p.m. on March 7, 2020, Mexico City's Zócalo was transformed into a scene of feminist resistance. On the eve of what would become a historic collective demonstration of female and feminist solidarity for #8M, hundreds if not thousands of women gathered in the city center ready to bring about a reckoning. Vivir Quintana's live debut of "Canción sin miedo" set the tone for that evening's concert and the march the following day—it has since become a powerful anthem against feminicide in Mexico and beyond.[1] Quintana's performance dealt a deafening blow to the nation's heteropatriarchal complicity as gender violence statistics increase year after year. The concert was organized by the Tiempo de Mujeres festival, which brings discussions, workshops, and theater performances both to the capital's metropolitan regions and to the periphery. The main artists that evening were Chilean Mon Laferte, Franco-Chilean Ana Tijoux, and Guatemalan Sara Curruchich, though Quintana has since become the evening's protagonist.[2] Joining Laferte on stage, Quintana and the all-female choir known as El Palomar became a collective of exasperated and enraged voices from across the Americas clamoring for justice. With lyrics like "que tiemble el Estado, los cielos, las calles / Que tiemblen los jueces y los judiciales" (the state should quiver, the heavens and streets as well / The judges and officers should quiver) and "Yo todo lo incendio, yo todo lo rompo" (I'll burn it all down, I'll break it all apart), the words resound against those in power as a furious recrimination for their disinterest and propagation of impunity.[3] If in 2007 the audible contours of the Zócalo proclaimed Andrés Manuel López the nation's rightful president, in 2020 the tables had turned. Quintana and the female collective commanded, "No olvide sus nombres, por favor, señor president" (Do not forget their names, please, Mr. President), a direct challenge to AMLO's legitimacy as the number of women murdered each day had risen to eleven and counting under his watch.

Unlike the 2007 event I described at the beginning of this book, a plaza divided in its celebration of the nation's Independence, on this March evening the space was united. The goal was to materialize another kind of liberation, one that is best represented by the hashtag #sevacaer (#itsgoingdown), targeting historically violent *machista* institutions. These tensions between the past and present, tradition and change, were made audible through the lyrics and musical arrangement of "Canción sin miedo." To start, the song's lyrics symbolically and rhetorically takes aim at Mexico's national anthem, adopted in 1853. While Quintana does not technically rewrite the anthem, she mimics its alexandrine poetic structure, meaning lines comprised of twelve syllables. The anthem's use of this European style, dating back to the twelfth century, associated with renown authors like Spanish Juan Ruiz or French Victor Hugo, reflects an intentional performance of literacy and worldliness that becomes astutely adopted by Quintana in the twenty-first century. Carefully crafting each line to follow the alexandrine style, Quintana firmly situates her feminist discourse within the realm of intellectualism, making it difficult to simply dismiss her words as propaganda. In terms of content, "Canción sin miedo," much like the anthem, invokes moments of conflict and bloodshed, suggesting that resistance is vital to preserving sovereignty. In the case of the 2020 production, the vitality of the female and female-presenting body, conceived of as its own territory deserving of protections and safety, is at stake.

In the event Quintana's calculated references to the national anthem were not clear, she concludes the song with an overt and unmistakable connection. Modifying the following lines from the anthem's refrain, "y retiemble en sus centros la tierra / Al sonoro rugir del cañon" (and the land shakes to its core / at the sound of the cannon's roar), "Canción sin miedo" concludes, "Y retiemblen sus centros la tierra / Al sororo rugir del amor" (and they are shaken to their core / upon hearing the roar of female solidarity and love).[4] Considering that the Ley sobre el Escudo, la Bandera y el Himno Nacional (Law regarding the Emblem, Flag, and National Anthem) details acceptable environments where the anthem can and should be performed, and unsurprisingly, protests, especially those meant to recriminate the president, are not on that approved list.[5] More importantly, the law strictly prohibits modifications to the lyrics or compositional style, making Quintana's decision is a bold move, to say the least.[6] The singer's decision to debut the song in such a public way, in front of thousands of people, reflects her own desire to "cantar sin miedo" (sing without fear) in spite of potential retaliation.

Beyond the politically charged lyrics, the performatic style of "Canción sin miedo" conjures familiar sonic cues associated with the *ranchera* genre

I described in Chapter 1. In this March 2020 performance, the aural references reverberate by way of acoustic guitars, a chorus of voices that accompany Laferte and Quintana, the sounds of excited whistles, and emulations of a "grito." Similar to Father Miguel Hidalgo's rallying cries associated with the Independence movement, the *ranchera* often incorporates its own kind of "grito" meant to express a man's emotional anguish over lost love. The sounds of masculine voices emitting high-pitched screams of "¡ay, yay, yay!" are almost always accompanied by a male chorus of whistles and cheers, as if communicating solidarity and encouragement. In "Canción sin miedo," the "grito" similarly expresses anguish and pain but is very literally associated with the war waged against female and female-presenting bodies throughout the nation. For Quintana and her chorus of accompanying voices, the sonic cry becomes a call to arms. For example, following the heart-wrenching lyric, "Soy la niña que subiste por la fuerza" (I'm the girl you took by force), Quintana's screams collide with the collective vocals of the all-female chorus that responds with whistles and by repeating the word "justice." By making these sounds and shouting "justice" over and over again, El Palomar reveals not simply enthusiasm for collective action, but also a firm repudiation of violence.

The vocals of Laferte, Quintana, and El Palomar became markers that March afternoon of female dissidence that fervently reject the *ranchera*'s historical association with masculine dominance. This resistance is further reinforced by the quality of the voices themselves, as throughout the song they sound like contained screams, voices on the edge of breaking from strain. Regardless, they remain strong, especially as they name some of the nation's better-known victims: "Soy Claudia, soy Esther y soy Teresa / Soy Ingrid, soy Fabiola y soy Valeria" (I am Claudia, I am Esther, and I am Teresa / I am Ingrid, I am Fabiola, and I am Valeria). In identifying the murdered women, this litany is a performative act of making them once again *¡presente!* The singing voices continue:

> Por todas las compas marchando en Reforma
> Por todas las morras peleando en Sonora
> Por las comandantes luchando por Chiapas
> Por todas las madres buscando en Tijuana[8]

> *For all the women marching down Reforma*
> *For all the women battling in Sonora*
> *For all the women fighting across Chiapas*
> *For all the mothers searching in Tijuana*

These clearly articulated and audible geographical reference points tether the nation's borders from north to south, while the imagery of women marching, fighting, leading, and searching reproduce the experiences of war that have guided this book. In this case, however, the women are fighting a war within a war. They organize themselves collectively to ensure that the perpetrators collaborating and complicit in feminicide "caiga con fuerza" (be forcefully overthrown).

As a means of giving voice to their demands, the March 7 performance becomes one of many sonic acts dedicated to promoting a woman's right to live and protect her body. The concert echoed the November 25, 2019, use of silent glitter bombs and raucous sounds of spray paint, chants, and fires heard throughout the capital city, sonic strategies geared to lay bare the rising numbers of cases of gender violence. These gatherings demonstrate the extent to which female declarations of power can be heard reverberating through city streets across the Americas. While I was not present for the 2020 concert, its transmission via digital platforms made it the shot heard round the world. It traveled within Mexico's borders and to international spaces almost instantaneously, thanks to livestreaming and Youtube. In fact, Quintana's composition has been adapted by groups in Uruguay, Brazil, Colombia, Ecuador, Panama, and Puerto Rico, signaling the terrifying ubiquity of gendered violence. Moreover, "Canción sin miedo" joins a series of musical creations that blend the division between protest song and popular music, such as the Chilean song "El violador eres tú," or Chocolate Remix's "Ni una menos" that I analyze in Chapter 4.[9] Resounding through public spaces, vibrating in and around government buildings, elite theatres, and other spaces inhabited by those in power, these feminist anthems capture "what popular music can offer about the debates that continue to trouble the world and some of its cities."[10] They become the means by which Mexico's women publicly express their nonconformity and their desire for social transformation. These anthems are the sounds of resistance.[11]

I conclude *Sonic Strategies: Performing Mexico's War on Drugs, Mourning, and Feminicide* with "Canción miedo" as an example of sonic and physical occupation of the Zócalo to round out my final chapter's consideration of musical declarations against feminicide. The song also allows me to bring the book full circle. I end where I began: the heart of Mexico City, the nation's most contested stage.[12] Occupying this space of political, cultural, and social significance, the September 2007 Independence celebration and March 2020 feminist musical intervention exemplify the imperative to be more attuned to sound in the humanities, as it is sound is too vast and loud to be ignored. Though sound arguably acquires meaning by way of interpretation, and sociocultural and historical contexts, the 2007 and 2020 events in the city's main plaza point to the audible realm as a mechanism for understanding contemporary Mexico. Importantly, these two sonic events are performances of social struggles after 2006. During the first, edgy rock bands proclaimed AMLO leader of the nation, and over a decade later, "Canción sin miedo" highlights the public's rapidly deteriorating trust in his decisions as president.

Throughout the book's four chapters, *Sonic Strategies* has focused less on stand-alone musical performances, such as those performed in the Zócalo, and has instead maintained the importance of sounds performed on stages across Mexico. Concretely, this study has analyzed sonic stimuli, understood as music, audience sounds, unplanned interjections, and noise as crucial to theater and performance works after 2006, the start of the nation's War on Drugs. Although there is no monolithic way to process or understand the magnitude of this conflict, this book has explored some of the obvious outcomes, which have included the rise of *narco*-related crimes, violent cartel feuds, the forced disappearances of Mexican youth, local and federal police corruption, and necropolitical legal practices. This project has also considered the way the war has shaped immigration flows, abuses along the border, and rampant gendered violence toward women, female-presenting bodies, and nonnormative figures. What makes theater and performance compelling sites to examine the vast and varied impact of war is their ability to facilitate the shared act of experiencing a live performance, giving rise to a temporary community, what Jorge Dubatti refers to as *convivio*.[13] These spaces of conviviality and embodied practice activate the senses of the artists involved and the audience members in attendance. And yet, theater and performance researchers tend to privilege linguistic and visual cues on stage, despite the way aurality offers unique opportunities for intellectual inquiry. In the case of Mexico, the seemingly ubiquitous nature of *narco* language and visual markers of violence makes it easy to understand how and why scholars have often zeroed in on the spectacular qualities of war onstage and off. At the same time, the War on Drugs has indelibly shaped the sonicscape of the nation.

By emphasizing the centrality of sonic triggers in performance works, *Sonic Strategies* diversifies perspectives on how war is enacted and perceived not just within the realm of theater and performance studies, but also across disciplines that seek to analyze the ramifications of violent conflict. Notably, each performance included in this study emphasizes the complexities, nuances, and aftershocks of war by way of audible geographies. These geographies—sometimes physical, sometimes metaphorical—map a suffering nation, and the undergirding connective thread of sound illustrates how citizens internalize, manifest, and reimagine the audible contours of a wounded country. Whether via Las Reinas Chulas' sonic disidentifications with Mexico's Golden Age cinema or Enrique Ježik's, Hugo Salcedo's, and Lechedevirgen Trimegisto's enactments of the progressive sounds of Mexico's War on Drugs, aurality is evidence of how artists make myriad victims heard and knowable in a nation that routinely denies casualties of war the dignity of recognition. Moreover, from Violeta Luna's and Lukas Avendaño's nonverbal and silent embodiments of the nation's Antigones to the soundtracks of Las Pussy Queers, La Mafia Cabaret, and César Enríquez as radical cartographies that refuse feminicide and transfeminicide, sonic stimuli provide performers with creative ways to remember bodies, make the weight of the disappeared felt despite their painful absence, and give the forcibly silenced a new voice.

In amplifying the auditory realm, my aim has been to demonstrate the impact of sound within the theatre space, as well as within and upon us as spectators, scholars, and listeners. Each of the works in this study highlights how sonic sensations invade, fold, envelop, ricochet, and maneuver through space and time. From revised Gloria Trevi to haunting techno music, the sonic reverberations and vibrations enhance the verbal, embodied, and visual gestures onstage and in written texts, creating opportunities to appreciate meaning that may otherwise go unnoticed. As such, *Sonic Strategies* has attempted to answer key questions about what sound can teach us when we turn our ear toward the aural realm within theater and performance arenas. In effect, each chapter has illustrated, in very real ways, what Les Back calls "the art of listening," as the variety of works, theoretical considerations, personal discourses, and intimate reflections demonstrate what happens when we let our sources speak for themselves and, importantly, be heard.

Notes

INTRODUCTION

1. James Patrick Kiernan, "Grito de Dolores," *Américas* 62, no. 6 (2010): 64. All translations are by the author, unless otherwise indicated.
2. I use the word "legitimate" in quotation marks because those in support of Andrés Manuel López Obrador repeated the refrain "el president legítimo" (the legitimate president) for well over a year after the election. For more, see "El Grito de Independencia de AMLO como 'presidente legítimo' en 2007," *Zona Guadalajara*, September 18, 2007, https://zonaguadalajara.com/grito-independencia-amlo-2007, and "López Obrador se proclama 'presidente legítimo' de México," *El País*, November 20, 2006, https://elpais.com/internacional/2006/11/21/actualidad/1164063605_850215.html. For a short clip of Andrés Manuel López Obrador's "legitimate" 2007 Grito, see "Grito de Independencia de AMLO (15 de septiembre de 2007)," Youtube, uploaded by xhglc, September 18, 2007, https://www.youtube.com/watch?v=jz4zxb31qiY.
3. Ileana Diéguez, *Cuerpos sin duelo: Iconografías y teatralidades del dolor* (Córdoba, Argentina: Ediciones Documenta/Escénicas, 2013). Diéguez asserts, "México se ha llenado de muertos. Pero la muerte no es una cifra, es un límite real, una dimensión matérica, un olor. Y su expansión desmedida nos contamina" (Mexico is filled with dead bodies. Yet, death it not just a number, it is also a real limit, a material dimension, a smell. Moreover, it spreads uncontrollably and contaminates us all). Diéguez, *Cuerpos*, 29.
4. I consciously employ the term feminicide throughout this manuscript, following Marcela Lagarde y de Los Ríos's argument that femicide is homologous to homicide of women whereas feminicide designates "genocide against women." For more see, Marcela Lagarde y de Los Ríos, "Preface: Feminist Keys for Understanding Feminicide: Theoretical, Political, and Legal Construction," in *Terrorizing Women: Feminicide in the Américas*, edited by Rosa-Linda Fregoso and Cynthia Bejarano (Durham, NC: Duke University Press, 2010), xi–xxvi.

5. I am inspired by the title of Cristina Rivera Garza's book *Grieving: Dispatches from a Wounded Country*, translated by Sara Booker (New York: Feminist Press, 2020), a collection of journalistic-style pieces and personal essays on systemic violence in Mexico and along the US–Mexico border.
6. When I say sound has power, I am inspired by Tia DeNora's assertion that music "does much more than convey signification through non-verbal means. At the level of daily life, music has power." Tia DeNora, *Music in Everyday Life* (Cambridge: Cambridge University Press, 2009), 17.
7. Jean-Luc Nancy, *Listening*, translated by Charlotte Mandell (New York: Fordham University Press, 2002), 5
8. Nancy, *Listening*, 12–14.
9. Phelan states that performance's only life is in the present; "it cannot be saved, recorded, documented, or otherwise participate in the circulation of representations *of* representations: Once it does so it becomes something other than performance." Peggy Phelan, *Unmarked: The Politics of Performance* (New York: Routledge, 1991), 146.
10. Cecilia Sotres, *Introducción al cabaret (con albur)* (Mexico City: Paso de Gato, 2016), 22.
11. Jorge Dubatti, *Filosofía del Teatro I: Convivio, Experiencia, Subjetividad* (Buenos Aires: Atuel. 2007). According to Dubatti, *convivio* is the gathering of two or more people resulting in an encounter experienced at the crossroads outside of daily life. This basic definition becomes the base of his philosophy of theater, a happening rooted in liveness, the shared act of being there. Dubatti, *Filosofía del Teatro I*, 43.
12. Rodolfo Sánchez Alvarado, a sound engineer for innumerable radio, theater, dance, and film productions between 1957 and 2011, refers to his work as "escenofonía," the space where all that is sonic becomes part of the scenic action. See Leandro Luis Rey, "La Escenografía de Rodolfo Sánchez Alvarado. De la musicalización del teatro hacia la teatralización de la música," *Argus-a: Artes y Humanidades* 10, no. 38 (December 200): 4. In speaking of her work, Violeta Luna refers to the "musical architecture," though her musical partner, David Molina, does not use this same terminology. Renowned Argentine sound designer Zypce refers to his work as "sonic dramaturgy."
13. Samuel Araújo and Grupo Musicultura, "Sound Praxis: Music, Politics, and Violence in Brazil," in *Music and Conflict*, edited by John Morgan O'Connell and Salwa El-Shawan Castelo-Branco (Urbana: University of Illinois Press, 2010), 2017.
14. Key edited volumes that have helped shape conversations in the aforementioned fields, as well as my own ideas, include *Music, Politics, and Violence*, edited by Susan Fast and Kip Pegley (Middletown, CT: Wesleyan University Press, 2012), and *Music and Conflict*, edited by John Morgan O'Connell and Salwa El-Shawan Castelo-Branco (Chicago: University of Illinois Press, 2010).

15. Salwa El-Shawan Castelo-Branco, "Epilogue: Ethnomusicologists as Advocates," in *Music and Conflict*, edited by John Morgan O'Connell and Salwa El-Shawan Castelo-Branco (Chicago: University of Illinois Press, 2010), 245.
16. J. Martin Daughtry, *Listening to War: Sound, Music, Trauma, and Survival in Wartime Iraq* (Oxford: Oxford University Press, 2015), 6.
17. Steve Goodman, *Sonic Warfare: Sound, Affect, and the Ecology of Fear* (Cambridge, MA: MIT Press, 2009), xiv.
18. Carol Martin, *Theatre of the Real* (New York: Palgrave Macmillan, 2013), 4.
19. Lindsey Mantoan, *War as Performance: Conflicts in Iraq and Political Theatricality* (New York: Palgrave Macmillan, 2018), 5. Also see Jennifer Hughes, *Performance in a Time of Terror: Critical Mimesis and the Age of Uncertainty* (Manchester: Manchester University Press, 2011), 5.
20. Paola S. Hernández, *Staging Lives in Latin American Theater: Bodies, Objects, Archives* (Evanston, IL: Northwestern University Press, 2021), 4.
21. Lynne Kendrick, *Theatre Aurality* (New York: Palgrave, 2017), xv-xix.
22. George Home-Cook, *Theatre and Aural Attention: Stretching Ourselves* (New York: Palgrave, 2015), 173; emphasis in original.
23. Fred Moten's *In the Break: The Aesthetics of the Black Radical Tradition* (Minneapolis: University of Minnesota press, 2003) positions shrieks and breaks as critical hermeneutic tools for listening to Frederick Douglass, Amiri Baraka, and Duke Ellington, among others. Alexandra T. Vásquez's *Listening in Detail: Performances of Cuban Music* (Durham, NC: Duke University Press, 2013) leverages Caribbean musical performance in the US to study migratory routes, memory-making practices, refugee community formation, and reparative acts in the wake of dispossession. Roshanak Kheshti's *Modernity's Ear: Listening to Race and Gender in World Music* (New York: NYU Press, 2015) analyzes how white women listen to music made by and for diasporic groups as a reflection of biopolitics and the contemporary US music industry.
24. Josefina Alcázar, *Performance un arte del yo: Autobiografía, cuerpo e identidad* (Mexico City: Siglo xxi editors, 2014). Alcázar states, "el performance se despliega en y desde el cuerpo.... Los artistas de performance buscan estrechar la distancia entre el arte y la vida" (performance unfolds within and from the body.... Performance artists seek to reduce the distance between life and art). Alcázar, *Performance un arte del yo*, 8.
25. For a powerful aural analysis of protests in the wake of Ayotzinapa, see Jorge Velasco García, *El Sonido de la resistencia: Patrimonio musical. El canto popular en los movimientos sociales del siglo XXI en México* (Mexico City: FONCA, 2017). Anthony W. Rasmussen, "Resistance Resounds: Hearing Power in Mexico City" (PhD diss., University of California Riverside, 2017), dedicates chapter 4 to the sounds of public protests and Ayotzinapa, and for more specifically on Las Hijas de la Violencia, see 180–85. Los Macuanos' song is available on Youtube, "Los Macuanos - Sangre, Bandera, Cruz," uploaded by azucatto,

December 21, 2016, https://www.youtube.com/watch?v=YDSw9n70OTE. A fragment of Reyes' installation is available on Youtube, "Pedro Reyes - Disarm," uploaded by Carnegie Museum of Art, August 27, 2018, https://www.youtube.com/watch?v=rHjsxdONSpw.

CHAPTER 1

1. Ana Francis Mor et al., *Nosotras las proles*, performance, Coyoacán, Mexico, August 16, 2013.
2. "Hija de Peña Nieto califica de 'pendejos' y 'prole' a los críticos de su padre." *Vanguardia*, September 23, 2015, https://vanguardia.com.mx/hijadepenanieto-calificadependejosyprolealoscriticosdesupadre-1162731.html.
3. Rosa Elvira Vargas, "Hija de Peña Nieto causa ira en Twitter al renviar mensaje que insulta a críticos." *La Jornada*, December 6, 2011, https://www.jornada.com.mx/2011/12/06/politica/013n1pol.
4. Peter Brooks, *The Melodramatic Imagination: Balzac, Henry James, Melodrama and the Mode of Excess* (New Haven, CT: Yale University Press, 1976). According to Brooks, melodrama "appears to have first been used in this sense by Rousseau, to describe a play in which he sought a new emotional expressivity through the mixture of spoken soliloquy, pantomime, and orchestral accompaniment." Brooks, *The Melodramatic Imagination*, 14.
5. Thomas Elsaesser, "Tales of Sound and Fury: Observations on the Family Melodrama," in *Imitations of Life: A Reader on Film and Television Melodrama*, edited by Marcia Landy (Detroit, MI: Wayne State Press, 1991), 74.
6. Ana M. López, "Mexico," in *The International Film Musical*, edited by Corey K. Creekmur and Linda Y. Mokdad (Edinburgh: Edinburgh University Press, 2012), 122. For a broader consideration of the melodrama in Latin America, see Darlene J. Sadlier, ed., *Latin American Melodrama: Passion, Pathos, and Entertainment* (Urbana: University of Illinois Press, 2009).
7. Jacqueline Avila, *Cinesonidos: Film Music and National Identity during Mexico's Época de Oro* (New York: Oxford University Press, 2019), 3.
8. Avila, *Cinesonidos*, 3.
9. Néstor García Canclini, *Consumers and Citizens: Globalization and Multicultural Conflicts*, translated by George Yúdice (Minneapolis: University of Minnesota Press, 2001), 113.
10. Ana Francis Mor, personal interview, August 18, 2013.
11. For key studies on the relationship between cinema and cultural formation, see Carlos Monsiváis, *Escenas de pudor y liviandad* (Barcelona: Editorial Grijalbo, 1981); Carlos Monsiváis, "And All the People Came and Did Not Fit onto the Screen: Notes on the Cinema Audience in Mexico," in *Mexican Cinema*, edited by Paulo Antonio Parangaguá and translated by Ana López (London: British Film Institute, 1995), 145–51; and Carlos Monsiváis, "Mythologies," in *Mexican Cinema*, edited by Paulo Antonio Parangaguá and translated by Ana López (London: British Film Institute, 1995), 117–27.

12. Susan Denver, *Celluloid Nationalism and Other Melodramas: From Post-Revolutionary Mexico to fin de siglo Mexamérica* (Albany: State University of New York Press, 2003), 110.
13. Gilbert Joseph, Anne Rubenstein, and Eric Zolov, eds., *Fragments of a Golden Age: The Politics of Culture in Mexico Since 1940* (Durham, NC: Duke University Press, 2001), 6
14. Manthia Diawara, "Black British Cinema: Spectatorship and Identity Formation in *Territories*," *Public Culture* 3, no.1 (Fall 1990): 36.
15. bell hooks, *Black Looks: Race and Representation* (Boston: South End, 1992), 4. hooks further explores the notion of the oppositional gaze in her article, "The Oppositional Gaze: Black Female Spectators," in *The Film Theory Reader: Debates and Arguments*, edited by Marc Furstenau (New York: Routledge, 2010): 229–41.
16. Anne Friedberg, "A Denial of Difference: Theories of Cinematic Identification" in *Psychoanalysis and Cinema*, edited by E. Ann Kaplan (New York: Routledge, 1990): 36–45. The author argues that women generally found themselves in a position to reject or oppose the screen story: "her *difference* from the screen star is vanquished, she is neither the female-as-represented nor is she the male-as-represented." Friedberg, "A Denial of Difference," 42.
17. Here, my observation is inspired by Sara Ahmed's *Queer Phenomenology: Orientations, Objects, Others.* (Durham, NC: Duke University Press, 2006). I am especially drawn to the notion that "compulsory heterosexuality produces a 'field of heterosexual objects,' by the very requirement that the subject 'give up' the possibility of other love objects." Ahmed, *Queer Phenomenology*, 87. By extension, as Ahmed proposes, "bodies become straight by 'lining up' with lines that are already given," meaning those objects are socioculturally reinforced as ideal benchmarks for achievement and identity. Ahmed, *Queer Phenomenology*, 23.
18. Rebecca Schneider, *Performing Remains: Art and War in Times of Theatrical Reenactment* (New York: Routledge, 2011), 17.
19. Elizabeth Freeman, *Time Binds: Queer Temporalities, Queer Histories* (Durham, NC: Duke University Press, 2010), 7.
20. Jose Esteban Muñoz, *Disidentifications: Queers of Color and Performance of Politics* (Minneapolis: University of Minnesota Press, 1999), 4.
21. Muñoz, *Disidentifications*, 31.
22. Muñoz, *Disidentifications*, 6.
23. Armando María y Campos, *El teatro de género chico en la Revolución Mexicana* (Mexico City: Biblioteca del Instituto Nacional de Estudios Históricos de la Revolución Mexicana, 1956), 23.
24. Socorro Merlín, *Vida y Milagros de las carpas: La carpa en México, 1930–1950*, 1st ed. (Mexico City: CITRU, 1995), 12.
25. Laura Gutiérrez, *Performing Mexicanidad: Vendidas y Cabareteras on the Transnational Stage* (Austin: University of Texas Press, 2010), 82.

26. Gutiérrez, *Performing Mexicanidad*, 82.
27. For more on the development of *teatro de carpa* in Mexico, see Socorro Merlín's in-depth study, *Vida y Milagros de las carpas*.
28. Jacqueline Avila, "Juxtaposing Teatro de Revista and Cine: Music in the 1930s Comedia Ranchera," *Journal of Film Music* 5 no. 1–2 (2012): 123–25.
29. For more information on *teatro-cabaret*'s development as a genre and its relationship to dissidence and neoliberalism, see Gastón Alzate, *Teatro de Cabaret: Imaginarios Disidentes* (Irvine: Ediciones de GESTOS, 2002). For works that consider how *teatro-cabaret* negotiates definitions of *mexicanidad*, see Christina Baker, "Queering Mexicanidad in Cabaret and Film: Redefining Boundaries of Belonging." (PhD diss., University of Wisconsin-Madison, 2015), and Gutiérrez's, *Performing Mexicanidad*. For more on the early stages of *teatro-cabaret*, see Diana Taylor, "'High Aztec' or Performing Anthro Pop: Jesusa Rodríguez and Liliana Felipe in 'Cielo de abajo.'" *TDR: The Drama Review* 37, no. 3 (1993): 142–52.
30. Lisa Appignanesi, *The Cabaret* (New Haven, CT: Yale University Press, 2004), 6.
31. Gastón Alzate, "Dramaturgia, ciudadanía y anti-neoliberalismo: El cabaret mexicano contemporáneo." *Latin American Theatre Review* 41 no.2 (2008): 50.
32. Achy Obejas, "It Hurts to Laugh: Even Performance Artists are Numbered by Mexico's Crises," *Chicago Tribune*, April 11, 1996.
33. Sotres, *Introducción al cabaret*, 21.
34. Sotres, *Introducción al cabaret*, 22.
35. For more on Ayotzinapa, see Grupo Interdisciplinario de Expertos Independientes, 2016, *Informe Ayotzinapa II: Avances y nuevas conclusiones sobre la investigación, búsqueda y atención a las víctimas*, https://prensagieiayotzi.wixsite.com/giei-ayotzinapa/informe-; Comisión Nacional de Derechos Humanos, "Pronunciamiento de la CNDH sobre la investigación de violaciones graves a los derechos humanos con motivo de los ocurridos los días 26 y 27 de septiembre de 2014, en Iguala, Guerrero," March 25, 2021, https://www.cndh.org.mx/documento/pronunciamiento-de-la-cndh-sobre-la-investigacion-de-violaciones-graves-los-derechos; and Lucina Melesio, "Ayotzinapa 43 Four Years On: Renewed Hope for Finding Truth," *Al Jazeera*, September 27, 2018, www.aljazeera.com/news/2018/09/ayotzinapa-43-years-renewed-hope-finding-truth-180927033943677.html. For more on the causes for and ramifications of Mexico's "War on Drugs," see George Grayson, *Mexico: Narco-Violence and a Failed State?* (New Brunswick, NJ: L Transaction, 2010) and George Grayson, *The Impact of President Felipe Calderón's War on Drugs on the Armed Forces: The Prospects for Mexico's "Militarization" and Bilateral Relations* (Carlisle Barracks, PA: Strategic Studies Institute, 2012). Also see Comisión Mexicana de Defensa y Promoción de los Derechos Humanos, 2015, *Violaciones graves a derechos humanos en la guerra contra las drogas en México*, https://www.cmdpdh.org/publicaciones-pdf/cmdpdh-violaciones-graves-a-ddhh-en-la-guerra-contra-las-drogas-en-mexico.pdf. For a critique of the way the Mexican government fictionalized and mythologized the *narco*, see Oswaldo

Zavala, "Imagining the U.S.-Mexico Drug War: The Critical Limits of Narco-narratives." *Comparative Literature* 66, no.3 (2014): 340–60 and Oswaldo Zavala, *Los cárteles no existen: Narcotráfico y cultura en México*. (Mexico City: Malpaso, 2018). For more on the escalating rates at which women are murdered each day in Mexico, see "Asesinan en México a 9 mujeres al día, denuncia la ONU," 2018. *Excelsior*, November 11, 2018, https://www.excelsior.com.mx/nacional/en-mexico-diario-asesinan-a-9-mujeres-denuncia-la-onu/1280023; Ariadna García, "Asesinan a 9 mujeres al día en México, asegura Segob." *El universal*, March 17, 2019, https://www.eluniversal.com.mx/nacion/politica/asesinan-9-mujeres-al-dia-en-mexico-asegura-segob; and Nallely Jiménez, "Alarmante: Van más de 760 feminicidios durante 2018 en todo México." *Infobae*, December 29, 2018, https://www.infobae.com/america/mexico/2018/12/29/alarmante-van-mas-de-760-feminicidios-durante-2018-en-todo-mexico.

36. Gastón Alzate, "'Fiesten' una pastorela cabaretera," *Letras femeninas* 37, no.1 (2011): 71–86. Alzate explains: "como grupo Las Reinas Chulas existen desde el año 2000 aunque su trayectoria comenzó desde antes cuando trabajan con Tito Vasconcelos. . . . Luego se unieron a Jesusa Rodríguez y Liliana Felipe en el Teatro Bar El Hábito del 2002 al 2005" (as a group, Las Reinas Chulas has officially existed since the year 2000, though their trajectory began before that when they worked with Tito Vasconcelos. . . . They later joined Jesusa Rodríguez and Liliana Felipe in Teatro Bar El Hábito from 2002–2005). Alzate, "Fiesten," 74.

37. Rosana Blanco-Cano, *Cuerpos disidentes del México imaginado: Cultura, género, etnia y nación más allá del Proyecto posrevolucionario* (Madrid: Iberoamericana Editorial Vervuert), 2014.

38. Alzate, "Dramaturgia," 57.

39. Las Reinas Chulas, "Perspectiva de cabaret," n.d., https://www.lasreinaschulasac.org/perspectiva-de-cabaret. It is worth noting that once Ana Francis Mor and Marisol Gasé were elected as congresswomen in 2021, their continued participation in the civil association would represent a conflict of interest. Only Nora Huerta and Cecilia Sotres remain active participants.

40. The FONCA no longer exists under that name but underwent a transition in 2020. The organization is now referred to as the Sistema de Apoyos a la Creación y Proyectos Culturales.

41. Huerta was awarded the honor of *Mejor Revelación Femenina* in its inaugural year. It was last awarded in 2018. See "Lista de ganadores del Ariel 2015," *El Universal*, May 27, 2015, https://archivo.eluniversal.com.mx/espectaculos/2015/lista-ganadores-ariel-2015-1103204.html.

42. Muñoz, *Disidentifications*, 11.

43. In his 2019 keynote at the annual Festival Internacional de Cabaret, Gastón Alzate planted important questions regarding the role of art under President AMLO, particularly a growing tendency not to critique the nation's leader. He implored contemporary practitioners to be alert regarding uncritical

productions, noting that "hay que afrontar y debatir esos cuestionamientos especialmente desde ese scenario tan naturalmente plural, diverso y heterodoxo como es el cabaret" (We must confront and debate these issues, especially from this natural site of plurality, diversity, and heterodoxy that characterizes cabaret).

44. Vargas, "Hija de Peña Nieto." While the original version of *teatro-cabaret* work is from 2008, throughout this chapter I use 2013 as its official date due to the title change and content modifications made at that time.

45. Alzate, "'Fiesten,'" 76.

46. For more on Peña Nieto's energy reform plan, see Georgina Olson, "Apuesta histórica; Peña propone cambiar la Constitución en materia energética," *Excelsior*, August 8, 2013, https://www.colimanoticias.com/apuesta-historica-pena-propone-cambiar-la-constitucion-en-materia-energetica; "Peña Nieto busca incrementar las exportaciones de petróleo a China," *CNN México*, April 4, 2013, available online at https://expansion.mx/nacional/2013/04/04/pena-nieto-busca-incrementar-las-exportaciones-de-petroleo-a-china. In regard to Elba Esther Gordillo's arrest, see "Detienen a Elba Esther Gordillo, PRG la acusa de malversación de fondos" *Excélsior*, February 26, 2013, https://www.excelsior.com.mx/nacional/2013/02/26/886284; "Encarcelan a poderosa líder de gremio docente," *Peru21*, February 28, 2013, https://peru21.pe/opinion/encarcelan-poderosa-lider-gremio-docente-95084-noticia. For more on Romero Deschamps and PEMEX, see Jorge Pérez Albarrán, "Revelan que Romero Deschamps regresó 'desahuciado' de Houston." *Proceso*, October 5, 2012, https://www.proceso.com.mx/nacional/2012/10/5/revelan-que-romero-deschamps-regreso-desahuciado-de-houston-109266.html. For more on the teacher strikes, see Mauricio Torres, "7 puntos clave de la nueva ley para evaluar a los profesores," *CNN México*, September 6, 2013, available online at https://expansion.mx/nacional/2013/09/06/7-puntos-clave-de-la-nueva-ley-para-evaluar-a-los-profesores; Lisbeth Padilla Fajardo, "La reforma educativa, la propuesta 'más costosa' de Peña Nieto," *CNN México*, September 9, 2013, available online at https://expansion.mx/nacional/2013/09/09/la-reforma-educativa-la-propuesta-mas-costosa-de-pena-nieto.

47. Jorge Ayala Blanco, *La aventura del cine mexicano en la época de oro y después* (Barcelona: Editorial Grijalbo, 1993), 97; Carlos Monsiváis, *Pedro Infante: Las leyes de querer* (Mexico City: Aguilar, 2008), 27. Also see Valentín Tejada, *Pedro Infante, ídolo popular* (Mexico City: Editorial Tejada, 1958).

48. José Ernesto Infante Quintanilla, *Pedro Infante, el ídolo inmortal* (Mexico City: Editorial Oceano, 2006). Infante Quintanilla states, "Pedro Infante y Blanca Estela destacaron los elementos esenciales del melodrama" (Pedro Infante and Blanca Estela highlighted the essential elements of melodrama). Quintanilla, *Pedro Infante*, 67. In *A través del espejo: El cine mexicano y su publico* (Mexico City: Ediciones El Milagro, 1994), Carlos Monsiváis and Carlos Bonfil explain that the melodrama is characterized by "los conflictos y los desgarramientos

se suceden en un vértigo apenas aliviado por unos cuantos chistes y canciones, y refrendan la naturaleza del melodrama-a-la-mexicana" (conflicts and confrontations happen at a vertigo-inducing speed, only to be briefly interrupted by a few jokes and songs, all of which affirm the nature of the Mexican melodrama). Monsiváis and Bonfil, *A través del espejo*, 148.
49. According to Monsiváis and Bonfil, "el vestuario, las costumbres, el gozo de vivir sin privacidad, el tono de voz canturreado, y el habla carente de refinamiento, alejada de cualquier pretensión" (costumes, habits, the sense of enjoying a life without privacy, the tone of a sing-song voice, and a speech pattern lacking in refinement or sense of pretension). Monsiváis and Bonfil, *A través del espejo*, 148.
50. Muñoz, *Disidentifications*, 25.
51. The performance is an excellent example of what Michael Kirby would call "complex acting." See Michael Kirby, "On Acting and Not-Acting," *TDR: The Drama Review* 16 no.1 (1972): 9.
52. It is worth brief mention that this on-stage 2013 depiction does not differ greatly from Ata's cinematic depiction, where he also stutters and seems incapable of protecting Chachita from terrible circumstances. In general, I would argue that his character, both on screen and on stage, represents weak masculinity, in stark contrast to the masculinity represented by Pepe "el Toro."
53. Carlos Monsiváis, *Pedro Infante*, 136.
54. *Nosotros los pobres*, directed by Ismael Rodríguez (Film by Producciones Rodríguez Hermanos, 1948).
55. Here, I am inspired by Michael Bull's concept of the audiovisual iPod. He posits that our mobile listening practices shape how we understand our surroundings and forge personal connections to them. See Michael Bull, "The audio-visual iPod," in *The Sound Studies Reader*, edited by Jonathan Sterne (New York: Routledge, 2012), 197–208.
56. Mor et al. *Nosotras las proles* (Unpublished script, 2013), 2.
57. Ayala Blanco refers to Pedro Infante as "el tenorio del pueblo" (the people's tenor). Ayala Blanco, *La aventura*, 61.
58. For more on gendered vocal performance and bodily spaces, see Simon Frith, *Performing Rites: On the Values of Popular Music* (Cambridge, MA: Harvard University Press, 1996), John Shepherd, *Music as Social Text* (Cambridge: Polity, 1991), Angela McRobbie, "Recent Rhythms of Sex and Race in Popular Music," *Media, Culture and Society* 17, no. 2 (1995): 323–31, and Susan McClary, *Feminine Endings: Music, Gender, and Sexuality* (Minneapolis: University of Minnesota Press, 1991).
59. Mor et al., *Nosotras las proles*, 2.
60. While none of the women would necessarily classify themselves as part of Mexico's upper class, they arguably live comfortable middle-class lives. Hence, aligning themselves with the prole can certainly be called into question, but given that the term "prole" was used by Peña Nieto's daughter to insult anyone

who critiques her father, regardless of socio-economic status, Las Reinas Chulas fits this broad definition. Moreover, most *teatro-cabaret* practitioners, including Rodríguez, Felipe, Vasconcelos, and Hadad, could be considered part of Mexico's middle-to-upper class. However, their ability to attend university, occupy performance spaces in Coyoacán, and live in areas like La Romita, Avenida Reforma, or Polanco signal their economic comfort does not exclude them from being able to critique government actions that have a direct impact on Mexico's "prole."

61. For more information about educational reforms, see Torres, "7 puntos," and Padilla Fajardo, "La reforma educativa"
62. Mor et al., *Nosotras las proles*, 1.
63. Monsiváis and Bonfil, *A través del espejo*, 148.
64. Mor et al., *Nosotras las proles*, 17.
65. Mor et al., *Nosotras las proles*, 3.
66. Mor et al., *Nosotras las proles*, 16.
67. Mor et al., *Nosotras las proles*, 16.
68. Mor et al., *Nosotras las proles*, 18.
69. Mor et al., *Nosotras las proles*, 18.
70. Jesús Amezcua Castillo, *Pedro Infante: Medio siglo de idolatría* (Mexico City: Ediciones B, 2007), 62.
71. Avila, "Juxtaposing," 122.
72. Olga Nájera-Ramírez, "Engendering Nationalism: Identity, Discourse and the Mexican Charro," *Anthropology Quarterly* 67 no. 1 (1994): 1.
73. Avila, *Cinesonidos*, 158.
74. Avila, *Cinesonidos*, 158–60.
75. Jack Halberstam, *Female Masculinity* (Durham, NC: Duke University Press, 1998), 232. Halberstam also claims that "performances of masculinity seem to demand a different genre of humor and performance." Halberstam, *Female Masculinity*, 238. Sarah Murray echoes this notion: "it is difficult to imagine successful female-to-male drag that doesn't make fun of masculinity. In fact, making fun of masculinity seems unavoidable, as men's seriousness about being male is one of their most prominent characteristics." Sarah Murray, "Dragon Ladies, Draggin' Men: Some Reflections on Gender, Drag and Homosexual Communities," *Public Culture* 6 (1994), 358.
76. Mor, personal interview.
77. Mor et al., *Nosotras las proles*, 5.
78. Mor et al., *Nosotras las proles*, 5.
79. Monsiváis, *Pedro Infante*, 78.
80. Avila, *Cinesonidos*, 191.
81. The entire plot revolves around how three cousins compete over a shared love interest: "*Los tres García* relata, en primera instancia, el cortejo sentimental de tres primos hermanos a una prima nacida en el extranjero" (*Los tres García* relates, above all, the way three cousins try to court their foreign-born female cousin). Ayala Blanco, *La aventura*, 59.

82. Mor et al., *Nosotras las proles*, 6.
83. Elizabeth Freeman, "Time Binds, or Erotohistoriography," *Social Text* 23, nos. 3–4 (Fall–Winter 2005): 58.
84. Mor et al., *Nosotras las proles*, 5.
85. Mor et al., *Nosotras las proles*, 6.
86. Nájera-Ramírez, "Engendering," 9.
87. Alejandro L. Madrid and Robin D. Moore. *Danzón: Circum-Caribbean Dialogues in Music and Dance* (New York: Oxford University Press, 2013), 109.
88. Ayala Blanco, *La aventura*, 61.
89. Anne Rubenstein, "Bodies, Cities, Cinema: Pedro Infante's Death as Political Spectacle" in *Fragments of a Golden Age: The Politics of Culture in Mexico Since 1940*, edited by Gilbert Joseph, Anne Rubenstein, and Eric Zolov (Durham, NC: Duke University Press, 2001), 212.
90. Avila, *Cinesonidos*, 188.
91. Vicente Fernández, "Para Siempre," *Para siempre* (Sony Music Entertainment Mexico, 2007) Spotify, http://open.spotify.com/track/ouyVgmoXDbwS1ubv8AurVZ?si=PM5DJjK6TIiLBIzmmWUBJg.
92. Mladen Dolar, *A Voice and Nothing More* (Cambridge, MA: MIT Press, 2006), 22.
93. Dolar, *A Voice and Nothing More*, 14.
94. See Mary-Lee Mulholland, "Mariachis Machos and Charros Gays: Masculinities in Guadalajara," in *Masculinity and Sexuality in Modern Mexico*, edited by Víctor M. Macías-Gónzalez and Anne Rubenstein (Albuquerque: University of New Mexico Press, 2012), 233–61. Guadalajara is often "reputed to be home to the authentic Mexican macho: the tequila-drinking, singing charro. Paradoxically, Guadalajara is known as being Mexico's 'gayest' city." Mullholland, "Mariachis Machos," 237.
95. Mulholland, "Mariachis Machos and Charros Gays," 234.
96. On rumors regarding Alejandro Fernández's sexuality, see "Con esta publicación, Alejandro Fernández habría confirmado su homosexualidad," *Yosoitú*, October 29, 2019, https://yosoitu.com/entretenimiento/2019/10/29/con-esta-publicacion-alejandro-fernandez-habria-confirmado-su-homosexualidad-60823.html.
97. For coverage on Vicente Fernández's health and transplant, see "Vicente Fernández rechazó un trasplante de hígado por si el donante era 'homosexual o drogadicto," *El país*, May 10, 2019, https://elpais.com/elpais/2019/05/10/gente/1557475198_989117.html.
98. Mor et al. *Nosotras las proles*, 7–8.
99. García Canclini, *Consumers and Citizens*, 118.
100. Sergio de la Mora, *Cinemachismo: Masculinities and Sexuality in Mexican Film* (Austin: University of Texas Press, 2006), 86.
101. Theodore Cohen, *Finding Afro-Mexico: Race and Nation after the Revolution* (Cambridge: Cambridge University Press, 2020), 245.
102. Joanne Herschfield, "Race and Ethnicity in the Classical Cinema" in *Mexico's Cinema: A Century of Film and Filmmakers*, edited by Joanne Herschield and

David R. Maciel (New York: SR Books, 1996), 96.
103. Marco Polo Hernández Cuevas, *African Mexicans and the Discourse on Modern Nation* (Dallas, TX: University Press of America, 2004), 76.
104. Hernández Cuevas, *African Mexicans*, 76.
105. Mónica G. Moreno Figueroa and Emiko Saldívar Tanaka, "'We Are Not Racists, We Are Mexicans': Privilege, Nationalism and Post-Race Ideology in Mexico," *Critical Sociology* 42, nos. 4–5 (2016): 520.
106. Moreno Figueroa and Saldívar Tanaka, "'We Are Not Racists, We Are Mexicans,'" 516. For more on the erasure and silencing of black bodies from definitions of *mexicanidad*, see Bobby Vaughn, "México Negro: From the Shadows of Nationalist Mestizaje to New Possibilities in Afro-Mexican Identity," *Journal of Pan African Studies* 6 no.1 (2016): 227–4, and Cohen's *Finding Afro-Mexico*. For more on the scholarly research on coloniality, Afro-Mexicans, and mestizaje, see Ben Vinson III, "La historia del estudio de los negros en México," in *Afroméxico: El pulso de la población negra en México: Una historia recordada, olvidada y vuelta a recordar*, edited by Ben Vinson III and Bobby Vaughn (Mexico City: Fondo de Cultura Económica, 2004), 13–48, and Ben Vinson III, *Before mestizaje: The Frontiers of Race and Caste in Colonial Mexico* (Cambridge: Cambridge University Press, 2018).
107. Hernández Cuevas, *African Mexicans*, 73.
108. Theresa Delgadillo, "Singing 'Angelitos Negros': African Diaspora Meets Mestizaje in the Americas," *Latin American Quarterly* 58, no. 2 (2006): 417.
109. B. Christine Arce, *Mexico's Nobodies: The Cultural Legacy of the Soldadera and Afro-Mexican Women* (Albany: State University of New York Press, 2017), 209.
110. Alex M. Saragoza and Graciela Berkovich, "Intimate Connections: Cinematic Allegories of Gender, the State and National Identity," in *The Mexican Cinema Project*, edited by Chon A. Noriega and Steven Ricci (Los Angeles: UCLA Film and Television Archive, 2004), 27.
111. Jill Lane has extensively studied blackface in Cuban theater during the nineteenth century in her monograph, *Blackface Cuba, 1840–1895* (Philadelphia: University of Pennsylvania Press, 2005). With an emphasis on the United States, Daniel H. Foster's "From Minstrel Shows to Radio Shows: Racism and Representation in Blackface and Blackvoice," *Journal of American Drama and Theatre* 17, no. 2 (Spring 2005): 7–16 offers provocative considerations of audiovisual invocations of blackface.
112. Laura G. Gutiérrez, "*El derecho de re-hacer*: Signifyin(g) Blackness in Contemporary Mexican Political Cabaret," *Arizona Journal of Hispanic Cultural Studies* 16 (2012): 164.
113. Talia Weltman-Cisneros and Candelaria Donají Méndez Tello, "Negros-Afromexicanos: Recognition and the Politics of Identity in Contemporary Mexico," *Journal of Pan African Studies* 6 no. 1 (2013): 143.
114. Hernández Cuevas, *African Mexicans*, 76.
115. Hettie Malcomson, "The Expediency of Blackness: Racial Logics and Danzón in the Port of Veracruz, Mexico," in *Afro-Latin@s in Movement: Critical*

Approaches to Blackness and Transnationalism in the Americas, edited by Petra R. Rivera-Rideau, Jennifer A. Jones, and Tianna Paschel (New York: Palgrave Macmillan), 43. For more on Golden Age cinematic depictions of Cubanness and the resulting stereotypes, see Gabriela Pulido Llano, *Mulatas y negros cubanos en la escena Mexicana, 1920–1950* (Mexico City: Instituto Nacional de Antropología e Historia, 2010), and Arce's, *Mexico's Nobodies*.

116. Mor et al. *Nosotras las proles*, 9.
117. Mor et al. *Nosotras las proles*, 9.
118. Talia Weltman-Cisneros, "Cimarronaje Cultural: Towards a Counter-Cartography of Blackness and Belonging in Mexico," *Journal of Pan African Studies* 6, no. 1 (2013): 128.
119. Arce, *Mexico's Nobodies*, 8.
120. Arce, *Mexico's Nobodies*, 8.
121. Mor et al. *Nosotras las proles*, 9-10.
122. Mor et al. *Nosotras las proles*, 9.
123. Cohen, *Finding Afro-Mexico*, 11.
124. For more on Sosa, see Mark Holston, "Remembering Mercedes Sosa," *Americas* 62, no. 1 (2010): 64, and Robert Neustadt, "Music as Memory and Torture: Sounds of Repression and Protest in Chile and Argentina," *Chasqui* 33, no. 1 (2004):128–37. For more on *Nueva Canción*, see Ignacio Guzmán Roldán "The Political Song in Chilean nueva canción: Víctor Jara and Quilapayún—A Case Study (1969–1973)" (Thesis, Universidad Alberto Hurado, 2011); J. Patrice McSherry, *Chilean New Song: The Political Power of Music, 1960s–1973* (Philadelphia: Temple University Press, 2015); and Juan Pablo González's articles, "Hegemony and Counter-Hegemony of Music in Latin-America: The Chilean Pop," *Popular Music and Society* 15, no 2.2 (1991): 63–78, and "Nueva Canción Chilena en dictadura: Divergencia, memoria, escuela (1973–1983)," *Estudios interdisciplinarios de América Latina y el Caribe* 27, no. 1 (2016): 63–82.
125. Delgadillo, "Singing 'Angelitos Negros,'" 407. From the poem, filmic José Carlos sings to Belén, "Aunque la Virgen sea blanca / píntame angelitos negros / que también se van al cielo / todos los negritos buenos. Pinto si pintas con amor / por qué desprecias su color / si sabes que en el cielo / también los quiere Dios" (Even though the Virgin Mary is white / paint me little black angels / that too go to heaven / all the good black people. I paint if you paint with love / why do you hate the color of your skin / if you know that in heaven / God will love you too).
126. Delgadillo, "Singing 'Angelitos Negros,'" 407.
127. Weltman-Cisneros, "Cimarronaje Cultural," 128.
128. For Sosa's performance, see "Mercedes Sosa – Duerme negrito (en directo, 10.03.1976)," Youtube, uploaded by Miguel Toston Cienfuegos, March 30, 2022, https://www.youtube.com/watch?v=0zmXK1zo3eM.
129. Mor et al. *Nosotras las proles*, 12.
130. Anita González, *Afro-Mexico: Dancing between Myth and Reality* (Austin: University of Texas Press, 2010), 88.

131. Arce, *Mexico's Nobodies*, 4.
132. Rafael Figueroa Hernández, *Salsa mexicana: Transculturación e identidad* (Xalapa: Con Clave, 1996), 35.
133. Pulido Llano, *Mulatas y negros*, 104.
134. Arce, *Mexico's Nobodies*, 211.
135. Herman Bennett, *Colonial Blackness: A History of Afro-Mexico* (Bloomington: Indiana University Press, 2009), 15.

CHAPTER 2

1. This chapter is derived in part from an article published in *Symposium: A Quarterly Journal in Modern Literatures* in Fall 2017. Copyright Taylor & Francis, available online: doi.org/10.1080/00397709.2017.1386480.
2. Grayson, *Impact*, 3. For an assessment of Mexico and the War on Drugs from an international affairs perspective, see Grayson, *Mexico: Narco-Violence*.
3. Grayson, *Impact*, 2; Gabriela Calderón et al. "The Beheading of Criminal Organizations and the Dynamics of Violence in Mexico," *Journal of Conflict Resolution* 59, no. 8 (2015): 1456.
4. Munmun De Choudhury et al, "'Narco' Emotions: Affect and Desensitization in Social Media during the Mexican Drug War," *Proceedings of the 32nd Annual ACM Conference on Human Factors in Computing Systems* (Toronto, Canada: CHI 2014): 3564.
5. Ordorika Imaz states, "tenemos desde el 2006 más de 150 mil personas asesinadas, desde el 2011 tenemos más de 280 mil personas desplazadas por la violencia" (since 2006, we have more than 150,000 people murdered, and since 2011, we have more than 280,000 displaced by the violence). She goes on to say, "la tortura se ha vuelto generalizada en nuestro país. Creo que los riesgos de las policías prohibicionista rebasan por mucho los riesgos que las mismas políticas pueden llegar a generar" (torture has become a generalized phenomenon in our country. I think that the risks created by prohibitive policies stem from the very risks that the same policies can generate). Cited in Juan Luis García Hernández, "Los 150 mil muertos prueban que la guerra contra las drogas fracasó, a México le queda legalizar: ONGs," *Sin Embargo*, April 19, 2016, https://www.sinembargo.mx/19-04-2016/1650116. For more information on human rights abuses during Calderón's presidency, see Comisión Mexicana de Defensa y Promoción de los Derechos Humanos, *Violaciones graves a derechos humanos en la guerra contra las drogas en México*, 2015, https://www.cmdpdh.org/publicaciones-pdf/cmdpdh-violaciones-graves-a-ddhh-en-la-guerra-contra-las-drogas-en-mexico.pdf.
6. Rossana Reguillo, "The Narco-Machine and the Work of Violence: Notes toward Its Decodification," *e-misférica* 8 no. 2 (2010). https://hemisphericinstitute.org/en/emisferica-82/reguillo5.html.
7. Grayson, *Impact*, 30.
8. Dolar, *A Voice and Nothing More*, 119.

9. Giorgio Agamben, *State of Exception*, translated by Kevin Attell (Chicago: University of Chicago Press, 2005), 37.
10. "Presidente Calderón: Discurso completo en el auditorio," *El Universal.com.mx*, December 1, 2006, https://archivo.eluniversal.com.mx/notas/391513.html.
11. Rafael Saldívar Arreola and Ignacio Rodríguez Sánchez, "Análisis del léxico en diferentes registros textuales en la construcción del imaginario social del narcotráfico en México," *Literatura y Lingüística*, no. 37 (2018): 386. Also see Zavala, "Imagining," and *Los cárteles no existen*.
12. Cited in Alonso Vásquez Moyers and Germán Espino Sánchez, "La producción discursive en la Guerra contra el narcotráfico en el sexenio de Calderón: En busca de la legitimidad," *Discurso y Sociedad* 9, no. 4 (2015): 502.
13. Melissa W. Wright, "Necropolitics, Narcopolitics, and Femicide: Gendered Violence on the Mexico–US Border," *Signs: Journal of Women in Culture and Society* 36, no. 3 (2011): 722.
14. Slavoj Žižek, *Violence: Six Sideways Reflections* (New York: Picador, 2008), 2.
15. Reguillo, "The Narco-Machine."
16. For Žižek, this kind of violence "is invisible since it sustains the very zero-level standard against which we perceive something as subjectively violent." Žižek, *Violence*, 2.
17. Ileana Diéguez, "Necroteatro. Iconografías del cuerpo roto y sus registros punitivos," *Investigación Teatral* 3, no. 5 (Winter 2013–2014): 12.
18. Agamben, *State of Exception*, 2.
19. Agamben, *State of Exception*, 28.
20. Achille Mbembe, *Necro-politics*, translated by Steven Corcoran (Durham, NC: Duke University Press, 2019), 66.
21. Mbembe, *Necro-politics*, 77.
22. Mbembe, *Necro-politics*, 74.
23. R. Guy Emerson, *Necropolitics: Living Death in Mexico* (New York: Palgrave MacMillan, 2019), 30.
24. R. Murray Schafer, *The Soundscape: Our Sonic Environment and the Tuning of the World* (Rochester, VT: Destiny Books, 1977), 50.
25. Daughtry's *Listening to War* represents a growing interest in the field of ethnomusicology which explores the relationship between violence and popular music styles. Other examples of this include Goodman's *Sonic Warfare*, and Bruce Johnson and Martin Cloonan, eds., *Dark Side of the Tune: Popular Music and Violence* (New York: Taylor and Francis, 2008). In their introduction, Johnson and Cloonan argue that "popular music is always mercenary," functioning as a stratagem to invade across multiple geographies and temporal moments. Martin and Cloonan, "Introduction," 4. Fast and Pegley's introduction to *Music, Politics, and Violence* explicitly takes up Žižek's understanding of violence to suggest that musical practices "participate directly in the production of objective and subjective violence." Fast and Pegley, "Introduction," 3. Similarly, Araújo argues that musical practice can deploy sonic

triggers that enact and reinforce "socially orchestrated power." Araújo, "Sound Praxis," 217.
26. Daughtry, *Listening to War*, 33.
27. While not engaging Diéguez, Jeffrey Coleman does apply Mbembe's necropolitics as a lens through which he analyzes immigration, race, and death as depicted in Spanish theater in *The Necropolitical Theatre: Race and Immigration on the Contemporary Spanish Stage* (Evanston, IL: Northwestern University Press, 2020).
28. Diéguez, *Cuerpos*, 78.
29. Enrique Ježik, "Entrevista con Enrique Ježik," interview by Tomáš Pospiszyl, 2008, http://enriquejezik.com/entrevista-por-tomas-pospiszyl.
30. Néstor García Canclini, "Mexico: Cultural Globalization in a Disintegrating City," *American Ethnologist* 22, no. 4 (1995): 748.
31. Enrique Ježik, "Entrevista: Enrique Ježik," interview by Pamela Ballesteros. *GASTV*, January 2015, http://gastv.mx/entrevista-enrique-jezik.
32. Ježik states: "empiezan a despertar muchas conciencias y mucha gente ha decidido ya no bajar la cabeza" (people begin to wake up to events around them and many people have decided not to look away any longer) (2015).
33. Kate Bonansinga, *Curating at the Edge: Artists Respond to the U.S./Mexico Border* (Austin: University of Texas Press, 2010). As Bonansinga explains, "This work references *El Siluetazo /The Silhouette*, a public intervention that took place in Buenos Aires in 1983, during the last days of the military dictatorship, and consisted of human-sized silhouettes, representing disappeared people, traced on paper and pasted on exterior walls throughout the city." Bonansinga, *Curating at the Edge*, 210. For more on Ježik's work, see Gabriela Galindo, "*Obstruir, Destruir, Ocultar*: Retrospectiva de Enrique Ježik," *Répilica21*, December 20, 2011, https://www.replica21.com/archivo/articulos/g_h/617_galindo_jezik.html#.; Xavier Antich, "Arte y activism: El siluetazo," *La Vanguardia*, July 8, 2009, https://www.lavanguardia.com/cultura/20090708/53739900388/arte-y-activismo-el-siluetazo.html.; Daniel Garza-Usabiaga, "Enrique Ježik. Formas de la violencia," *Revista Exist Express*, November 2009, http://enriquejezik.com/texto-de-daniel-garza-usabiaga-en-exit.; and Pilar Villela, "Violencia y escritura. Algunas notas sobre la obra de Enrique Ježik," Exposition text for "Práctica (200 cartuchos calibre 12, 78 balas 9mm)," Centro Cultural Tlatelolco, 2009, http://enriquejezik.com/anterior/sitejezik/textos/PV-violencia_txt.htm.
34. For example, *La Fiesta de las Balas* (2011; The Party of Bullets) was a museum installation of three panes of glass shot riddled with dozens of bullet holes, accompanied by a soundtrack of Ježik himself shooting the guns. Earlier pieces include the 2002 work titled *154 cartuchos calibre 12* (154 12-Caliber Cartridges) and the 2003 installation called *Estructura construida por albañiles y quinientos cartuchos calibre 12* (Structure Created by Day Laborers and 500 12-Caliber Cartridges). These are showcased on his artist page: http://enriquejezik.com/obras.

As Gabriela Galindo states, "la fascinación de Ježik con el poderío de las armas puede en ocasiones cruzar la línea entre la denuncia de la violencia y la estetización de la misma" (Ježik's fascination with the power of firearms can, on occasion, cross the line between denouncing violence and aestheticizing it). Galindo, *"Obstruir."*

35. The festival is sometimes referred to as the XII Muestra Nacional de Performance. For more, see Pancho López, "Arranca la XII Muestra Internacional de Performance," Crónica.com.mx, November 9, 2006, https://www.cronica.com.mx/notas/2006/270375.html.
36. Diana Taylor, *The Archive and the Repertoire: Performing Cultural Memory in the Americas* (Durham, NC: Duke University Press, 2003), 19–20.
37. Enrique Ježik, *Ejercicio de Percusión*, performance, El Teresa Arte Actual, Mexico City, Mexico, November 2006, available online, Youtube, uploaded by Enrique Ježik, July 3, 2013, https://www.youtube.com/watch?v=orR_h8rqCXI. For context and photographic images provided by the artist, see Enrique Ježik, "Ejercicio de percusión," 2006, http://enriquejezik.com/2006-ejercicio-de-percusion.
38. Calderón et al., "The Beheading," 1456.
39. "Ex Teresa Arte Actual," *INBAL*, https://inba.gob.mx/recinto/55/ex-teresa-arte-actual.
40. Black Wolfette, "Ex-Templo de Santa Teresa la Antigua," *Loquaris: Diálogos con México*, March 11, 2009, https://web.archive.org/web/20090619101430/http://dialogos.pideundeseo.org/inmuebles-notables/extemplo-santa-teresa-la-antigua#more-462.
41. See Ana Martínez, *Performance in the Zócalo: Constructing History, Race, and Identity in Mexico's Central Square from the Colonial Era to the Present* (Ann Arbor: University of Michigan Press, 2020). In this in-depth study of the Zócalo as simultaneously a performance space and a performative place, Martinez describes the area as a palimpsest to denote the "Zócalo's singular simultaneity of past and present materialized in its buildings." Martínez, *Performance in the Zócalo*, 1.
42. Ross Brown, *Sound: A Reader in Theatre Practice* (New York: Palgrave Macmillan, 2010), 170.
43. Here I am using the term, inspired by Brandon LaBelle, *Acoustic Territories: Sound Culture and Everyday Life*. (New York: Bloomsbury Academic & Professional, 2010). LaBelle "traces the soundways of the contemporary metropolis, rendering a topography of auditory life through a spatial structure." LaBelle, *Acoustic Territories*, xx. In turning to auditory knowledge, the author demonstrates how the connective elements of sonic stimuli are not only political, but also able to "reconfigure the spatial distinctions of inside and outside, to foster confrontations between one and another, and to infuse language with degrees of immediacy." LaBelle, *Acoustic Territories*, xxi.
44. Johnson and Cloonan, "Introduction," 4.
45. Jacques Attali, *Noise: The Political Economy of Music*, translated by Brian Massumi (Minneapolis: University of Minnesota Press, 1985), 6.

46. Attali, *Noise*, 4.
47. Daughtry, *Listening to War*, 164.
48. Agamben, *State of Exception*, 37.
49. Martin, *Theatre of the Real*, 9.
50. Richard Schechner, *Performance Studies: Introduction* (New York: Routledge, 2002), 64.
51. Richard Schechner, *Between Theatre and Anthropology* (Philadelphia: University of Pennsylvania Press, 1985), 36; Schechner, *Performance Studies*, 29.
52. Reguillo, "The Narco-Machine." Referencing times of war, Elaine Scarry notes that, except for body counts, "the movements and actions of the armies are emptied of human content and occur as a rarefied choreography of disembodied events." See Elaine Scarry, *The Body in Pain: The Making and Unmaking of the World* (New York: Oxford University Press, 1985), 70.
53. Raul Rodríguez, director, *Música de balas*, performance, Real Escuela Superior de Arte Dramático, Madrid, Spain, September 26–October 13, 2013. Paola Hernández, director, *Música de balas*, performance, University of Wisconsin–Madison, Madison, Wisconsin, May 5, 2015. Naoli Eguiarte, director, *Música de balas*, performance, Centro Dramático de Michoacán, Pátzcuaro, Mexico, December 8–December 14, 2019, available online, Youtube, uploaded by Cedram Difusion, March 30, 2020, https://www.youtube.com/watch?v=ZbUHvWuLoJo&t=1473s.
54. Hugo Salcedo, *Música de balas* (Mexico City: Universidad Autónoma Metropolitana, 2012), 29.
55. Estela Leñero Franco, "Premio Nacional de Dramaturgia a Hugo Salcedo," *Proceso*, December 29, 2011, https://www.proceso.com.mx/cultura/2011/12/29/premio-nacional-de-dramaturgia-hugo-salcedo-96766.html.
56. Jorge Celaya, "Teatro de frontera en México," in *Teatro de frontera II*, edited by Jorge Celaya (Durango: Siglo XXI), 2004), 18.
57. For more on postdramatic theater, see Hans-Thies Lehmann, *Postdramatic Theatre*, translated by Karen Jürs-Munby (New York: Routledge, 2006). Lehmann, states that postdramatic theater "signals the continuing association and exchange between theatre and text. Nevertheless, the discourse of *theatre* is at the center of this book and the text therefore is considered only as one element, one layer, or as a 'material' of the scenic creation, not as its master." Lehmann, *Postdramatic Theatre*, 17. For information on documentary theater, see Thomas Irmer, "A Search for New Realities: Documentary Theatre in Germany," *TDR: The Drama Review* 50, no. 3 (Autumn 2006): 16–28, in which he traces three periods of its development in the German context. Carol Martin suggests that "documentary theatre takes the archive and turns it into repertory, following a sequence form behavior to archived records of behavior to the restoration of behavior as public performance" Carol Martin, "Bodies of Evidence," *Drama Review* 50, no. 3 (2006): 10. In the Mexican context, see Vicente Leñero, *Vivir del teatro* (Mexico City: Fondo de Cultura Económica, 2012) for how documentary

theater and its political efforts were incorporated into textual and performatic means. Antonin Artaud in *The Theatre and Its Double*, translated by Mary Caroline Richards (New York: Grove Weidenfeld, 1958), argues that a theater of cruelty emerges when theater rids itself of ornamentation and diversion to expose the vulnerabilities of the body. As a result, audiences are cruelly shaken from a state of complacency and into a state of analytical action (84–100).

58. Cited in Armando Partida Tayzán, "La novísima dramaturgia Mexicana," in *Teatro mexicano reciente: Aproximaciones críticas*, edited by Samuel Gordon (Austin: University of Texas Press, 2005), 19.
59. Hugo Salcedo, personal interview, October 6, 2016.
60. For a comparative approach to three Salcedo pieces, see Peter Beardsell, "Crossing the Border in Three Plays by Hugo Salcedo," *Latin American Theatre Review* 29, no. 2 (1996): 71–84. Among several shared qualities, Beardsell suggests that by referencing sound, the plays afford the audience a greater connection to the themes of tragedy, loss, and impinging US cultural products. Priscilla Melendez dedicates substantial space to analyzing sound in *El viaje de los cantores*, and specifically, "whether these poetic and musical expressions actually become a soothing presence or a disturbing and ironic one." Priscilla Melendez, "The Body and the Law in the Mexico/U.S. Borderlands: Violence and Violations in *El viaje de los cantores* by Hugo Salcedo and *Backyard* by Sabina Berman," *Modern Drama* 55, no. 1 (Spring 2011): 30.
61. Salcedo, personal interview.
62. Iani del Rosario Moreno explains that the prize "was awarded jointly by the Universidad Autónoma Metropolitana, Universidad de Guadalajara, and the Secretaría de Cultura del Gobierno del Distrito Federal." Iani Del Rosario Moreno, *Theatre of the Borderlands: Conflict, Violence, and Healing* (Lanham, MD: Lexington Books, 2015),142.
63. Del Rosario Moreno, *Theatre of the Borderlands*, 142.
64. Leñero Franco, "Premio Nacional."
65. Salcedo, *Música de balas*, 17.
66. Brian Kane, "Acousmatic Fabrications: Les Paul and the 'Les Paulverizer,'" *Journal of Visual Culture* 10, no. 212 (2011): 215.
67. Salcedo, *Música de balas*, 17.
68. Salcedo, *Música de balas*, 17.
69. Javier Trevino-Rangel, "Silencing Grievance: Responding to Human Rights Violations in Mexico's War on Drugs," *Journal of Human Rights* 17, no. 4 (2018): 491.
70. Scarry, *The Body in Pain*, 73.
71. See Felipe Calderón, "Interview Transcript: Felipe Calderón," interview by Adam Thomson, *Financial Times*, January 23, 2007, https://www.ft.com/content/317c1bbc-ab01-11db-b5db-0000779e2340.
72. Felipe Calderón, "El presidente de México en los Desayunos de TVE," *Desayunos de TVE*, May 18, 2010, https://www.rtve.es/alacarta/videos/los-desayunos-

de-tve/desayunos-presidente-mexico-desayunos-tve/774692. Also see Claudia Herrera Beltrán and Armango G. Tejeda, "Los criminals no se convertirán de pronto en santos, dice Calderón," *La Jornada*, May 19, 2010, https://www.jornada.com.mx/2010/05/19/politica/005n1pol.

73. Calderón, "El president de México."
74. Saldívar Arreola and Rodríguez Sánchez, "Análysis del léxico," 384. Dolar also explores the accent, suggesting it as an indicator of social bonds and political relationships: "as if the voice were the very epitome of a society that we carry with us and cannot get away from. We are social beings by the voice and through the voice; it seems that voice stands at the axis of our social bonds, and that voices are the very texture of the social." Dolar, *A Voice and Nothing More*, 14.
75. Salcedo, *Música de balas*, 29.
76. Salcedo, *Música de balas*, 29.
77. Alacranes Musical starts their version with the upbeat sounds of *norteña* music, followed immediately by the sounds of automatic rifles being shot and loaded even before the first lyrics are sung, "500 balazos / armas automáticas / pecheras portaban, / de cuerno las ráfagas / los altos calibres, tumbaban civiles / también por igual" (500 gun shots / automatic rifles / vests they wore / bursts of shooting / with large calibre rifles, took down civilians / equally well). Throughout the entirety of the song, the sounds of gunfire are heard. "Alacranes Musical 500 Balazos," uploaded by Jesús Flores, April 16, 2012, https://www.youtube.com/watch?v=-P3_aml2-gc. Yet, the lyrical references to bullets flying seem to be sufficient for other renditions of the song—first by Voz de Mando in 2010, followed by versions by Calibre 50, El Komander, Larry Hernández, and Javier Rosas—no other versions include the sounds of gunfire.
78. See Alejandro L. Madrid, *Music in Mexico: Experiencing Music, Expressing Culture* (New York: Oxford University Press, 2013). Madrid explains that though *banda* and *norteña* are used interchangeably with some musical styles, they hold different meanings: "throughout the twentieth century, *norteña* music became an indicator of northeastern Mexican identity while *banda* music symbolized northwestern Mexican identity, and neither was to be confused with the other even though the performed musical genres were often the same—in many cases, the same *corridos* or songs." Madrid, *Music in Mexico*, 92.
79. Eric Lara, "'Salieron de San Isidro . . .' El corrido, El narcocorrido y tres de sus categorías de análisis: El hombre, la mujer y el soplón. Un acercamiento etnográfico." *Revista de Humanidades: Tecnológico de Monterrey*, no. 015 (2003): 211.
80. Lara, "'Salieron de San Isidro . . .'" 211.
81. Madrid, *Music in Mexico*, 99.
82. Hermann Herlinghaus, *Violence without Guilt: Ethical Narratives from the Global South* (New York: Palgrave Macmillan, 2009), 33.
83. Salcedo, personal interview.

84. For a more in-depth exploration of this trend of emulating Chalino Sánchez, see Helena Simonett "Narcocorridos: An Emerging Micromusic of Nuevo L.A.," *Ethnomusicology* 45, no. 2 (Spring-Summer 2001): 321–22, 328.
85. César Jesús Burgos Dávila, "Narcocorridos: Antecedentes de la tradición corridística y del narcotráfico en México," *Studies in Latin American Popular Culture* 31 (2013): 172.
86. Salcedo, *Música de balas*, 19.
87. Salcedo, *Música de balas*, 19.
88. Salcedo, *Música de balas*, 20.
89. Salcedo, *Música de balas*, 20.
90. Salcedo, *Música de balas*, 20.
91. Salcedo, *Música de balas*, 20.
92. Herlinghaus, *Violence without Guilt*, 47.
93. The FONCA no longer exists under that name; it underwent a transition in 2020 and is now referred to as the Sistema de Apoyos a la Creación y Proyectos Culturales.
94. Felipe Osornio, "Lechedevirgen Trimegisto: Artista de performance," http://www.lechedevirgen.com/lechedevirgen.
95. Felipe Osornio, *México exhumado*, performance, Centro Universitario de Teatro, Black Box Theatre, Mexico City, June 10, 2019, available online, Hemispheric Institute Digital Video Library, https://hemisphericinstitute.org/es/encuentro-2019-performances/item/2935-lechedevirgen.html.
96. Felipe Osornio, personal interview, April 14, 2020. In many ways, *México exhumado* expands on one of Lechedevirgen's earlier performances called *Infierno Varieté*. This piece, as they describe it, is a perverse and twisted adaptation of the cabaret variety sketch model. For an in-depth analysis of the piece, see Xiomara Verenice Cervantes-Gómez, "Lechedevirgen Trimegisto's *Infierno Varieté*, Queer Mexicanness, and the Aesthetics of Risk," *ASAP Journal* 6, no. 1 (2021): 95–122.
97. Deborah R. Vargas, "Rita's Pants: The *charro traje* and Trans-Sensuality," *Women and Performance: A Journal of Feminist Theory* 20, no. 1 (2010): 7.
98. Nájera-Ramírez, "Engendering," 9.
99. Nájera-Ramírez, "Engendering," 8.
100. Avila, *Cinesonidos*, 151.
101. For more on the construction of the masculine *charro* and the feminine *china poblana*, see Jeanne, Gillespie, "Gender, Ethnicity, and Piety: The Case of the China Poblana," in *Imagination beyond Nation*, edited by Eva P. Bueno and Terry Caesar (Pittsburgh: University of Pittsburgh Press, 1998): 19–40; Christina Baker, "Ranchera Rebel: Transgressive Expression and the Voice of Lucha Reyes," in "Historical Rebels in the Mexican Imaginary," special issue of *Hispanic Journal* 38, no. 2 (2017): 107–24; and Marie Sarita Gaytán, *¡Tequila!: Distilling the Spirit of Mexico* (Palo Alto, CA: Stanford University Press, 2014).

102. Christopher Conway, "Charros: A Critical Introduction," in *Modern Mexican Culture: Critical Foundations*, edited by Stuart A. Day (Tucson: University of Arizona Press, 2017), 68.
103. See Paul Chavez, "Rosa Mexicano," *Medium*, November 18 2018, https://medium.com/these-unanswered-questions/rosa-mexicano-151fb01ccaoa and Yanin Alfaro, "¿Por qué se llama rosa mexicano?: 3 datos curiosos" Paredro.com, September 16, 2014, https://www.paredro.com/por-que-se-llama-rosa-mexicano-3-datos-curiosos.
104. Paola Gerez Levy, "Un homenaje al rosa mexicano (y a todas las veces en las que los muros se confundieron con las buganvilias)," *Travesías*, June 15, 2020, https://travesiasdigital.com/cultura/de-donde-viene-el-rosa-mexicano. As Gerez Levy explains, while *rosa mexicano* is a relatively new term, Valdiosera found the color used throughout Mexico, heralding back to sites of indigenous pasts, such as Mayan and Aztec lands, suggesting a much deeper past and significance.
105. Chavez, "Rosa Mexicano."
106. Osornio, personal interview. The idea of dark tourism was, in part, inspired by *México bizarro: El país que no quieres recordar* (Mexico City: Editorial Planeta, 2017) by Julio Patán and Alejandro Rosas. The book is a series of anecdotes about Mexico that expose its surreal qualities and stranger-than-fiction moments.
107. Frith, *Performing Rites*, 187.
108. Felipe Osornio, *México exhumado* (Unpublished script, 2019), 1.
109. Felipe Osornio, *México exhumado*, 1.
110. Felipe Osornio, *México exhumado*, 2.
111. Felipe Osornio, *México exhumado*, 3.
112. While I am using concepts from the realm of theater studies to consider the effect of Lechedevirgen's voice, Madlen Dolar offers a useful consideration, positing that "intonation is another way in which we can be aware of the voice, for the particular tone of the voice, its particular melody and modulation, its cadence and inflection, can decide meaning." Dolar, *A Voice and Nothing More*, 21.
113. Bertolt Brecht, *Brecht on Theatre: The Development of an Aesthetic*, edited and translated by John Willett (New York: Hill and Wang, 1954), 192.
114. Osornio, personal interview.
115. Diéguez, *Cuerpos*, 79.
116. Emerson, *Necropolitics*, 6. For more on phenomenology as Emerson is using the concept, see Maurice Merleau-Ponty's *Phenomenology of Perception* (New York: Routledge, 2012).
117. Dolar, *A Voice and Nothing More*, 22.
118. According to numerology, the number seven, symbolizes completion (Osornio, personal interview).
119. Including Colosio as the opening wound is symbolic and strategic (Osornio, personal interview). It refers to a moment that has been recently revived via numerous television series and films, such as *Crime Diaries: The Candidate* (2019)

and *1994* (2019), both on Netflix, that signal 1994 as a watershed moment for Mexico, politically and economically. The decision was also inspired by the way Patán and Rosas frame Colosio's potential for change as a myth (57–59).

120. For more, see "Hallan a seis personas vivas con las manos cortadas," ElQuintanaRoo.mx, October 18, 2016, https://elquintanaroo.mx/hallan-a-seis-personas-vivas-con-las-manos-cortadas; Raúl Torres, "Cortan las manos a seis personas en Tlaquepaque," *El Universal*, October 18, 2016, available online at http://www.tvbus.tv/web/2016/10/18/cortan-las-manos-a-seis-personas-en-tlaquepaque.

121. For Lechedevirgen, this moment of spectacularized violence was a pivotal moment in the War on Drugs and what would follow, notably the government's inability to control the violence. Osornio, personal interview. For more, see Misael Habana de Los Santos, "Decapitan a un comandante y un oficial en Acapulco," *La Jornada*, April 21, 2006, https://www.jornada.com.mx/2006/04/21/index.php?section=politica&article=021n1pol. Also see, Antonio Ortega Ávila "Las decapitaciones, nuevo lenguaje de los 'narcos,'" *El País*, May 22, 2008, https://elpais.com/diario/2008/05/23/internacional/1211493607_850215.html.

122. This is a reference to José Antonio Elena Rodríguez, who was killed by a US Border Patrol agent. The young boy was killed on Mexican soil, as the officer, Lonnie Swartz, shot him in the back through the border fence. Swartz was found "not guilty" of murder in federal court. See Rory Carroll, "Border Patrol Agent Found Not Guilty of Murder in Mexican Teen's 2012 Death," *Guardian*, April 24, 2018, https://www.theguardian.com/us-news/2018/apr/23/border-patrol-shooting-jose-antonio-elena-rodriguez-lonnie-swartz; E. J. Montini, "Did the Supreme Court Deny Justice for a Mexican Boy Shot 10 Times in the Back and Head?" *azcentral*, March 3, 2020, https://www.azcentral.com/story/opinion/op-ed/ej-montini/2020/03/03/supreme-court-denies-justice-mexican-boy-shot-border-agent/4936609002.

123. For more, see Kenny Juárez "Asesinan a balazos a joven en Neza," *Quadratin Exomex*, March 25, 2018, https://edomex.quadratin.com.mx/asesinan balazos-joven-neza.

124. According to Lechedevirgen, he chose to include Santa Anna because, just as Colosio, he is well-known as a mythical figure tied to violence and war. Osornio, personal interview. His story also directly precedes Colosio's in *México bizarro* (60–62), so putting them together in the sketch seemed logical for the structure of national wounds. Osornio, personal interview.

125. For more, see "Matan a mujer por resistirse a asalto, cerca de La Raza," *Noticieros Televisa*, May 29, 2019, https://noticieros.televisa.com/ultimas-noticias/asalto-hoy-asesinan-mujer-resistirse-la-raza.

126. My use of sound wounds is inspired by Sidra Lawrence's work on sonic memory and the US justice system. Lawrence argues that when victims of sexual violence are asked to recount their experiences as part of their testimony, the auditory description of the events wounds both the speaker and the listeners

in the courtroom. Sidra Lawrence, "Sounding Trauma: Justice, Audibility, and Sexual Violence" (presentation at the Society for Ethnomusicology Conference [online], October 22, 2020).

127. This voice and the on-stage body unite, but in a way that is distinct from the voice existing as separate from its source, as proposed by Michel Chion's notion of acousmatization. Michel Chion, *Audio-Vision: Sound on Screen* (New York: Columbia University Press, 1994), 4. The performatic approach in *México exhumado* is also distinct from the "coming together" of the unseen voice and its body that often happens in theater. Kendrick, *Theatre Aurality*, 88.
128. Emerson, *Necropolitics*, 46.
129. Osornio, personal interview.
130. Emerson, *Necropolitics*, 46.
131. Emerson, *Necropolitics*, 46.
132. Bruce Johnson, "Music and Violence in History," in *Dark Side of the Tune: Popular Music and Violence*, edited by Bruce Johnson and Martin Cloonan (New York: Taylor and Francis, 2008), 46.
133. Osornio, personal interview.
134. Osornio, personal interview.
135. Goodman, *Sonic Warfare*, xvii.
136. Jonathan Pieslak, "Sound Targets: Music and the War in Iraq," *Journal of Musicological Research* 26, nos. 2–3 (2007): 129.
137. See Suzanne Cuzik, "'You Are in a Place That Is Out of This World . . .': Music in the Detention Camps of the 'Global War on Terror,'" *Journal of the Society for American Music* 2, no. 1 (2008): 1–26.
138. Black Asteroid, "Black Asteroid on Lessons from Prince and Visually," interview by Neal Gustafson, *Reverb News*, February 28, 2018, https://reverb.com/news/black-asteroid-on-lessons-from-prince-visually-inspired-songwriting-and-telling-stories-with-synths.
139. Asteroid, "Black Asteroid."
140. Asteroid, "Black Asteroid."
141. Black Asteroid, "Interview: Black Asteriod," *FNGRS CRSSD*, April 27, 2018, https://web.archive.org/web/20191021133839/http://crssd.com/interview-black-asteroid (original site accessed October 26, 2020; site inactive on July 12, 2023).
142. Annalisa P. Cignitti, "Michele Lamy," *Rocaille*, May 23, 2012, https://www.rocaille.it/michele-lamy.

Lamy is perhaps most widely known as the wife and muse of fashion designer Rick Owens. Recognized for blurring the divisions between fashion and mixed-media art, Owens and Lamy are a visionary duo.
143. Pieslak, "Sound Targets," 139.
144. Dolar, *A Voice and Nothing More*, 30.
145. Daughtry proposes the term *belliphonic* "to encompass sonic material that is less directly or conventionally associated with warfare: the omnipresent civilian gas generators that appeared throughout Iraq after the partial destruction

of the electric grid in the wake of major combat operations in 2003; the sirens and the other warning signals that punctuated life on military bases and urban areas during the war . . . musical genres that refracted and memorialized wartime violence." Daughtry, *Listening to War*, 5.
146. Scarry, *The Body in Pain*, 40.

CHAPTER 3

1. Jean Baudrillard, *Why Hasn't Everything Already Disappeared?*, translated by Chris Turner (New York: Seagull Books, 2009), 9.
2. Reguillo, "The Narco-Machine."
3. I use the following website for this information, using the dates December 1, 2006, to July 17, 2023, and the category "Personas desaparecidas y no localizadas": Gobierno de México, Comisión Nacional de Búsqueda, Versión Pública RNPDNO, "Aviso para la persona usuaria," https://versionpublicarnpdno.segob.gob.mx/Dashboard/Index.
4. Comisión Nacional de los Derechos Humanos, "Informe Especial de la Comisión Nacional de Los Derechos Humanos sobre desaparición de personas y fosas clandestinas en México," April 6, 2017, http://informe.cndh.org.mx/menu.aspx?id=30100. According to this report, "en 2012, 3,343 casos; en 2013, 3,878 casos; en 2014, 4,196 casos; en 2015, 3,768 casos; y hasta octubre de 2016, 3,805 casos." Comisión Nacional de los Derechos Humanos, "Informe Especial," 15.
5. Efraín Tzuc, "CBN lleva un año de retraso en la publicación del registro de personas desaparecidas," *A dónde van los desaparecidos*, May 1, 2020, https://adondevanlosdesaparecidos.org/2020/04/30/cnb-lleva-un-ano-de-retraso-en-la-publicacion-del-registro-de-personas-desaparecidas.; Tzuc, Efraín, "Presentan plataforma de personas desaparecidas pero no abren datos," *Revista Proceso*, July 13, 2020. https://www.proceso.com.mx/nacional/2020/7/13/presentan-plataforma-de-personas-desaparecidas-pero-no-abren-datos-246102.html.
6. Data Cívica, *Análisis y evaluación de registros oficiales de personas desaparecidas: Hacia el nuevo registro nacional*, March 2019, https://registros-desaparecidos.datacivica.org/informe/FINAL_Anaìlisis_y_evaluacioìn_de.pdf, 16–18.
7. Comisión Nacional de los Derechos Humanos, "Análisis Situacional de los Derechos Humanos de las Personas Desaparecidas y No Localizadas," 2018, http://informe.cndh.org.mx/menu.aspx?id=40062#lda40330.
8. Inter-American Commission on Human Rights, "The Human Rights Situation in Mexico," *Inter-American Commission on Human Rights*, December 31, 2015, http://www.oas.org/en/iachr/reports/pdfs/mexico2016-en.pdf, 46.
9. Inter-American Commission on Human Rights, "Chapter V: Follow-up to Recommendations Made by the IACHR in its Country or Thematic Reports," *Inter-American Commission on Human Rights*, 2019, https://www.oas.org/en/iachr/docs/annual/2019/docs/IA2019cap5MX-en.pdf, 687–774.
10. United States State Department, *Mexico 2018 Human Rights Report*, 2018 https://www.state.gov/reports/2018-country-reports-on-human-rights-practices/mexico, 3.

11. United States State Department, *Mexico 2019 Human Rights Report*, 2019, https://www.state.gov/reports/2019-country-reports-on-human-rights-practices/mexico, 3.
12. Inter-American Commission on Human Rights, "Chapter V," 703.
13. United States State Department, *Mexico 2018*, 3.
14. "Conferencia de prensa matutina, desde Palacio Nacional." Youtube, uploaded by Andrés Manuel López Obrador, streamed live on January 29, 2021, https://www.youtube.com/watch?v=XHyGoSm3EMk. Also see, "México encontró 599 fosas," *DW*, January 30, 2020, https://www.dw.com/es/méxico-encontró-559-fosas-clandestinas-en-2020/a-56389269.
15. See Saldívar Arreola and Rodríguez Sánchez, "Análisis del léxico."
16. Judith Butler, *Frames of War: When Is Life Grievable?* (New York: Verso, 2009), 31.
17. Butler, *Frames*, 31.
18. See Judith Butler, *Precarious Life: The Powers of Mourning and Violence* (New York: Verso, 2004).
19. Butler, *Frames*, 26.
20. See Melissa Wright, "Epistemological Ignorances and Fighting for the Disappeared: Lessons from Mexico," *Antipode* 49 no. 1 (2017): 259.
21. For more on the events of Ayotzinapa, see Grupo Interdisciplinario de Expertos Independientes, *Informe Ayotzinapa II*; Comisión Nacional de Derechos Humanos, "Pronunciamiento de la CNDH"; Marchando con letras, *Ayotzinapa: La Travesía de las tortugas* (Mexico City: Marchando con letras, 2015); and Melesio, "Ayotzinapa 43." For more on forced disappearance as a strategy of terror, see Federico Mastrogiovanni, *Ni vivos ni Muertos: La desaparición forzada en México como estrategia de terror* (Mexico City: Debolsillo, 2017). For more on citizen responses to disappearance and Mexico's War on Drugs, see Raúl Diego Rivera Hernández, *Narratives of Vulnerability in Mexico's War on Drugs*, translated by Isis Sadek (New York: Palgrave MacMillan, 2020).
22. Inter-American Commission on Human Rights, "The Human Rights Situation," 32.
23. Cited in Tommaso Gravante "Forced Disappearance as a Collective Cultural Trauma in the Ayoztinapa Movement," *Latin American Perspectives* 47, no. 6 (November 2020): 88.
24. Rossana Reguillo, "La turbencia en el paisaje: De jóvenes, necropolítica y 43 esperanzas," in *Juvencidio: Ayotzinapa y las vidas precarias en América Latina*, edited by José Manuel Valenzuela Arce (Barcelona: Ned Ediciones, 2015), 59–77. Reguillo explains that, "el hashtag #TodosSomosAyotzinapa se convirtió rápidamente en un espacio que permitía el amplio reconocimiento principalmente de jóvenes, que han sido los que han comandado la protesta y la imaginación en los nuevos lenguajes de la resistencia activa" (the hashtag #TodosSomos Ayotzinapa rapidly became a space that allowed for the wide-spread recognition of young people, principally those that had been leading the protest,

and also an example of how imagination can shape the language of resistance movements). Reguillo, "La turbencia," 72. For more on hashtags and activism, see Gerardo Blanco Ramírez and Amy Scott Metcalfe, "Hashtivism as Public Discourse: Exploring Online Student Activism in Response to State Violence and Forced Disappearances in Mexico," *Research in Education* 97, no. 1 (2017): 56–75; Marcela Fuentes, "#Niunamenos: Hashtag Performativity, Memory, and Direct Action against Gender Violence in Argentina," in *Women Mobilizing Memory*, edited by Aye GI Altnay et al. (New York: Colombia University Press, 2019), 172–91.

25. While outside the scope of my discussion, it is important to recognize that this discourse about the nation's future as embodied in the Ayotzinapa 43 is paradoxical, given that they possess Indigenous features and dark-skinned Mexicans often face discrimination and erasure from national representation. For more on this, see Melissa Wright, "Against the Evils of Democracy: Fighting Forced Disappearance and Neoliberal Terror in Mexico," *Annals of the American Association of Geographers* 108, no. 2 (2018): 330–33.
26. Wright, "Against the Evils," 322.
27. Butler, *Frames*, 38.
28. Diéguez, *Cuerpos*, 173.
29. Attending to the question of producing literature in the Mexican context after 2006, in her book, *The Restless Dead: Necrowriting and Disappropriation*, translated by Robin Myers (Nashville, TN: Vanderbilt University Press, 2020), Cristina Rivera Garza offers a concept similar to Diéguez's *communitas de dolor*. Rivera Garza declares communalities of writing as "survival strategies based on mutual care and the protection of the common good, challenging the ease and apparent immanence that marks the languages of global capitalism." Rivera Garza, *The Restless Dead*, 5.
30. Brenda Werth's *Theatre, Performance, and Memory Politics in Argentina* (New York: Palgrave Macmillan, 2010) dedicates chapter 2 to the figure of Antigone in contemporary drama. For more on Yuyachkani's *Antígona*, see Taylor's *The Archive and the Repertoire*, particularly chapter 8. Also see chapter 3 in Anne Lambright's *Andean Truths: Transitional Justice, Ethnicity, and Cultural Production in Post-Shining Path Peru* (Liverpool: Liverpool University Press, 2016). For more on Gambaro's work, see Nancy Kason Poulson's "In Defense of the Dead: *Antígona Furiosa*, by Griselda Gambaro," *Romance Quarterly* 59 no. 1 (2012): 48–54. For a detailed reading of Sara Uribe's poem, see Tamara Williams's "Wounded Nation, Voided State: Sara Uribe's *Antígona González*," *Romance Notes* 57, no. 1 (2017): 3–14.
31. Judith Butler, *Antigone's Claim: Kinship between Life and Death* (New York: Columbia University Press, 2000), 2.
32. My questions are inspired by Rebecca Schneider's *Performing Remains*. Though she studies reenactments of war, particularly in the United States, the notion

of remains, both as the body in war as well as a kind of permanence in memory, is powerful.
33. Julia Kristeva, "Antigone: Limit and Horizon," in *Feminist Readings of Antigone*, edited by Fanny Söderbäck (Albany: State University of New York Press, 2010), 222.
34. Victor Turner, *From Ritual to Theatre: The Human Seriousness of Play* (New York: PAJ Publications, 1982), 79.
35. Paul Connerton, *How Societies Remember* (Cambridge: Cambridge University Press, 1989), 45.
36. Jason Castle and William L. Phillips, "Grief Rituals: Aspects That Facilitate Adjustment to Bereavement," *Journal of Loss and Trauma* 8, no. 1 (2003): 50.
37. Rivera Garza, *Grieving*, 7.
38. Tara Bailey and Tony Walter, "Funerals against Death," *Mortality* 21, no. 2 (2016): 163
39. Douglas Davies, *Death, Ritual, and Belief: The Rhetoric of Funerary Rites*, 3rd ed. (New York: Bloomsbury Academic, 2017), 4.
40. Butler, *Antigone's Claim*, 27.
41. Fanny Söderbäck, "Impossible Mourning: Sophocles Reversed," in *Feminist Readings of Antigone*, edited by Fanny Söderbäck (Albany: State University of New York Press, 2010), 70.
42. Diéguez, "Necroteatro, 13; Diéguez, *Cuerpos*, 227.
43. By unspeakability, I am reminded of Theodor Adorno's declaration that "what the Nazis did to the Jews was unspeakable: language has no word for it." Theodor Adorno, "Messages in a Bottle," translated by Edmund Jephcott, *New Left Review* 1, no. 200 (1993): 6. Yet, I use the term, inspired by how Naomi Mandel implores us to speak and write of horrors, lest silence become complicity. Naomi Mandel, *Against the Unspeakable: Complicity, the Holocaust, and Slavery in America* (Charlottesville: University of Virginia Press, 2006). She states that "the movement from a focus on the unspeakable to an ethics of complicity, then, is paralleled by a movement from a focus on language, representation, and its limits on the one hand to an engagement with the corporeal on the other." Mandel, *Against the Unspeakable*, 13.
44. Butler, *Frames*, 61.
45. Violeta Luna, personal interview, April 28, 2020.
46. Violeta Luna, "About the Artist," http://www.violetaluna.com/About.html.
47. Violet Luna, "Cor-po/etics: A Poetics of the Body in Performance." Presentation at the University of Wisconsin–Madison, April 20, 2021.
48. Paola Marín, "Migrant Bodies, Flowing Rituals: The Performance Art of Violeta Luna," *Latin American Theatre Review* 52, no. 1 (Fall 2018): 97.
49. Alexander Stein, "Music, Mourning, and Consolation," *JAPA* 52, no. 3 (2004): 791, 793.
50. This piece was originally envisioned for the 2012 Hemispheric Institute of Politics and Performance Encuentro in Mexico City. However, due to

unforeseen circumstances, this event was canceled and rescheduled in 2013 in São Paolo, Brazil. For more on the piece, see Marín, "Migrant Bodies," 88–91.
51. For more, see Marín, "Migrant Bodies," 92–94. Also see Violeta Luna, Ileana Diéguez, and Rián Lozano, "Imaginario—Necromachines," presentation at the Hemispheric Institute of Politics and Performance Encuentro, Mexico City, June 14, 2019, available online, Vimeo, uploaded by Hemispheric Institute, July 29, 2019, https://vimeo.com/349664038.
52. Luna, personal interview.
53. Violeta Luna, *Réquiem #3: Fosas Cuerpo/Body Graves*, performance, Centro Universitario de Teatro, Black Box Theatre, Mexico City, Mexico, June 11, 2019, available online, Hemispheric Institute Digital Video Library, https://hemisphericinstitute.org/es/encuentro-2019-performances/item/2936-violeta-luna.html.
54. For a detailed description of the 2017 FLACC performance, see Juan Manuel Aldape Muñoz, "Choreotopias: Performance, State Violence, and the Near Past." (PhD diss., University of California, Berkeley, 2020), 77.
55. Marín, "Migrant Bodies," 91.
56. Luna, personal interview.
57. Luna, personal interview.
58. Turner, *From Ritual to Theatre*, 81.
59. Turner, *From Ritual to Theatre*, 50.
60. Luna, personal interview.
61. Butler, *Frames*, 15.
62. Butler, *Frames*, 79.
63. James E. Young, *The Texture of Memory: Holocaust Memorials and Meaning* (New Haven, CT: Yale University Press, 1993), 3.
64. Kristeva, "Antigone," 226.
65. Söderbäck, "Impossible Mourning, 70.
66. Söderbäck, "Impossible Mourning, 77.
67. Movimiento por nuestros desaparecidos en México began in March 2015 as a conglomerate of 35 collectives that came together "para luchar por la existencia e implementación de la primera Ley General en materia de desapariciones en México" (to fight for the existence and implementation of the first General Law on disappearances in Mexico). Movimiento por nuestros desaparecidos en México. "Acerca de," n.d., https://memoriamndm.org/sobre-el-movndmx.
68. See Alma E. Muñoz, "Madre de policía federal desaparecido exige que el Estado no evada su responsabilidad," *La Jornada*, February 21, 2016, https://www.jornada.com.mx/2016/02/21/politica/010n1pol. Also see, "Luis Ángel León Rodríguez." *CMDPDH*, http://cmdpdh.org/no-olvidamos/luis-angel.
69. Comisión Mexicana de Defensa y Promoción de los Derechos Humanos, "A 10 años de la desaparición forzada de Luis Ángel León Rodríguez," *CMDPDH Blog*, November 14, 2019, http://cmdpdh.org/2019/11/a-10-anos-de-la-desaparicion-forzada-de-luis-angel-leon-rodriguez-policia-federal-aun-se-desconoce-su-paradero.

70. Ramona Mosse, "Thinking Theatres beyond Sight: From Reflection to Resonance," *Anglia* 136, no. 1 (2018): 141.
71. Luna, personal interview.
72. Bailey and Walter, "Funerals against Death," 161.
73. Butler, *Antigone's Claim*, 11.
74. Bailey and Walter, "Funerals against Death," 161; emphasis in original.
75. Luce Irigaray, "The Eternal Irony of the Community," translated by Gillian C. Gill, in *Feminist Readings of Antigone*, edited by Fanny Söderbäck (Albany: State University of New York Press, 2010), 103.
76. Melissa W. Wright, "Visualizing a Country without a Future: Posters for Ayotzinapa, Mexico and Struggles against State Terror," *Geoforum* 102 (2019): 237.
77. Wright, "Visualizing," 237; emphasis in original.
78. David Molina, personal interview, May 12, 2020.
79. Molina, personal interview.
80. Molina, personal interview.
81. Molina, personal interview.
82. Tazewell Thompson, "The Art of Looking with the Ear," in *Sound and Music for the Theatre: The Art and Technique of Design*, edited by Deena Kaye, James LeBrecht, and Davied Budries (New York: Routledge, 2016), xxix–xxx.
83. Janieke Bruin-Mollenhorst, "The Musical Eulogy and Other Functions of Funeral Music," *OMEGA* 82, no. 1 (2018): 34–36.
84. Molina, personal interview.
85. David Roesner and Lynne Kendrick, introduction to *Theatre Noise: The Sound of Performance*, edited by David Roesner and Lynne Kendrick (Cambridge: Cambridge Scholars Publishing, 2011), xxv.
86. Nicholas Ridout, "Welcome to the Vibratorium," *Senses and Society* 3, no. 2 (2008): 231.
87. Thompson, "The Art of Looking," xxx.
88. Tia DeNora, *After Adorno: Rethinking Music Sociology* (Cambridge: Cambridge University Press, 2009), 83.
89. I use the term here inspired by Teresa Brennan's *The Transmission of Affect* (Ithaca, NY: Cornell University Press, 2004), 6.
90. Paola Hernández *Staging Lives in Latin American Theater*, 3.
91. The waterphone is named after its inventor, Richard Waters, and consists of a series of rods of different lengths and thickness attached to the rim of a bowl, usually made of metal (Molina, personal interview).
92. DeNora, *After Adorno*, 100; emphasis in original.
93. Although "grounded terrain," may seem redundant, I refer to it as such to emphasize the bodies hidden deep within the earth as opposed to those found on sidewalks, dispersed in pieces above ground, or left to decay in basins or other containers.
94. Glenys Caswell, "Beyond Words: Some Uses of Music in the Funeral Setting," *OMEGA* 64, no. 4 (2011–2012): 327.

95. Bruin-Mollenhorst, "The Musical Eulogy," 35.
96. Stein, "Music, Mourning," 793.
97. Molina, personal interview.
98. Daniela Valdez, "Lukas Avendaño: Interview," *Revista 192*, June 18, 2020, https://revista192.com/lukas-avendan%CC%830.
99. Of this decision, Avendaño states, "when my father broke the logic of remaining indio and became an 'illegal' (immigrant) in the United States, we all broke the chain of being indio," and once broken, Avendaño felt like he could pursue his own path. Rafael E. Lozano, "Lukas Avendaño: A Successful Case of Failure," *Que Pasa Oaxaca*, August 27, 2019, https://www.quepasaoaxaca.com/lukas-avendano-un-caso-exitoso-del-fracaso.
100. Valdez, "Lukas Avendaño."
101. See Lozano, "Lukas Avendaño,"; Patxi Beltzaiz Traba, "Lukas Avendaño. Bailando Bruno." *De la utre cote du charco* blog. March 18, 2020, http://delautrecoteducharco.org/2020/03/18/lukas-avendano-bailando-bruno-en-espanol.
102. Traba, "Lukas Avendaño."
103. For more on *Réquiem para un alcaraván*, see Antonio Prieto Stambaugh, "'RepresentaXión' de un *muxe*," *Latin American Theatre Review* 48, no. 1 (Fall 2014): 31–53. To understand Avendaño's inpiration for *No soy hombre, soy mariposa*, see "Lechedevirgen: Pensamiento Puñal." *Lechedevirgen*. https://www.lechedevirgen.com/textos/pensamiento-punal. This text, from 2012, became the basis for Avendaño's discourse used in the performance.
104. Antonio Prieto Stambaugh, "The Queer/*Muxe* Performance of Disappearance: Lukas Avendaño's Butterfly Utopía," in *Performances that Changed the Americas*, edited by Stuart A. Day (New York: Routledge, 2021), 185.
105. Samuel Rutter, and Caitlin Younquist, "10 Queer Indigenous Artists on Where Their Inspirations Have Led Them," *New York Times*, April 23, 2021, https://www.nytimes.com/2021/04/23/t-magazine/queer-indigenous-artists.html.
106. See Riansares Lozano de la pola, "¿Dónde está Bruno Avendaño? La práctica artística como 'espacio de aparición.'" *El ornitorrinco tachado*, no. 8 (November–April 2019): 29–39.
107. According to Avendaño: "nadie vio nada ni oyó nada. Fue como si Bruno se hubiera desvanecido en el aire" (no one saw or heard anything. It was as if Bruno disappeared into thin air). Traba, "Lukas Avendaño."
108. "Bruno Avendaño vuelve a casa, pero la búsqueda de justicia continúa," Youtube, uploaded by Rompeviento TV, December 4, 2020, https://www.youtube.com/watch?v=2TFqXJefusU.
109. "Pedirán por la desaparición forzada Bruno Avendaño en México," *ANRed*, October 8, 2018, https://www.anred.org/2018/10/08/pediran-por-la-desaparicion-forzada-bruno-avendano-en-mexico.
110. Traba, "Lukas Avendaño"; Sandra Vicente, "Quiero pensar que con el arte puedo convertir la impotentica de la desaparición de mi hermano en algo alegre," interview with Lukas Avendaño, *Catalunya Plural*, June 26, 2018,

https://catalunyaplural.cat/es/quiero-pensar-que-con-el-arte-puedo-convertir-la-impotencia-de-la-desaparicion-de-mi-hermano-en-algo-alegre.

111. "Después de 30 meses, encuentran sin vida a Bruno Avendaño, marino desaparecido en Oaxaca," *Aristegui Noticias*, December 3, 2020, https://aristeguinoticias.com/0312/mexico/despues-de-30-meses-encuentran-sin-vida-a-bruno-avendano-marino-desaparecido-en-oaxaca.

112. "Encuentran sin vida a Bruno Avendaño, desaparecido en 2018 en Tehuantepec," *EDUCA*, December 4, 2020, https://www.educaoaxaca.org/encuentran-sin-vida-a-bruno-avendano-desaparecido-en-2018-en-tehuantepec.

113. Lukas Avendaño, "Gratia Plena," Facebook post, December 4, 2020, https://www.facebook.com/lukas.avendano.39/posts/10221569862027880 2020.

114. For more on State-sponsored repression of Zapotec activists in the Loxicha region in 1996, see Kristen Norget, "Caught in the Crossfire: Militarization, Paramilitarization, and State Violence in Oaxaca Mexico," in *When States Kill: Latin America, the U.S., and Technologies of Terror*, edited by Cecilia Menjívar and Néstor Rodríguez (Austin: University of Texas Press, 2005), 115–42.

115. Alejandra Favela, "Lasting Lessons from Oaxaca: Teachers as Luchadores Sociales: An Inside Account of the Historic 2006 Oaxacan Teachers' Movement and Why It Is Still Relevant Today," *Radical Teacher* 1, no. 88 (2010): 63–72.

116. Biologist Ramiro Aragón Pérez, and teachers Elionai Santiago Sánchez and Juan Gabriel Ríos, were falsely charged, tortured, and imprisoned by governmental forces because of their perceived participation in subversive efforts, such as the 2006 APPO uprising. See Lynn Stephen, "Testimony and Human Rights Violations in Oaxaca," *Latin American Perspectives* 38, no. 6 (2011): 52.

117. Diana Denham, Patrick Lincoln, and Chris Thomas, introduction to *Teaching Rebellion: Stories from the Grassroots Mobilization in Oaxaca*, edited by Diana Denham and the C.A.S.A. collective (Oakland, CA: PM Press, 2008), 38.

118. Inter-American Commission on Human Rights, "Chapter V," 741; United States State Department, *Mexico 2019*, 3.

119. Alexander Dunlap, "Wind Energy: Toward a 'Sustainable Violence' in Oaxaca," *NACLA Report on the Americas* 49, no. 4 (2017): 488; Isabel Altamirano-Jiménez, "Indigenous women refusing the violence of resource extraction in Oaxaca," *AlterNative* 17, no. 2 (2021): 219.

120. The violence in Oaxaca's Juchitán has become so common that artists, like the group Juchirap, have produced music detailing the landscape of fear and terror. For more, see Citali López Velázquez, "'Juchitán de las balas', el rap que llama a no normalizer la violencia en Oaxaca," *La silla rota*, February 15, 2022, https://lasillarota.com/estados/juchitan-de-las-balas-el-rap-que-llama-a-no-normalizar-la-violencia-en-oaxaca/617283. Much of this increased violence is related to cartels spreading throughout the region. For more, see "Nuevo grupo armado amenaza a policías en Oaxaca: 'Tenemos ubicados a municipals y estatales,'" *infobae*, February 2, 2021, https://www.infobae.com/america/mexico/2021/02/02/nuevo-grupo-armado-amenaza-a-policias-en-oaxaca-tenemos-ubicados-a-todos-los-municipales-y-estatales.; Alondra Olivera "'El Chapo de Oaxaca',

el líder del cartel de Juchitán," *La silla rota*, Abril 24, 2017, https://lasillarota.com/estados/el-chapo-de-oaxaca-el-lider-del-cartel-de-juchitan/145027.; and Alberto Nájar, "Minería, el nuevo negocio de los carteles mexicanos," *BBC Mundo*, March 18, 2016, https://www.bbc.com/mundo/noticias/2014/03/140318_mexico_mineria_nuevo_negocio_carteles_narcotrafico_templarios_zetas_an. Over the last several years, journalists have also alluded to the role of cartel participation in mining efforts as well as the mining industry as a form of financial and land conquest. See Jesús J. Lemus, "Opinión: A 500 años de la Conquista, elterritorio mexicano es botín de empresas mineras transnacionales," *Los Angeles Times*, August 14, 2021, https://www.latimes.com/espanol/opinion/articulo/2021-08-14/opinion-a-500-anos-de-la-conquista-el-territorio-mexicano-es-botin-de-empresas-mineras-trasnacionales.
121. Prieto Stambaugh, "RepresentaXión," 31.
122. Prieto Stambaugh, "The Queer/*Muxe*," 176.
123. See "Mexico's Third Gender," Youtube, uploaded by Great Big Story, June 19, 2018, https://youtu.be/aEZEiiNS3Ew?si=mZQ9GOEdpIFywUwy; "Muxes 'El tercer género de México' – Entrevista a Lukas Avendaño," Youtube, uploaded by Conecta Estudio, July 27, 2020, https://youtu.be/U_PKeRdCn-U?si=whevmPSPJa5yrczZ.
124. Heather Vrana, "An 'Other' Woman?: Juchitec Muxes in Marie Claire and Documentary," *Michigan Feminist Studies* 21 (Fall 2008): 1.
125. Lukas Avendaño, "Queer: No. Queer-Po Muxe: Yes," translated by Robin Myers, *Goethe-Institut Mexiko*, May, 2019, https://www.goethe.de/ins/us/en/m/kul/wir/swl/qpe/21586998.html.
126. Alfredo Mirandé, *Behind the Mask: Gender Hybridity in a Zapotec Community* (Tucson: University of Arizona Press, 2017), 5.
127. Charles Brasseur, "The Didjazá," translated by Lorna Scott Fox, *Artes de México*, no. 49 (2000): 83.
128. See Miguel Covarrubias, "A Southward View," *Artes de México*, no. 49 (2000): 86; Sergei Eisenstein, "Life," translated by Richard Moszka, *Artes de México*, no. 49 (2000): 83.
129. Aída Sierra, "The Creation of a Symbol," translated by Richard Moszka, *Artes de México*, no. 49 (2000): 84–85.
130. Avendaño, "Queer: No."
131. Marinella Miano Borruso, "Gays tras bambalinas. Historia de belleza, pasiones e identidades," *Debate Feminista* 18 (1998): 186–236; Marinella Miano Borruso, *Hombre, mujer y* muxe' *en el Istmo de Tehuantepec* (Mexico City: Instituto Nacional de Antropología e Historia, 2002).
132. Lynn Stephen defines the vela in the following way: "*Velas* are elaborate several-day celebrations involving processions, masses, food preparation and blessing, drinking, and dancing organized around neighborhoods and families." Lynn Stephen, "Sexualities and Genders in Zapotec Oaxaca," *Latin American Perspectives* 29, no. 2 (March 2000): 43. For more on *velas*, see Mirandé *Behind the Mask*, 33–38; Islas *Muxes*; Marinella Miano Borruso, "Género y Homosexualidad entre los Zapotecos del Istmo de Tehuantepec: El Caso de los Muxe," in

Actas del IV Congreso Chileno de Antropología (Santiago: Colegio de Antropólogos de Chile A. G. 2001), 685–89; and Marinella Miano Borruso, "Muxe: 'Nuevos Liderazgos' y Fenómenos Mediáticos," *Revista Digital Universitaria* 11, no. 9 (September 2010): 3–15. Every November, over a period of four days, Las Intrépidas, buscadores de peligro organize their own *vela*. For more on Las Intrépidas, their *vela*, and activism efforts in the *Istmo*, see "Las intrépidas buscadoras de peligro," Youtube, uploaded by VICE en Español, May 4, 2016, https://www.youtube.com/watch?v=nTY-7dfyy68.

133. Gustavo Subero "*Muxeninity* and the Institutionalization of a Third Gender Identity in Alejandra Isla's *Muxes: Auténticas, intrépidas, buscadores de peligro*," *Hispanic Research Journal* 14 no. 2 (2013): 181,188. Also see Dominika Gasiorowski, "The *muxes* of Juchitán: Representations of Non-binary Gender Identities in Contemporary Photography from Mexico," *Bulletin of Hispanic Studies* 85 no. 8 (2018): 895–914.

134. Avendaño, "Queer: No."

135. Amaranta Gómez, "Trascendiendo," *Desacatos*, nos. 15–16 (Fall 2004): 203. Gómez prefers the spelling *muxhe*, as it relates to the Zapotec understanding of the Spanish word for woman, *mujer*.

136. Ángelo Néstore, "La autotraducción al servicio de la visibilidad de discursos disidentes: El caso de la poeta y traductora cuir* muxe' Elvis Guerra," *Revista Letral*, no. 24 (2020): 225. Alejandra Elizabeth Urbioa Solís et al. make a similar observation in "Expresión y trabajo de los Muxe' del Istmo de Tehuantepec, en Juchitán de Zaragoza, México," *Nova Scientia* 9, no. 19 (2017): 502–27. They state, "un muxe' se auto denomina como tal en tanto tiene una práctia sexo-genérica identificada como diferente de mujer y diferente de hombre, se es muxe' si el sujeto se identifica como zapoteca y al reconocerse como descendiente de zapotecas y hablar zapoteco" (A "muxe" defines oneself as such if they identify with a certain sexual and gendered practice and if they identify as different from both a woman and man. One can be "muxe" if the subject also identifies as Zapotec, recognizes themselves as a descendent of Zapotecs, and they speak Zapotec). Urbioa Solís et al., "Expresión y trabajo," 506.

137. Avendaño, "Queer: No."

138. Modestomigato, "Conversación con Lukas Avendaño: Primera parte," *Heredad Blog*, March 21, 2021, https://www.heredadpalabras.com/post/conversación-con-lukas-avendaño-primera-parte.

139. Stephen states that the Juchitán is unique in "the people's strong sense of local nationalism tied to a history of political struggles to maintain regional and local autonomy." Stephen, "Sexualities and Genders," 42. Echoing this, Sierra explains that during the postrevolutionary efforts to create an understanding of *mexicanidad*, the Isthmus "was far from peaceful, nor was it known to be so, given that since the nineteenth century its inhabitants had become notorious for being a courageous and indomitable people." Sierra, "The Creation of a Symbol," 85. Also see Mirandé, *Behind the Mask*, 19–25.

140. See Marianella Miano Borruso, "Género y Homosexualidad," 685–89.
141. Urbiola Solís, "Expresión y trabajo," 511.
142. Miano Borruso, "Gays," 234; Miano Borruso, *Hombre, mujer y muxe'*, 165–69.
143. Avendaño, "Queer: No."
144. Lukas Avendaño, *Buscando a Bruno*, performance, Museo Universitario del Chopo, Mexico City, Mexico, February 6, 2019, available online, Youtube, uploaded by Museo Universitario del Chopo, March 30, 2020, at https://www.youtube.com/watch?v=qnFf-QZZfRA; Lukas Avendaño, *Buscando a Bruno*, performance, Museo Universitario de Arte Moderno, Mexico City, Mexico, June 9, 2019, available online, Hemispheric Institute Digital Video Library, https://hemisphericinstitute.org/en/encuentro-2019-performances/item/2821-performances-007.html.
145. Adriana Cavarero, "On the Body of Antigone," in *Feminist Readings of Antigone*, edited by Fanny Söderbäck (Albany: State University of New York Press, 2010), 56.
146. Cecilia Sjöholm, *The Antigone Complex: Ethics and the Invention of Feminine Desire* (Palo Alto, CA: Stanford University Press, 2004), xiii.
147. Vicente, "Quiero pensar."
148. Sjöholm, *The Antigone Complex*, 125.
149. Butler, *Antigone's Claim*, 11.
150. See Alba Aragón, "Uninhabited Dresses: Frida Kahlo, from Icon of Mexico to Fashion Muse," *Fashion Theory* 18, no. 5 (2004): 537; Deborah Poole, "An Image of 'Our Indian': Type Photographs and Racial Sentiments in Oaxaca, 1920–1940," *Hispanic American Historical Review* 84, no. 1 (2004): 67; Francie Chassen-López, "The Traje de Tehuana as National Icon: Gender, Ethnicity, and Fashion in Mexico," *The Americas* 71, no. 2 (2014): 307.
151. Poole, "An Image of 'Our Indian,'" 67–68.
152. Annegret Hesterberg, "A Second Skin," translated by Johannes Weber, *Artes de México*, no. 49 (2000): 88.
153. Hesterberg, "A Second Skin," 89.
154. Vicente, "Quiero pensar."
155. Prieto Stambaugh, "The Queer/*Muxe*," 190.
156. Butler, *Antigone's Claim*, 80.
157. Butler, *Antigone's Claim*, 80.
158. Prieto Stambaugh, "The Queer/*Muxe*," 185.
159. Lozano de la pola 2019, 36; Alejo Medina "¿Dónde está Bruno? / Where is Bruno?: Lukas Avendaño's Autobiography as a Political Act," *Performance Research* 27, no. 7 (2019): 57.
160. On multiple occasions Avendaño has clarified that his work is not a copy of Kahlo's painting. For Avendaño, Kahlo is the one who appropriated clothing from a culture not entirely her own. He often makes sure to explain that, as a Zapotec person from the Istmo, this is his culture, not an imitation or variation. See Rutter and Youngquist "10 Queer"; Vicente "Quiero pensar."

161. Of Kahlo's use of the Tehuana, "we know she began to wear the traje at the request of her husband." Chassen-López, "The Traje," 312. For more on Kahlo's self-fashioning of a mestiza identity, one that mixed indigenous groups, see Aragón, "Uninhabited."
162. See Rutter and Youngquist, "10 Queer."
163. Miguel Covarrubias comments, "the most spectacular garment of the Tehuanas is a headdress of starched, pleated lace seen on important ceremonial occasions. It is called 'head-huipil' or 'great huipil.'" Covarrubias, "A Southward View," 88. Similarly, Hesterberg explains, "the *huipil grande* often worn as a headdress at fiestas consists of a lace blouse with *faux* sleeves that are purely decorative and lace trimming on the hem and neckline." Hesterberg, "A Second Skin," 89.
164. Covarrubias, "A Southward View," 88.
165. Sadly, there is no video archive of this performance. Avendaño generally works with his own videographer, who did not accompany him to the Encuentro because the Hemispheric Institute of Politics and Performance promised Avendaño that the piece would be filmed. It was not. Lukas Avendaño, personal interview, May 12, 2020.
166. Banda Princesa Donají was formed in 1964 in Santa María by Nicolás Vichido Rito and Margarito M. Guzmán. Their goal was to preserve the music of the region. Since its formation, Banda Princesa Donají has performed at local events around the Istmo with notable appearances over the years in Mexico City, Acapulco, Texcoc and Veracruz. See "Princesa Donají: Biografía," Last.fm, updated October 9, 2011, https://www.last.fm/es/music/Princesa+Donashii/+wiki.
167. "*Sonidos de la Nación Zapoteca* define plan de trabajo," *Guidxizá, una mirada a nuestros pueblos*, cultural supplement of *Comité Melendre* 1, no. 8 (September 17, 2012). http://comitemelendre.blogspot.com/2012/12/sonidos-de-la-nacion-zapoteca-define.html.
168. Edgar Cartas Orozco, personal interview, April 22, 2020.
169. Avendaño, personal interview.
170. Avendaño, personal interview.
171. Sarah B. Barber and Mireya Olvera Sánchez, "A Divine Wind: The Arts of Death and Music in Terminal Formative Oaxaca," *Ancient Mesoamerica* 23, no. 1 (2012): 9.
172. Charles V. Heath, *The Inevitable Bandstand: The State Band of Oaxaca and the Politics of Sound* (Lincoln: University of Nebraska Press, 2015), 3.
173. Xóchitl C. Chávez, "Oaxacan Indigenous Women Musicians' Collective Songwriting Process on the Title Track of *Mujeres*," *Americas: A Hemispheric Music Journal* 29 (2020): 121-122; Xóchitl C. Chávez, "La creación de Oaxacalifornia mediante tradiciones culturales entre jóvenes oaxaqueños de Los Ángeles, California." *Desacatos* 62 (Jan.-Apr. 2020): 172-73.
174. Kristin Norget, *Days of Death, Days of Life: Ritual in the Popular Culture of Oaxaca* (New York: Columbia University Press, 2006), 115.

175. Norget, *Days of Death, Days of Life*, 116.
176. Stein, "Music, Mourning," 793.
177. George Home-Cook, "Aural Acts: Theatre and the Phenomenology," in *Theatre Noise: The Sound of Performance*, edited by David Roesner and Lynne Kendrick (Cambridge: Cambridge Scholars Publishing, 2011), 103.
178. Home-Cook, "Aural Acts," 103.
179. Bruin-Mollenhorst, "The Musical Eulogy," 36.
180. Bruin-Mollenhorst, "The Musical Eulogy," 36.
181. Reguillo, "The Necro-Machine."
182. Natalia Cruz, "'Luto por derecho,' de Atilano Morales Jiménez," *Guidxizá, una mirada a nuestros pueblos*, cultural supplement of *Comité Melendre* 1, no. 1 (July 29, 2012), available online at http://comitemelendre.blogspot.com/2012/12/luto-por-derecho-de-atilano-morales.html.
183. Cruz, "'Luto.'"
184. "Dolor profundo – Banda Princesa Donají [Autor. Atilano Morales]." *Comité Melendre*, http://comitemelendre.blogspot.com/search?q=dolor+profundo.
185. DeNora, *After Adorno*, 83.
186. Caswell, "Beyond Words," 324.
187. Cartas Orozco, personal interview.
188. Cartas Orozco, personal interview.
189. Norget, *Days of Death*, 114.
190. Sandra Garrido and Waldo F. Garrido, "The Psychological Function of Music in Mourning Rituals," in *Music and Mourning*, edited by Jane W. Davidson and Sandra Garrido (New York: Routledge, 2016), 64.
191. Kendrick, *Theatre Aurality*, 103.
192. Turner, *From Ritual to Theatre*, 44-45.

CHAPTER 4

1. Jill Radford and Diana Russell, *Femicide: The Politics of Woman Killing* (New York: Twayne. 1992), xiv.
2. Radford and Russell, *Femicide*, 7.
3. Marcela Lagarde y de Los Ríos, "Preface: Feminist Keys for Understanding Feminicide: Theoretical, Political, and Legal Construction," in *Terrorizing Women: Feminicide in the Américas*, edited by Rosa-Linda Fregoso and Cynthia Bejarano (Durham: Duke University Press, 2010), xv.
4. Lagarde y de Los Ríos, "Preface," xv.
5. Rosa-Linda Fregoso and Cynthia Bejarano, eds. *Terrorizing Women: Feminicide in the Américas*, 1.
6. "En 25 años van 1,779 feminicidios en Ciudad Juárez." *El Heraldo de México*, February 15, 2018, https://heraldodemexico.com.mx/nacional/2018/2/15/en-25-anos-van-1779-feminicidios-en-ciudad-juarez-32735.html. As Diana Washington Valdéz, reports, "many women's murders, regardless of the motive, [are] unpunished crimes, and that made their deaths an issue of justice." Diana

Washington Valdez, *The Killing Fields: Harvest of Women* (Atlanta: Peace at the Border, 2006), 65. Since many of the women are never found, or are found dismembered, local citizens and family members erect pink crosses bearing the women's names, which in lieu of official gravesites have become emblematic of Ciudad Juárez's losses.

7. Julia Monárrez Fragoso, "The Victims of the Ciudad Juárez Feminicide: Sexually Fetishized Commodities," translated by Sara Koopman, in *Terrorizing Women*, 69.
8. Wright, "Necropolitics, Narcopolitics," 713–14.
9. See Monárrez Fragoso, "The Victims of the Ciudad Juárez Feminicide," 69; Wright Necropolitics, Narcopolitics," 710; Rita Laura Segato, *La escritura en el cuerpo de las mujeres asesinadas en Ciudad Juárez: Territorio, soberanía y crímenes de segundo estado* (Mexico City: Universidad del Claustro de Sor Juana, 2006), 27.
10. Rita Laura Segato, *La guerra contra las mujeres* (Madrid: Traficantes de sueños, 2016), 21.
11. Segato, *La guerra*, 149.
12. Instituto Nacional de Estadística y Geografía (INEGI). "Estadísticas a propósito del día internacional de la eliminación de la violencia contra la mujer (25 de noviembre)." *INEGI*, November 23, 2017, https://www.inegi.org.mx/contenidos/saladeprensa/aproposito/2017/violencia2017_Nal.pdf, 12.
13. "Feminicidios en México: Asesinaron a más de 56,000 mujeres desde 1990," *infobae*, December 18, 2020, https://www.infobae.com/america/mexico/2020/12/18/feminicidios-en-mexico-asesinaron-a-mas-de-56000-mujeres-desde-1990.
14. "Mexico rompió cifra histórica de mujeres asesinadas por homicidio doloso en el 2022; los feminicidios no bajan," *infobae*, February 5, 2023, https://www.infobae.com/mexico/2023/02/05/mexico-rompio-cifra-historica-de-mujeres-asesinadas-por-homicidio-doloso-en-el-2022-los-feminicidios-no-bajan.
15. Carolina Romero, "El riesgo de ser transexual en México." *El Universal*, October 15. 2018, https://www.eluniversal.com.mx/nacion/el-riesgo-de-ser-transexual-en-mexico; Pedro Matías, "Aumenta 47% asesinatos de mujeres trans; México segundo lugar mundial con 422 crímenes." *Página 3*, August 15, 2018, https://pagina3.mx/2018/08/aumenta-47-asesinatos-de-mujeres-trans-mexico-segundo-lugar-mundial-con-422-crimenes.
16. "Liz, Nicole, Kimberley, Martha y Karen: Cinco transfemicidios en los primeros diez días de noviembre en México," Agenciapresentes.org, November 17, 2022, https://agenciapresentes.org/2022/11/17/mexico-registro-cinco-transfemicidios-durante-noviembre; "CDMX reconoció el primer caso de feminicidio a una mujer trans," *infobae*, December 8, 2022, https://www.infobae.com/america/mexico/2022/12/08/cdmx-reconocio-el-primer-caso-de-feminicidio-a-una-mujer-trans.
17. Sayak Valencia, *Gore Capitalism* (South Pasadena, CA: Semiotext(e), 2018), 20.
18. Segato, *La escritura*, 9.
19. Wright, "Epistemological," 259.

20. Melissa W. Wright, "Gender and Geography II: Bridging the Gap—Feminist, Queer, and the Geographical Imaginary," *Progress in Human Geography* 34, no. 1 (2010): 57.
21. Melissa W. Wright, *Disposable Women and Other Myths of Global Capitalism* (New York: Routledge, 2006), 2.
22. Butler, *Precarious Life*, 10.
23. Segato, *La guerra*, 70.
24. "'La música es el mar por el que navega el cabaret', como dice Jesusa Rodríguez. . . . La música es un elemento indispensable en el cabaret" ("Music is the sea that cabaret navagates," as Jesusa Rodríguez says. . . . Music is an indispensable element in cabaret). Sotres, *Introducción al cabaret*, 68.
25. Also see Nick Castree et al., *The Point Is to Change It: Geographies of Hope and Survival in an Age of Crisis* (Oxford: Wiley-Blackwell, 2013).
26. Jose Esteban Muñoz, *Cruising Utopia: The Then and There of Queer Futurity* (New York: NYU Press, 2009), 1.
27. Valencia, *Gore Capitalism*, 218.
28. As a result of the COVID-19 pandemic, Las Pussy Queers has been forced to take an indefinite hiatus as Polaco relocated to Oaxaca, Mexico and Lima now resides in Madrid, Spain.
29. Mer, "'La desnudez asusta y seduce', Las Pussy Queers en El Vicio," Chicas.mx, May 18, 2018, https://www.chicas.mx/autor/almondomi.
30. Larissa Polaco and Irakere Lima, personal interview, April 7, 2020.
31. Irakere Lima and Larissa Polaco, *Ni una menos*, performance, Teatro Bar El Vicio, Coyoacán, Mexico, June 14, 2019, available online, Hemispheric Institute Digital Video Library, https://hemisphericinstitute.org/en/encuentro-2019-trasnocheo/item/3221-las-pussy-queers-not-one-woman-less.html.
32. Ella Jessel, "Chocolate Remix: The Lesbian Reggaetón Artista Taking on the 'Supermachos,'" *Guardian*, May 7, 2017, https://www.theguardian.com/music/2017/may/07/chocolate-remix-lesbian-reggaeton-taking-on-supermacho.
33. Mer, "La desnudez."
34. Hector Calderón, "Conversación con Aldo Acuña de Maldita Vecindad," *Aztlán* 31, no. 1 (2006): 122.
35. Calderón, "Conversación con Aldo Acuña de Maldita Vecindad," 120.
36. Noehmy Solórzano-Thompson, "Performative Masculinities: The Pachuco and the Luchador in the Songs of Maldita Vecindad and Café Tacuba," *Studies in Latin American Pop Culture* 26 (2007): 83.
37. Solórzano-Thompson, "Performative Masculinities," 85.
38. Solórzano-Thompson, "Performative Masculinities," 85. For more, see Soledad Lujan, "En medio de un gran circo: La ciudad de México a tráves de las crónicas musicales de Maldita Vecindad y Los Hijos del 5° Patio." (MA thesis, University of California–Santa Cruz, 2014).
39. Anthony W. Rasmussen, "Acoustic Patriarchy: Hearing Gender Violence in Mexico City's Public Spaces," *Women and Music: A Journal of Gender and Culture* 23 (2019): 21. I am using the notion of "acoustic patriarchy" in relation to

musical production, though Anthony Rasmussen proposes the idea as a means of analyzing the sounds of everyday Mexico City, such as street harassment. For more on notions of sound production and power structures, see Rasmussen, "Resistance Resounds: Hearing Power in Mexico City."

40. Polaco and Lima, personal interview.
41. Maldita Vecindad, "Morenaza," *Maldita Vecindad y los Hijos del Quinto Patio* (Sony Music Entertainment, 2015), Spotify, https://open.spotify.com/track/6MaTImJcG82qYwx6fJkm84?si=rEnB6Ex3SjexczZ330Wg5Q.
42. Alfredo Nieves Moreno, "A Man Lives Here: Reggaetón's Hypermasculine Resident," translated by Héctor Fernández L'Hoeste, in *Reggaetón*, edited by Raquel Z. Rivera, Wayne Marshall, and Deborah Pacini Hernández (Durham, NC: Duke University Press, 2009), 255–56.
43. For more on the organization's development and goals, see the website for Ni Una Menos, http://niunamenos.org.ar. For more on their organized events, see Fuentes, "#Niunamenos"; Marcela A. Fuentes, *Performance Constellations: Networks of Protest and Activism in Latin America* (Ann Arbor: University of Michigan Press, 2019).
44. Jessel, "Chocolate."
45. Wayne Marshall, Raquel Z. Rivera, and Deborah Pacini Hernandez, 2009. "Introduction: Reggaeton's Socio-Sonic Circuitry," in *Reggaetón*, edited by Raquel Z. Rivera, Wayne Marshall, and Deborah Pacini Hernández (Durham, NC: Duke University Press, 2009), 11.
46. Wayne Marshall, "From Música Negra to Reggaeton Latino: The Cultural Politics of Nation, Migration, and Commercialization," in *Reggaetón*, 34.
47. Marshall, Rivera, and Hernandez, "Introduction," 8.
48. Marshall, Rivera, and Hernandez, "Introduction," 11.
49. Félix Jiménez, "(W)rapped in Foil: Glory at Twelve Words a Minute," in *Reggaetón*, 248.
50. Jiménez, "(W)rapped in Foil," 248.
51. Petra R. Rivera-Rideau, *Remixing Reggaetón: The Cultural Politics of Race in Puerto Rico* (Durham, NC: Duke University Press, 2015), 105.
52. Jessel, "Chocolate." For more on Ivy Queen, see Dara E. Goldman, "Walk Like a Woman, Talk Like a Man: Ivy Queen's Troubling of Gender," *Latino Studies* 15 (2017): 439–57.
53. For more on feminist trends and female artists in reggaetón, see Mariana Viera, "Reggaeton's Leading Ladies Combat Exclusion with Unfiltered Sexual Expression," *Vibe*, October 26, 2018, https://www.vibe.com/features/viva/reggaeton-women-sexual-liberation-612019; Raquel Reichard, "Meet the New Generation of Women in Reggaetón and Latin Trap," *Popsugar*, July 9, 2020, https://www.popsugar.com/latina/meet-new-generation-women-in-reggaetón-latin-trap-47598774; and Núria Araüna, Iolanda Tortajada, and Mònica Figueras-Maz. "Feminist Reggaeton in Spain: Young Women Subverting Machismo Through 'Perreo,'" *YOUNG* 28, no. 1 (2020): 32–49.

54. Agustín Gómez Cascales, "Chocolate Remix: 'Que una mujer lesbiana cante reguetón ya es un hecho político en sí mismo,'" *Shangay*, July 13, 2019, https://shangay.com/2019/07/13/chocolate-remix-mujer-lesbiana-regueton-argentina-entrevista; Zani, Alejandra M. "La madre del reggaetón lésbica aterriza en Madrid: 'Todo supermacho guarda adentro una loba,' *El Mundo*, April 29, 2018, www.elmundo.es/cultura/musica/2018/04/29/5ae2f3b746163fee1d8b4609.html.
55. Lucía Blasco, "Chocolate Remix, la argentina que reta a los 'reggaetoneros machos' con su sexual 'reggaetón lésbico,'" *BBC mundo*, October 2, 2017, https://www.bbc.com/mundo/noticias-41414563.amp.
56. Chocolate Remix, "Ni una menos," *Sátira* (Chocolate Remix, 2017) Spotify, https://open.spotify.com/track/4XfX4gnuhGbWO5UQx4I61V?si=YZbi8ceTTC2KLfXhZ8FfTQ.
57. Polaco and Lima, personal interview.
58. Liliana Papalotl, Irakere Lima, and Pako Reyes, personal interview, July 2, 2019.
59. Unfortunately, due to the COVID-19 pandemic, the group could not continue to perform the piece or secure future funding. Additionally, the group decided to take a break to pursue individual interests. Lima now lives in Madrid, Spain, Papalotl resides in Veracruz, Mexico, and Reyes has remained in Mexico City, Mexico.
60. "Interdisciplina: Hernán Del Riego, Todavía," FONCA, available at https://web.archive.org/web/20170202003716/http://fonca.cultura.gob.mx/encuentro/hernan-del-riego. Born into a family of musicians, Del Riego concurrently studied music and composition along with acting in his college days. Hernan Del Riego, personal interview, April 4, 2020. This combination of skills led Del Riego to become an esteemed member of Mexico's theatre community. In a more recent turn toward the big and small screen, Del Riego is known for his roles in popular television series such as *Juana Inés* (2016), *Ingobernable* (2017), and *Historia de un crimen: Colosio* (2019), and feature films like *Cantinflas* (2011), just to name a few. Despite his busy filming schedule, the man of many talents has also found a way to keep active in the world of music. His work *La Bola: Cancionero para resistir* (2017) is more like a Youtube series in which Del Riego breathes new life into some of Mexico's most traditional songs and musical styles. He has also fostered collaboration across the theatre community, participating in projects where he often composes scores based on lyrics and ideas that actors, dramaturges, and performers send him.
61. Carlos Acuña, "Hernán del Riego: Resistir a punta de canciones y cantar para hallar una identidad," *máspormás*, November 21, 2017, https://www.maspormas.com/especiales/hernan-del-riego-esperanza-iris.
62. Liliana Papalotl, Irakere Lima, and Pako Reyes, *El Desierto de Las Leonas*, performance, Teatro Bar El Vicio, Coyoacán, Mexico City, Mexico, January–February 2019.
63. Andrés Henestrosa was credited as the lyrical composer, and there are versions by Lila Downs and Hernán Del Riego, for example.

64. Papalotl, Lima, and Reyes, personal interview.
65. Papalotl, Lima, and Reyes, personal interview.
66. Papalotl, Lima, and Reyes, personal interview.
67. Liliana Papalotl, Irakere Lima, and Pako Reyes. *El Desierto de Las Leonas* (Unpublished Script, 2017), 13.
68. Papalotl, Lima, and Reyes, *El Desierto de Las Leonas*, 2.
69. Papalotl, Lima, and Reyes, *El Desierto de Las Leonas*, 2.
70. Papalotl, Lima, and Reyes, *El Desierto de Las Leonas*, 3.
71. Madrid, *Music in Mexico*, 83.
72. Helena Simonett, *Banda: Mexican Musical Life across Borders* (Middletown, CT: Wesleyan University Press, 2001), 224.
73. Anna Férnandez Poncela, *Pero vas a estar muy triste y así te vas a quedar: Construcciones de género en la canción popular Mexicana* (Mexico City: Instituto Nacional de Antropología e Historia, 2002), 84.
74. See Simonett, *Banda*, 221; Madrid, *Music in Mexico*, 84.
75. Fernández Poncela, *Pero vas a estar muy triste*, 88, 93.
76. María Herrera-Sobek, *The Mexican Corrido: A Feminist Analysis* (Bloomington: Indiana University Press, 1990), 92.
77. Papalotl, Lima, and Reyes, *El Desierto de Las Leonas*, 3.
78. Yolanda Moreno Rivas, *Historia de la música popular mexicana* (Mexico City: Alianza Editorial Mexicana,
79. 1979), 186.
80. Moreno Rivas, *Historia de la música*, 186.
81. For more on Lucha Reyes's vocal qualities, see Baker, "Ranchera Rebel," and Marie Sarita Gaytán and Sergio de la Mora, "Queening/Queering *Mexicanidad*: Lucha Reyes and the *Canción Ranchera*," *Feminist Formations* 28, no. 3 (Winter 2006): 196–221.
82. Olga Nájera-Ramírez, "Unruly Passions: Poetics, Performance and Gender in the Ranchera Song," in *Chicana Feminisms: A Critical Reader*, edited by Gabriela F. Arredondo et. al. (Durham, NC: Duke University Press, 2003), 199.
83. For more on vocal performance and gender expectations in musicological terms, see Frith, *Performing Rites*; Shepherd, *Music as Social Text*, McRobbie, "Recent Rhythms, and McClary, *Feminine Endings*.
84. Segato, *La guerra*, 69.
85. Papalotl, Lima, and Reyes, *El Desierto de Las Leonas*, 3.
86. Papalotl, Lima, and Reyes, *El Desierto de Las Leonas*, 3.
87. This refrain has become a popular battle cry for Mexican and Latin American feminists at rallies that draw attention to startling rates of feminicide and gendered violence.
88. Papalotl, Lima, and Reyes, *El Desierto de Las Leonas*, 9.
89. Papalotl, Lima, and Reyes, *El Desierto de Las Leonas*, 11.
90. Papalotl, Lima, and Reyes, *El Desierto de Las Leonas*, 12.
91. Papalotl, Lima, and Reyes, *El Desierto de Las Leonas*, 12.

92. Taylor, *The Archive and The Repertoire*, 168.
93. Fabio Correa, "Quitarse la ropa y cantando al sexo: Gloria Trevi y la trampa rockera de la juventud mexicana," *Latin American Music Review* 16, no. 1 (Spring-Summer 1995): 79.
94. Olivia Cosentino, "Starring Mexico: Female Stardom, Age, and Mass Media Trajectories in the Twentieth Century," in *The Routledge Companion to Gender, Sex and Latin American Culture*, edited by Frederick Luis Aldama (New York: Routledge, 2018), 201.
95. Cosentino, "Starring Mexico," 201; Correa, "Quitarse la ropa," 82.
96. Gloria Trevi, "Todos me miran," *La Trayectoria* (Univision Records, 2006) Spotify, https://open.spotify.com/track/4pmRDyDRRiZ5Pq7hm4WTpb?si=2y6qONskQHWs33eCRsV8Ow.
97. Correa, "Quitarse la ropa," 91.
98. Papalotl, Lima, and Reyes, *El Desierto de Las Leonas*, 17.
99. Papalotl, Lima, and Reyes, *El Desierto de Las Leonas*, 18.
100. Papalotl, Lima, and Reyes, *El Desierto de Las Leonas*, 14.
101. Ileana Diéguez puts it beautifully when she refers to physical objects and tangible spaces as "una especie de depósito de memoria" (a kind of memory bank), much like the chest on stage in *El Desierto de Las Leonas*. Diéguez, *Cuerpos*, 225.
102. Papalotl, Lima, and Reyes, *El Desierto de Las Leonas*, 14.
103. Papalotl, Lima, and Reyes, *El Desierto de Las Leonas*, 7.
104. Papalotl, Lima, and Reyes, *El Desierto de Las Leonas*, 21.
105. Papalotl, Lima, and Reyes, *El Desierto de Las Leonas*, 22.
106. Acuña, "Hernán del Riego."
107. Del Riego wrote "Somos más" in 2017 after the murder of Javier Valdez. Del Riego was working on *La Bola*, publishing new videos approximately every two weeks, and when Valdez was murdered, he could not bring himself to concentrate on the project. Rather, he wrote and composed "Somos más" as a declaration of resistance. His plan was always to perform it with other artists, and in the 2017 performance of *La Bola* in el Teatro de la Ciudad, he invited a series of well-known journalists to perform the song with him. After that performance, Pako Reyes asked to use the song as part of this *teatro-cabaret* piece. Del Riego, personal interview.
108. Papalotl, Lima, and Reyes, *El Desierto de Las Leonas*, 22.
109. Papalotl, Lima, and Reyes, *El Desierto de Las Leonas*, 23.
110. Portions of this section were previously published as Christina Baker, "Soundtrack of an (After) Life: Transfemicide, Mourning, and Pop Music in La Prietty Guoman by César Enríquez," *Latin American Theatre Review* 53, no. 2 (Spring 2020): 5-31.
111. For example, Vasconcelos is foundational to the LGBTQ+ movement in Mexico, Rodríguez is currently a senator for the Morena party, and several members of Las Reinas Chulas have been vocal supporters of AMLO.

112. *Teatro de carpa* is a particularly Mexican performance genre that developed at the turn of the twentieth century. *Carpa* refers to the tents where performances were housed, and, as generally mobile constructions, they created opportunities for performers and shows to travel to the margins of Mexico City. This mobility allowed those who could not otherwise access "elite" cultural productions a way to engage with content. Moreover, by combining elements from Spanish performance styles, such as the *zarzuela*, and influences from body-centric circus acts, *carpa* was one of the earliest styles in which the popular classes saw themselves reflected. For more, see Merlín, *Vida y Milagros*, 12; Gutiérrez, *Performing Mexicanidad*, 82; Baker, "Queering Mexicanidad," 10–12; Alzate, "Dramaturgia,"; Monsiváis, "And All the People Came." Known for its biting critiques of social and political events and humorous renditions of neighborhood archetypes, *carpa* influenced Mexico's Golden Age of cinema and contemporary *teatro-cabaret* practices.

113. César Enríquez, *La Prietty Guoman*, performance, Centro Cultural Helénico Mexico City, Mexico, June 11, 2019, available online, Hemispheric Institute Digital Video Library, https://hemisphericinstitute.org/en/encuentro-2019-performances/item/2827-performances-012.html. When describing audio-visual aspects of the piece, I am referring to this performance.

114. Enríquez, personal interview, October 6, 2018.

115. On humor, power, and victimization, see Sotres, *Introducción al cabaret*, 65–66.

116. The US Department of State 2018 report on human trafficking suggests Mexico is a "tier 2" nation, detailing that as of 2017, "proceedings were initiated against 609 individuals in federal and state cases," and authorities identified "429 victims of sex trafficking." US Department of State, *Mexico 2018*, 301–302. Additionally, investigative journalists have recently called the small city of Tenanginco, just hours from Mexico City, the "sex-trafficking capital of the world." See Natasha Bertrand, "This Mexican Town is the Sex-Trafficking Capital of the World," *Business Insider*, February 10, 2015, https://www.businessinsider.com/this-mexican-town-is-the-sex-trafficking-capital-of-the-world-2015-2, and Hernández, *Tierra de padrotes: Tenancingo, Tlaxcala, un velo de impunidad* (Mexico City: Tusquets, 2015). For more on gendered violence in Mexico, see Instituto Nacional de Estatística y Geografía (INEGI), "Estadísticas," and for more on the violence and sexual labor of women on an international scale, see International Labour Organization. *Global Estimates of Modern Slavery: Forced Labour and Forced Marriage*. Geneva: International Labour Organization and Walk Free Foundation, 2017. https://www.ilo.org/global/publications/books/WCMS_575479/lang--en/index.htm.

117. Lydia Cacho, *Esclavas del poder: Un viaje al corazón de la trata sexual de mujeres y niñas en el mundo* (Mexico City: Debolsillo, 2016), 142–43.

118. Cacho, *Esclavas del poder*, 146.

119. In a Facebook post about the way La Prietty transformed over the years, Enríquez mentions the four transwomen murdered just a week before Orlando.

I have not been able to find news sources; however, the tragedy likely did not make national or even local news, and possibly the deaths were not reported as transfeminicides at all. See Enríquez, "Cosas que seguro no sabían entre la Prietty y yo que hoy deseo compartir," Facebook, October 25, 2017, https://www.facebook.com/cesarenriquezcabaret/posts/10211907458894795.
120. César Enríquez, "Cosas que seguro." While La Prietty's discourse tackles transfeminicide, she also makes jokes throughout about Veracruz as a corrupt state, focusing on topics ranging from ex-governor Javier Duarte to violence toward journalists. See "Mexican Photojournalist Found Dead Was Likely Tortured, Activists Say," *Guardian*, August 2, 2015, https://www.theguardian.com/world/2015/aug/02/mexican-photojournalist-killed-ruben-espinosa-tortured; James North, "Welcome to Veracruz, Mexico, One of the Most Dangerous Places in the World to be a Journalist," *Nation*, March 23, 2018, https://www.thenation.com/article/archive/welcome-to-veracruz-mexico-one-of-the-most-dangerous-places-in-the-world-to-be-a-journalist; and Adalberto Ruiz Mójica, "Javier Duarte: El ladrón más grande en la historia de México," Contralinea.com.mx, April 10, 2018, https://www.contralinea.com.mx/archivo-revista/2018/04/10/javier-duarte-el-ladron-mas-grande-en-la-historia-de-mexico.
121. Valencia, *Gore Capitalism*, 9.
122. Enríquez, personal interview.
123. Butler, *Precarious Life*, 32.
124. César Enríquez, *La Prietty Guoman* (Unpublished Script, 2017), 3. While Enríquez did provide me with an unpublished translation by Enrique Urueta, I use my own translations throughout to best represent the original text, rather than language adapted to fit US vernacular.
125. Enríquez, *La Prietty Guoman*, 3.
126. Valencia, *Gore Capitalism*, 11.
127. Enríquez, *La Prietty Guoman*, 3.
128. Enríquez, *La Prietty Guoman*, 23.
129. Muñoz, *Cruising Utopia*, 1.
130. Enríquez, personal interview.
131. Esther Newton, *Mother Camp: Female Impersonators in America* (Chicago: University of Chicago Press, 1971), 43.
132. Elizabeth Freeman, "Packing History, Count(er)ing Generations," *New Literary History* 31, no. 4 (2000): 728.
133. Nicole Eschen, "Embodying the Past: Citing and Circulating Celebrity," *Extensions: The Online Journal of Embodiment and Technology* 4 (2008): 32. The kind of drag Enríquez performs and the challenge it poses to Butler's issue with citationality is not unique to him but rather a general phenomenon in drag culture. Eschen's work, for example, makes a connection between representing a famous figure and reimagining them as a site for potential change, which is an important component of not just Enríquez's drag, but also the work of famous performers like Lypsinka and El Vez.

134. Muñoz, *Cruising Utopia*, 1.
135. As Muñoz would say, La Prietty becomes "the one who dreams for many." *Cruising Utopia*, 3.
136. Frith, *Performing Rites*, 97.
137. Enríquez, *La Prietty Guoman*, 4.
138. Enríquez, *La Prietty Guoman*, 5.
139. To literally walk in their shoes, Enríquez initially could not bear to wear the boots for more than ten minutes and had to build up his stamina and strength to do this show, full of dance choreography and nonstop action. Enríquez, personal interview.
140. Enríquez, *La Prietty Guoman*, 5.
141. Enríquez, *La Prietty Guoman*, 4.
142. Of course, the place of the indigenous citizen within contemporary Mexican society is routinely contested. Oaxaca, Guerrero, and Chiapas are routinely the poorest states in the nation, and unsurprisingly the states with the highest number of indigenous groups. Recent debates about Yalitza Aparicio's role and subsequent nominations for her performance in the Oscar-winning film *Roma* reflect deeply entrenched racism. Many online forums and public commentary have homed in on her indigenous features, as she is a member of the Mixtec indigenous group, even suggesting she should not have been allowed on screen nor given feature stories in international press outlets. For an overview of racist indigenous parodies on Mexican television over the last fifty years, see Dorany Pineda, "Long before *Roma*'s Yalitza Aparicio, Mexican TV and Cinema often Parodied Indigenous People," *Los Angeles Times*, March 9, 2019, www.latimes.com/entertainment/la-et-mn-yalitza-aparicio-brownface-history-20190309-story.html. For an overview of critical and racist comments toward Aparicio see "Sergio Goyri llama 'pinche india' a Yalitza Aparicio," *Nación 321*, February 19, 2019, https://www.nacion321.com/ciudadanos/video-sergio-goyri-llama-pinche-india-a-yalitza-aparicio; and David Agren, "'We Can Do It': Yalitza Aparicio's Vogue Cover Hailed by Indigenous Women," *Guardian*, December 21, 2018, www.theguardian.com/film/2018/dec/21/yalitza-aparicio-vogue-mexico-cover-roma-indigenous.
143. Muñoz, *Cruising Utopia*, 3.
144. Enríquez, *La Prietty Guoman*, 10.
145. González, *Afro-Mexico*, 1.
146. Arce, *Mexico's Nobodies*, 31.
147. Weltman-Cisneros and Méndez Tello, "Negros-Afromexicanos," 141.
148. For more on trends in scholarly research from the colonial period to present, see Vinson, "La historia." For more on routes of slavery and the presence of enslaved people in Mexico City during the colonial period, see Bennett, *Colonial Blackness*.
149. For more on archeological sites and slave maroonage practices, see Adela Amaral, "Social Geographies, the Practice of Marronage and the Archaeology of Absence in Colonial Mexico," *Archaeological Dialogues* 24, no. 2 (2017):

207–23. For more on Oaxaca and Guerrero as sites of research regarding Afro-Mexicans, see Vaughn, "México Negro," and Weltman-Cisneros, "Cimarronaje Cultural."
150. For more on Cuban representations and archetypes in Mexican cinema, see Pulido Llano, *Mulatas y negros*.
151. Enríquez, *La Prietty Guoman*, 6.
152. Enríquez, *La Prietty Guoman*, 6.
153. Enríquez, *La Prietty Guoman*, 7.
154. Enríquez, *La Prietty Guoman*, 8.
155. Valencia, *Gore Capitalism*, 20.
156. Enríquez, *La Prietty Guoman*, 8.
157. Enríquez, *La Prietty Guoman*, 24.
158. See Michael Krumholtz, "Mexico Trans Women Fight for Justice as Murder Unpunished," Associated Press, September 10, 2019, apnews.com/d5abd5bbee0a4e4b871d1f6d9aa08940.
159. Enríquez, *La Prietty Guoman*, 25.
160. Valencia, *Gore Capitalism*, 10.
161. Muñoz, *Cruising Utopia*, 1.
162. Enríquez, *La Prietty Guoman*, 12.
163. See Muñoz, *Cruising Utopia*, 106–10.
164. Enríquez, *La Prietty Guoman*, 12.
165. Enríquez, *La Prietty Guoman*, 20.
166. Enríquez, *La Prietty Guoman*, 23.
167. Valencia, *Gore Capitalism*, 28.
168. Enríquez, *La Prietty Guoman*, 23.
169. Justin Torres, "In Praise of Latin Night at the Queer Club," in *Queer Dance: Meanings & Makings*, edited by Clare Croft (Oxford: Oxford University Press, 2017), 182.
170. Enríquez, *La Prietty Guoman*, 26.
171. Valencia, *Gore Capitalism*, 295.
172. Enríquez, *La Prietty Guoman*, 27.

CONCLUSION

1. See Vivir Quintana, Mon Laferte, and El Palomar, "Canción sin miedo," performance, Zócalo, Mexico City, Mexico, March 7, 2019, available online, Youtube, uploaded by México en el Arte, March 8, 2020, https://www.youtube.com/watch?v=LdArO2jV9h0. For more on the performance, see Sara Cáceres Huerta, "La historia detrás del himno al feminismo: 'Canción sin miedo,' por Vivir Quintana," *Rolling Stone Mexico*, March 8, 2021, https://es.rollingstone.com/la-historia-detras-del-himno-al-feminismo-cancion-sin-miedo-por-vivir-quintana; "'Canción sin miedo': El himno de las protestas feministas," *infobae*, March 8, 2021, https://www.infobae.com/america/entretenimiento/2021/03/08/cancion-sin-miedo-el-himno-de-las-protestas-feministas-que-pone-voz-al-dolor-de-mujeres-en-mexico.

2. Elsa Núñez, "Checa el programa complete del festival Tiempo de Mujeres 2020 en CDMX," animal.mx, March 3, 2020, https://animal.mx/2020/03/festival-tiempo-de-mujeres-2020-cdmx-programa-mon-laferte.
3. Vivir Quintana, "Canción sin miedo," (Universal Music Mexico, 2020) Spotify, https://open.spotify.com/track/5w3AsUEG0aCuBhDp14umuy?si=ByjQyoM7SVSlu6yVsAAn9w.
4. Cámara de Diputados del H. Congreso de la Unión, "Ley sobre el Escudo, la Bandera y el Himno Nacionales," Diputados.Gob.mx, January 19, 2023, https://www.diputados.gob.mx/LeyesBiblio/pdf/LEBHN.pdf, 14; Quintana, "Canción sin miedo."
5. As stipulated by articles thirty-nine and forty of the law, all performances of the national anthem are required to obtain prior authorization. Additionally, the anthem is meant to be performed in part, or in full, "en actos solemnes de carácter oficial, cívico, cultural, escolar o deportivo, y para rendir honores tanto a la Bandera Nacional como al Presidente de la República." Cámara de Diputados del H. Congreso de la Unión, "Ley," 11.
6. According to article 39 of the law, "queda estructamente prohibido alterar la letra o música del Himno Nacional y ejecutarlo total o parcialmente con composiciones o arreglos" (altering the lyrics or the music of the National Anthem with different arrangements, in part or in its totality, it is strictly prohibited). Cámara de Diputados del H. Congreso de la Unión, "Ley," 11.
7. "¡Presente!" is common refrain uttered or shouted at mourning rituals and serves as an homage to those who have been lost. Here the term brings those who are missing or dead back into the present; it renders them unforgotten. I also use the word as a reference to Diana Taylor's most recent book, *¡Presente! The Politics of Presence* (Durham, NC: Duke University Press 2020), an astute analysis of resistance efforts through presence and practice in the Americas.
8. Quintana, "Canción sin miedo."
9. For more on LASTESIS, the Chilean artists behind "El violador eres tú," see Rocío Montes, "'El violador eres tú,' el himno que Chile export al mundo," *El País*, December 7, 2019, https://elpais.com/sociedad/2019/12/07/actualidad/1575742572_306059.html. For the song's lyrics, see "La letra de 'El violador eres tú,' el himno feminista que se extiende por el mundo," *El País*, December 8, 2019, https://elpais.com/sociedad/2019/12/07/actualidad/1575750878_441385.html. For a video example, see "El violador eres tú – LETRA COMPLETA del HIMNO FEMINISTA Un violador en tu camino," Youtube posted by La Nación Costa Rica, December 5, 2019, https://www.youtube.com/watch?v=tB1cWh27rmI&t=2s.
10. Lashua, Brett et al., eds, *Sounds and the City: Volume 2* (New York: Palgrave MacMillan, 2019), 2.
11. Here I am using the idea of sounds of resistance as proposed by Jorge Velasco in his book, *El Sonido de la resistencia: Patrimonio musical. El canto popular en los movimientos sociales del siglo XXI en México* (Mexico City: FONCA,

2017). In surveying protests throughout Mexico City, Velasco declares the use of sound to be vital to expressing "inconformidad ante la situación de dominio que viven y para proyectar sus anhelos y necesidad de transformación social" (inconformity when facing the situation of dominance under which people live, and to communicate their desires and need for social transformation). Velasco, *El Sonido de la resistencia*, 11.

12. Ana Martínez declares, "today, the Zócalo is Mexico's most disputed public space, as presidents and governments stage official celebrations, while revolutionary, political, and social groups create performances questioning the state." Martínez, *Performance in the Zócalo*, 4.

13. *Convivio* is the term coined by Jorge Dubatti to reference the act of coming together as fundamental to the theater experience. Dubatti, *Filosofía del Teatro I*, 43.

Bibliography

Acuña, Carlos. "Hernán del Riego: Resistir a punta de canciones y cantar para hallar una identidad." *máspormás*, November 21, 2017. https://www.maspormas.com/especiales/hernan-del-riego-esperanza-iris.
Adorno, Theodor. "Messages in a Bottle." Translated by Edmund Jephcott. *New Left Review* 1, no. 200 (1993): 5–15.
Agamben, Giorgio. *State of Exception*. Translated by Kevin Attell. Chicago: University of Chicago Press, 2005.
Agren, David. "'We Can Do It': Yalitza Aparicio's Vogue Cover Hailed by Indigenous Women." *Guardian*, December 21, 2018. https://www.theguardian.com/film/2018/dec/21/yalitza-aparicio-vogue-mexico-cover-roma-indigenous.
Ahmed, Sara. *Queer Phenomenology: Orientations, Objects, Others*. Durham, NC: Duke University Press, 2006.
Alacranes Musical. "500 Balazos." On *Nuestra historia de voces*, BMI Records, 2013.
Alcázar, Josefina. *Performance un arte del yo: Autobiografía, cuerpo e identidad*. Mexico City: Siglo xxi editores, 2014.
Aldape Muñoz, Juan Manuel. "Choreotopias: Performance, State Violence, and the Near Past." PhD diss., University of California, Berkeley, 2020.
Alfaro, Yanin. "¿Por qué se llama rosa mexicano?: 3 datos curiosos" Paredro.com, September 16, 2014. https://www.paredro.com/por-que-se-llama-rosa-mexicano-3-datos-curiosos.
Altamirano-Jiménez, Isabel. "Indigenous women refusing the violence of resource extraction in Oaxaca." *AlterNative* 17, no. 2 (2021): 215–223. https://doi.org/10.1177/11771801211015316.
Alzate, Gastón. "Jesusa Rodríguez: Cabaret, disidencia y legitimación en el teatro mexicanocontemporáneo." *Gestos* 28 (1999): 81–102.
———. *Teatro de Cabaret: Imaginarios Disidentes*. Irvine: Ediciones de GESTOS, 2002.
———. "Dramaturgia, ciudadanía y anti-neoliberalismo: El cabaret mexicano contemporáneo." *Latin American Theatre Review* 41, no. 2 (2008): 49–66.
———. "'Fiesten' una pastorela cabaretera." *Letras femeninas* 37, no. 1 (2011): 71–86.

———. "¿Es burgués el cabaret politico mexicano?: La historia del arte y los chairos o los chairos en la historia del arte (una lectura teórico-cabaretera del arte en las sociedades progresistas)." Keynote address at the Festival Internacional de Cabaret, Mexico City, Mexico, August 26, 2019.

Amaral, Adela. "Social Geographies, the Practice of Marronage and the Archaeology of Absence in Colonial Mexico." *Archaeological Dialogues* 24, no. 2 (2017): 207–223.

Amezcua Castillo, Jesús. *Pedro Infante: Medio siglo de idolatría*. Mexico City: Ediciones B, 2007.

Antich, Xavier. "Arte y activism: El siluetazo" *La Vanguardia*, July 8, 2009. https://www.lavanguardia.com/cultura/20090708/53739900388/arte-y-activismo-el-siluetazo.html.

Appiah, K. Anthony. "Identity, Authenticity, Survival: Multicultural Societies and Social Reproduction." In *Multiculturalism*, edited by Amy Gutmann, 149–63. Princeton, NJ: Princeton University Press, 1994.

Appignanesi, Lisa. *The Cabaret*. New Haven: Yale University Press, 2004.

Aragón, Alba. "Uninhabited Dresses: Frida Kahlo, from Icon of Mexico to Fashion Muse." *Fashion Theory* 18, no. 5 (2014): 517–49.

Araújo, Samuel, and Grupo Musicultura. "Sound Praxis: Music, Politics, and Violence in Brazil." In *Music and Conflict*, edited by John Morgan O'Connell and Salwa El-Shawan Castelo-Branco, 217–31. Urbana: University of Illinois Press, 2010.

Araüna, Núria, Iolanda Tortajada, and Mònica Figueras-Maz. "Feminist Reggaeton in Spain: Young Women Subverting Machismo Through 'Perreo.'" *YOUNG* 28, no. 1 (2020): 32–49.

Arce, B. Christine. *Mexico's Nobodies: The Cultural Legacy of the Soldadera and Afro-Mexican Women*. Albany: State University of New York Press, 2017.

Artaud, Antonin. *The Theatre and Its Double*. Translated by Mary Caroline Richards. New York: Grove Weidenfeld, 1958.

"Asesinan en México a 9 mujeres al día, denuncia la ONU." *Excelsior*, November 11, 2018. https://www.excelsior.com.mx/nacional/en-mexico-diario-asesinan-a-9-mujeres-denuncia-la-onu/1280023.

Asteroid, Black. "Black Asteroid on Lessons from Prince and Visually." Interview by Neal Gustafson, *Reverb News*, February 28, 2018. https://reverb.com/news/black-asteroid-on-lessons-from-prince-visually-inspired-songwriting-and-telling-stories-with-synths.

———. "Interview: Black Asteriod." *FNGRS CRSSD*, April 27, 2018. http://www.crssd.com/interview-black-asteroid (accessed October 26,2020; site inactive on July 12, 2023).

Attali, Jacques. *Noise: The Political Economy of Music*. Translated by Brian Massumi. Minneapolis: University of Minnesota Press, 1985.

Avendaño, Lukas. *Buscando a Bruno*. Performance. Barcelona, Spain, 2018. Available online, Vimeo, uploaded by Lukas Avendaño, June 29, 2018, https://vimeo.com/277627522.

———. *Buscando a Bruno*. Performance. Museo Universitario del Chopo, Mexico City, Mexico, February 6, 2019. Available online, Youtube, uploaded by Museo Universitario del Chopo, March 30, 2020, at https://www.youtube.com/watch?v=qnFf-QZZfRA.

———. *Buscando a Bruno*. Performance. Museo Universitario de Arte Moderno, Mexico City, Mexico, June 9, 2019. Available online, Hemispheric Institute Digital Video Library, https://hemisphericinstitute.org/en/encuentro-2019-performances/item/2821-performances-007.html.

———. "Queer: No. Queer-Po Muxe: Yes." Translated by Robin Myers. *Goethe-Institut Mexiko*, May 2019. https://www.goethe.de/ins/us/en/m/kul/wir/swl/qpe/21586998.html.

———. "Gratia Plena." Facebook post, December 4, 2020. https://www.facebook.com/lukas.avendano.39/posts/10221569862027880.

Avila, Jacqueline. "Juxtaposing Teatro de Revista and Cine: Music in the 1930s Comedia Ranchera." *Journal of Film Music* 5, nos. 1–2 (2012): 121–26.

———. *Cinesonidos: Film Music and National Identity during Mexico's Época de Oro*. New York: Oxford University Press, 2019.

Ayala Blanco, Jorge. *La aventura del cine mexicano en la época de oro y después*. Barcelona: Editorial Grijalbo, 1993.

Back, Les. *The Art of Listening*. New York: Berg, 2007.

Bailey, Tara, and Tony Walter. "Funerals against Death." *Mortality* 21, no. 2 (2016): 149–66. https://doi.org/10.1080/13576275.2015.1071344.

Baker, Christina. "Staging *Narcocorridos*: Las Reinas Chulas' Dissident Audio-Visual Performance." *Latin American Theatre Review* 47, no. 1 (2014): 93–113.

———. "Queering Mexicanidad in Cabaret and Film: Redefining Boundaries of Belonging." PhD diss., University of Wisconsin-Madison, 2015.

———. "Ranchera Rebel: Transgressive Expression and the Voice of Lucha Reyes." In "Historical Rebels in the Mexican Imaginary," special issue of *Hispanic Journal* 38, no. 2 (2017): 107–24.

———. "Sounds of a Modern Nation: From Narcocorridos to Hugo Salcedo's *Música de balas*." *Symposium: A Quarterly Journal in Modern Literatures* 71, no. 4 (Fall 2017): 179–94.

———. "Soundtrack of an (After) Life: Transfemicide, Mourning, and Pop Music in *La Prietty Guoman* by César Enríquez." *Latin American Theatre Review* 53, no. 2 (Spring 2020): 5–31.

Barber, Sarah B., and Mireya Olvera Sánchez. "A Divine Wind: The Arts of Death and Music in Terminal Formative Oaxaca." *Ancient Mesoamerica* 23, no. 1 (2012): 9–24.

Baudrillard, Jean. *Why Hasn't Everything Already Disappeared?* Translated by Chris Turner. New York: Seagull Books, 2009.

Beardsell, Peter. "Crossing the Border in Three Plays by Hugo Salcedo." *Latin American Theatre Review* 29, no. 2 (1996): 71–84.

Bennett, Herman. *Colonial Blackness: A History of Afro-Mexico*. Bloomington: Indiana University Press, 2009.

Bennet, Jane. *Vibrant Matter*. Durham, NC: Duke University Press, 2009.

Bennholdt-Thomsen, Veronika, editor. *Juchitán, la ciudad de las mujeres*. Oaxaca: Instituto Oaxaqueño de Las Culturas, 1997.

Bertrand, Natasha. "This Mexican Town is the Sex-Trafficking Capital of the World." *Business Insider*, February 10, 2015. https://www.businessinsider.com/this-mexican-town-is-the-sex-trafficking-capital-of-the-world-2015-2.

Blanco-Cano, Rosana. *Cuerpos disidentes del México imaginado: Cultura, género, etnia y nación más allá del Proyecto posrevolucionario*. Madrid: Iberoamericana Editorial Vervuert, 2014.

Blanco Ramírez, Gerardo, and Amy Scott Metcalfe. "Hashtivism as Public Discourse: Exploring Online Student Activism in Response to State Violence and Forced Disappearances in Mexico." *Research in Education* 97, no. 1 (2017): 56–75. https://doi.org/10.1177/0034523717714067.

Blasco, Lucía. "Chocolate Remix, la argentina que reta a los 'reggaetoneros machos' con su sexual 'reggaetón lésbico'." *BBC mundo*, October 2, 2017. https://www.bbc.com/mundo/noticias-41414563.amp.

Bonansinga, Kate. *Curating at the Edge: Artists Respond to the U.S./Mexico Border*. Austin: University of Texas Press, 2010.

Brasseur, Charles. "The Didjazá." Translated by Lorna Scott Fox. *Artes de México* 49 (2000): 83.

Brecht, Bertolt. *Brecht on Theatre: The Development of an Aesthetic*. Edited and translated by John Willett. New York: Hill and Wang, 1954.

Brennan, Teresa. *The Transmission of Affect*. Ithaca, NY: Cornell University Press, 2004.

Brooks, Peter. *The Melodramatic Imagination: Balzac, Henry James, Melodrama and the Mode of Excess*. New Haven, CT: Yale University Press, 1976.

———. "The Melodramatic Imagination." In *Imitations of Life: A Reader on Film and Television Melodrama*, edited by Marcia Landy, 50–67. Detroit, MI: Wayne State University Press, 1991.

Brown, Ross. "The Theatre Soundscape and the End of Noise." *Performance Research* 10, no. 4 (2005): 105–19.

———. *Sound: A Reader in Theatre Practice*. New York: Palgrave Macmillan, 2010.

Bruin-Mollenhorst, Janieke. "The Musical Eulogy and Other Functions of Funeral Music." *OMEGA* 82, no. 1 (2018): 24–41. https://doi.org/10.1177/0030222818799939.

"Bruno Avendaño vuelve a casa, pero la búsqueda de justicia continúa." Youtube, uploaded by Rompeviento TV, December 4, 2020. https://www.youtube.com/watch?v=2TFqXJefusU.

Bull, Michael. "The audio-visual iPod." In *The Sound Studies Reader*, edited by Jonathan Sterne, 197–208. New York: Routledge, 2012.

Burgos Dávila, César Jesús. "Narcocorridos: Antecedentes de la tradición corridística y del narcotráfico en México." *Studies in Latin American Popular Culture* 31 (2013): 157–183.

Butler, Judith. *Antigone's Claim: Kinship between Life and Death*. New York: Columbia University Press, 2000.
———. *Precarious Life: The Powers of Mourning and Violence*. New York: Verso, 2004.
———. *Frames of War: When Is Life Grievable?* New York: Verso. 2009.
Cáceres Huerta, Sara. "'Canción sin miedo,' por Vivir Quintana." *Rolling Stone Mexico*, March 8, 2021. https://es.rollingstone.com/la-historia-detras-del-himno-al-feminismo-cancion-sin-miedo-por-vivir-quintana.
Cacho, Lydia. *Esclavas del poder: Un viaje al corazón de la trata sexual de mujeres y niñas en el mundo*. Mexico City: Debolsillo, 2016.
Calderón, Felipe. "Interview Transcript: Felipe Calderón." Interview by Adam Thomson. *Financial Times*, January 23, 2007. https://www.ft.com/content/317c1bbc-ab01-11db-b5db-0000779e2340.
———. "El presidente de México en los Desayunos de TVE." *Desayunos de TVE*, May 18, 2010. https://www.rtve.es/alacarta/videos/los-desayunos-de-tve/desayunos-presidente-mexico-desayunos-tve/774692.
Calderón, Gabriela, Gustavo Robles, Alberto Díaz-Cayeros, and Beatriz Magaloni. "The Beheading of Criminal Organizations and the Dynamics of Violence in Mexico." *Journal of Conflict Resolution* 59, no. 8 (2015): 1455–85.
Calderón, Hector. "Conversación con Aldo Acuña de Maldita Vecindad." *Aztlán* 31, no. 1 (2006): 119–37.
Cámara de Diputados del H. Congreso de la Unión. "Ley General en Materia de Desaparición Forzada de Personas, Desaparición Cometida por Particulares y del Sistema Nacional de Búsqueda de Personas." Diputados.Gob.mx, November 17, 2017. http://www.diputados.gob.mx/LeyesBiblio/pdf/LGMDFP_190221.pdf.
———. "Ley sobre el Escudo, la Bandera y el Himno Nacionales." Diputados.Gob.mx, January 19, 2023. https://www.diputados.gob.mx/LeyesBiblio/pdf/LEBHN.pdf.
"'Canción sin miedo': El himno de las protestas feministas." *infobae*, March 8, 2021. https://www.infobae.com/america/entretenimiento/2021/03/08/cancion-sin-miedo-el-himno-de-las-protestas-feministas-que-pone-voz-al-dolor-de-mujeres-en-mexico.
Carroll, Rory. "Border Patrol Agent Found Not Guilty of Murder in Mexican Teen's 2012 Death." *Guardian*, April 24, 2018. https://www.theguardian.com/us-news/2018/apr/23/border-patrol-shooting-jose-antonio-elena-rodriguez-lonnie-swartz.
Castelo-Branco, Salwa El-Shawan. "Epilogue: Ethnomusicologists as Advocates." In *Music and Conflict*, edited by John Morgan O'Connell and Salwa El-Shawan Castelo-Branco, 243–63. Urbana: University of Illinois Press, 2010.
Castle, Jason, and William L. Phillips. "Grief Rituals: Aspects That Facilitate Adjustment to Bereavement." *Journal of Loss and Trauma* 8, no. 1 (2003): 41–71.
Castree, Nick, et. al. *The Point Is to Change It: Geographies of Hope and Survival in an Age of Crisis*. Oxford: Wiley-Blackwell, 2013.

Caswell, Glenys. "Beyond Words: Some Uses of Music in the Funeral Setting." *OMEGA* 64, no. 4 (2011–2012): 319–34. https://doi.org/10.2190/OM.64.4.c.

Cavarero, Adriana. "On the Body of Antigone." In *Feminist Readings of Antigone*, edited by Fanny Söderbäck, 45–63. Albany: State University of New York Press, 2010.

"CDMX reconoció el primer caso de feminicidio a una mujer trans." *infobae*, December 8, 2022. https://www.infobae.com/america/mexico/2022/12/08/cdmx-reconocio-el-primer-caso-de-feminicidio-a-una-mujer-trans.

Celaya, Jorge. "Teatro de frontera en México." In *Teatro de frontera II*, edited by Jorge Celaya, 1–26. Durango: Siglo XXI, 2004.

Cervantes-Gómez, Xiomara Verenice. "Lechedevirgen Trimegisto's *Infierno Varieté*, Queer Mexicanness, and the Aesthetics of Risk. *ASAP Journal* 6, no. 1 (2021): 95–122.

Chassen-López, Francie. "The Traje de Tehuana as National Icon: Gender, Ethnicity, and Fashion in Mexico." *The Americas* 71, no. 2 (2014): 281–314.

Chavez, Paul. "Rosa Mexicano." *Medium*, November 18, 2018. https://medium.com/these-unanswered-questions/rosa-mexicano-151fb01ccaoa.

Chávez, Xóchitl C. "La creación de Oaxacalifornia mediante tradiciones culturales entre jóvenes oaxaqueños de Los Ángeles, California." *Desacatos* 62 (Jan.–Apr. 2020): 172–81.

———. "Oaxacan Indigenous Women Musicians' Collective Songwriting Process on the Title Track of *Mujeres*." *Americas: A Hemispheric Music Journal* 29 (2020): 121–33. https://doi.org/10.1353/ame.2020.0007.

Chion, Michel. *Audio-Vision: Sound on Screen*. New York: Columbia University Press, 1994.

———. *The Voice in Cinema*. Translated by Claudia Gorbman. New York: Columbia University Press, 1999.

Chocolate Remix. "Ni una menos." *Sátira*, Chocolate Remix, 2017. Spotify, https://open.spotify.com/track/4XfX4gnuhGbWO5UQx4I61V?si=YZbi8ceTTC2KLfXhZ8FfTQ.

Cignitti, Annalisa P. "Michele Lamy." *Rocaille*, May 23, 2012. https://www.rocaille.it/michele-lamy.

Cohen, Theodore. *Finding Afro-Mexico: Race and Nation after the Revolution*. Cambridge: Cambridge University Press, 2020.

Coleman, Jeffrey. *The Necropolitical Theatre: Race and Immigration on the Contemporary Spanish Stage*. Evanston, IL: Northwestern University Press, 2020.

Comisión Mexicana de Defensa y Promoción de los Derechos Humanos. *Violaciones graves a derechos humanos en la guerra contra las drogas en México*. 2015. https://www.cmdpdh.org/publicaciones-pdf/cmdpdh-violaciones-graves-a-ddhh-en-la-guerra-contra-las-drogas-en-mexico.pdf.

———. "2,555 días sin Luis Ángel y contando." Youtube, uploaded by CMDPDH, November 22, 2016. https://www.youtube.com/watch?v=m4CVXrw2srk.

———. "A 10 años de la desaparición forzada de Luis Ángel León Rodríguez." *CMDPDH Blog*, November 14, 2019. http://cmdpdh.org/2019/11/a-10-anos-de-la-desaparicion-forzada-de-luis-angel-leon-rodriguez-policia-federal-aun-se-desconoce-su-paradero.

Comisión Nacional de los Derechos Humanos. "Informe Especial de la Comisión Nacional de Los Derechos Humanos sobre desaparición de personas y fosas clandestinas en México." April 6, 2017. http://informe.cndh.org.mx/menu.aspx?id=30100.

———. "Análisis Situacional de los Derechos Humanos de las Personas Desaparecidas y No Localizadas." 2018. http://informe.cndh.org.mx/menu.aspx?id=40062#lda40330.

———. "Pronunciamiento de la CNDH sobre la investigación de violaciones graves a los derechos humanos con motivo de los ocurridos los días 26 y 27 de septiembre de 2014, en Iguala, Guerrero." March 25, 2021. https://www.cndh.org.mx/documento/pronunciamiento-de-la-cndh-sobre-la-investigacion-de-violaciones-graves-los-derechos.

"Con esta publicación, Alejandro Fernández habría confirmado su homosexualidad." *Yosoitú*, October 29, 2019. https://yosoitu.com/entretenimiento/2019/10/29/con-esta-publicacion-alejandro-fernandez-habria-confirmado-su-homosexualidad-60823.html.

"Conferencia de prensa matutina, desde Palacio Nacional." Youtube, uploaded by Andrés Manuel López Obrador, streamed live on January 29, 2021. https://www.youtube.com/watch?v=XHyG0Sm3EMk.

Connerton, Paul. *How Societies Remember*. Cambridge: Cambridge University Press, 1989.

Conway, Christopher. "Charros: A Critical Introduction." In *Modern Mexican Culture: Critical Foundations*, edited by Stuart A. Day, 66–83. Tucson: University of Arizona Press, 2017.

Cook, Guy and Tony Walter. "Rewritten Rites: Language and Social Relations in Traditional and Contemporary Funerals." *Discourse and Society* 16, no. 3 (2005): 365–91.

Correa, Fabio. "Quitarse la ropa y cantando al sexo: Gloria Trevi y la trampa rockera de la juventud mexicana." *Latin American Music Review* 16, no. 1 (Spring-Summer 1995): 78–92.

Cosentino, Olivia. "Starring Mexico: Female Stardom, Age, and Mass Media Trajectories in the 20th Century." In *The Routledge Companion to Gender, Sex and Latin American Culture*, edited by Frederick Luis Aldama, 196–206. New York: Routledge, 2018.

Covarrubias, Miguel. "A Southward View." *Artes de México* 49 (2000): 86–88.

Cruz, Natalia. "'Luto por derecho,' de Atilano Morales Jiménez." *Guidxizá, una mirada a nuestros pueblos*, cultural supplement of *Comité Melendre*, 1, no. 1 (July 29, 2012). Available online at http://comitemelendre.blogspot.com/2012/12/luto-por-derecho-de-atilano-morales.html.

Cusik, Suzanne. "'You Are in a Place That Is Out of This World . . .': Music in the Detention Camps of the 'Global War on Terror.'" *Journal of the Society for American Music* 2, no. 1 (2008): 1–26. https://doi.org/10.1017/S1752196308080012.

Data Cívica. *Análisis y evaluación de registros oficiales de personas desaparecidas: Hacia el nuevo registro nacional.* March 2019. https://registros-desaparecidos.datacivica.org/informe/FINAL_Anaìlisis_y_evaluacioìn_de.pdf.

Daughtry, J. Martin. *Listening to War: Sound, Music, Trauma, and Survival in Wartime Iraq.* Oxford: Oxford University Press, 2015.

Davies, Douglas. *Death, Ritual, and Belief: The Rhetoric of Funerary Rites.* 3rd ed. New York: Bloomsbury Academic, 2017.

De Choudhury, Munmun, et al. "'Narco' Emotions: Affect and Desensitization in Social Media during the Mexican Drug War." *Proceedings of the 32nd Annual ACM Conference on Human Factors in Computing Systems* (Toronto, Canada: CHI 2014), 3563–72.

de la Mora, Sergio. *Cinemachismo: Masculinities and Sexuality in Mexican Film.* Austin: University of Texas Press, 2006.

Delgadillo, Theresa. "Singing 'Angelitos Negros': African Diaspora Meets Mestizaje in the Americas." *Latin American Quarterly* 58, no. 2 (2006): 407–30.

del Rosario Moreno, Iani. *Theatre of the Borderlands: Conflict, Violence, and Healing.* Lanham, MD: Lexington Books, 2015.

Denham, Diana, Patrick Lincoln, and Chris Thomas. Introduction to *Teaching Rebellion: Stories from the Grassroots Mobilization in Oaxaca,* edited by Diana Denham and the C.A.S.A. collective, 25–49. Oakland, CA: PM Press, 2008.

DeNora, Tia. *After Adorno: Rethinking Music Sociology.* Cambridge: Cambridge University Press, 2009.

———. *Music in Everyday Life.* Cambridge: Cambridge University Press, 2009.

Denver, Susan. *Celluloid Nationalism and Other Melodramas: From Post-Revolutionary Mexico to* fin de siglo *Mexamérica.* Albany: State University of New York Press, 2003.

"Después de 30 meses, encuentran sin vida a Bruno Avendaño, marino desaparecido en Oaxaca." *Aristegui Noticias* December 3, 2020. https://aristeguinoticias.com/0312/mexico/despues-de-30-meses-encuentran-sin-vida-a-bruno-avendano-marino-desaparecido-en-oaxaca.

"Detienen a Elba Esther Gordillo, PRG la acusa de malversación de fondos" *Excélsior,* February 26, 2013. https://www.excelsior.com.mx/nacional/2013/02/26/886284.

Diawara, Manthia. "Black Spectatorship: Problems of Identification and Resistance." *Screen* 29, no. 4 (1988): 66–76.

———. "Black British Cinema: Spectatorship and Identity Formation in *Territories.*" *Public Culture* 3, no.1 (Fall 1990): 33–48.

Díaz, Gloria Leticia. "De más de 37 mil desapariciones, sólo 170 ocurrieron a manos de Fuerzas Armadas, señala Peña en informe." *Proceso,* September 1, 2018. https://www.proceso.com.mx/nacional/2018/9/1/de-mas-de-37-mil-desapariciones-solo-170-ocurrieron-manos-de-fuerzas-armadas-senala-pena-en-informe-211431.html.

Diéguez, Ileana. *Cuerpos sin duelo: Iconografías y teatralidades del dolor*. Córdoba, Argentina: Ediciones Documenta/Escénicas, 2013.

———. "Necroteatro. Iconografías del cuerpo roto y sus registros punitivos." *Investigación Teatral* 3, no. 5 (Winter 2013–2014): 9–28.

Dolar, Mladen. *A Voice and Nothing More*. Cambridge: Massachusetts Institute of Technology Press, 2006.

"Dolor profundo – Banda Princesa Donají [Autor. Atilano Morales]." *Comité Melendre*, n.d. http://comitemelendre.blogspot.com/search?q=dolor+profundo.

Dubatti, Jorge. *Filosofía del Teatro I: Convivio, Experiencia, Subjetividad*. Buenos Aires: Atuel, 2007.

Dunlap, Alexander. "Wind Energy: Toward a 'Sustainable Violence' in Oaxaca." *NACLA Report on the Americas* 49, no. 4 (2017): 483–488. https://doi.org/10.10 80/10714839.2017.1409378.

Edberg, Mark Cameron. *El Narcotraficante: Narcocorridos and the Construction of a Cultural Persona on the U.S.-Mexico Border*. Austin: University of Texas Press, 2004.

Eguiarte, Naoli, director. *Música de balas*. Performance. Centro Dramático de Michoacán, Pátzcuaro, Mexico, December 8–14, 2019. Available online on Youtube, uploaded by Cedram Difusion, March 30, 2020, https://www.youtube.com/watch?v=ZbUHvWuLoJo&t=1473s.

Eisenstein, Sergei. "Life." Translated by Richard Moszka. *Artes de México* 49 (2000): 83.

Elsaesser, Thomas. "Tales of Sound and Fury: Observations on the Family Melodrama." In *Imitations of Life: A Reader on Film and Television Melodrama*, edited by Marcia Landy, 68–92. Detroit, MI: Wayne State Press, 1991.

Emerson, R. Guy. *Necropolitics: Living Death in Mexico*. New York: Palgrave MacMillan, 2019.

"Encarcelan a poderosa líder de gremio docente." *Peru21*, February 28, 2013. https://peru21.pe/opinion/encarcelan-poderosa-lider-gremio-docente-95084-noticia.

"Encuentran sin vida a Bruno Avendaño, desaparecido en 2018 en Tehuantepec." *EDUCA*, December 4, 2020. https://www.educaoaxaca.org/encuentran-sin-vida-a-bruno-avendano-desaparecido-en-2018-en-tehuantepec.

Enríquez, César. "Cosas que seguro no sabían entre la Prietty y yo que hoy deseo compartir." Facebook, October 25, 2017. https://www.facebook.com/cesarenriquezcabaret/posts/10211907458894795.

———. *La Prietty Guoman*. Unpublished Script, 2017.

———. *La Prietty Guoman*. Performance. Centro Cultural Helénico, Mexico City, Mexico, June 11, 2019. Available online, Hemispheric Institute Digital Video Library, https://hemisphericinstitute.org/en/encuentro-2019-performances/item/2827-performances-012.html.

"En 25 años van 1,779 feminicidios en Ciudad Juárez." *El Heraldo de México*, February 15, 2018. https://heraldodemexico.com.mx/nacional/2018/2/15/en-25-anos-van-1779-feminicidios-en-ciudad-juarez-32735.html.

Eschen, Nicole. "Embodying the Past: Citing and Circulating Celebrity." *Extensions: The Online Journal of Embodiment and Technology* 4 (2008): 32–43.

"Ex Teresa Arte Actual." n.d. *INBAL*. https://inba.gob.mx/recinto/55/ex-teresa-arte-actual.

Fast, Susan, and Kip Pegley. Introduction to *Music, Politics, and Violence*, edited by Susan Fast and Kip Pegley, 1–34. Middletown, CT: Wesleyan University Press, 2012.

Favela, Alejandra. "Lasting Lessons from Oaxaca: Teachers as Luchadores Sociales: An Inside Account of the Historic 2006 Oaxacan Teachers' Movement and Why It Is Still Relevant Today." *Radical Teacher* 1, no. 88 (2010): 63–72.

Fein, Seth. "Myths of Cultural Imperialism and Nationalism in Golden Age Mexican Cinema." In *Fragments of a Golden Age: The Politics of Culture in Mexico Since 1940*, edited by Gilbert Joseph, Anne Rubenstein, and Eric Zolov, 159–98. Durham, NC: Duke University Press, 2001.

"Feminicidios en México: Asesinaron a más de 56,000 mujeres desde 1990." *infobae*, December 18, 2020. https://www.infobae.com/america/mexico/2020/12/18/feminicidios-en-mexico-asesinaron-a-mas-de-56000-mujeres-desde-1990.

Fernández, Vicente. "Para Siempre." *Para siempre*, Sony Music Entertainment Mexico, 2007. Spotify, http://open.spotify.com/track/ouyVgmoXDbwS1ubv8AurVZ?si=PM5DJjK6TliLBIzmmWUBJg.

Férnandez Poncela, Anna M. *Pero vas a estar muy triste y así te vas a quedar: Construcciones de género en la canción popular mexicana*. Mexico City: Instituto Nacional de Antropología e Historia, 2002.

Figueroa Hernández, Rafael. *Salsa mexicana: Transculturación e identidad*. Xalapa: Con Clave, 1996.

Foster, Daniel H. "From Minstrel Shows to Radio Shows: Racism and Representation in Blackface and Blackvoice." *Journal of American Drama and Theatre* 17, no. 2 (Spring 2005): 7–16.

Freeman, Elizabeth. "Packing History, Count(er)ing Generations." *New Literary History* 31, no. 4 (2000): 727–44.

———. "Time Binds, or Erotohistoriography." *Social Text* 23, nos. 3–4 (Fall–Winter 2005): 57–68.

———. *Time Binds: Queer Temporalities, Queer Histories*. Durham, NC: Duke University Press, 2010.

Fregoso, Rosa-Linda, and Cynthia Bejarano, eds. *Terrorizing Women: Feminicide in the Américas*. Durham, NC: Duke University Press, 2010.

Friedberg, Anne. "A Denial of Difference: Theories of Cinematic Identification." In *Psychoanalysis and Cinema*, edited by E. Ann Kaplan, 36–45. New York: Routledge, 1990.

Frith, Simon. *Performing Rites: On the Values of Popular Music*. Cambridge, MA: Harvard University Press, 1996.

Fuentes, Marcela A. "#Niunamenos: Hashtag Performativity, Memory, and Direct Action against Gender Violence in Argentina." In *Women Mobilizing Memory*, edited by Aye GI Altnay et al., 172–91. New York: Colombia University Press, 2019.

———. *Performance Constellations: Networks of Protest and Activism in Latin America*. Ann Arbor: University of Michigan Press, 2019.

"fuga de 'El Chapo' refleja un 'abismo de incredulidad': NYT, La." *Aristegui noticias*, August 7, 2015. aristeguinoticias.com/0708/mexico/la-fuga-de-el-chapo-refleja-un-abismo-de-incredulidad-nyt.

Galindo, Gabriela. "*Obstruir, Destruir, Ocultar*: Retrospectiva de Enrique Ježik." *Répilica21*, December 20, 2011. https://www.replica21.com/archivo/articulos/g_h/617_galindo_jezik.html#.

García, Ariadna. "Asesinan a 9 mujeres al día en México, asegura Segob." *El universal*, March 17, 2019. https://www.eluniversal.com.mx/nacion/politica/asesinan-9-mujeres-al-dia-en-mexico-asegura-segob.

García Canclini, Néstor. "Mexico: Cultural Globalization in a Disintegrating City." *American Ethnologist* 22, no. 4 (1995): 743–55.

———. *Consumers and Citizens: Globalization and Multicultural Conflicts*. Translated by George Yúdice. Minneapolis: University of Minnesota Press, 2001.

García Hernández, Juan Luis. "Los 150 mil muertos prueban que la guerra contra las drogas fracasó, a México le queda legalizar: ONGs." *Sin Embargo*, April 19, 2016. https://www.sinembargo.mx/19-04-2016/1650116.

Garcia-Orozco, Antonia. "Lucha Reyes la Reina del estilo Bravío." *Estudios sobre las Culturas Contemporáneas* 19 (2013): 127–55.

———. "Cucurrucucu palomas: The *estilo bravío* of Lucha Reyes and the Creation of Feminist Consciousness via the *canción ranchera*." PhD diss., Claremont Graduate University, 2005.

García Riera, Emilio. *Breve historia del cine mexicano: Primer siglo 1897–1997*. Zapopan, Jalisco: Ediciones Mapa, 1998.

Garrido, Sandra, and Waldo F. Garrido. "The Psychological Function of Music in Mourning Rituals" In *Music and Mourning*, edited by Jane W. Davidson and Sandra Garrido, 55–68. New York: Routledge, 2016.

Garza-Usabiaga, Daniel. "Enrique Ježik. Formas de la violencia." *Revista Exist Express*, November 2009. http://enriquejezik.com/texto-de-daniel-garza-usabiaga-en-exit.

Gasiorowski, Dominika. "The *muxes* of Juchitán: Representations of Non-binary Gender Identities in Contemporary Photography from Mexico." *Bulletin of Hispanic Studies* 85, no. 8 (2018): 895–914. https://doi.org/10.3828/bhs.2018.52.

Gaspar de Alba, Alicia, and Georgina Guzmán, eds. *Making a Killing: Femicide, Free Trade, and* La Frontera. Austin: University of Texas Press, 2010.

Gaytán, Marie Sarita.*¡Tequila!: Distilling the Spirit of Mexico*. Palo Alto, CA: Stanford University Press, 2014.

Gaytán, Marie Sarita, and Sergio de la Mora. "Queening/Queering *Mexicanidad*: Lucha Reyes and the *Canción Ranchera*" *Feminist Formations* 28, no. 3 (Winter 2006): 196–221.

Gerez Levy, Paola. "Un homenaje al rosa mexicano (y a todas las veces en las que los muros se confundieron con las buganvilias)." *Travesías*, June 15, 2020. https://travesiasdigital.com/cultura/de-donde-viene-el-rosa-mexicano.

Gilbert, Joseph, Anne Rubenstein, and Eric Zolov, eds. *Fragments of a Golden Age: The Politics of Culture in Mexico Since 1940.* Durham, NC: Duke University Press, 2001.

Gillespie, Jeanne. "Gender, Ethnicity, and Piety: The Case of the China Poblana." In *Imagination beyond Nation*, edited by Eva P. Bueno and Terry Caesar, 19–40. Pittsburgh, PA: University of Pittsburgh Press, 1998.

Goldman, Dara E. "Walk Like a Woman, Talk Like a Man: Ivy Queen's Troubling of Gender." *Latino Studies* 15 (2017): 439–57.

Gómez, Amaranta. "Trascendiendo." *Desacatos*, nos. 15–16 (Fall 2004): 199–208.

Gómez Cascales, Agustín. "Chocolate Remix: 'Que una mujer lesbiana cante reguetón ya es un hecho político en sí mismo.'" *Shangay*, July 13, 2019. https://shangay.com/2019/07/13/chocolate-remix-mujer-lesbiana-regueton-argentina-entrevista.

González, Anita. *Afro-Mexico: Dancing between Myth and Reality.* Austin: University of Texas Press, 2010.

González, Juan Pablo. "Hegemony and Counter-Hegemony of Music in Latin-America: The Chilean Pop." *Popular Music and Society* 15, no. 2.2 (1991): 63–78.

———. "Nueva Canción Chilena en dictadura: Divergencia, memoria, escuela (1973–1983)." *Estudios interdisciplinarios de América Latina y el Caribe* 27, no. 1 (2016): 63–82.

Goodman, Steve. *Sonic Warfare: Sound, Affect, and the Ecology of Fear.* Cambridge, MA: MIT Press, 2009.

Gravante, Tommaso. "Forced Disappearance as a Collective Cultural Trauma in the Ayoztinapa Movement." *Latin American Perspectives* 47, no. 6 (November 2020): 87–102. https://doi.org/10.1177/0094582X20951773.

Grayson, George W. *Mexico: Narco-Violence and a Failed State?* New Brunswick, NJ: L Transaction, 2010.

———. *The Impact of President Felipe Calderón's War on Drugs on the Armed Forces: The Prospects for Mexico's "Militarization" and Bilateral Relations.* Carlisle Barracks, PA: Strategic Studies Institute, 2013.

"Grito de Independencia de AMLO como 'presidente legítimo' en 2007, El." *Zona Guadalajara*, September 18, 2007. https://zonaguadalajara.com/grito-independencia-amlo-2007.

Grupo Interdisciplinario de Expertos Independientes. *Informe Ayotzinapa II: Avances y nuevas conclusiones sobre la investigación, búsqueda y atención a las víctimas.* 2016. prensagieiayotzi.wixsite.com/giei-ayotzinapa/informe-.

Gutiérrez, Laura G. *Performing Mexicanidad: Vendidas y Cabareteras on the Transnational Stage.* Austin: University of Texas Press, 2010.

———. "*El derecho de re-hacer*: Signifyin(g) Blackness in Contemporary Mexican Political Cabaret." *Arizona Journal of Hispanic Cultural Studies* 16 (2012): 163–76.

Guzmán Roldán, Ignacio. "The Political Song in Chilean nueva canción: Víctor Jara and Quilapayún—A Case Study (1969-1973)." Thesis, Universidad Alberto Hurado, 2011.

Habana de Los Santos, Misael. "Decapitan a un comandante y un oficial en Acapulco," *La Jornada*, April 21, 2006. https://www.jornada.com.mx/2006/04/21/index.php?section=politica&article=021n1pol.

Halberstam, Jack. *Female Masculinity*. Durham, NC: Duke University Press, 1998.

"Hallan a seis personas vivas con las manos cortadas." ElQuintanaRoo.mx, October 18, 2016. Available online at http://www.tvbus.tv/web/2016/10/18/cortan-las-manos-a-seis-personas-en-tlaquepaque.

Heath, Charles V. *The Inevitable Bandstand: The State Band of Oaxaca and the Politics of Sound*. Lincoln: University of Nebraska Press, 2015.

Herlinghaus, Hermann. *Violence without Guilt: Ethical Narratives from the Global South*. New York: Palgrave Macmillan, 2009.

Hernández, Evangelina. *Tierra de padrotes: Tenancingo, Tlaxcala, un velo de impunidad*. Mexico City: Tusquets, 2015.

Hernández, Paola, director. *Música de balas*. Performance. University of Wisconsin–Madison, Madison, WI, May 5, 2015.

———. *Staging Lives in Latin American Theater: Bodies, Objects, Archives*. Evanston, IL: Northwestern University Press, 2021.

Hernández Cuevas, Marco Polo. *African Mexicans and the Discourse on Modern Nation*. Dallas: University Press of America, 2004.

Herrera Beltrán, Claudia, and Armango G. Tejeda. "Los criminals no se convertirán de pronto en santos, dice Calderón." *La Jornada*, May 19, 2010. https://www.jornada.com.mx/2010/05/19/politica/005n1pol.

Herrera-Sobek, María. *The Mexican Corrido: A Feminist Analysis*. Bloomington: Indiana University Press, 1990.

Herschfield, Joanne. "Race and Ethnicity in the Classical Cinema." In *Mexico's Cinema: A Century of Film and Filmmakers*, edited by Joanne Herschield and David R. Maciel, 81–101. New York: SR Books, 1999.

Hesterberg, Annegret. "A Second Skin." Translated by Johannes Weber. *Artes de México* 49 (2000): 88–89.

"Hija de Peña Nieto califica de 'pendejos' y 'prole' a los críticos de su padre." *Vanguardia*, September 23, 2015. https://vanguardia.com.mx/hijadepenanietocalificadependejosyprolealoscriticosdesupadre-1162731.html.

Holston, Mark. "Remembering Mercedes Sosa." *Americas* 62, no. 1 (2010): 64.

Home-Cook, George. "Aural Acts: Theatre and the Phenomenology." In *Theatre Noise: The Sound of Performance*, edited by David Roesner and Lynne Kendrick, 97–110. Cambridge: Cambridge Scholars Publishing, 2011.

———. *Theatre and Aural Attention: Stretching Ourselves*. New York: Palgrave, 2015.

hooks, bell. *Black Looks: Race and Representation*. Boston, MA: South End, 1992.

———. "The Oppositional Gaze: Black Female Spectators." In *The Film Theory Reader: Debates and Arguments*, edited by Marc Furstenau, 229–41. New York: Routledge, 2010.

Hughes, Jenny. *Performance in a Time of Terror: Critical Mimesis and the Age of Uncertainty*. Manchester: Manchester University Press, 2011.
Human Rights Watch. "Informe Mundial 2019: Mexico Eventos de 2018." *Human Rights Watch*. 2019. https://www.hrw.org/es/world-report/2019/country-chapters/325538#.
Infante Quintanilla, José Ernesto. *Pedro Infante, el ídolo inmortal*. Mexico City: Editorial Oceano, 2006.
Instituto Nacional de Estadística y Geografía (INEGI). "Estadísticas a propósito del día internacional de la eliminación de la violencia contra la mujer (25 de noviembre)." *INEGI*, November 23, 2017. https://www.inegi.org.mx/contenidos/saladeprensa/aproposito/2017/violencia2017_Nal.pdf.
Inter-American Commission on Human Rights. "The Human Rights Situation in Mexico." *Inter-American Commission on Human Rights*, December 31, 2015. http://www.oas.org/en/iachr/reports/pdfs/mexico2016-en.pdf.
———. "Chapter V: Follow-up to Recommendations Made by the IACHR in its Country or Thematic Reports." *Inter-American Commission on Human Rights*, 2019. 687–774. https://www.oas.org/en/iachr/docs/annual/2019/docs/IA2019cap5MX-en.pdf.
International Labour Organization. *Global Estimates of Modern Slavery: Forced Labour and Forced Marriage*. Geneva: International Labour Organization and Walk Free Foundation, 2017. https://www.ilo.org/global/publications/books/WCMS_575479/lang--en/index.htm.
"intrépidas buscadoras de peligro, Las." Youtube, uploaded by VICE en Español, May 4, 2016. https://www.youtube.com/watch?v=nTY-7dfyy68.
Irigaray, Luce. "The Eternal Irony of the Community." Translated by Gillian C. Gill. In *Feminist Readings of Antigone*, edited by Fanny Söderbäck, 99–110. Albany: State University of New York Press, 2010.
Irmer, Thomas. "A Search for New Realities: Documentary Theatre in Germany." *TDR: The Drama Review* 50, no. 3 (Autumn 2006): 16–28.
Islas, Alejandra, director. *Muxes: Auténticas, intrépidas, buscadores de peligro*. Instituto Mexicano de Cinematografía, 2005.
Jessel, Ella. "Chocolate Remix: The Lesbian Reggaetón Artista Taking on the 'Supermachos.'" *Guardian*, May 7, 2017. https://www.theguardian.com/music/2017/may/07/chocolate-remix-lesbian-reggaeton-taking-on-supermacho.
Ježik, Enrique. *Ejercicio de Percusión*, performance, El Teresa Arte Actual, Mexico City, Mexico, November 2006, available online, Youtube, uploaded by Enrique Ježik, July 3, 2013, https://www.youtube.com/watch?v=orR_h8rqCXI.
———. "Ejercicio de percusión." 2006. http://enriquejezik.com/2006-ejercicio-de-percusion.
———. "Entrevista con Enrique Ježik." Interview by Tomáš Pospiszyl, 2008. http://enriquejezik.com/entrevista-por-tomas-pospiszyl.
———. "Entrevista: Enrique Ježik." Interview by Pamela Ballesteros. *GASTV*, January 2015. http://gastv.mx/entrevista-enrique-jezik.

Jiménez, Félix. "(W)rapped in Foil: Glory at Twelve Words a Minute." In *Reggaetón*, edited by Raquel Z. Rivera, Wayne Marshall, and Deborah Pacini Hernández, 229–51. Durham, NC: Duke University Press, 2009.

Jiménez, Nallely. "Alarmante: Van más de 760 feminicidios durante 2018 en todo México." *Infobae*, December 29, 2018. https://www.infobae.com/america/mexico/2018/12/29/alarmante-van-mas-de-760-feminicidios-durante-2018-en-todo-mexico.

Johnson, Bruce. "Music and Violence in History." In *Dark Side of the Tune: Popular Music and Violence*, edited by Bruce Johnson and Martin Cloonan, 31–47. New York: Taylor and Francis, 2008.

Johnson, Bruce, and Martin Cloonan. Introduction to *Dark Side of the Tune: Popular Music and Violence*, edited by Bruce Johnson and Martin Cloonan, 1–12. New York: Taylor and Francis, 2008.

Juárez, Kenny. "Asesinan a balazos a joven en Neza." *Quadratin Exomex*, March 25, 2018. https://edomex.quadratin.com.mx/asesinan-balazos-joven-neza.

Kahlo, Frida. *Las dos Fridas*. 1939. Museo de Arte Moderno, Mexico City.

Kane, Brian. "Acousmatic Fabrications: Les Paul and the 'Les Paulverizer.'" *Journal of Visual Culture* 10, no. 212 (2011): 212–31.

Kendrick, Lynne. *Theatre Aurality*. New York: Palgrave, 2017.

Kenny, Paul, and Mónica Serrano. "Introduction: Security Failure Versus State Failure." In *Mexico's Security Failure: Collapse into Criminal Violence*, edited by Paul Kenny et al., 1–26. New York: Routledge, 2012.

Kheshti, Roshanak. *Modernity's Ear: Listening to Race and Gender in World Music*. New York: New York University Press, 2015.

Kiernan, James Patrick. "Grito de Dolores." *Américas* 62 no. 6 (2010): 64.

Kirby, Michael. "On Acting and Not-Acting." *TDR: The Drama Review*, 16 no. 1 (1972): 3–15.

Kristeva, Julia. "Antigone: Limit and Horizon." In *Feminist Readings of Antigone*, edited by Fanny Söderbäck, 215–29. Albany: State University of New York Press, 2010.

Krumholtz, Michael. "Mexico Trans Women Fight for Justice as Murder Unpunished." Associated Press, September 10, 2019. https://apnews.com/article/d5abd5bbee0a4e4b871d1f6d9aa08940.

LaBelle, Brandon. *Acoustic Territories: Sound Culture and Everyday Life*. New York: Bloomsbury Academic & Professional, 2010.

Lagarde y de Los Ríos, Marcela. "Preface: Feminist Keys for Understanding Feminicide: Theoretical, Political, and Legal Construction." In *Terrorizing Women: Feminicide in the Américas*, edited by Rosa-Linda Fregoso and Cynthia Bejarano, xi–xxvi. Durham, NC: Duke University Press, 2010.

Laing, Heather. *The Gendered Score: Music in 1940s Melodrama and the Woman's Film*. Aldershot: Ashgate, 2007.

Lambright, Anne. *Andean Truths: Transitional Justice, Ethnicity, and Cultural Production in Post-Shining Path Peru*. Liverpool: Liverpool University Press, 2016.

Lane, Jill. *Blackface Cuba, 1840–1895*. Philadelphia: University of Pennsylvania Press, 2005.

Lara, Eric. "'Salieron de San Isidro…' El corrido, El narcocorrido y tres de sus categorías de análisis: El hombre, la mujer y el soplón. Un acercamiento etnográfico." *Revista de Humanidades: Tecnológico de Monterrey* 015 (2003): 209–30.

Lashua, Brett et al., eds. *Sounds and the City: Volume 2*. New York: Palgrave MacMillan, 2019.

Las Reinas Chulas. "Perspectiva de cabaret." n.d. https://www.lasreinaschulasac.org/perspectiva-de-cabaret.

Lawrence, Sidra. "Sounding Trauma: Justice, Audibility, and Sexual Violence." Presentation at the Society for Ethnomusicology Conference (online), October 22, 2020.

Lehmann, Hans-Thies. *Postdramatic Theatre*. Translated by Karen Jürs-Munby. New York: Routledge. 2006.

Lemus, J. Jesús. "Opinión: A 500 años de la Conquista, elterritorio mexicano es botín de empresas mineras transnacionales." *Los Angeles Times*, August 14, 2021. https://www.latimes.com/espanol/opinion/articulo/2021-08-14/opinion-a-500-anos-de-la-conquista-el-territorio-mexicano-es-botin-de-empresas-mineras-trasnacionales.

Leñero, Vicente. *Vivir del teatro*. Mexico City: Fondo de Cultura Económica, 2012.

Leñero Franco, Estela. "Premio Nacional de Dramaturgia a Hugo Salcedo." *Proceso*, December 29, 2011. https://www.proceso.com.mx/cultura/2011/12/29/premio-nacional-de-dramaturgia-hugo-salcedo-96766.html.

"letra de 'El violador eres tú,' el himno feminista que se extiende por el mundo, La." *El País*, December 8, 2019. https://elpais.com/sociedad/2019/12/07/actualidad/1575750878_441385.html.

Lima, Irakere, and Larissa Polaco. *Ni una menos*. Performance. Teatro Bar El Vicio, Coyoacán, Mexico, June 14, 2019. Available online, Hemispheric Institute Digital Video Library, https://hemisphericinstitute.org/en/encuentro-2019-trasnocheo/item/3221-las-pussy-queers-not-one-woman-less.html.

"Lista de ganadores del Ariel 2015," *El Universal*, May 27, 2015, https://archivo.eluniversal.com.mx/espectaculos/2015/lista-ganadores-ariel-2015-1103204.html.

"Liz, Nicole, Kimberley, Martha y Karen: Cinco transfemicidios en los primeros diez días de noviembre en México." Agenciapresentes.org, November 17, 2022. https://agenciapresentes.org/2022/11/17/mexico-registro-cinco-transfemicidios-durante-noviembre.

López, Ana M. "The Melodrama in Latin America: Films, Telenovelas, and the Currency of a Popular Form." In *Imitations of Life: A Reader on Film and Television Melodrama*, edited by Marcia Landy, 596–606. Detroit, MI: Wayne State Press, 1991.

———. "Mexico." In *The International Film Musical*, edited by Corey K. Creekmur and Linda Y. Mokdad, 121–40. Edinburgh: Edinburgh University Press, 2012.

López, Pancho. "Arranca la XII Muestra Internacional de Performance." Crónica.com. mx, November 9, 2006. https://www.cronica.com.mx/notas/2006/270375.html.

"López Obrador se proclama 'presidente legítimo' de México." *El País*, November 20, 2006. https://elpais.com/internacional/2006/11/21/actualidad/1164063605_850215.html.

López Velázquez, Citalli. "'Juchitán de las balas', el rap que llama a no normalizer la violencia en Oaxaca." *La silla rota*, February 15, 2022. https://lasillarota.com/estados/juchitan-de-las-balas-el-rap-que-llama-a-no-normalizar-la-violencia-en-oaxaca/617283.

Lozano, Rafael E. "Lukas Avendaño: A Successful Case of Failure." *Que Pasa Oaxaca*, August 27, 2019. https://www.quepasaoaxaca.com/lukas-avendano-un-caso-exitoso-del-fracaso.

Lozano de la pola, Riansares. "¿Dónde está Bruno Avendaño? La práctica artística como 'espacio de aparición.'" *El ornitorrinco tachado*, no. 8 (November–April 2019): 29–39.

"Luis Ángel León Rodríguez." *CMDPDH*. n.d. http://cmdpdh.org/no-olvidamos/luis-angel.

Lujan, Soledad. "En medio de un gran circo: La ciudad de México a tráves de las crónicas musicales de Maldita Vecindad y Los Hijos del 5º Patio." MA thesis, University of California–Santa Cruz, 2014. https://escholarship.org/uc/item/2xd1n48b

Luna, Violeta. *Réquiem II*. Performance. San Francisco, California, 2011.

———. *Réquiem para una tierra Perdida/Requiem for a lost land*. Performance. São Paolo, Brazil, January 2013. Available online, Hemispheric Institute Digital Video Library, https://hemisphericinstitute.org/en/enc13-performances1/item/2021-enc13-vluna-requiem.html.

———. *Réquiem #3: Fosas Cuerpo/Body Graves*. Performance. Centro Universitario de Teatro, Black Box Theatre, Mexico City, Mexico, June 11, 2019. Available online, Hemispheric Institute Digital Video Library, https://hemisphericinstitute.org/es/encuentro-2019-performances/item/2936-violeta-luna.html.

———. "Cor-po/etics: A Poetics of the Body in Performance." Presentation at the University of Wisconsin–Madison, Madison, WI, April 20, 2021.

———. "About the Artist." n.d. http://www.violetaluna.com/About.html.

Luna, Violeta, Ileana Diéguez, and Rián Lozano. "Imaginario—Necromachines." Presentation at the Hemispheric Institute of Politics and Performance Encuentro, Mexico City, Mexico, June 14, 2019. Available online, Vimeo, uploaded by Hemispheric Institute, July 23, 2019, https://vimeo.com/349664038.

Madrid, Alejandro L. *Los sonidos de la nación moderna*. Havana: Casa de las Américas, 2008.

———. *Music in Mexico: Experiencing Music, Expressing Culture*. New York: Oxford University Press, 2013.

Madrid, Alejandro L., and Robin D. Moore. 2013. *Danzón: Circum-Caribbean Dialogues in Music and Dance*. New York: Oxford University Press.

Malcomson, Hettie. "The Expediency of Blackness: Racial Logics and Danzón in the Port of Veracruz, Mexico." In *Afro-Latin@s in Movement: Critical Approaches to Blackness and Transnationalism in the Americas*, edited by Petra R. Rivera-Rideau, Jennifer A. Jones, and Tianna Paschel, 35–57. New York: Palgrave Macmillan, 2016.

Maldita Vecindad. "Morenaza," *Maldita Vecindad y los Hijos del Quinto Patio*, Sony Music Entertainment, 2015. Spotify, https://open.spotify.com/track/6MaTImJcG82qYwx6fJkm84?si=rEnB6Ex3SjexczZ330Wg5Q.

Mandel, Naomi. *Against the Unspeakable: Complicity, the Holocaust, and Slavery in America*. Charlottesville: University of Virginia Press, 2006.

Mantoan, Lindsey. *War as Performance: Conflicts in Iraq and Political Theatricality*. New York: Palgrave, 2018.

Marchando con letras. *Ayotzinapa: La travesía de las tortugas*. Mexico City: Marchando con letras, 2015.

María y Campos, Armando. *El teatro de género chico en la Revolución Mexicana*. Mexico City: Biblioteca del Instituto Nacional de Estudios Históricos de la Revolución Mexicana, 1956.

Marín, Paola. "Migrant Bodies, Flowing Rituals: The Performance Art of Violeta Luna." *Latin American Theatre Review* 52, no. 1 (Fall 2018): 83–100.

Marshall, Wayne. "From Música Negra to Reggaeton Latino: The Cultural Politics of Nation, Migration, and Commercialization." In *Reggaetón*, edited by Raquel Z. Rivera, Wayne Marshall, and Deborah Pacini Hernández, 19–76. Durham, NC: Duke University Press, 2009.

Marshall, Wayne, Raquel Z. Rivera, and Deborah Pacini Hernandez. 2009. "Introduction: Reggaeton's Socio-Sonic Circuitry." In *Reggaetón*, edited by Raquel Z. Rivera, Wayne Marshall, and Deborah Pacini Hernández, 1–16. Durham, NC: Duke University Press, 2009.

Martin, Carol. "Bodies of Evidence." *Drama Review* 50, no. 3 (2006): 8–15.

———, ed. *Dramaturgy of the Real on the World Stage*. New York: Palgrave MacMillan, 2010.

———. *Theatre of the Real*. New York: Palgrave Macmillan, 2013.

Martínez, Ana. *Performance in the Zócalo: Constructing History, Race, and Identity in Mexico's Central Square from the Colonial Era to the Present*. Ann Arbor: University of Michigan Press, 2020.

Martín Sánchez, María Isabel. "Violeta Luna: Dramaturgía y performatividad de la desaparición." *Latin American Theatre Review* 56, no. 1 (Fall 2022): 63–84.

Mastrogiovanni, Federico. *Ni vivos ni Muertos: La desaparición forzada en México como estrategia de terror*. Mexico City: Debolsillo, 2017.

"Matan a mujer por resistirse a asalto, cerca de La Raza." *Noticieros Televisa*, May 29, 2019. https://noticieros.televisa.com/ultimas-noticias/asalto-hoy-asesinan-mujer-resistirse-la-raza.

Matías, Pedro. "Aumenta 47% asesinatos de mujeres trans; México segundo lugar mundial con 422 crímenes." *Página 3*, August 15, 2018. https://pagina3.mx/2018/08/aumenta-47-asesinatos-de-mujeres-trans-mexico-segundo-lugar-mundial-con-422-crimenes.

Mbembe, Achille. *Necro-politics*. Translated by Steven Corcoran. Durham, NC: Duke University Press, 2019.

McClary, Susan. *Feminine Endings: Music, Gender, and Sexuality*. Minneapolis: University of Minnesota Press, 1991.

McDougall, Christopher. "The Martyred Mexican Madonna." *New York Times*, November 14, 2004.

McRobbie, Angela. "Recent Rhythms of Sex and Race in Popular Music." *Media, Culture and Society* 17, no. 2 (1995): 323–31.

McSherry, J. Patrice. *Chilean New Song: The Political Power of Music, 1960s–1973*. Philadelphia, PA: Temple University Press, 2015.

Medina, Alejo. "¿Dónde está Bruno? / Where is Bruno?: Lukas Avendaño's Autobiography as a Political Act." *Performance Research* 27, no. 7 (2019): 56–60. https://doi.org/0.1080/13528165.2019.1717865.

Melendez, Priscilla. "The Body and the Law in the Mexico/U.S. Borderlands: Violence and Violations in *El viaje de los cantores* by Hugo Salcedo and *Backyard* by Sabina Berman." *Modern Drama* 55, no. 1 (Spring 2011): 24–44.

Melesio, Lucina. "Ayotzinapa 34 Four Years On: Renewed Hope for Finding Truth." *Al Jazeera*, September 27, 2018. www.aljazeera.com/news/2018/09/ayotzinapa-43-years-renewed-hope-finding-truth-180927033943677.html.

Mendoza, Vicente T. *La canción Mexicana: Ensayo de clasificación y antología*. Mexico City: Universidad Nacional Autónoma de México, 1961.

Mer. "'La desnudez asusta y seduce', Las Pussy Queers en El Vicio." *Chicas.mx*, May 18, 2018. https://www.chicas.mx/autor/almondomi.

Merleau-Ponty, Maurice. *Phenomenology of Perception*. New York: Routledge, 2012.

Merlín, Socorro. *Vida y Milagros de las carpas: La carpa en México, 1930–1950*. 1st ed. Mexico City: CITRU, 1995.

"Mexican Photojournalist Found Dead Was Likely Tortured, Activists Say." *Guardian*, August 2, 2015. https://www.theguardian.com/world/2015/aug/02/mexican-photojournalist-killed-ruben-espinosa-tortured.

"México encontró 599 fosas clandestinas en 2020." *DW*, January 30, 2020. https://www.dw.com/es/méxico-encontró-559-fosas-clandestinas-en-2020/a-56389269.

"Mexico rompió cifra histórica de mujeres asesinadas por homicidio doloso en el 2022; los feminicidios no bajan." *infobae*, February 5, 2023. https://www.infobae.com/mexico/2023/02/05/mexico-rompio-cifra-historica-de-mujeres-asesinadas-por-homicidio-doloso-en-el-2022-los-feminicidios-no-bajan.

"Mexico's Third Gender." Youtube, uploaded by Great Big Story, June 19, 2018. https://www.youtube.com/watch?v=aEZEiiNS3Ew.

Miano Borruso, Marinella. "Gays tras bambalinas. Historia de belleza, pasiones e identidades." *Debate Feminista* 18 (1998): 186–236.

———. "Género y Homosexualidad entre los Zapotecos del Istmo de Tehuantepec: El Caso de los Muxe." In *Actas del IV Congreso Chileno de Antropología*, 685–90. Santiago: Colegio de Antropólogos de Chile A. G, 2001.

———. *Hombre, mujer y muxe' en el Istmo de Tehuantepec*. Mexico City: Instituto Nacional de Antropología e Historia, 2002.

———. "Muxe: 'Nuevos Liderazgos' y Fenómenos Mediáticos" *Revista Digital Universitaria* 11, no. 9 (September 2010): 3–15.

Mirandé, Alfredo. *Behind the Mask: Gender Hybridity in a Zapotec Community*. Tucson: University of Arizona Press, 2017.

Modestomigato. "Conversación con Lukas Avendaño: Primera parte." *Heredad Blog*, March 21, 2021. https://www.heredadpalabras.com/post/conversación-con-lukas-avendaño-primera-parte.

———. "Conversación con Lukas Avendaño: Segunda parte." *Heredad Blog*, March 28, 2021. https://www.heredadpalabras.com/post/conversación-con-lukas-avendaño-segunda-parte.

Monárrez Fragoso, Julia. "The Victims of the Ciudad Juárez Feminicide: Sexually Fetishized Commodities." Translated by Sara Koopman. In *Terrorizing Women: Feminicide in the Américas*, edited by Rosa-Linda Fregoso and Cynthia Bejarano, 59–69. Durham, NC: Duke University Press, 2010.

Monsiváis, Carlos. *Escenas de pudor y liviandad*. Barcelona: Editorial Grijalbo, 1981.

———. "And All the People Came and Did Not Fit onto the Screen: Notes on the Cinema Audience in Mexico." In *Mexican Cinema*, edited by Paulo Antonio Paranagaguá and translated by Ana López, 145–51. London: British Film Institute, 1995.

———. "Mythologies." In *Mexican Cinema*, edited by Paulo Antonio Paranagaguá and translated by Ana López, 117–27. London: British Film Institute, 1995.

———. *Pedro Infante: Las leyes de querer*. Mexico City: Aguilar, 2008.

Monsiváis, Carlos, and Carlos Bonfil. *A través del espejo: El cine mexicano y su publico*. Mexico City: Ediciones El Milagro, 1994.

Montes, Rocío. "'El violador eres tú,' el himno que Chile export al mundo." *El País*, December 7, 2019. https://elpais.com/sociedad/2019/12/07/actualidad/1575742572_306059.html.

Montini, E. J. "Did the Supreme Court Deny Justice for a Mexican Boy Shot 10 Times in the Back and Head?" *azcentral*, March 3, 2020. https://www.azcentral.com/story/opinion/op-ed/ej-montini/2020/03/03/supreme-court-denies-justice-mexican-boy-shot-border-agent/4936609002.

Mor, Ana Francis, Cecilia Sotres, Nora Huerta, and Marisol Gasé. *Nosotras las proles*. Unpublished script, 2013.

Mor, Ana Francis, Cecilia Sostres, Marisol Gase, and Nora Huerta. *Nosotras las proles*. Performance. Coyoacán, Mexico, August 16, 2013.

Moreno Figueroa, Mónica G., and Emiko Saldívar Tanaka. "'We Are Not Racists, We Are Mexicans': Privilege, Nationalism and Post-Race Ideology in Mexico." *Critical Sociology* 42, nos. 4–5 (2016): 515–33.

Moreno Rivas, Yolanda. *Historia de la música popular mexicana*. Mexico City: Alianza Editorial Mexicana, 1979.

Mosse, Ramona. "Thinking Theatres beyond Sight: From Reflection to Resonance." *Anglia* 136, no. 1 (2018): 138–53.

Moten, Fred. *In the Break: The Aesthetics of the Black Radical Tradition*. Minneapolis: University of Minnesota Press, 2003.

Movimiento por nuestros desaparecidos en México. "Acerca de." n.d. https://memoriamndm.org/sobre-el-movndmx.

Mulholland, Mary-Lee. "Mariachis Machos and Charros Gays: Masculinities in Guadalajara." In *Masculinity and Sexuality in Modern Mexico*, edited by Víctor M. Macías-Gónzalez and Anne Rubenstein, 233–61. Albuquerque: University of New Mexico Press, 2012.

Muñoz, Alma E. "Madre de policía federal desaparecido exige que el Estado no evada su responsabilidad." *La Jornada*, February 21, 2016. https://www.jornada.com.mx/2016/02/21/politica/010n1pol.

Muñoz, Jose Esteban. *Disidentifications: Queers of Color and Performance of Politics*. Minneapolis: University of Minnesota Press, 1999.

———. *Cruising Utopia: The Then and There of Queer Futurity*. New York: NYU Press, 2009.

Murray, Sarah E. "Dragon Ladies, Draggin' Men: Some Reflections on Gender, Drag and Homosexual Communities." *Public Culture* 6 (1994): 343-363.

"Muxes 'El tercer género de México' – Entrevista a Lukas Avendaño." Youtube, uploaded by Conecta Estudio, July 27, 2020. https://www.youtube.com/watch?app=desktop&v=U_PKeRdCn-U.

Nájar, Alberto. "Minería, el nuevo negocio de los carteles mexicanos." *BBC Mundo*, March 18, 2014. https://www.bbc.com/mundo/noticias/2014/03/140318_mexico_mineria_nuevo_negocio_carteles_narcotrafico_templarios_zetas_an.

———. "Masacrar familias enteras, la creciente práctica de terror de los narcos en México." *BBC Mundo*, July 28, 2016. https://www.bbc.com/mundo/noticias-america-latina-36901152.

Nájera-Ramírez, Olga. "Engendering Nationalism: Identity, Discourse and the Mexican Charro." *Anthropology Quarterly* 67 no. 1 (1994): 1–14.

———. "Unruly Passions: Poetics, Performance and Gender in the Ranchera Song." In *Chicana Feminisms: A Critical Reader*, edited by Gabriela F. Arredondo et al., 184–210. Durham, NC: Duke University Press, 2003.

Nancy, Jean-Luc. *Listening*. Translated by Charlotte Mandell. New York: Fordham University Press, 2002.

Néstore, Ángelo. "La autotraducción al servicio de la visibilidad de discursos disidentes: El caso de la poeta y traductora cuir* muxe' Elvis Guerra." *Revista Letral* 24 (2020): 221–36. http://dx.doi.org/10.30827/RL.v0i24.15472.

Neustadt, Robert. "Music as Memory and Torture: Sounds of Repression and Protest in Chile and Argentina." *Chasqui* 33, no. 1 (2004): 128–37.

Newbold Chiñas, Beverly. *The Isthmus Zapotecs: A Matrifocal Culture of Mexico*. 2nd ed. Fort Worth, TX: Harcourt Brace Jovanovich College, 1992.

Newton, Esther. *Mother Camp: Female Impersonators in America*. Chicago: University of Chicago Press, 1971.
Nieves Moreno, Alfredo. "A Man Lives Here: Reggaetón's Hypermasculine Resident." Translated by Héctor Fernández L'Hoeste. In *Reggaetón*, edited by Raquel Z. Rivera, Wayne Marshall, and Deborah Pacini Hernández, 252–79. Durham, NC: Duke University Press, 2009.
Norget, Kristin. "Caught in the Crossfire: Militarization, Paramilitarization, and State Violence in Oaxaca Mexico." In *When States Kill: Latin America, the U.S., and Technologies of Terror*, edited by Cecilia Menjívar and Néstor Rodríguez, 115–142. Austin: University of Texas Press, 2005.
———. *Days of Death, Days of Life: Ritual in the Popular Culture of Oaxaca*. New York: Columbia University Press, 2006.
North, James. "Welcome to Veracruz, Mexico, One of the Most Dangerous Places in the World to be a Journalist." *Nation*, March 23, 2018. https://www.thenation.com/article/archive/welcome-to-veracruz-mexico-one-of-the-most-dangerous-places-in-the-world-to-be-a-journalist.
"Nuevo grupo armado amenaza a policías en Oaxaca: 'Tenemos ubicados a municipals y estatales.'" *infobae*, February 2, 2021. https://www.infobae.com/america/mexico/2021/02/02/nuevo-grupo-armado-amenaza-a-policias-en-oaxaca-tenemos-ubicados-a-todos-los-municipales-y-estatales.
Núñez, Elsa. "Checa el programa complete del festival Tiempo de Mujeres 2020 en CDMX." animal.mx, March 3, 2020. https://animal.mx/2020/03/festival-tiempo-de-mujeres-2020-cdmx-programa-mon-laferte.
Obejas, Achy. "It Hurts to Laugh: Even Performance Artists are Numbered by Mexico's Crises." *Chicago Tribune*, April 11, 1996.
Olivera, Alondra. "'El Chapo de Oaxaca', el líder del cartel de Juchitán." *La silla rota*, April 24, 2017. https://lasillarota.com/estados/el-chapo-de-oaxaca-el-lider-del-cartel-de-juchitan/145027.
Olson, Georgina. "Apuesta histórica; Peña propone cambiar la Constitución en materia energética." *Excelsior*, August 8, 2013. https://www.colimanoticias.com/apuesta-historica-pena-propone-cambiar-la-constitucion-en-materia-energetica.
Ortega Ávila, Antonio. "Las decapitaciones, nuevo lenguaje de los 'narcos.'" *El País*, May 22, 2008. https://elpais.com/diario/2008/05/23/internacional/1211493607_850215.html.
Osornio, Felipe. "Lechedevirgen: Pensamiento Puñal." 2012. https://www.lechedevirgen.com/textos/pensamiento-punal.
———. *México exhumado*. Unpublished script. 2019.
———. *México exhumado*. Performance. Centro Universitario de Teatro, Black Box Theatre, Mexico City, Mexico, June 10, 2019. Available online, Hemispheric Institute Digital Video Library, https://hemisphericinstitute.org/es/encuentro-2019-performances/item/2935-lechedevirgen.html.
———. "Lechedevirgen Trimegisto: Artista de performance." n.d. http://www.lechedevirgen.com/lechedevirgen.

Padilla Fajardo, Lisbeth. "La reforma educativa, la propuesta 'más costosa' de Peña Nieto." *CNN México*, September 9, 2013. Available online at https://expansion.mx/nacional/2013/09/09/la-reforma-educativa-la-propuesta-mas-costosa-de-pena-nieto.

Papalotl, Liliana, Irakere Lima, and Pako Reyes. *El Desierto de Las Leonas.* Unpublished Script, 2017.

———. *El Desierto de Las Leonas.* Performance. Teatro Bar El Vicio, Coyoacán, Mexico, January–February 2019.

Partida Tayzán, Armando. "La novísima dramaturgia Mexicana." In *Teatro mexicano reciente: Aproximaciones críticas*, edited by Samuel Gordon, 15–34. Austin: University of Texas Press, 2005.

Paz, Octavio. *El laberinto de la soledad*. First published 1952. New York: Penguin Books, 1997.

"Pedirán por la desaparición forzada Bruno Avendaño en México." *ANRed*, October 8, 2018. https://www.anred.org/2018/10/08/pediran-por-la-desaparicion-forzada-bruno-avendano-en-mexico.

"Peña Nieto busca incrementar las exportaciones de petróleo a China." *CNN México*, April 4, 2013. Available online at https://expansion.mx/nacional/2013/04/04/pena-nieto-busca-incrementar-las-exportaciones-de-petroleo-a-china.

"Peña consuma la reforma educativa pese a la oposición magisterial." *CNN México*, September 10, 2013. Available online at https://expansion.mx/nacional/2013/09/10/pena-nieto-consuma-la-reforma-educativa-a-pesar-de-las-protestas.

Pérez Albarrán, Jorge. "Revelan que Romero Deschamps regresó 'desahuciado' de Houston." *Proceso*, October 5, 2012. https://www.proceso.com.mx/nacional/2012/10/5/revelan-que-romero-deschamps-regreso-desahuciado-de-houston-109266.html.

Phelan, Peggy. *Unmarked: The Politics of Performance*. New York: Routledge, 1991.

Pieslak, Jonathan R. "Sound Targets: Music and the War in Iraq." *Journal of Musicological Research* 26, no. 2–3 (2007): 123–49. DOI: 10.1080/01411890701360153.

Pineda, Dorany. "Long before Roma's' Yalitza Aparicio, Mexican TV and Cinema often Parodied Indigenous People." *Los Angeles Times*, March 9, 2019. www.latimes.com/entertainment/la-et-mn-yalitza-aparicio-brownface-history-20190309-story.html.

Poole, Deborah. "An Image of 'Our Indian': Type Photographs and Racial Sentiments in Oaxaca, 1920–1940." *Hispanic American Historical Review* 84, no. 1 (2004): 37–82.

Poulson, Nancy Kason. "In Defense of the Dead: *Antígona Furiosa*, by Griselda Gambaro." *Romance Quarterly* 59, no. 1 (2012): 48–54.

"Presidente Calderón: Discurso completo en el auditorio." El Universal.com.mx, December 1, 2006. https://archivo.eluniversal.com.mx/notas/391513.html.

Prieto Stambaugh, Antonio. "'RepresentaXión' de un *muxe*: La identidad performática Lukas Avendaño." *Latin American Theatre Review* 48, no. 1 (Fall 2014): 31–53.

———. "The Queer/*Muxe* Performance of Disappearance: Lukas Avendaño's Butterfly Utopia." In *Performances that Changed the Americas*, edited by Stuart A. Day, 176–201. New York: Routledge, 2021.

Pulido Llano, Gabriela. *Mulatas y negros cubanos en la escena Mexicana, 1920–1950*. Mexico City: Instituto Nacional de Antropología e Historia, 2010.

Quintana, Vivir. "Canción sin miedo." Universal Music Mexico, 2020. Spotify, https://open.spotify.com/track/5w3AsUEGoaCuBhDp14umuy?si=ByjQyoM7SVSlu6yVsAAn9w.

Quintana, Vivir, Mon Laferte, and El Palomar. "Canción sin miedo." Performance. Zócalo, Mexico City, Mexico. March 7, 2020. Available online, Youtube, uploaded by México en el arte, March 8, https://www.youtube.com/watch?v=LdArO2jV9ho.

Radford, Jill, and Diana Russell. *Femicide: The Politics of Woman Killing*. New York: Twayne, 1992.

Rasmussen, Anthony W. "Resistance Resounds: Hearing Power in Mexico City." PhD diss., University of California Riverside, 2017.

———. "Acoustic Patriarchy: Hearing Gender Violence in Mexico City's Public Spaces." *Women and Music: A Journal of Gender and Culture* 23 (2019): 15–42. https://doi.org/10.1353/wam.2019.0001.

Reguillo, Rossana. "The Narco-Machine and the Work of Violence: Notes toward Its Decodification." *e-misférica* 8, no. 2 (2010). https://hemisphericinstitute.org/en/emisferica-82/reguillo5.html.

———. "La turbencia en el paisaje: De jóvenes, necropolítica y 43 esperanzas." In *Juvencidio: Ayotzinapa y las vidas precarias en América Latina*, edited by José Manuel Valenzuela Arce, 59–77. Barcelona: Ned Ediciones, 2015.

Reichard, Raquel. "Meet the New Generation of Women in Reggaetón and Latin Trap." *Popsugar*, July 9, 2020. https://www.popsugar.com/latina/meet-new-generation-women-in-reggaetón-latin-trap-47598774.

Rey, Leandro Luis. "La Escenografía de Rodolfo Sánchez Alvarado. De la musicalización del teatro hacia la teatralización de la música." *Argus-a: Artes y Humanidades* 10, no. 38 (December 2020): 1–9.

Ridout, Nicholas. "Welcome to the Vibratorium." *Senses and Society* 3, no. 2 (2008): 221–31.

Rivera, Raquel Z., Wayne Marshall, and Deborah Pacini Hernández, eds. *Reggaetón*. Durham, NC: Duke University Press, 2009.

Rivera Garza, Cristina. *Grieving: Dispatches from a Wounded Country*. Translated by Sara Booker. New York: Feminist Press, 2020.

———. *The Restless Dead: Necrowriting & Disappropriation*. Translated by Robin Myers. Nashville, TN: Vanderbilt University Press, 2020.

Rivera Hernández, Raúl Diego. *Narratives of Vulnerability in Mexico's War on Drugs*. Translated by Isis Sadek. New York: Palgrave MacMillan, 2020.

Rivera-Rideau, Petra R. *Remixing Reggaetón: The Cultural Politics of Race in Puerto Rico*. Durham, NC: Duke University Press, 2015.

Rodríguez, Ismael, dir. *Los tres García*. Film by Producciones Rodríguez Hermanos, 1947.

Rodríguez, Ismael, dir. *Nosotros los pobres*. Film by Producciones Rodríguez Hermanos, 1948.

Rodríguez, Joselito, dir. *Ángelitos negros*. Film by Producciones Rodríguez Hermanos, 1948.

Rodríguez, Raul, director. *Música de balas*. Performance. Real Escuela Superior de Arte Dramático, Madrid, Spain, September 26–October 13, 2013.

Roesner, David, and Lynne Kendrick. Introduction to *Theatre Noise: The Sound of Performance*, edited by David Roesner and Lynne Kendrick, xiv–xxxv. Cambridge: Cambridge Scholars Publishing, 2011.

———, eds. *Theatre Noise: The Sound of Performance*. Cambridge: Cambridge Scholars Publishing. 2011.

Romero, Carolina. "El riesgo de ser transexual en México." *El Universal*, October 15, 2018. https://www.eluniversal.com.mx/nacion/el-riesgo-de-ser-transexual-en-mexico.

Rosas, Alejandro, and Julio Patán. *México bizarro: El país que no quieres recordar*. Mexico City: Editorial Planeta, 2017.

Rubenstein, Anne. "Bodies, Cities, Cinema: Pedro Infante's Death as Political Spectacle." In *Fragments of a Golden Age: The Politics of Culture in Mexico Since 1940*, edited by Gilbert Joseph, Anne Rubenstein, and Eric Zolov, 199–233. Durham, NC: Duke University Press, 2001.

Ruiz Mójica, Adalberto. "Javier Duarte: El ladrón más grande en la historia de México." Contralinea.com.mx, April 10, 2018. https://www.contralinea.com.mx/archivo-revista/2018/04/10/javier-duarte-el-ladron-mas-grande-en-la-historia-de-mexico/.

Rutter, Samuel, and Caitlin Younquist. "10 Queer Indigenous Artists on Where Their Inspirations Have Led Them." *New York Times*, April 23, 2021. https://www.nytimes.com/2021/04/23/t-magazine/queer-indigenous-artists.html.

Sadlier, Darlene J. editor. *Latin American Melodrama: Passion, Pathos, and Entertainment*. Urbana: University of Illinois Press, 2009.

Salcedo, Hugo. *Música de balas*. Mexico City: Universidad Autónoma Metropolitana, 2012.

Saldívar Arreola, Rafael, and Ignacio Rodríguez Sánchez. "Análisis del léxico en diferentes registros textuales en la construcción del imaginario social del narcotráfico en México." *Literatura y Lingüística* 37 (2018): 381–400.

Salgado López, Melanie del Carmen. "Declaro la Guerra contra de ¿quién? El discurso de Guerra contra el Narcotráfico de Calderón. Análisis Crítico del Discurso." B.A. Thesis, Universidad Nacional Autónoma de México, 2012.

Saragoza, Alex M. and Graciela Berkovich. "Intimate Connections: Cinematic Allegories of Gender, the State and National Identity." In *The Mexican Cinema Project*, edited by Chon A. Noriega and Steven Ricci, 25–32. Los Angeles: UCLA Film and Television Archive, 1994.

Sassafras_Ghost. "Biografía: Banda Princesa Donashii." Last.fm, October 9, 2011. https://www.last.fm/es/music/Princesa+Donashii/+wiki

Sauceda, Jonathan. "Smuggling, Betrayal, and the Handle of a Gun: Death, Laughter, and the *Narcocorrido*." *Popular Music and Society* 37, no. 4 (2014): 425–43.

Scarry, Elaine. *The Body in Pain: The Making and Unmaking of the World*. New York: Oxford University Press, 1985.

Schafer, R. Murray. *The Soundscape: Our Sonic Environment and the Tuning of the World*. Rochester, VT: Destiny Books, 1977.

Schechner, Richard. *Between Theatre and Anthropology*. Philadelphia: University of Pennsylvania Press, 1985.

———. *Performance Studies: Introduction*. New York: Routledge, 2002.

Schneider, Rebecca. *Performing Remains: Art and War in Times of Theatrical Reenactment*. New York: Routledge, 2011.

Secretaría de Gobernación. *Informe Anual 2016: Registro Nacional de Datos de Personas Extraviadas o Desaparecidas (RNPED)*. August 2017. https://infosen.senado.gob.mx/sgsp/gaceta/63/3/2017-09-12-1/assets/documentos/Informe_Anual_RNPED_2016_FINAL.pdf.

Segato, Rita Laura. *La escritura en el cuerpo de las mujeres asesinadas en Ciudad Juárez: Territorio, soberanía y crímenes de segundo estado*. Mexico City: Universidad del Claustro de Sor Juana, 2006.

———. *La guerra contra las mujeres*. Madrid: Traficantes de sueños, 2016.

"Sergio Goyri llama 'pinche india' a Yalitza Aparicio." *Nación 321*, February 19, 2019. https://www.nacion321.com/ciudadanos/video-sergio-goyri-llama-pinche-india-a-yalitza-aparicio.

Shepherd, John. *Music as Social Text*. Cambridge: Polity, 1991.

Sierra, Aída. "The Creation of a Symbol." Translated by Richard Moszka. *Artes de México* 49 (2000): 84–85.

Simonett, Helena. *Banda: Mexican Musical Life across Borders*. Middletown, CT: Wesleyan University Press, 2001.

———. "Narcocorridos: An Emerging Micromusic of Nuevo L.A." *Ethnomusicology* 45, no. 2 (Spring–Summer 2001): 315–37.

Sjöholm, Cecilia. *The Antigone Complex: Ethics and the Invention of Feminine Desire*. Palo Alto, CA: Stanford University Press, 2004.

Söderbäck, Fanny. "Impossible Mourning: Sophocles Reversed." In *Feminist Readings of Antigone*, edited by Fanny Söderbäck, 65–82. Albany: State University of New York Press, 2010.

———. "Introduction: Why Antigone Today?" In *Feminist Readings of Antigone*, edited by Fanny Söderbäck, 1–13. Albany: State University of New York Press, 2010.

Solórzano-Thompson, Nohemy. "Performative Masculinities: The Pachuco and the Luchador in the Songs of Maldita Vecindad and Café Tacuba." *Studies in Latin American Pop Culture* 26 (2007): 79–96.

"Sonidos de la Nación Zapoteca define plan de trabajo." *Guidxizá, una mirada a nuestros pueblos*, cultural supplement of *Comité Melendre* 1, no. 8 (September 17, 2012.). http://comitemelendre.blogspot.com/2012/12/sonidos-de-la-nacion-zapoteca-define.html.

Sosa, Mercedes. "Mercedes Sosa – Duerme negrito (en directo, 10.03.1976)," Youtube, uploaded by Miguel Toston Cienfuegos, March 30, 2022, https://www.youtube.com/watch?v=ozmXK1zo3eM.

Sotres, Cecilia. *Introducción al cabaret (con albur)*. Mexico City: Paso de Gato, 2016.

Stein, Alexander. "Music, Mourning, and Consolation." *JAPA* 52, no. 3 (2004): 783–811.

Stephen, Lynn. "Sexualities and Genders in Zapotec Oaxaca." *Latin American Perspectives* 29, no. 2 (March 2002): 41–49.

———. *Zapotec Women: Gender, Class, and Ethnicity in Globalized Oaxaca*. Durham, NC: Duke University Press, 2005.

———. "Testimony and Human Rights Violations in Oaxaca." *Latin American Perspectives* 38, no. 6 (2011): 52-68. Doi: 10.1177/0094582X11414684.

Subero, Gustavo. "*Muxeninity* and the Institutionalization of a Third Gender Identity in Alejandra Isla's *Muxes: Auténticas, intrépidas, buscadores de peligro*." *Hispanic Research Journal* 14, no. 2 (2013): 175–93.

Taylor, Diana. "'High Aztec' or Performing Anthro Pop: Jesusa Rodríguez and Liliana Felipe in 'Cielo de abajo.'" *TDR: The Drama Review* 37, no. 3 (1993): 142–52.

———. *The Archive and the Repertoire: Performing Cultural Memory in the Americas*. Durham, NC: Duke University Press, 2003.

———. *¡Presente! The Politics of Presence*. Durham, NC: Duke University Press, 2020.

Tejada, Valentín. *Pedro Infante, ídolo popular*. Mexico City: Editorial Tejada, 1958.

Thompson, Tazewell. "The Art of Looking with the Ear." In *Sound and Music for the Theatre: The Art & Technique of Design*, edited by Deena Kaye, James LeBrecht, and Davied Budries, xxvii–xxx. New York: Routledge, 2016.

Torres, Justin. "In Praise of Latin Night at the Queer Club." In *Queer Dance: Meanings & Makings*, edited by Clare Croft, 181–84. Oxford: Oxford University Press, 2017.

Torres, Mauricio. "7 puntos clave de la nueva ley para evaluar a los profesores." *CNN México*, September 6, 2013. Available online at https://expansion.mx/nacional/2013/09/06/7-puntos-clave-de-la-nueva-ley-para-evaluar-a-los-profesores.

Torres, Raúl. "Cortan las manos a seis personas en Tlaquepaque." *El Universal*, October 18, 2016. https://www.eluniversal.com.mx/articulo/estados/2016/10/18/cortan-las-manos-seis-personas-en-tlaquepaque.

Traba, Patxi Beltzaiz. "Lukas Avendaño. Bailando Bruno." *De la utre cote du charco* blog. March 18, 2020. http://delautrecoteducharco.org/2020/03/18/lukas-avendano-bailando-bruno-en-espanol.

Trevi, Gloria. "Todos me miran." *La Trayectoria*, Univision Records, 2006. Spotify, https://open.spotify.com/track/4pmRDyDRRiZ5Pq7hm4WTpb?si=2y6qONsk QHWs33eCRsV8Ow.

Trevino-Rangel, Javier. "Silencing Grievance: Responding to Human Rights Violations in Mexico's War on Drugs." *Journal of Human Rights* 17, no. 4 (2018): 485–501. doi: 10.1080/14754835.2018.1487777.

Turner, Victor. *From Ritual to Theatre: The Human Seriousness of Play*. New York: PAJ Publications, 1982.

Tzuc, Efraín. "CBN lleva un año de retraso en la publicación del registro de personas desaparecidas." *A dónde van los desaparecidos*, May 1, 2020. https://adondevanlosdesaparecidos.org/2020/04/30/cnb-lleva-un-ano-de-retraso-en-la-publicacion-del-registro-de-personas-desaparecidas.

———. "Presentan plataforma de personas desaparecidas pero no abren datos." *Revista Proceso*, July 13, 2020. https://www.proceso.com.mx/nacional/2020/7/13/presentan-plataforma-de-personas-desaparecidas-pero-no-abren-datos-246102.html.

United States State Department. *Country Reports on Human Rights Practices: Mexico*. 2019. https://www.state.gov/reports/2019-country-reports-on-human-rights-practices/mexico.

———. *Mexico 2017 Human Rights Report*. 2017. https://www.state.gov/reports/2017-country-reports-on-human-rights-practices/mexico.

———. *Mexico 2018 Human Rights Report*. 2018. https://www.state.gov/reports/2018-country-reports-on-human-rights-practices/mexico.

———. *Mexico 2019 Human Rights Report*. 2019. https://www.state.gov/reports/2019-country-reports-on-human-rights-practices/mexico.

———. *Trafficking in Persons Report*. 2018. https://www.state.gov/reports/2018-trafficking-in-persons-report.

Urbiola Solís, Alejandra Elizabeth, et al. "Expresión y trabajo de los Muxe' del Istmo de Tehuantepec, en Juchitán de Zaragoza, México." *Nova Scientia* 9, no. 19 (2017): 502–27.

Valdez, Daniela. "Lukas Avendaño: Interview" *Revista 192*, June 18, 2020. https://revista192.com/lukas-avendan%CC%83o.

Valencia, Sayak. *Gore Capitalism*. South Pasadena, CA: Semiotext(e), 2018.

Vargas, Deborah R. "Rita's Pants: The *charro traje* and Trans-Sensuality." *Women and Performance: A Journal of Feminist Theory* 20, no. 1 (2010): 3–14.

Vargas, Rosa Elvira. "Hija de Peña Nieto causa ira en Twitter al renviar mensaje que insulta a críticos." *La Jornada*, December 6, 2011. https://www.jornada.com.mx/2011/12/06/politica/013n1pol.

Vasconcelos, José. *La raza cósmica*. Mexico: Espasa-Calpe Mexicana, 1966.

Vásquez, Alexandra T. *Listening in Detail: Performances of Cuban Music*. Durham, NC: Duke University Press, 2013.

Vásquez Moyers, Alonso, and Germán Espino Sánchez. "La producción discursive en la Guerra contra el narcotráfico en el sexenio de Calderón: En busca de la legitimidad." *Discurso y Sociedad* 9, no. 4 (2015): 492–518.

Vaughn, Bobby. "México Negro: From the Shadows of Nationalist Mestizaje to New Possibilities in Afro-Mexican Identity." *Journal of Pan African Studies* 6, no. 1 (2016): 227–40.

Velasco García, Jorge. *El Sonido de la resistencia: Patrimonio musical. El canto popular en los movimientos sociales del siglo XXI en México.* Mexico City: FONCA, 2017.

Vicente, Sandra. "Quiero pensar que con el arte puedo convertir la impotentica de la desaparición de mi hermano en algo alegre." Interview with Lukas Avendaño. *Catalunya Plural*, June 26, 2018. https://catalunyaplural.cat/es/quiero-pensar-que-con-el-arte-puedo-convertir-la-impotencia-de-la-desaparicion-de-mi-hermano-en-algo-alegre.

"Vicente Fernández rechazó un trasplante de hígado por si el donante era 'homosexual o drogadicto." *El país*, May 10, 2019. https://elpais.com/elpais/2019/05/10/gente/1557475198_989117.html.

Viera, Mariana. "Reggaeton's Leading Ladies Combat Exclusion with Unfiltered Sexual Expression." *Vibe*, October 26, 2018. https://www.vibe.com/features/viva/reggaeton-women-sexual-liberation-612019.

Villela, Pilar. "Violencia y escritura. Algunas notas sobre la obra de Enrique Ježik" Exposition text for "Práctica (200 cartuchos calibre 12, 78 balas 9mm)," Centro Cultural Tlatelolco, Mexico City, Mexico, 2009. http://enriquejezik.com/anterior/sitejezik/textos/PV-violencia_txt.htm.

Vinson, Ben, III. "La historia del estudio de los negros en México." In *Afroméxico: El pulso de la población negra en México: Una historia recordada, olvidada y vuelta a recordar*, edited by Ben Vinson III and Bobby Vaughn, 13–48. Mexico City: Fondo de Cultura Económica, 2004.

———. *Before mestizaje: The Frontiers of Race and Caste in Colonial Mexico.* Cambridge: Cambridge University Press, 2018.

Vrana, Heather. "An 'Other' Woman?: Juchitec Muxes in Marie Claire and Documentary." *Michigan Feminist Studies* 21 (Fall 2008): 1–23.

Washington Valdéz, Diana. *The Killing Fields: Harvest of Women*. Atlanta: Peace at the Border, 2006.

Weltman-Cisneros, Talia. "Cimarronaje Cultural: Towards a Counter-Cartography of Blackness and Belonging in Mexico." *Journal of Pan African Studies* 6 no. 1 (2013): 125–39.

Weltman-Cisneros, Talia, and Candelaria Donají Méndez Tello. "Negros-Afromexicanos: Recognition and the Politics of Identity in Contemporary Mexico." *Journal of Pan African Studies* 6, no. 1 (2013): 140–56.

Werth, Brenda. *Theatre, Performance, and Memory Politics in Argentina.* New York: Palgrave Macmillan, 2010.

Williams, Tamara. "Wounded Nation, Voided State: Sara Uribe's *Antígona González*." *Romance Notes* 57, no. 1 (2017): 3–14.

Wolfette, Black. "Ex-Templo de Santa Teresa la Antigua." *Loquaris: Diálogos con México*, March 11, 2009. https://web.archive.org/web/20090619101430/http://

dialogos.pideundeseo.org/inmuebles-notables/extemplo-santa-teresa-la-antigua#more-462.

Wright, Melissa W. *Disposable Women and Other Myths of Global Capitalism.* New York: Routledge, 2006.

———. "Gender and Geography II: Bridging the Gap—Feminist, Queer, and the Geographical Imaginary." *Progress in Human Geography* 34, no. 1 (2010): 56–66.

———. "Necropolitics, Narcopolitics, and Femicide: Gendered Violence on the Mexico-U.S. Border." *Signs: Journal of Women in Culture and Society* 36, no. 3 (2011): 707–31.

———. "Epistemological Ignorances and Fighting for the Disappeared: Lessons from Mexico." *Antipode* 49, no. 1 (2017): 249–69. https://doi.org/10.1111/anti.12244.

———. "Against the Evils of Democracy: Fighting Forced Disappearance and Neoliberal Terror in Mexico." *Annals of the American Association of Geographers* 108, no. 2 (2018): 327–36.

———. "Visualizing a Country without a Future: Posters for Ayotzinapa, Mexico and Struggles against State Terror." *Geoforum* 102 (2019): 235–41.

Yeguas del Apocalipsis. *Las dos Fridas.* Performance. Santiago, Chile,1989.

———. "1989/Las dos Fridas." 2018. http://www.yeguasdelapocalipsis.cl/1989-las-dos-fridas.

Young, James E. *The Texture of Memory: Holocaust Memorials and Meaning.* New Haven: Yale University Press, 1993.

Zani, Alejandra M. "La madre del reggaetón lésbica aterriza en Madrid: 'Todo supermacho guarda adentro una loba.'" *El Mundo*, April 29, 2018. www.elmundo.es/cultura/musica/2018/04/29/5ae2f3b746163fee1d8b4609.html.

Zavala, Oswaldo. "Imagining the U.S.-Mexico Drug War: The Critical Limits of Narconarratives." *Comparative Literature* 66, no. 3 (2014): 340–60.

———. *Los cárteles no existen: Narcotráfico y cultura en México.* Mexico City: Malpaso, 2018.

Žižek, Slavoj. *Violence: Six Sideways Reflections.* New York: Picador, 2008.

Zuazo, Eñaut. "Vicente Fernández había rechazado un trasplante por si el donante era 'homosexual o drogadicto.'" *La Vanguardia*, December 13, 2021. https://www.lavanguardia.com/gente/20211213/7924754/cantante-vicente-fernandez-habia-rechazado-trasplante-donante-homosexual-drogadicto-mmn.html.

Index

Page numbers in *italic* refer to illustrations.

Abarca Velázquez, José Luis, 99
activism
   disappeared persons and, 105
   environmental, 119–20
   hashtag, 8, 188
   teatro-cabaret and, 24
   See also feminism; protests; resistance
Acuña, Aldo, 145
Adorno, Theodor, 220n43
affect, 4, 6, 13, 87, 114, 116–18, 133
Afro-Cuban musicians, 50, 55–56
Afro-Mexicans, 17, 46–57, 178
afterlife, 9, 142, 172–74, 180, 186
Agamben, Giorgio, 60, 62, 69
Ahmed, Sara, 197n17
Alacranes Musical, 78, 212n77
Alcázar, Josefina, 10, 195n24
Alemán, Miguel, 84
alienation, 62, 85, 87
Alzate, Gastón, 23, 199n36, 199n43
Amezcua Castillo, Jesús, 37
AMLO. *See* López Obrador, Andrés Manuel
Angelitos negros (Black Angels, 1948), 16, 26, 46–57, *51*, 205n125
Ángel Mancera, Miguel, 84
Antigone figure, 10, 100–103, 107–10, 113–17, 124–26, 134, 192
antiriot police, 67–69

Aparicio, Yalitza, 238n142
Aragón Pérez, Ramiro, 224n116
Araújo, Samuel, 7, 207n25
Arce, Christine, 52, 56
archetypes, 21–22, 27, 55, 145, 159
archival memory, 65, 165–68
Argentina
   Dirty War, 64–65, 208n33
   Ni una menos (NUM; Not one woman less) movement, 148–49
Artaud, Antonin, 211n57
arte acción (performance), 10
Attali, Jacques, 68
audience
   collective resistance and, 184–85
   distance between performer and, 106–7
   fear experienced by, 67–69
   sonic ethereal realm and, 114–15
   See also communitas de dolor
Avendaño, Lukas, 81, *122*, 192, 223n99
   Buscando a Bruno (Searching for Bruno, 2018), 10, 95–96, 100–103, *127*, *129*, 223n107
   career, 117–18
   Lukas y José (Lukas and José, 2017), 128
   No soy Hombre, soy Mariposa (I Am Not a Man, I Am a Butterfly, 2014), 118

Avendaño, Lukas (*continued*)
　Réquiem para un alcaraván (Requiem for a Stone-Curlew, 2012), 118, 128, 130
　Utopía de la mariposa (The Butterfly's Utopia, 2019), 118
Avendaño Martínez, Bruno Alonso, 95–96, 118
Avila, Jacqueline, 17, 38, 42, 83
Ayotzinapa 43 (disappeared students), 2, 10, 99–100, 110, 218n24, 219n25

Back, Les, 192
Bad Bunny, 149
Bailey, Tara, 102, 110
Banda Femenil Regional "Mujeres del Viento Florido," 131
banda music, 78, 212n78
Banda Princesa Donahí, 130, 228n166
Barber, Sara, 131
battle soundscapes, 63, 167. *See also* gunfire sounds; ricochet noises
Baudrillard, Jean, 96
Beardsell, Peter, 211n60
Beckett, Samuel, *All That Fall*, 9
Becky G, 149
Bejarano, Cynthia, 139
belliphonic, 216n146
belonging, 17, 20, 22, 170, 174, 182
　national, 38
　race and, 46, 169–72, 177
　tehuana clothing and, 125
Bennett, Herman, 48, 56, 178
Bennholdt-Thomsen, Veronika, 121
Bernardo, Romina, 148. *See also* Chocolate Remix
Betancourt, Óscar, 91
biopower, 62
Black Asteroid (Bryan Black), 91–92
blackface, 47–50, 55–57, 204n111
blackness, 178
　black aesthetics, 195n23
　See also Afro-Cuban musicians; Afro-Mexicans; race

Blanco, Andrés Eloy, "Píntame angelitos negros," 53
Blanco, Ayala, 201n57
Boliver, Rocío (La Congelada de Uva), 65
Bonasinga, Kate, 208n33
Bonfil, Carlos, 27, 200n48, 201n49
border crossings, 33, 70, 72, 179–80, 215n122
Brecht, Bertolt, 85, 87, 168
Brooks, Peter, 196n4
Brown, Ross, 9, 65
Bruin-Mollenhorst, Janieke, 116, 132
Bull, Michael, 201n55
Burgos Dávila, César Jesús, 79
burlesque, 143–44, 148
Buscando a Bruno (Searching for Bruno, 2018), 10, 95–96, 100–103, *127*, *129*, 223n107
Butler, Judith, 98, 100, 126, 237n133

cabaret theater
　European styles of, 21–23
　See also teatro-cabaret
Cacho, Lydia, 170–71
cacophony, 2, 5, 91
Calderón, Felipe
　presidency and War on Drugs, 1–3, 60–63, 65, 68–70, 72, 94, 96, 119, 141 (*see also* War on Drugs)
　rhetoric of collateral damage, 74–76
"Canción sin miedo" (song), 187–91
Canclini, García, 46
capos, 2, 59, 76
Carey, Mariah, 179
Caribbean region, 50. *See also* Cuba
Cartas Orozco, Edgar, 129–33
cartels
　government efforts against (*see* War on Drugs)
　in Oaxaca, 120, 224n120
　violence of, 2–3, 59–60, 75–81, 191
　See also narco violence

Casas, Francisco, 128
catharsis, 6, 68, 94, 107
Celaya, Jorge, 71
Centro Cultural Helénico, 169
Centro Nacional de las Artes (CENART), 59
Centro Universitario de Teatro (CUT), 82, 103
Chabaud, Jaime, 71
charro (cowboy) masculinity, 38–46, 83–84
Chávez, Xóchitl C., 131
Chiapas, 238n142
Chicago Latino Theatre Alliance, 170
Chile, 128
china poblana, 83
Chion, Michel, 216n127
Chocolate Remix, "Ni una menos," 144, 148–52, 186, 190
"Cielito lindo" (song), 42–43
cinema. *See* Golden Age cinema
circuses, 21, 236n112
Ciudad Juárez, Mexico, 34, 64, 139–40, 229n6
clandestine graves. *See* mass graves
class
    race and, 48
    See also elites; lower class; middle class; poverty
Cloonan, Martin, 68, 90, 207n25
Cohen, Theodore, 48
Coleman, Jeffrey, 208n27
collateral damage, 73–76, 98–99, 134
collective action, 168
colonialism, 65, 121
Colosio, Luis Donaldo, 86–89, 214n119, 215n124
comedia ranchera. See *ranchera* genre
Comisión Mexicana en Defensa y Promoción de los Derechos Humanos (CMDPDH), 60

Comisión Nacional de Búsqueda (CNB; National Search Commission), 96–97
Comisión Nacional de los Derechos Humanos (CNDH; National Human Rights Commission), 97, 108
Comisión Nacional para Prevenir y Erradicar la Violencia contra las Mujeres (Conavim; National Commision for the Prevention and Erradication of Violence Against Women), 140
commedia dell'arte, 168
commemoration, 105–7, 127, 132. *See also* funeral rites; memory
communitas de dolor (communities of pain and loss), 6, 100, 102, 107–9, 112, 116, 127, 132, 219n29
confusion, 67, 69, 73, 93
Connerton, Paul, 102
Consejo Nacional de Fomento Educativo (CONAFE; National Council on Educational Development), 117
convivio, 6, 191, 194n11, 241n13
Conway, Christopher, 83
Correa, Fabio, 162
corrido genre, 2, 78–81, 157–60, 212n78
corruption
    disappeared persons and, 97
    police, 72, 84–85, 108, 191
    political, 2, 23, 48, 51, 82, 184, 237n120
    resistance against, 120
    violence and, 82
    War on Drugs and, 4, 62
Cortázar, Julio, 72
Cosentino, Olivia, 162–63
Covarrubias, Miguel, 121, 228n163
COVID-19 pandemic, 25, 231n28, 233n59

Coyoacán, Mexico, 15–16
cruelty
  misogynist, 156
  pedagogy of, 140
  resistance against, 142
  theater of, 211n57
cruising, 173–74
Cruz, Celia, 9, 179, 184
Cuba, 50, 55–56, 177–78
cubanidad, 56, 178
cuerno de chivo, 2
Curruchich, Sara, 187
Cusik, Suzanne G., 7, 91

Daddy Yankee, 149
dark tourism, 82–85, 214n106
Daughtry, J. Martin, 7, 63, 68, 91–92, 207n25, 216n146
Davies, Douglas, 102
de Aguilar y Seixas, Don Francisco, 65
death. *See* disappeared and missing persons; feminicide; homicide rates; mass graves; trans feminicide
defiance, 107–8, 126
  of gendered violence, 142
  music and, 132–33
  muxe identity and, 123, 125
  See also Antigone figure
dehumanization, 52, 98, 143, 146–48, 179–80
de la Madrid, Miguel, 23
de la Mora, Sergio, 47
del Carmen Salgado López, Melanie, 61
Delgadillo, Theresa, 47, 53, 205n125
de los Ángeles Pineda Villa, María, 99
Del Riego, Hernán, 153–54, 233n60
"Somos más" (song), 166–68, 186, 235n107
del Rosario Moreno, Iani, 72, 211n62
DeNora, Tia, 115, 194n6
derealized bodies
  of disappeared and missing persons,

98–99, 103, 107–8, 124, 131, 134–35
  female, 144, 148
  See also erasure
Desierto de Las Leonas, El (The Desert of the Lionesses, 2017), 138, 141–42, 152–68, *158*, *162*, *169*, 186
Diawara, Manthia, 19
Diéguez, Ileana, 63, 86, 100, 102, *127*, 193n3, 219n29, 235n101
digital political economy, 8
disappeared and missing persons, 10, 95, 142, 169, 191
  absence of bodies, 101–3, 106
  in Argentina's Dirty War, 64–65, 208n33
  closure and, 107, 134
  female, 99–100, 140
  male, 99–100
  numbers of, 34, 96–97
  remembering, 192
  sonic representations of, 102–3
  state attempts to derealize, 98–99, 103, 107–8, 124, 131
  War on Drugs and, 2, 23
  See also Ayotzinapa 43; mass graves
discrimination, 17, 51–52, 117, 170, 219n25, 238n142
disidentification, 20. *See also* sonic disidentification
dismemberment, 2, 34, 82, 85–86, 106, 110, 140–41, 150, 230n6
displaced persons, 2, 60, 206n5
dissonance, 2, 5, 72, 90–93
divas, pop culture, 174–75, 179, 183
DNA of performance, 161–62
documentary theater, 8, 210n57
Dolar, Mladen, 43, 60, 87, 92, 212n74, 214n112
"Dolor profundo" (song), 132–33
dos Fridas, Las (Two Fridas), 128
drag
  female-to-male, 28, 38–39, 155, 202n75

male-to-female, 163, 169, 174, 182, 237n133
  racial, 49–50
drug trade
  music industry and, 78
  See also cartels; *narco* violence; War on Drugs
Duarte, Javier, 237n120
Dubatti, Jorge, 6, 191, 194n11, 241n13
"Duerme Duerme Negrito" (song), 53–55

education reforms, 32
Eguiarte, Naoli, 70, 73, 76–77, 80
Eisenstein, Sergei, 121
Ejercicio de percusión (Percussion Exercise, 2006), 7–8, 63–69, 74, 89, 93–94
elections, presidential, 1, 25, 31, 119, 193n2
Elena Rodríguez, José Antonio, 215n122
El Faro Oriente (neighborhood in Mexico City), 15
El Foro Teatro Contemporáneo, 168
El Hábito (performance space), 15, 24, 199n36
elites, 32, 46
El Palomar, 187, 189
Elsaesser, Thomas, 17
El Salvador, 111
El Vez (performer), 237n133
El Vicio (performance space), 15, 24, 153, 169
Emerson, R. Guy, 86, 90
Encinas, Alejandro, 98
energy reform, 26, 31
Enríquez, César, 168–69, 192
  La Prietty Guoman (The Prietty Woman, 2017), 9, 53, 138, 142, 168–86, *175*, *181*, *185*, 236n119, 237n120, 237n133, 238n135, 238n139
enslavement. *See* slavery
environmental activists, 119–20

ephemerality
  of performance, 5–6, 65
  of rituals, 134
erasure, 107, 169–70, 180–81. *See also* derealized bodies
eroticism, 143, 154
escenofonía, 6, 194n12
Eschen, Nicole, 237n133
Espino Sánchez, Germán, 61
Estefan, Gloria, 181
Estela, Blanca, 27
ethnomusicology, 5, 7, 207n25
exclusion, 7, 9, 20, 40, 49
exploitation, 34–37, 40–41
Ex Teresa Arte Actual (performance space), 65–69

Fast, Susan, 207n25
fear, 62, 73
  experienced by audiences, 67–69
  freedom from, 164
  in Oaxaca, 224n120
  power and, 64
  sound and, 6, 67–69, 83–85, 88
  See also terror
Federal Police, 108, 191
Felipe, Liliana, 15, 22, 24, 199n36, 202n60
Félix, María, 157
female sexuality, 143, 154, 163
femicide, use of term, 138–39, 193n4
feminicide, 2, 34, 72, 82
  in Ciudad Juárez, 34, 139–40, 229n6
  derealized female bodies and, 144, 148
  mourning for victims of, 104–5 (*see also* mourning)
  performances as resistance against, 138–86, 192
  rates of, 9, 24, 137–38, 140–41, 151–52, 184, 187, 234n87
  records of, 180–81
  use of term, 138–39, 193n4
  See also transfeminicide

feminism, 25, 142, 150
    popular music and, 187–90
    revolutionary tactics, 156–68
    See also activism; protests; resistance
Fernández, Alejandro, 44, 203n96
Fernández, Vicente, 42, 44–45, 203n91
Fernández Poncela, Anna, 158
Ferrer, Vincent, 120
Festival of Latin American Contemporary Choreographers (FLAC), 105
Figueroa Hernández, Rafael, 55
film studies, 7
Fiscalía General de la República (FGR; Mexico's Office of the Attorney General), 118, 125
Fiscalía General del Estado de Oaxaca (Oaxaca's District Attorney's Office), 118
Fondo de Ayudas para las Artes Escénicas Iberoamericanas, 25
Fondo Nacional para la Cultura y las Artes (FONCA), 24, 82
forced disappearances. See disappeared and missing persons
Foro A Poco No (performance space), 153
Foucault, Michel, 62
Fox, Vicente, 60
Freeman, Elizabeth, 40
Fregoso, Rosa-Linda, 139
French cabaret, 22–23
Fresh Festival, 105
Friedberg, Anne, 197n16
Frith, Simon, 84, 175
Fuentes, Marcela A., 8
funeral rites
    music in, 112
    Oaxacan *música fúnebre*, 9–10, 124, 131–34
    symbolic, 101–3, 107, 112, 116, 124, 133–34
futurity, 142–43, 156, 173. See also utopia

Galindo, Gabriela, 208n34
Gambaro, Griselda, 100
García Canclini, Néstor, 18, 64
Garcia-Orozco, Antonia, 42
Gasé, Marisol, 24–25, 57, 199n39
Gatz (elevator repair service), 9
gendered violence, 100, 190–91
    as genocide, 139–40
    government narratives on, 8–9
    rates of, 234n87
    research on, 138
    statistics on, 141, 187
    See also feminicide; street harassment; trans feminicide
gender fluidity and nonconformity, 83, 124–25, 142–43, 163–64. See also drag; LGBTQ+ people; *muxe* identity
genre, 10
geographies
    audible, 191–92
    exclusionary, 9
    imagined, 11
    songs and, 30
    See also radical geographies of hope and survival
Gerez Levy, Paola, 214n104
German Kabarett, 23
Golden Age cinema (Mexico, 1930–1960), 11, 177, 184, 236n112
    critiques of idealized *mexicanidad* in, 16–20, 25–57
    gender roles in, 17–20 (*see also* heteronormativity)
    genres of, 22
    popularity of, 18
    sonic tropes, 16–18
Gómez, Amaranta, 122–23
Gómez Peña, Guillermo, 82, 118
González, Anita, 178
Goodman, Steve, 7, 91, 207n25
Gordillo, Elba Esther, 26

grief, 126–27
  music and, 132–33
  sonic registers of, 114–17
  women's public, 100–101
  See also mourning
"Grito," 1–2, 189
grounded terrain, 115–16, 222n93
Guadalupe Posadas, José, 110
Guerrero, 178, 238n142
gunfire sounds, 59, 63, 65, 68–70, 73, 76, 80–81, 94, 208n34, 212n77
Gutiérrez, Laura, 21, 49
Guzmán, Margarito M., 228n166

Hadad, Astrid, 15, 22, 202n60
Halberstam, Jack, 38, 202n75
harmony, 5, 167
hashtag activism, 8, 188
Heath, Charles, 131
Hemispheric Institute of Politics and Performance, 105
Hemispheric Institute of Politics and Performance Encuentro, 82, 104–5, 124, 143, 170, 228n165
Herlinghaus, Hermann, 79
Hernández, Paola S., 8, 10, 70, 74, *75*, 76–77, *77*, 80, *81*
Herrera-Sobek, María, 158–59
Herschfield, Joanna, 47
Hesterberg, Annegret, 228n163
heteronormativity, 160, 197n17
  masculinity and, 83
  melodramatic family unit, 26–37
  mexicanidad and, 17–20, 22, 25–26, 29–30, 34, 38, 41–46, 57
Hidalgo y Costilla, Miguel, 1, 189
hip-hop, 149
history, 7, 11, 21–24, 46, 94, 141–42, 156, 236n112
Home-Cook, George, 9, 132
homicide rates, 9, 34, 60, 98, 206n5. See also disappeared and missing persons; feminicide; trans feminicide
homoerotic desire, 41. See also queerness
homophobia, 17, 43–44, 57, 138. See also LGBTQ+ people, persecution of
hooks, bell, 19
hope. See radical geographies of hope and survival
Houston, Whitney, 179, 183, *185*, 186
Huerta, Nora, 24–25, 57, 153, 199n39, 199n41
Hughes, Jenny, 8
Hugo, Victor, 188
human geography, 3. See also geographies
human rights, 28, 97, 99, 119–20, 156, 224n116
human rights studies, 8
human trafficking, 2, 236n116. See also sex trafficking

Ibarra, Xandra, 65
"I Have Nothing" (song), 183, *185*
imagination, 4, 11, 21, 101, 171–80, 219n24
immersive sound, 66–69, 146
immigrants, 33, 70–71, 79, 103, 111–12, 117, 149, 191, 223n99. See also border crossings
impunity, 97, 99, 113, 116, 120, 140, 180, 187
inclusion, 20, 47, 57, 182
Independence movement, 1–2, 189
Indigenous people
  conquest of, 65
  cultural practices, 117–18
  discrimination against, 219n25, 238n142
  female musicians, 131
  gender and sexual practice, 120–21
  mestiza identity and, 228n161

Indigenous people (*continued*)
  queer Indigenous artists, 118
  skin color and, 176–78
  violence towards, 119–20
  See also muxe identity; race; Zapotec communities
industrial techno music, 90–93
inequalities, 16, 49, 51. *See also* discrimination; poverty
Infante, Pedro, 17, 26–30, 34, 37–38, 42–45, 47–48, 53, 83, 155, 201n57
Infante Quintanilla, José Ernesto, 200n48
Instituto Nacional de Mujeres (Inmujeres; National Institute of Women), 140
instruments, 112–13, 115–16
Inter-American Commission on Human Rights (IACHR), 97
International Cabaret Festival, 15, 24, 143, 169, 199n43
International Tribunal on Crimes against Women, 138
International Women's Day, 170
intersectionality, 120
intonation, 32, 214n112
Iraq, US war in, 7, 63, 68, 76, 216
"Isla Bonita, La" (song), 179
Islas, Alejandra, 122
Istmo de Tehuantepec, 120–23, 130, 132, 226n139
Ivy Queen, 149
"I Will Survive" (song), 9, 184–86
Izquierdo, Paola, 152

Jamaican dancehall, 149
Ježik, Enrique, 192, 208n32
  Ejercicio de percusión (Percussion Exercise, 2006), 7–8, 63–69, 74, 89, 93–94
  La Fiesta de las Balas (The Party of Bullets, 2011), 208n34
  Práctica (Practice, 2007), 65

Valla (Fence, 2007), 65
Johnson, Bruce, 68, 90, 207n25
Juana Gallo (1961), 157
Juana Gallo (mythical figure, character), 153–67, *158*, *169*
"Juana Gallo" (song), 157–61
Juárez Frías, Ernesto, 159
Juchirap, 224n120
Juchitán, 120, 224n120, 226n139

Kahlo, Frida, 128, 227n160, 228n161
Karol G, 149
Kendrick, Lynn, 9
Kheshti, Roshanak, 9, 195n23
kidnapping, 84–85, 179–80
Kirby, Michael, 201n51
knowledge hierarchies, 4, 9
Kristeva, Julia, 101, 107–8

LaBelle, Brandon, 209n43
La Candelaria, 101
La Capilla (performance space), 169
La Casa del Humor, 25
Laferte, Mon, 187, 189
La Fura del Baus, 82
Lagarde y de Los Ríos, Marcela, 138–39, 193n4
Lagartijas Tiradas al Sol, 10
La Mafia Cabaret, 3, 59, 152, 192
  El Desierto de Las Leonas (The Desert of the Lionesses, 2017), 138, 141–42, 152–68, *158*, *162*, *169*, 186
laments, 102, 113, 116–17, 132–33
Lamy, Michèle, 92–93, 216n143
La Pocha Nostra, 65, 81, 103, 118
Lark Fellowship, 170
Las Hijas de Violencia, 10
Las Intrépidas, Buscadores de Peligro, 122, 225–26n132
Las Madres de la Plaza de Mayo, 100
Las Pussy Queers, 192, 231n28, 233n59
  Ni una menos (Not One Woman Less, 2019), 9, 138, 141–52, 168, 186

Las Reinas Chulas, 5–6, 24–25, 49,
    152–53, 192, 199n36, 235n111
  El derecho de dudar (The Right to
    Doubt, 2006), 49
  Está de moda ser negro (It's
    Fashionable to be Black, 2009), 49
  Marty, Luty, Kin: I Have a Drink
    (2013), 49
  Nosotras las proles (We, the Plebs,
    2013), 15–20, 23–57, *28*, *37*, *46*,
    51, 84
  Petroleo en la sangre (Petroleum in
    the Blood, 2008), 26, 49
Las Yeguas del Apocalipsis, *Las dos
    Fridas*, 128
Lawrence, Sidra, 215n126
Lechedevirgen Trimegisto, 81–82, 118, 192
  Infierno Varieté, 212n96
  México exhumado (Mexico
    Exhumed, 2019), 8, 63–64, 81–93,
    86, *89*, *93*, 105
Lehmann, Hans-Thies, 210n57
Lemebel, Pedro, 128
Leñero Franco, Estela, 71–72
León Rodríguez, Luis Ángel, 105, 108,
    124
Ley General (2018), 96–97, 125, 221n67
LGBTQ+ people
  lesbians and bisexual women, 19, 25,
    150, 164, 182
  persecution of, 2, 17, 34, 44, 57, 128,
    171, 184 (*see also* trans feminicide)
  resistance and activism, 174, 182–83,
    235n111
  See also gender fluidity and
    nonconformity; homoerotic
    desire; queerness
"Like a Virgin" (song), 179
Lima, Irakere, 143, 145, 148, 152–54,
    231n28, 233n59
liminality, 89, 101, 125, 134
listening practices
  "art of listening," 192

  engaged, 5–6, 103
  mobile, 201n55
  of women in public spaces, 146
lo mexicano, 27
López, Ana, 17
López, Valeriano, 132
López Obrador, Andrés Manuel
    (AMLO), 1–3, 8–9, 25–26, 187, 191,
    193n2, 199n43, 235n111
Los Macuano, 10
loss, 62–63, 73, 90
  legitimacy of, 107–8
  mourning and, 101, 106–8
  sonic registers of, 114–15
  See also *communitas de dolor*
Los Tigres del Norte, 78
Los tres García (The Three García,
    1947), 16, 26, 37–46, *46*, 57,
    202n81
lower class, 22, 27, 30–37. See also
    poverty
Luna, Violeta, 103–4, 192, 194n12
  *Réquiem #3: Fosas Cuerpo/Body
    Graves* (2017), 3, 100–117, *109*, *113*,
    115, 124, 134
"Luto por derecho" (song), 132–33
Lypsinka, 237n133
lyrical composition, 4
  in *corridos*, 158
  dehumanization of women in,
    147–48
  in *La Prietty Guoman*, 176–77, 182,
    185
  in *Nosotras la proles*, 28, 44–46, 57
  resistance to gendered violence,
    150–52
  unintelligible, 92

Madonna, 179, *181*, 182, 186
Madrid, Alejandro L., 42, 157, 212n78
Magdalena Project, 103
Mandel, Naomi, 220n43
Mantoan, Lindsey, 8

marginalized populations, 34–37, 40, 169–70. *See also* Indigenous people; LGBTQ+ people
Margules, Ludwik, 168
María y Campos, Armando, 21–22
Marín, Paola, 103
Marshall, Wayne, 149
Martin, Carol, 8, 69, 210n57
Martínez, Ana, 209n41, 241n12
masculinity
  disidentification with, 20, 25–46
  drag performances of, 28, 38–39, 155, 202n75
  in Guadalajara, 44, 203n94
  hegemonic, 123
  heterosexual, 34
  marginalized, 145
  mexicanidad and, 17–20, 25–46, 57
  narco violence and, 78
  race and, 48
  visual representations of, 154–55
  weak, 201n52
  See also heteronormativity
mass graves
  clandestine, 2, 84–85, 97–99, 101, 109, 119, 156
  sonic and material representations of, 109–10, 115–16
matriarchy, 121
Maytorena, Sabrina, 154, 166, 168
Mbembe, Achille, 62–63, 208n27
Melendez, Priscilla, 211n60
melodrama
  characteristics of, 200n48
  disidentification and, 57 (*see also* sonic disidentification)
  excess and, 34–37, 47
  music in, 17, 27
  origin of term, 196n4
  popularity of, 18–19
  See also Golden Age cinema
memory, 105–7, 192
  archival, 65, 165–68

of murdered women, 165–68, 184
  See also commemoration
Mendoza, Vincente T., 42, 158
Merlín, Socorro, 21–22
mestizo identity, 17–20, 26–27, 47–57, 128–29, 177, 228n161
mexicanidad (Mexicanness)
  heteronormativity and, 17–20, 22, 25–26, 29–30, 34, 38, 41–46, 57
  idealized images in Golden Age films, 16–20, 25–57
  masculinity and, 17–20, 25–46, 57
  musical styles and, 2, 38
  postrevolutionary era, 226n139
  race and, 46–53, 178
  whitened mestizo physique and, 17–20, 26–27, 47–57
Mexican Revolution, 21–22, 154–55, 157, 160–61
Mexico
  border with United States, 33, 70, 72, 179–80, 215n122
  economic crises, 22–23
  national anthem, 188, 240nn5–6
  official government narratives, 8–9 (*see also* Calderón, Felipe; López Obrador, Andrés Manuel (AMLO); Peña Nieto, Enrique)
  See also neoliberal politics; state of exception; War on Drugs
Mexico City, 10–11
  cabaret festival in, 15
  city center, 65–66
  street harassment in, 144–48, 232n39
  theater and performance artists in, 64
  Zócalo plaza, 1, 187–91, 209n41, 241n12
México exhumado (Mexico Exhumed, 2019), 8, 63–64, 81–93, *86*, *89*, *93*, 105
Miano Borruso, Marinella, 121
Mictecacíhuatl, 106

Mictlán (Aztec underworld), 110–11, 114
middle class, 22, 201n60
militarization, 3, 23, 59–60
  collateral damage, 73–76, 98–99, 134
  sounds of, 68–69, 74–75, 93–94
  See also gunfire sounds; War on Drugs
mining industry, 120, 225n120
minority subjects, 20, 27. See also marginalized populations
minstrelsy, 49. See also blackface
Misemer, Sarah, 8
misogyny, 138–39, 142, 156. See also feminicide; gendered violence; trans feminicide
missing persons. See disappeared and missing persons
Mixe region, 131
Mixtec (indigenous group), 238n142
Molina, David R., 3, 106, 111–17, 194n12
Monárrez Fragoso, Julia, 139
Monsiváis, Carlos, 27, 29, 200n48, 201n49
Mor, Ana Francis, 18–19, 24–25, 30, 38, 57, 199n39
  Entre Villa y una Mujer Desnuda (Between Villa and a Nude Woman, 2020), 25
  La Testosterona (The Testosterone Woman, 2018), 25
  Lo que soñé mientras dormías (What I Dreamt while You Slept, 2017), 25
Morales Jiménez, Atilano, 132–33
Morena party, 25–26, 235n111
"Morenaza" (song), 144–48, 150–51
Moreno, Lucha, 159–60
Moreno Figueroa, Mónica G., 47
Moreno Rivas, Yolanda, 159
Moten, Fred, 9, 195n23
mothers
  of disappeared persons, 100–101, 105–6, 110, 116–18, 134, 189
  feminist resistance, 161–62
  in Golden Age films, 47–54
  grandmothers, 38–39, 42
  laments of, 116–17
Moulin Rouge, 23
mourning
  Antigone figure and, 10, 100–103, 107–10, 113–17, 124–26, 134, 192
  clothing and, 128–29
  for disappeared persons, 3, 98–135
  for murdered trans women, 183
  "presente" shouts and, 189, 240n7
  reparative acts of, 101, 134
  silence and, 183
  sound and, 129–34
  See also *communitas de dolor*; grief
Movimiento por nuestros desaparecidos en México (Movement for Our Disappeared in Mexico), 108, 221n67
Ms. Nina, 149
MUAC esplanade, 128, 130, 132, 134
Muestra Nacional de Teatro (2017), 170
Mujeres México (NGO), 140
Muñoz, José Esteban, 20, 45, 142, 156, 173, 179, 181–82, 238n135
murders. See disappeared and missing persons; feminicide; homicide rates; trans feminicide
Murray, Sarah, 202n75
Museo el Chopo, 130, 132, 134
music, 4
  communitas de dolor and, 112
  critique through sonic disidentification, 28–31, 38, 53–55, 57
  distorted and amplified, 90–93
  power of, 7
  used in torture, 91, 93
  as voice of silenced female and feminized bodies, 9, 142–44, 148–52, 174–86, 190
  in war zones, 7, 91, 216n146

Música de balas (Music of the Bullets, 2011), 3, 69–81, *75*, *77*, *81*, 89, 94
musical architecture, 6, 194n12
música norteña genre, 2
musicology, 3, 5, 7
mutilation, 3, 59, 140
muxeidad, 123–26, 129
muxe identity, 10, 120–24, 226n136

NAFTA, 119
Nájera-Ramírez, Olga, 83, 160
Nancy, Jean-Luc, 4
narcocorrido genre, 78–81
narcofosa, 2
Narcos: Mexico (2018–), 78
narco-telenovelas, 78
narco violence, 2, 23, 61–62, 104, 191
  against Indigenous and environmental activists, 119–20
  territory wars, 72
  See also cartels; War on Drugs
national anthem, 188, 240nn5–6
National Association of Latino Arts and Cultures (NALAC), 103
National Autonomous University of Mexico (UNAM), 24–25, 130, 152
  Centro Cultural Universitario, 134
  Centro Universitario de Teatro (CUT), 82, 103
nationalism, 29, 38, 75, 226n139
National Theater Company, 25
Natti Natasha, 149
natural resources, 37–46, 120, 225n120. *See also* petroleum industry
necroauralities, 63, 65, 70, 83, 94
necropolitics, 62–63, 84, 90, 98, 104, 191, 208n27
necroteatro, 63, 86
Negrete, Jorge, 83
neocolonialism, 65
neoliberal politics
  disenfranchisement and, 2

gendered violence and, 141
opposition to, 119
wounding tendencies of, 26, 30–31, 37, 40–42, 50, 57
Newbold Chiñas, Beverly, 121
Newton, Esther, 174
Nieves, Yurief, 45
"¡Ni hablar mujer!" (song), 29–31, 36–37
Ni una menos (Argentinian movement), 148–49
Ni una menos (play; Not One Woman Less, 2019), 9, 138, 141–52, 168, 186
"Ni una menos" (song), 144, 148–52, 186, 190
noises, 3, 63, 65–68, 71–72, 74, 82, 90–93, 109–10, 114–16, 134, 191
nonbinary identity, 81, 83
Norget, Kristin, 131, 133
Noriega, Manuel, 91
norteña music, 2, 78, 212nn77–78
Nosotras las proles (We, the Plebs, 2013), 15–20, 23–57, *28*, *37*, *46*, *51*, 84
Nosotros los pobres (We the Poor, 1948), 15–16, 18–19, 26–37, *28*, 39, 48, 57
novísima dramaturgia, 71
Nueva Canción (New Song) movement, 53

Oaxaca, 64–65, 118–20, 125, 178, 238n142
  death-related rituals, 133–34
  música fúnebre (funeral music), 9–10, 124, 131–34
  State Band, 131
Oaxaqueño, 155
Ókin Frioli, Nicola, 122
Olvera Sánchez, Mireya, 131
Operation "Just Cause," 91
oppositional gaze, 19

oppression, 24, 29, 35, 45, 49, 62, 64, 78, 143, 156
Orbison, Roy, "Oh, Pretty Woman," 171–73, 176–77
Ordorika Imaz, Amaya, 60, 206n5
Orozco, Regina, 49
Osornio, Felipe. *See* Lechedevirgen Trimegisto
Otherness, 7, 9
   disidentification and, 20
   erasure and, 180–81
   female, 121
   queer, 57, 143
   racial, 47, 55, 57, 178
   tropicalized, 50
Owens, Rick, 216n143

Pacini Hernandez, Deborah, 149
pain, 62
   mourning and, 101, 106
   music and, 132–33
   weaponized sound and, 90–93
   See also *communitas de dolor*; mourning
Panama, 149
Papalotl, Liliana, 152–56, 160, 233n59. See also La Mafia Cabaret
"Para siempre" (song), 42–44
Paredes, Américo, 158
Patán, Julio, 214n106, 215n119
patriarchal state
   failures of, 34–37, 48
   power and, 124–25
   resistance against, 25–26, 30, 43–45, 187 (*see also* protests; resistance)
patriarchy, acoustic, 145, 231n39
Paz, Octavio, 27
Pegley, Kip, 207n25
Peña Nieto, Enrique
   presidency, 2, 26, 31–32, 46
   "prole" comment and, 16, 26, 201n60
   War on Drugs and, 60, 96, 98–99

performance
   as art of the self, 10
   in the present, 194n9
   See also theater and performance
performative gesture, trace of, 5
Perleau-Ponty, Maurice, 86
petroleum industry, 26, 41, 46
Phelan, Peggy, 5, 194n9
photographs, 65
Pieslak, Jonathan, 91–92
Pinochet, Augusto, 128
Polaco, Larissa, 143, 145, 148, 231n28
police corruption, 72, 84–85, 108, 191
Popular Assembly of the Peoples of Oaxaca (APPO), 119, 224n116
Pornoterrorista, Diana, 82
postdramatic productions, 8, 10, 210n57
poverty, 2, 32–37
power
   biopower, 62
   fear and, 64
   of music, 7
   political, 124–25
   of sound, 4
   urban, 145
precarity, 98
Pretty Woman (1990), 170–73, 175–79
PRI, 31–32, 40, 45
Prieto Stambaugh, Antonio, 105, 120, 126
Prietty Guoman, La (The Prietty Woman, 2017), 9, 53, 138, 142, 168–86, *175, 181, 185*, 236n119, 237n120, 237n133, 238n135, 238n139
Procuraduría General de la República (PGR; Office of the Attorney General), 108
prostitution, 169–76, 179–80, 183. See *also* sex trafficking
protests, 10, 99, 119, 149, 187–90, 218n24, 240n11. *See also* activism; feminism; resistance

public spaces
  performances in, 130, 132, 134
  women in, 100–101, 124–25, 139–40, 144–48
  See also street harassment
Puerto Rico, 149
Pulido Llano, Gabriela, 56
Pulse massacre (Orlando, 2016), 171, 184

queer Indigenous artists, 118
queerness, 83
  futurity and, 142–43, 173
  imagined queer utopias, 120, 173, 181, 183
  as Other, 57, 143
  resistance and, 174
  See also LGBTQ+ people
queer studies, 3
Quetzalcoatl, 106
Quintana, Vivir, "Canción sin miedo" (song), 187–91

race
  belonging and, 169–72, 177
  class and, 48
  female bodies and, 142, 177
  in Golden Age cinema, 46–57, 177
  masculinity and, 48
  mexicanidad (Mexicanness) and, 46–53, 178
  protest songs and, 53–55
  racial discrimination, 17, 51–52, 117, 238n142
  See also Afro-Cuban musicians; Afro-Mexicans; blackface; blackness; Indigenous people; mestizo identity
Radford, Jill, 138
radical geographies of hope and survival, 142–43
  in *El Desierto de Las Leonas* (The Desert of the Lionesses, 2017), 138, 141–42, 152–68

in *La Prietty Guoman* (The Prietty Woman, 2017), 9, 138, 142, 168–86
  in *Ni una menos* (Not One Woman Less, 2019), 138, 141–52
ranchera genre, 2, 22, 37–46, 159, 188–89
Rasmussen, Anthony W., 145, 231n39
raza cósmica, La (The Cosmic Race,1925), 177
reggaetón, 148–50
Registro Nacional de Personas Desaparecidas y No Localizadas (RNPED; National Registry for Disappeared and Missing Persons), 96
Reguillo, Rossana, 61, 69, 96, 132, 218n24
Reina del Sur, La (The Queen of the South, 2011), 78
repertoire, 65
Réquiem #3: Fosas Cuerpo / Body Graves (2017), 3, 100–117, *109, 113, 115,* 124, 134
resistance, 4–6
  cabaret and, 24
  against feminicide and gendered violence, 136–82, 192
  growth of, 64–65
  Istmo and, 123
  nonverbal sonic acts of, 107–11
  against patriarchal heteronormativity, 25–26, 30, 43–45, 187
  queer, 174
  sonic disidentification and, 56 (*see also* sonic disidentification)
  sovereignty and, 188
  vocal performance and, 189–90
  See also activism; Antigone figure; feminism; protests
reverberations, sonic, 3–4, 20, 45, 144, 192
  activism and, 167–68, 185–86, 189–90

community and, 114, 116, 130
street harassment and, 146
war and violence, 63, 66, 68, 89, 91–94
revolution, 154–55, 157, 160–61, 164
Reyes, Lucha, 159–60, 234n81. See also *voz bravía*
Reyes, Pako, 59, 152–55, 233n59, 235n107
Reyes, Pedro, 10
ricochet noises, 65, 68
Ridout, Nicholas, 113–14
Ríos, Juan Gabriel, 224n116
ritual, 107. See also funeral rites
Rivera, Diego, 121, 128
Rivera, Raquel Z., 149
Rivera Garza, Cristina, 194n5, 219n29
Roberts, Julia, 171–72, 175–76, 178–79
rock en español genre, 2, 144–45
Rodríguez, Ismael, 27
Rodríguez, Jesusa, 15, 22–24, 199n36, 202n60, 231n24, 235n111
Rodríguez, Raul, 70, 74, 77, 80
Rodríguez Nava, Araceli, 101, 105, 107, 124
Rodríguez Sánchez, Ignacio, 61, 76–77
Roesner, David, 9
Roma (film), 238n142
Romero Deschamps, Carlos, 26, 50–51
rosa mexicano, 83–84, 214n104
Rosas, Alejandro, 214n106, 215n119
Rousseau, Jean-Jacques, 196n4
Ruiz, Juan, 188
rumbera dancers, 55–56, 184
rural communities, 37–46
Russell, Diana, 138

Salcedo, Hugo, 70–72, 192
  El viaje de los cantores (The Singers' Journey, 1989), 211n60
  Música de balas (Music of the Bullets, 2011), 3, 69–81, 75, 77, 81, 89, 94

Selena, la reina del tex-mex (Selena, the Queen of Tex-Mex, 1997), 72
Sinfonía en una botella (Symphony in a Bottle, 1990), 72
Saldívar Arreola, Rafael, 61, 76–77
Saldívar Tanaka, Emiko, 47
Salinas de Gortari, Carlos, 50–51, 91, 94
Sánchez, Chalino, 79–81
Sánchez, Luis Rafael, 100–101
Sánchez Alvarado, Rodolfo, 194n12
Santa Anna, 11, 94, 215n124
Santa María Mixtequilla, 130
Santiago Sánchez, Elionai, 224n116
San Ysidro, 72
satire, 17, 21–22, 24, 28, 30–32, 39, 44, 57, 148, 170
Scarry, Elaine, 93, 210n52
Schafer, R. Murray, 63, 167
Schechner, Richard, 69
Schedler, Andreas, 99
Schneider, Rebecca, 219n32
Secos & Mojados, 103
Segato, Rita Laura, 103, 140, 142, 160
Selena, 72
señor de los cielos, El (The Master of the Heavens, 2013–), 78
#sevacaer (#itsgoingdown), 188
sexism, 139
sex trafficking, 53, 170–71, 179–80. See also human trafficking; prostitution
Sierra, Aída, 121, 226n139
Sierra Mixe region, 131
silence, 8–9, 95–96, 124, 126, 133
  death and, 142
  mourning and, 183
  verbal, 135
Simmons, Merle E., 158
Simonett, Helena, 158
Sinaloa, 76–77, 79–80
Sistema de Apoyos a la Creación y Proyectos Culturales, 199n40, 213n93

Sjöholm, Cecilia, 124–25
skeletons, 110–11
slavery, 52–53, 62, 178. *See also* human trafficking; sex trafficking
Slim, Carlos, 50–51
solidarity, 31, 95, 100, 103, 142, 150, 152, 168, *169*, 186–89
Solórzano-Thompson, Nohemy, 145
"Somos más" (song), 166–68, 186, 235n107
sonic disidentification
  defined, 20
  with Mexico's Golden Age cinema, 17, 26–29, 34–35, 38–48, 51–57, 192
sonic dramaturgy, 6, 194n12
sonic ethereal realm, 114–15
sonicscape of War on Drugs, 3, 59–94, 192
sonic stimuli (in performances), 3–7. *See also* music; noises; sound
sonic wounds, 83, 85–93, 215n126
Sophocles, 108, 124–26. *See also* Antigone figure
Sosa, Cecilia, 8
Sosa, Mercedes, 53–55
Sotres, Cecilia, 5–6, 23–25, 57, 152, 199n39
sound
  characteristics of, 4–5
  definition of category, 3–4
  diegetic, 67
  immersive, 66–69, 146
  meaning of, 191
  plasticity of, 4–5
  power of, 4
  of violence, 6–8
  weaponized, 90–93
  See also gunfire sounds; ricochet noises
sound design, 111–12
sounds against death
  in Avendaño's *Buscando a Bruno*, 103, 124, 129–35

  in Luna's *Réquiem #3*, 103, 107–17, 135
sound studies, 5, 7
sound universe, 6
sovereignty, 188
state of exception, 62–63, 65, 69, 86, 89
Stein, Alexander, 104
Stephen, Lynn, 121, 225n132, 226n139
street harassment, 144–48, 232n39
street interventions, 8, 10
Subero, Gustavo, 122
subjective violence, 61, 89
suffering, 3–4, 32, 56, 62–63, 76–78, 95, 126, 138, 141, 192
surround sound, 65–66
survival, 4, 181. *See also* radical geographies of hope and survival
Swartz, Lonnie, 215n122

"Tangiers" (song), 92–93
Taylor, Diana, 65, 133, 161–62, 240n7
Taymor, Julie, 169
teatro-cabaret (cabaret theater), 10–11
  female and trans female performers, 142
  history of, 21–24, 236n112
  humor used in, 11, 23–24, 26, 44, 153, 170, 172
  musical numbers in, 11, 153–54, 231n24
  sociopolitical critique in, 11, 23–24, 26, 44, 137–38, 152–53, 170, 172
  See also Enríquez, César; Felipe, Liliana; Hadad, Astrid; La Mafia Cabaret; Las Pussy Queers; Las Reinas Chulas; Orozco, Regina; Rodríguez, Jesusa; Vasconcelos, Tito
teatro de carpa (tent theater), 21–22, 169, 236n112
teatro de revista (revue theater), 21–22
Teatro Línea de Sombra, 10
Teatro NH (performance space), 169

tehuana clothing, *122*, 125–26, 128–29, 228n161, 228n163
Tehuana women, 121
Tehuantepec, Oaxaca, 117–18, 130
Televisa, 18
temporal fluidity, 92–93, 154–55
Tenanginco, 236n116
Tenochtitlán, 65
Teresa "la Antigua," Saint, 65
terror, 59, 67–69, 73–74, 86–89, 120, 144, 224n120. *See also* fear
theater and performance
  coming together in (see *convivio*)
  ephemerality of, 5–6, 65
  as mechanism of resistance, 5–6 (*see also* resistance)
  sound and, 3–5 (*see also* sound)
  Spanish styles of, 21–22
theater and performance studies, 4–5, 7–9
theater of the real, 8
Thomasa la Real, 149
Thompson, Tazewell, 112
Tiempo de Mujeres festival, 143, 187
Tijoux, Ana, 187
Tirado, Katia, 65
Tirso de Molina prize, 70
Tizoc (1957), 16, 26, 47
Tlalpán (neighborhood in Mexico City), 15
Tlaxcala, 152, 170, 174, 180
Torres, Justin, 184
torture, 2, 76, 91, 93, 119, 206n5, 224n116
tourism, dark, 82–85, 214n106
transfeminicide, 9
  mourning for victims of, 183
  rates of, 137–38, 141, 184, 236n119
  records of, 180–81
  resistance against, 169–86, 192
  in Veracruz, 171
  See also feminicide
trans identity, 122, 175. See also *muxe* identity

trauma
  of feminicide, 34
  political, 101, 108
  sound and, 10, 88
  of violence in War on Drugs, 69, 82, 88
trauma studies, 3, 8
Trevi, Gloria, 162–64, 166, 192
Trevino-Rangel, Javier, 74
Turner, Victor, 101–2, 107, 134
TV Azteca, 18

United States
  border with Mexico, 33, 70, 72, 179–80, 215n122
  hip-hop, 149
  military forces, 91
  performances in, 170
  State Department, 97, 119–20, 236n116
  War on Terror, 7
  See also Iraq, US war in
Universidad Veracruzana-Xalapa, 117, 130
unspeakability, 102, 220n43
upper class, 48. *See also* elites
urban life, 27, 30–32. *See also* street harassment
Urbioa Solís, Alejandra Elizabeth, 226n136
Urdemalas, Pedro de, 27
Uribe, Sara, 101
Ustedes los ricos (You All, the Rich, 1948), 16, 25, 28
utopia, 142–43, 155–56, 175
  queer, 120, 173, 181, 183
  radical feminist, 159

Valdez, Javier, 235n107
Valencia, Sayak, 141, 171, 183
Varea, Roberto, 106
Vasconcelos, José, 177
Vasconcelos, Tito, 15, 22, 153, 199n36, 202n60, 235n111
Vásquez, Alexandra T., 9, 195n23

Vaughn, Bobby, 48
Vázquez Moyers, Alonso, 61
Vecindad, Maldita, "Morenaza," 144–48, 150–51
vela, 122, 225n132
Veracruz, 11, 87–88, 97–98, 141, 171, 173–74, 178–79, 237n120
vibratorium, 113–14
Vichido Rito, Nicolás, 228n166
video recordings, 65
Vinson, Ben, III, 178
"violador eres tú, El" (song), 190
violence
  normalization of, 87
  spectacularization of, 85
  subjective, 61, 89
  War on Drugs and, 2–4, 6–8, 23, 59–94, 191
  against women (*see* gendered violence)
  See also disappeared and missing persons; dismemberment; homicide rates; mass graves; militarization; mutilation; *narco* violence
visual studies, 8
vocal performance
  in *Nosotras las proles*, 28, 32–33, 57
  projection, 159–60
  resistance and, 189–90
  of sobs, tears, and wailing, 116–17, 184
  trans identity and, 175
  without emotion, 87
"Vogue" (song), 179, *181*, 182
voice en off (voiceover), 82, 86–89, 146
voz bravía (untamed voice), 159–60. *See also* Reyes, Lucha
Vrana, Heather, 120
vulnere voce (wounded voice), 87

Walter, Tony, 102, 110
Ward, Julie, 10

War on Drugs (Mexico)
  Calderón's declaration of, 2–3, 60–61, 94
  collateral damage, 73–76, 98–99, 134
  damaging impact of, 2–4, 6–8, 23, 59–94, 191
  death toll, 2, 62, 69, 73, 79
  sonicscape of, 3, 59–94, 192
  See also cartels; militarization; *narco* violence
War on Terror (United States), 7
war zones, music and sound in, 7, 91, 216n146
Washington Valdéz, Diana, 229n6
Waters, Richard, 222n91
weaponized sound, 90–93
Werth, Brenda, 8
whitened mestizo physique, 17–20, 26–27, 47–57
Wolffer, Lorena, 65
women
  as "disposable," 13, 142, 155
  murder of (*see* feminicide; trans feminicide)
  public grief of, 100–101
  in public sphere, 124–25, 139–40, 144–48
  subordination of, 139
  See also gendered violence; misogyny; sexism
wounded body, 83, 85–94, 214n119, 215n126
Wright, Melissa, 98, 100, 110, 141–42, 155

Yucatán, 178
Yugüe flute, 131
Yuyachkani, 101

Zapata, Emiliano, 154
zapateado, 76
Zapotec communities, 117–23, 131
  culture of, *122*, 125–26, 128–29, 227n160

muxe identity and, 226n136
  violence in, 119–20
zarzuela (Spanish performance style), 236n112

Žižek, Slajov, 61, 207n16, 207n25
Zócalo plaza (Mexico City), 1, 187–91, 209n41, 241n12
Zypce, 194n12

www.ingramcontent.com/pod-product-compliance
Lightning Source LLC
Chambersburg PA
CBHW030526230426
43665CB00010B/784